WELLINGTON AT WAR
1794–1815

WELLINGTON RIDING IN THE PYRENEES, 1813

From the painting by Thomas Heaphy

WELLINGTON
AT WAR
1794-1815

✳

A SELECTION OF HIS WARTIME LETTERS
EDITED AND INTRODUCED

BY

ANTONY BRETT-JAMES

LONDON
MACMILLAN & CO LTD
NEW YORK · ST MARTIN'S PRESS
1961

MACMILLAN AND COMPANY LIMITED
London Bombay Calcutta Madras Melbourne

THE MACMILLAN COMPANY OF CANADA LIMITED
Toronto

ST MARTIN'S PRESS INC
New York

PRINTED IN GREAT BRITAIN

PREFACE

THE military commanders of our own day are prone to set down their recollections of great days at war. Their motives for such authorship are varied. Field-Marshal the Viscount Montgomery of Alamein aimed 'to give to future generations the impressions I have gained in a life that has been full of interest, and to define the principles under which I have considered it my duty to think and act'. Field-Marshal the Viscount Slim, a writer of greater distinction and humanity, set out the several ways in which a general might write something of value. 'He might, as honestly as he could, tell of the problems he faced, why he took the decisions he did, what helped, what hindered, the luck he had, and the mistakes he made. He might, by showing how one man attempted the art of command, be of use to those who later may themselves have to exercise it. He might even give, to those who have not experienced it, some impression of what it feels like to shoulder a commander's responsibilities in war.'[1]

Some high-ranking memorialists have sought to justify their decisions, to allay or to rekindle controversy; whereas some have criticised their former comrades, be they superior or inferior to them in the wartime hierarchy, others have blamed only themselves and been almost too generous in avoiding mention of lapses on the part of men who had been their friends in barracks and cantonment, at staff college or on the battlefield. Several commanders have enlisted the aid of professional writers, either to sustain and improve their own literary efforts or to compile, after access to all personal papers and to the subject's recollections, a biography which may be critical, laudatory, or a balance between the two.

A century and more ago it was rare that a great soldier, sailor or politician, for that matter, wrote an autobiography or allowed someone to write a full account of him in his lifetime. General Sir George Napier, one of a splendid trio of brothers, did

---

[1] *Defeat into Victory*, p. vii.

relate his military experiences for the interest and instruction of his grandchildren, but most of the events described were lived through as a comparatively junior officer. Lieutenant-General Charles Stewart, Marquess of Londonderry, who had been Adjutant-General to Wellington in the Peninsular campaigns, wrote a narrative of that war, blending history with personal reminiscence and expressing himself with considerable candour. And that brave, brilliant and dashing fellow, Sir Harry Smith, wrote an autobiography of singular charm and freshness, though here again the general was looking back on the adventures of the youthful subaltern and field officer.

Such cases are few. For the most part it was left to sons or daughters or former comrades in arms to compile, often with a devotion that outstripped their skill, one or more weighty volumes of letters, diaries and memoirs.

The Duke of Wellington, who considered himself 'much exposed to authors', never wrote down his recollections. He was ready enough to talk about the past, though he would have been full of disapprobation if not horror had he known that, for the benefit of posterity, friends like Lord Mahon, afterwards the 5th Earl Stanhope, and the Marchioness of Salisbury were recording all they could remember of his spoken memories and comments. Dining at Apsley House in May 1834, he confessed that he had not read the recently published fourth volume of Sir William Napier's *History of the War in the Peninsula*. 'I am determined not to read any of it till the six volumes — or whatever they are — are all out, and then I will read them fairly through, I dare say with much entertainment. But I will not read them now. I might else be tempted into contradicting him — into authorising somebody to answer him for me. Now I will have nothing to do with writing a book.'

He had said much the same in 1827 when Samuel Rogers enquired why the Duke did not write a book himself. 'I have indeed no time to write, much as I might wish to do so, and I am still too much in the world to do it.' He might have made time after his retirement from politics, had it not been for a still stronger objection : 'I should much like to tell the truth ; but if I did, I should be torn to pieces here or abroad'.

Wellington held very firm views about the truth in military history. To John Wilson Croker, who had expressed his wish to write an account of Waterloo, the Duke replied from Paris on

August 8th, 1815 : 'The history of the battle is not unlike the history of a ball. Some individuals may recollect all the little events of which the great result is the battle won or lost; but no individual can recollect the order in which, or the exact moment at which, they occurred, which makes all the difference as to their value or importance. Then the faults or the misbehavior of some gave occasion for the distinction of others, and perhaps were the cause of material losses; and you cannot write a true history of a battle without including the faults and misbehavior of part at least of those engaged. Believe me that every man you see in a military uniform is not a hero. . . .' [1]

Harsh and scathing as he could often be, the Duke was always reluctant to hurt the feelings of other men, and this was a further reason against writing a book. He would have required the help of no professional writer, for his letters display not only a prolific output but a fluency and command of the English language that has had few rivals among men in his position. His letters reveal the man with honesty and modesty. They do tell us a great deal, and at first hand, of 'the problems he faced, why he took the decisions he did, what helped, what hindered, the luck he had, and the mistakes he made'. They show how one great man exercised the art of command and bore the manifold responsibilities of a commander in war. They show, too, how Lord Wellington dealt with men of widely differing race, with his own kin as well as with allies and enemies. They can teach some aspects of the art of letter writing as practised by a master, though it must be stressed that, unlike Lord Nelson, his letters were rarely intimate or emotional, and the personal is most often contained by the professional.

It is to be regretted that very few letters to his wife survive. Such as do exist, being terse, even impatient, reveal little of their relationship, which we know to have been far from ideal. They were subjected to prolonged separations, and whereas he grew in stature in the thick of crucial events, her development did not keep pace. Moreover, though the daughter of a peer, she was by nature ill-equipped to play the difficult public role of a hero's wife; and her quiet sweetness failed to offset the timidity which so irritated him.

Of letters to his family, by far the greatest number are addressed to three brothers : Richard, Marquess Wellesley,

[1] See letter no. 177.

with whom his relations were sometimes strained; Henry Wellesley, to whom he wrote regularly both in India and in the Peninsula; and William Wellesley-Pole. Some of his indignant references to the activities of Richard are exceedingly candid, if not coarse.

Among his most frequent official correspondents were two Secretaries of State for War to whom he was responsible — Lords Liverpool and Bathurst — and Henry Torrens, who, having been Wellington's Military Secretary during the 1808 campaign, served the Commander-in-Chief in London in a similar capacity for the rest of the war.

From the years spent in India two special friends stand out : Barry Close and John Malcolm, of whom details are given when they first appear in this volume; while in later years there is the 4th Duke of Richmond, under whom Arthur Wellesley served in Ireland — as Chief Secretary to Lord-Lieutenant — and with whose children he was on terms of affection.

He wrote to British Ambassadors like J. C. Villiers, Charles Stuart and John Hookham Frere, besides two of his brothers who held such diplomatic posts; to generals senior to himself like Harris in India and Sir John Moore; and to many of his corps, divisional and even regimental commanders. He corresponded with French marshals about the exchange of prisoners of war, with William Wilberforce about the slave trade, with Lady Frances Webster on the desirability of her remaining in Brussels on the eve of Waterloo. I have deliberately not included Wellington's official despatches describing his major battles, even Waterloo, largely because so much space in them is devoted to lists of officer casualties, to mention of commanders and staff officers whose conduct deserved commendation, to tributes to individual divisions and regiments, and to a record of captured guns and equipment. Rather, I have chosen more personal letters which refer to his many victories and few setbacks.

Interspersed among the correspondence are quotations from contemporary diaries, letters and recollections. These afford glimpses of Wellington at each stage in his wartime career, and by describing the scene at typical headquarters, in particular the towns and villages where Wellington settled for several months on end instead of for a day or a week, show the circumstances in which many of the letters were composed and Wellington's methods of handling administration, staffwork, diplomacy and senior members of his staff.

The introductory passages — to an individual campaign, period or year — are intended to give the general reader enough facts and background to follow the course of events, but they are not designed as chapters in a life of Lord Wellington or as a history of the several campaigns. The footnotes, besides explaining people and events mentioned in the text, often comprise extracts from the Duke's conversation or from letters which have had to be excluded from this volume but which give his further, or more detailed, views on topics discussed in the correspondence.

Unless otherwise stated, the letters are taken from Colonel Gurwood's edition of the *Dispatches* in twelve stout volumes containing over six thousand pages and two and a half million words. To these should be added a considerable proportion of the *Supplementary Despatches* which also include a host of letters addressed to the Duke. Of unpublished letters there are but three, taken from the Richmond Papers in the National Library of Ireland (number 161), and from the Additional MSS. in the British Museum (numbers 60 and 74). Among letters which have hitherto appeared in volumes having only a very limited sale or circulation are those to William Wellesley-Pole published in volume xviii of the *Camden Miscellany* for members of the Royal Historical Society (numbers 65, 67, 68, 72, 82, 85, 91, 98 and 100); and three from the *Mysore Letters and Dispatches* published in Bangalore in 1862 (numbers 16, 17 and 18).

I should like to record my gratitude to Countess Wavell, C.I., for allowing me to dedicate this book to the memory of her husband; to His Grace the Duke of Wellington, K.G., for granting me access to some of the papers in Apsley House, London, and to the Duke's Librarian, Mr. Francis Needham, for his valuable aid in finding particular documents and for his help and advice on a number of points; to Countess Walde-grave; to the Marquess of Salisbury, K.G.; to Marjorie, Lady Pentland; to Lord Saltoun, M.C. I am indebted to Lord Raglan, F.S.A., Sir Charles Webster, K.C.M.G., Litt.D., F.B.A., and the Council of the Royal Historical Society for permission to reprint letters first published in *The Camden Miscellany*, volume xviii, 1948; to Mr. Peter Quennell and Mr.

Alan Hodge, Editors of *History Today*, for allowing me to use as the basis of my Introduction an article which first appeared in that journal ; to Mr. A. S. Bennell, for giving me the benefit of his research into Indian history during the Wellesley period and for taking great pains to ferret out information. I also tender thanks to the Trustees of the British Museum for permission to reproduce three extracts from the diary of Lieutenant William Lambton and two letters from the Wellesley Papers ; to the Earl of Powis and the National Library of Wales for permission to include in facsimile a letter from the Clive Papers ; to the Trustees of the National Library of Ireland for allowing inclusion of a letter from the Richmond Papers ; to the Parker Gallery, London, for providing prints for two of the illustrations ; to Lieut.-Colonel C. B. Appleby, D.S.O., F.S.A., Director of the National Army Museum ; to Mr F. I. S. McEndrick.

Acknowledgment is due to William Heinemann Ltd. for allowing me to quote from *Memoirs of George Elers (1777–1842)*, edited by Lord Monson and George Leveson-Gower ; to Hurst and Blackett Ltd. for two passages from *Memoirs of William Hickey*, edited by Alfred Spencer ; to John Murray Ltd. for extracts from *The Creevey Papers*, edited by Sir Herbert Maxwell, and also for a letter in *A Great Man's Friendship*, edited by Lady Burghclere. Among others to whom this book owes a debt are : Miss Aileen Armstrong, Miss Anne Burns, Mr. E. P. Greenwood, Mr. T. G. F. Paterson, O.B.E., Mrs. Henrietta Phipps, Miss Anne Scott Elliott, Miss Maureen Sloan. I am glad to express my thanks to Miss Kay Hallett for typing most of the letters in her usual impeccable way, and to Miss Thelma Nye for her valued help with reading the proofs.

Finally, as with previous books, my mother afforded me very real aid in compiling the index, and gave support and encouragement at every stage, as did my father, who read the galley proofs but did not live to see the completed book.

A. B.-J.

MILL HILL and KENSINGTON

CONTENTS

Contents

PART FOUR

INTERIM : 1805–1807

Contents

B   xvii

Contents

xix

PART SIX

VICTORY IN FRANCE AND FLANDERS : 1814–1815

Contents

LIST OF ILLUSTRATIONS

MAPS

NAMES OF RECIPIENTS OF LETTERS

With reference numbers of letters addressed to them

Names of Recipients of Letters

INTRODUCTION

ONE July day at Apsley House Wellington remarked to Mr. George William Chad, who had just read the fourth volume of the Duke's published Dispatches : 'Aye, it quite interested me to look them over again — it recalled all the feelings of youth — especially the Indian Dispatches. I felt young again — all the enterprize and excitement of that time.'

'They are very valuable,' replied Chad. 'I had no idea of all the variety of knowledge necessary for a Commander in Chief. I wonder how you could suffice.'

'I never should if I had not been very young in command.' (Wellington had been forty-six at Waterloo, the last of his battles.) 'They are valuable as a professional book, more so than Caesar's Commentaries because Caesar wrote afterwards for effect. These are a Collection of the Instruments used at the Time — they were all written in my own hand.' [1]

To the Marchioness of Salisbury in 1834 the Duke expressed surprise to find his Dispatches so good : 'They are as good as I could write now. They show the same attention to details — to the pursuit of all the means, however small, that could promote success.'

As one reads through the twelve portly volumes of Gurwood's edition of the *Dispatches*, one cannot but be amazed by the variety of knowledge, the clarity of exposition, the attention to detail, the relentless supervision or inspiration of such manifold activities — military, administrative and diplomatic.

His letters from India, studded with local words like *amildars, brinjarries, pettahs, killadars, polygars, sumnuds*, or with such unfamiliar coinage as Bombay gold mohurs and star pagodas, are concerned with problems that range from the disposal of wives and concubines of native princes to roadmaking and the crossing of monsoon-swollen rivers by means of basket boats. One day we find Colonel Wellesley explaining to the Secretary of Government the difference between rice from

[1] *The Conversations of the First Duke of Wellington with George William Chad*, p. 19.

xxix

Bengal and from Canara, on another he is ordering the execution of thieves who infest the roads, or ascertaining the causes of mortality among draught cattle.

His Peninsular letters abound in details of bivouacs and bullocks, biscuits and blankets, wood and wine, pontoons and powder barrels. Now he is applying to Lord Liverpool for scythes with which to cut forage, now he is recommending that French prisoners at Lisbon and Oporto be moved to England, now he is requesting shirts and sheets for use in hospitals. He discusses the principles to be adopted in the grant of medals for distinguished conduct in battle with the same clarity and vigour as he claims an allowance for shoeing mules employed in the carriage of surgeons' medicine chests and the regimental paymasters' account books. If he is not coping with naval commanders and diplomats, he is grousing about barefaced anonymous letters from Portuguese dignitaries or the excessive delays in bringing officers to trial by court martial.

There are a few letters of condolence, and rather more letters in which Wellington recommends to the favour and protection of the British Government the widow and family — usually numerous and unprovided for — of a meritorious officer who has been killed in action or has died of his wounds. He takes time to thank Spaniards for the gift of a most beautiful set of pistols or of six Andalusian horses, and the Lord Mayor of London or the Speaker of the House of Commons for their welcome expressions of approbation.

One day he is concerned with a duel between two officers, or with complaints by Portuguese villagers against billeted soldiers; on another he has to deal with smuggling off Lisbon and reforms of abuses in the custom house there. Yet again he is busy drafting memoranda for his engineers or commissaries, or enquiring about stables for the cavalry and the state of roads in some corner of the Peninsula. He has to defend himself against reproaches of injustice by explaining why certain officers are not qualified to receive a medal, and why marks of distinction and favour have been conferred by the Spanish and Portuguese Governments upon some senior officers and not on others less fortunate.

There seems to be no subject that does not come within his jurisdiction and ken, be it white breeches cloth, the purchase of mules in Barbary, the activities of gunboats on the Tagus, the early closing of Lisbon coffee-houses, the enormous cost of military post-offices, or the relative merits of iron and tin camp kettles for cooking.

Complaints loom large in his letters, and Wellington certainly had much to contend with, much to irritate and anger him, many a source of disapprobation and disquiet. He rails at '*sharks* at Lisbon calling themselves British merchants . . . who, I verily believe, are the worst subjects His Majesty has'. He complains at the disadvantage of waging war against an enemy possessed of all the details of British defence works, guns, and troops which London newspapers so diligently revealed for French eyes to read. He deplores the almost useless entrenching and cutting tools supplied to his army : 'Is it not shameful that the French should have better cutlery than we have ?'

Often as he complained about the arrears of pay of the soldiers and the state of the army for want of money, a still more frequent cause of complaint was his allies. First in India, where he soon formed a poor opinion of the people as looters and liars, as tyrannical and impudent when likely to be supported, and as incapable of keeping a secret — 'if one black man ever hears of your plan, it may as well be published in the bazaar'. We have him stating bluntly that his fickle, self-seeking allies think 'that when once they have put the seal to a treaty with us, they have nothing to do but to amuse themselves and sleep', and that 'if my Mahratta allies did not know that I should hang any one that might be found plundering, not only I should have starved long ago, but most probably my own coat would have been taken off my back'. The native governments, characterised as they were by knavery, robbery and corruption, seemed all too often to adopt as their policy the following : 'never to give assistance to your friend when he stands in most need of it, and always to break your treaty with him at the moment when it would be most convenient to him that you should fulfil all its stipulations'.

Intricate and exasperating as were his dealings with the people of southern and central India, Wellington turned the experience to good account when he came to handle Spaniards and Portuguese in the Peninsula. The former, whom he described as 'visionaries and enthusiasts who will not look at things as they really are', would make next to no exertion for themselves ; and, being too sanguine by disposition, were quick to exaggerate their own strength and diminish that of the French,

while expecting success in objects for the attainment of which
they had adopted no effective measures. 'There never was anything', wrote Wellington late in 1809, 'like the madness, the
imprudence, and the presumption of the Spanish officers in the
way they risk their corps, knowing that the national vanity will
prevent them from withdrawing them from a situation of danger,
and that if attacked they must be totally destroyed. . . . Nothing
will answer except to fight great battles in plains, in which their
defeat is as certain as is the commencement of the battle.'

Handicapped by inexperience, vitiated by a mixture of
'haughtiness and low intrigue', the Spanish leaders, both civil
and military, so conducted themselves that every transaction
was, in Wellington's opinion, characterised by 'delay, weakness,
folly or treachery'. From Madrid in 1812 he assured Lord
Bathurst : 'They cry *viva* and are very fond of us, and hate the
French ; but they are, in general, the most incapable of useful
exertion of all the nations that I have known ; the most vain,
and at the same time the most ignorant, particularly of military
affairs, and above all of military affairs in their own country'.

An especial burden for Lord Wellington was having to cope
with the long-standing enmity between Portugal and Spain,
each his ally yet 'more like cat and dog than anything else, of
which no sense of common danger, or common interest, or any
thing, can get the better, even in individuals'. Though Wellington had more time for and sympathy with the Portuguese, they
did not escape his criticism. Impatient with the constant efforts
of their Government to 'indulge the caprice and ease of the
people of Lisbon at the expense of every other consideration',
he expressed himself no less surprised than disgusted by the
'frivolous and manifestly unfounded complaints' from Portuguese about billets ; and when one household complained at
having to lodge a British officer who had a wife and children
with him, Wellington let fly with a severe rebuke : 'It is not
very agreeable to any body to have strangers quartered in his
house ; nor is it very agreeable to us strangers, who have good
houses in our own country, to be obliged to seek for quarters
here. We are not here for our pleasure : the situation of your
country renders it necessary.'

Often his letters become more violent in tone than mere
complaint. He could explode with fury at 'the fraudulent and
disgusting tyranny of Buonaparte', or with exasperation because

'nobody in the British army ever reads a regulation or an order as if it were a guide for his conduct, or in any other manner than as an amusing novel'. Already in India we see him bursting with annoyance over 'a parcel of blockheads who know nothing and have no data', or 'a parcel of absurd, impracticable shop-keeping regulations under which no great undertaking could ever prosper'. He could on occasion be very violent in reference to those whom he despised. For instance, the Spanish Minister of War he termed 'the greatest of all blackguards', and a Spanish civilian attached to Wellington's army was bluntly described as 'not only the most useless and inefficient of God's creatures, but an impediment to all business ; and he cannot speak one word of truth'.

If his disparaging portrayal, to the British Ambassador in Lisbon, of one British General : 'He possesses no one military quality, and he has been repeatedly guilty of that worst of all tricks, which invariably defeats its own ends, viz., courting popularity with the common soldiers, by flattering their vices, and by impunity for their misconduct', seems hostile enough, it sounds pale beside his withering — and celebrated — diatribe against Major-General Lightburne 'whose conduct is really scandalous. I am not able to bring him before a court-martial as I should wish, but he is a disgrace to the army which can have such a man as a Major-General. Really, when I reflect upon the characters and attainments of some of the General officers of this army, and consider that these are the persons on whom I am to rely . . . I tremble ; and, as Lord Chesterfield said of the Generals of his day, "I only hope that when the enemy reads the list of their names he trembles as I do". . . . I pray God and the Horse Guards to deliver me from General Lightburne and Colonel Sanders.'

While it was rare for Wellington so far to lose control as to upbraid a man to his face, we do know that he reduced his Adjutant-General, Charles Stewart, to tears at one interview, and in October 1810 he asked a brigadier, who was making awkward excuses for doing badly in a battle, how old he was. 'Forty-four', came the reply. 'Ah !' retorted Wellington. 'You will be a great soldier by the time you are as old as I am.' The Commander of the Forces was then forty-one !

He was certainly no leader to overlook misconduct, not least because 'His Majesty's government, and the British public, will not hear excuses for failure in this country [Portugal]'. However, he was normally considerate, and was anxious that when an officer had to be removed from a post he was incapable of filling, nothing should be done to injure his feelings and no step be taken unless he could be otherwise provided for.

If he was often driven to indulge in sarcasm and wounding rebukes, he could also, though less frequently, be generous in his praise. After the capture of Dhoondiah Waugh in India in 1800, for example, he wrote to a colonel who had commanded one of the columns engaged in the chase : 'I cannot avoid returning you my thanks for the assistance I have uniformly received from you. You have had much fatigue, and have not been so fortunate as to fall in with the enemy ; but I assure you that your exertions have nevertheless been seriously felt, and will always be acknowledged by me.' This was gracious and considerate. So, too, was the letter he sent thirteen years later, this time in Spain, to Lieut.-General William Clinton : 'I do not know how I can request you to continue to hold a command for which you state that your health renders you unequal ; but if an expression of the entire satisfaction I have had in all my communications with you, and of my confidence in all your arrangements, can be an inducement to you to continue to exercise your command, or can be any gratification to you upon quitting it, it is but justice to you to express it.'

Wellington could use or turn a phrase most aptly, and though his letters do not abound in such felicities, there are quite enough examples to indicate his powers. 'This officer, although an excellent man, has more of the oak than the willow in his disposition' ; 'You know that, when the labouring oar is to fall upon him, he is not over sanguine' ; 'the officer to be employed in this manner must have been the best the British service could afford, probably so like black swans, that the service could afford very few of them' ; 'Malcolm is indefatigable, and leads the life of a canister at a dog's tail'.

For the rest, his style varies between the colloquial, the ironic and the austerely formal. Of the first manner we may quote such phrases as 'The battle of the 28th was fair *bludgeon* work', or 'I hear there was *hell to pay* at Cadiz', or again 'The ball is now at my foot, and I hope I shall have strength enough to give it a good kick'. The following reference to the British Government has a surprisingly modern ring : 'having got their cake, they want both to eat it and keep it'. By contrast, and it is a sharp contrast, Wellington adopts the more pompous and inflated style in which he 'takes the liberty of suggesting the propriety of requesting the Governor-General to . . .', takes the opportunity of reporting to the Commander-in-Chief his sense of a regiment's conduct, which both claims and receives his fullest approbation, refers to a good officer as 'an ornament to his profession', or mentions 'a wound which, I am happy to say, has not deprived me for a moment of the benefit of his assistance' — the last a most characteristic phrase. No less typical were the words 'advert' and 'animadvert' and an opening such as 'Upon the occasion of addressing myself to your Lordship, I cannot avoid adverting and drawing your Lordship's attention to . . .'

Then he was particularly skilled, from long practice, at respectfully deflecting a superior, like the Prince Regent, from what he deemed an ill-advised course of action. 'I am convinced that your Highness will see that it will not answer to . . .' or 'I believe your Highness labors under a mistake regarding . . .' show his deferential tact combined with a firmness which usually gained its ends.

Seldom as he went in for irony, his few indulgences were pointed enough. For instance : 'If nobody is to remain in a situation which he does not like, or is to do only what he likes we have undertaken a task which is too great for us'. Sometimes a more caustic note creeps in, and after a bout of absurd statements in newspapers which had excited in the public extravagant expectations which were inevitably followed by disappointment, we have Lord Wellington declaring : 'If I had been at any time capable of doing what these gentlemen expected, I should now, I believe, have been in the moon. They have long expected me at Bordeaux ; nay, I understand that there are many of their wise readers (amateurs of the military art) who are waiting to join the army till headquarters shall arrive in that city.' Or again : 'I do not know how Mr. —— has discovered that my channels of intelligence are of doubtful fidelity. I should find it very difficult to point out what channels of intelligence I have ; but probably Mr. —— knows.'

The twelve volumes of *Dispatches* contain close on two and a half million words, most if not all of them written in Wellington's own hand. To these may be added half as many from the

Supplementary Despatches. It is extraordinary that, in an age
when a military commander disposed of no wireless, telephone,
dictaphone, jeep, staff car, helicopter, armoured car or personal
aircraft, he should have been able to get through so immense a
volume of paper work and administration. He was never one
to scamp the work ; he wrote numerous memoranda for the
Government as well as for his engineers and commissaries ; and
returns of ammunition, medical strengths, casualty lists, the
proceedings of courts martial were checked by eyes trained to
discover even a wrong casting-up of totals. 'Lord Wellington
reads and looks into everything', noted his Judge-Advocate
General early in 1813, later making the admiring comment that
'he banishes the terms difficulty, impossibility and responsibility
from his vocabulary'.

Staffs were small. Messages were carried by aides-de-camp,
by dragoons, even by local peasants. If Wellington wished to
visit his divisions or outposts, it was always on horseback, whatever the weather. If he wished to travel to Lisbon or Cadiz, he
had to ride a relay of horses for up to five days on end.

He added to his burdens by his reluctance to delegate
authority and to trust subordinates, be they divisional commanders or heads of staff departments : 'I am obliged to be
every where', he complained once, 'and if absent from any
operation, something goes wrong'. And we have his confident
claim that 'the real reason why I succeeded in my own campaigns is because I was always on the spot and saw every thing
and did every thing myself'. It was fortunate that his constitution, despite a delicate boyhood, withstood the rigours of
climate and campaigning : almost alone of his generals he never
went home ill from the Peninsula. All went well so long as
Wellington neglected his papers for no more than a day or two,
but during campaigns this was not always possible, as occurred
early in 1814 when he was away from headquarters for five days
and so much had accumulated in his absence that he was quite
overwhelmed. 'When I went in with a great bundle to add to
them', writes his Judge-Advocate General, 'he put his hands
before his eyes and said, "Put them on that table ; and do not
say anything about them now, or let me look at them at all".'

When asked how he managed to write so many letters in the
midst of active operations, he replied : 'My rule always was to
do the business of the day in the day'. Yet he assured one

General in 1816 : 'Persons who, like me, have much to attend
to ought to have a double portion of time ; or those who must
be conscious that they can feel nothing towards them but good
wishes, and know that they have only the time allotted to other
mortals, should excuse them if they omit to perform all the
offices, or rather duties, of society and friendship'.

One reason why Wellington got through so much work so
fast was that, like many another great man, he was able to fall
asleep in any circumstances, to refresh himself with a timely
cat-nap. Stepney Cowell of the Coldstream Guards records a
conversation round the dinner-table at the end of 1810, when a
visitor to Headquarters, having expressed pleasure at finding
Lord Wellington in such good looks and health, said : 'With
the details you have to think of, the numerous affairs, both
political and diplomatic, you have to provide for, I cannot conceive how you can sleep in your bed'. To this came the reply :
'When I throw off my clothes I throw off my cares, and when I
turn in my bed it is time to turn out'.

Even when rolled in his boatcloak on the ground, his slum-
bers, we are told, were as peaceful and profound as those of
a child, not only when far from a battlefield but also, more
remarkable, when facing the French. On September 26th, 1811,
for example, his troops, outnumbered by some four to one at
Fuente Guinaldo, were anxious at the prospect of being crushed
by the superior French. Yet Wellington, 'seemingly tired of
waiting, and feeling drowsy, told one of his aides-de-camp to
call him if anything was the matter, wrapped himself in his
cloak, lay down in the broiling sun, and slept composedly and
soundly for more than two hours'.

General Picton related at dinner in London an instance of
the Peer's calmness of mind in a difficult situation. Just before
the battle of Orthez, Wellington worked extremely hard to
dispose his troops in such a way as to have the best chance of
dislodging the French from their very advantageous positions.
Having surveyed his dispositions, he thought for a moment,
then turned to Picton with the remark : 'I think we have done
all we can. Nothing more seems necessary.' Whereupon, dis-
mounting from his horse, he sat down and in a few minutes was
fast asleep. And Sir Hussey Vivian, a cavalry commander, has
recorded that the Duke, having on the morning of June 17th,
1815, given the order to retire on the Waterloo positions, 'laid

himself down on the ground, covered his head with one of the newspapers he had been reading, and appeared to fall asleep; and in this way he remained some time, when he again rose and mounted his horse and rode down the field in front of Quatre-Bras a little distance, and looked about with his glass'.[1]

Surrounded by procrastination both in India and the Peninsula, Wellington set an example of prompt despatch of business. He therefore found all the more intolerable that his time should ever be occupied by comparative trifles.

'In the transaction of public business', he wrote once in India, 'there is nothing so unpleasant, or which takes up so much time unnecessarily, as for those who are obliged to correspond upon it to draw nice logical distinctions upon words, or to give them a meaning they were not intended to convey.' When, in January 1802, a regimental commander forwarded to Sir Arthur Wellesley a letter from one of his majors, Wellesley penned the following reply : 'I have to observe that if the complaints which Major —— has to make of you are not better founded, or of a nature less futile and frivolous than those which he has written to me in his letter, he will do well to forego his intention of making them. It is certainly impossible for time to be thrown away with less advantage to the public than mine would be in reading, forwarding and commenting upon such complaints, and than that, still more valuable, of the Commander-in-Chief would be in considering them; and it is more than probable that his Excellency would pronounce an opinion upon them which would not be very agreeable to Major ——.'

Advantage to the public — that was always Wellington's standard for handling such matters. He believed firmly that officers in particular should carry on the service in a spirit of good temper and conciliation, and that every gentleman should, when convinced of his error, be prepared to make ample apology. As far back as 1803 he had effectively shamed an officer who had, maybe overcome by the Indian climate, sent him an offensive, ill-considered tirade by addressing him thus : 'My dear Colonel, we shall get on very well, but it will be better when you have a fit of the bile to keep it to yourself, and not give it me in a letter'.

Striking testimony as are the published *Dispatches* to Wellington's exceptional energy of mind and body, to his wide-ranging and penetrating grasp of detail, to his sound common

[1] *Richard Hussey Vivian*, p. 280.

sense, to his determination to win final victory, though at his own pace and not at the panicky behest of ministers or allies, they bear even more striking witness to the Duke's integrity as a military commander, an administrator, a public servant of his King and Country. Time and again he declared his principles of conduct, the diligent pursuit of which often led to his censure of weaker subordinates. 'I should be neglectful of my duty to the King, to the Prince Regent, and to the common cause', he wrote in 1810, 'if I could permit myself to be influenced by public clamour, or by fear, so as to modify the system of operations which I have adopted after mature deliberation, and which daily experience proves to be the only one which can bring the matter to a successful issue.' He told a French duke in 1814 that 'No power on earth shall induce me to depart from what I conceive to be my duty towards the Sovereigns I am serving'. Likewise in India he declared that 'The war will be eternal if nobody is ever to be forgiven ; and I certainly think that the British Government cannot intend to make the British troops the instruments of the Peshwah's revenge. . . . When the empire of the Company [East India] is so great, little dirty passions must not be suffered to guide its measures.'

The more tangled the intrigues about him, the straighter a path of conduct he felt compelled to follow. 'I would sacrifice Gwalior, or every frontier of India, ten times over', he wrote, 'in order to preserve our credit for scrupulous good faith, and the advantages and honor we gained by the late war and the peace ; and we must not fritter them away in arguments, drawn from overstrained principles of the laws of nations, which are not understood in this country. What brought me through many difficulties in the war and negotiations for peace ? The British good faith, and nothing else.'

Wellington could be cold, harsh and haughty ; he could be severe, and sometimes unjust as in his much criticised letter about the retreat from Burgos, and his still more notorious reference to 'the scum of the earth as common soldiers'. But though human warmth and emotion rarely surfaced from behind his hooked nose and judging eyes, and though his opinion of his fellow-men was often disillusioned and intolerant, he showed himself to be a military commander of the highest stature and a man of honour, patriotism, integrity and lack of self-seeking.

PART ONE

THE EARLY YEARS: 1769–1797

INTRODUCTION TO PART ONE

ARTHUR WESLEY, born on May 1st, 1769, in Merrion Street, Dublin, sprang from the Anglo-Irish Ascendancy — that small number of Protestant, English families which, living as 'foreigners' among an impoverished, subject, Catholic people, had for generations governed Ireland as an aristocratic, land-owning caste, secluded by birth, religion, social and financial state. True it is that Arthur's father, Garret Wesley, Earl of Mornington, might seem, as Professor of Music at Trinity College, Dublin, and as a composer of church music and glees, to have belonged to a cultural rather than a ruling *élite*, but he owned estates in County Meath, had married a peer's daughter, and descended from the Colleys, squires of long standing in the country to which they did not belong.

Arthur's boyhood was divided between, on the Irish side, Dublin, Dangan Castle in Meath, and the village school at Trim, and, in England, between a seminary in the King's Road, Chelsea, and Eton College, where as Wesley major — his younger brothers Gerald and Henry followed close behind — he showed scant promise, made few friends, and was notable for dreamy idleness rather than for achievements as scholar, athlete, or embryo empire-builder.

His brother Richard, nine years older and the second Earl of Mornington since the death of his father in 1781, was already a source of awe-inspiring pride to the family, having shone brilliantly at Harrow, at Eton, and at Christ Church, Oxford. But money was tight for the others, and at fifteen Arthur had to exchange the mellow brick of College for a lodging in Brussels, and the company of rowdy Etonians for that of a Yorkshire baronet's son and the disapproving presence of his mother, who despaired of her ugly, awkward son. Then a year of private tuition with a lawyer gave way to education as a cadet at Pignerol's academy at Angers on the Mayenne. Even here, where for Latin was substituted mathematics, fencing, horsemanship and dancing, Arthur Wesley scarcely stood out among his fellow cadets. Poor health obliged him to lie up on a sofa for many an hour, amusing himself with a devoted white terrier or else playing the violin as he had done in Brussels ; and he preferred the dinner-table conversation of local gentry to the noisy quarrels of his gambling companions.

Whereas Richard was by now a Junior Lord of the Treasury and Gerald had already decided to enter the Church, Arthur had reached no decision about his career. Therefore his mother's view that he was 'food for powder and nothing more' prevailed to the extent that Richard used influence to procure him a commission, dated March 7th, 1787, as ensign

3

in the 73rd (Highland) Regiment of Foot. At once Ensign Wesley showed an interest in the Army: 'since I had undertaken a profession I had better try to understand it'. His regiment being then in India, the family looked for better prospects nearer home and obtained the post of aide-de-camp to the Lord-Lieutenant of Ireland. Four further regimental exchanges between infantry and cavalry and a second evasion of India found Arthur a captain in the 58th Foot in the summer of 1791, mostly on duty at Dublin Castle amid viceregal splendour but drawing modest pay, getting into debt, and lodging with a bootmaker on a Liffey quayside.

Though he had no great enthusiasm for politics, he was elected to the Irish Parliament as member for the family borough of Trim. 'Ruddy-faced and juvenile in appearance', wearing red coat, high collar and epaulettes, he sat on a committee and he spoke without distinction in favour of Catholic franchise besides seconding the Address to the Sovereign in January 1793, just before the outbreak of the prolonged war against France.

At the Lord-Lieutenant's court he met and fell in love with Catherine Pakenham, Lord Longford's third daughter. His love was returned, but her brother, who had succeeded to the title, remained adamant in his objections to a match with an impecunious captain — by this time Wesley had exchanged into the 18th Light Dragoons. It became clear that in order to marry he must rise in his profession. To economise he renounced cards; he took up the habit of studying for some hours each day; and from Richard he borrowed enough money to buy himself a majority in the 33rd Foot, then part of the Irish garrison. He gained his new rank on April 30th, 1793, and exactly five months later he became lieutenant-colonel of the Regiment — he had reached that position from ensign in less than seven years.

There followed months of regimental routine in Dublin and in Cork, and not until June 1794 did the 33rd, along with other regiments, go on active service. They sailed to Ostend to reinforce the young Duke of York, whose army had been sent the previous year to help Prussia and Austria oust the French from the Netherlands, and was now, after some early successes, in a criticial position. The Austrians were about to be shattered after sustaining a melancholy series of reverses.

On the French capture of Bruges and Ypres, the Duke fell back on Malines, and it was here that Arthur Wesley joined him after evacuating Ostend, re-embarking his redcoats and landing at Antwerp. In September the British army began a northward retreat out of Belgium, and on the 15th Wesley and his men conducted themselves admirably in a sharp action in Dutch Brabant. The Colonel's rearguard brigade now covered the subsequent retreat to Nijmegen, then across the Waal, on the north bank of which river the 33rd held positions among ice-bound canals and bleak flats from October until January.

The first letter in this collection describes conditions during this period.

4

I

TO SIR CHICHESTER FORTESCUE [1]

Ysendoom, 20th December, 1794

. . . I intend to go to England in a few days, that is to say, if the French remain quiet, and if the regiment is relieved from the advanced post upon the river Waal, where it has been for above six weeks. At present the French keep us in a perpetual state of alarm; we turn out once, sometimes twice, every night; the officers and men are harassed to death, and if we are not relieved, I believe there will be few of the latter remaining shortly. I have not had my clothes off my back for a long time, and generally spend the greatest part of the night upon the bank of the river, notwithstanding which I have entirely got rid of that disorder which was near killing me at the close of the summer campaign. Although the French annoy us much at night, they are very entertaining during the day time; they are perpetually chattering with our officers and soldiers, and dance the *carmagnole* [2] upon the opposite bank whenever we desire them; but occasionally the spectators on our side are interrupted in the middle of the dance by a cannon-ball from theirs. . . .

It was now 1795 and the retreat was resumed — a terrible winter withdrawal beset by indiscipline, hunger, plunder and ill-will — across the north of Holland, over the frontier of Hanover to Ems, and then to Bremen. Here, on April 13th, the 33rd Foot embarked for Harwich, thankful to escape from a disastrous failure of a campaign which had taught Colonel Wesley 'what one ought not to do, and that is always something. . . . No one knew anything of the management of an army, though many of the regiments were excellent.'

Home from Germany, the Regiment settled at Warley in Essex, but Wesley travelled to Ireland, to resume his post as aide-de-camp at Dublin Castle — there was a new Lord-Lieutenant, the Earl of Camden. He spoke in Parliament, saw to his Trim constituents, and sought promotion, still better financial prospects, a new impetus to his career. He even thought of quitting the Army for a civilian post on the Revenue or

[1] Fortescue, born in June 1750, was a Rear-Admiral. He received a knighthood on succeeding his brother as Ulster King of Arms in 1787. His mother, Elizabeth Wesley, was a daughter of the 1st Earl of Mornington and thus an aunt of the future Duke of Wellington. Fortescue's elder brother, like Arthur Wellesley, married into the family of the Earl of Longford.

[2] A dance of the French Revolution, dating from about 1793.

Treasury Board if anything attractive could be procured, but to the blessing of Britain's military future his place-hunting efforts proved vain, despite heavy fraternal support.

So it was that in the autumn of 1795 he rejoined the 33rd, now waiting outside Southampton for a passage to the fever-ridden West Indies and the projected capture of Dutch colonies there. So many weeks went by that it was November before the convoy sailed, and then a gale blew up, wrecked seven transports and drove the rest to Portsmouth. They tried again in December but gales still lashed the Channel, and although some ships did find their scattered way to the Indies, thirty, among them Wesley's, were driven back to port. The winter was spent in Poole.

With the advent of 1796 came fresh orders to embark, this time for the East Indies, as India was then called. When the 33rd sailed in April, Arthur, now a full colonel, was convalescent in Dublin, yet the end of June saw him waiting for a fair wind and a fast frigate that would overtake his regiment before it rounded the Cape of Good Hope.

In his *Memoirs* Captain George Elers of the 12th Foot gives us a portrait of Colonel Wesley at this time : twenty-seven years of age. 'He was all life and spirits. In height he was about 5 feet 7 inches, with a long, pale face, a remarkably large aquiline nose, a clear blue eye, and the blackest beard I ever saw. He was remarkably clean in his person, and I have known him shave twice in one day, which I believe was his constant practice. . . . He spoke at this time remarkably quickly, with, I think, a very, very slight lisp. He had very narrow jawbones, and there was a great peculiarity in his ear, which I never observed but in one other person, Lord Byron — the lobe of the ear uniting to the cheek. He had a particular way, when pleased, of pursing up his mouth. I have often observed it when he has been thinking abstractedly.'

Very few of the Colonel's letters survive from the year 1797, but we catch sight of him several times in the memoirs of William Hickey, a Supreme Court Judge's clerk then residing in Calcutta. Hickey also had a house some thirty miles up the Hooghly at Chinsurah, the chief settlement of the Dutch in Bengal,[1] and it was here that he invited Major-General John St. Leger and his family to stay for the races.

'On the 31st of May we went up to Chinsurah together, as did Colonel Wellesley,[2] my friend John Scawen [a former school-fellow of Hickey at Westminster], and a nephew of his named Blunt, a young clergyman of very eccentric and peculiarly odd manners. Although I had no less than ten spare beds, my house was quite full. . . . The 1st, 2nd, and 3rd of June we each morning had admirable sport, the horses running in capital style ; two races were won by only half a neck. General St. Leger was quite delighted, positively saying what he had just seen could scarcely have been excelled at Newmarket. . . .

[1] The Dutch held Chinsurah for 180 years, and in 1826 ceded it to Britain in exchange for Sumatra.
[2] He changed his name from Wesley to Wellesley in May 1798. *See* p. 20, n. 1.

'The 4th being His Majesty's birthday I resolved to pay due honour thereto. I had procured a very fine turtle and half a tolerably fat deer, engaging an eminent French cook from Calcutta to dress the dinner. At three o'clock the following party sat down at table : Myself, whom I mention first as master of the house ; on my right hand, General St. Leger, on the left Colonel Wellesley, Mr. Van Citters, the Dutch Governor . . . making the number sixteen. The dinner was pronounced excellent by all, but especially by General St. Leger, a professed judge of every circumstance connected with good living. He likewise admitted that the turtle and venison were done justice to in respect of dressing. I had taken especial care to lay in a *quantum sufficit* of the best champagne that was procurable, my claret, hock, and madeira I knew were not to be surpassed in Bengal. The day went off with the utmost hilarity and good humour. We had several choice songs by Major Bradshaw [1] and Captain Forrest,[2] followed by delightful catches and glees by them and the Messieurs Birch.[3] General St. Leger in the course of the evening sang "The British Grenadiers" with high spirit ; in short in such perfect harmony were the whole party that we did not break up until two and three o'clock in the morning, when my guests retired to their respective apartments.

'At ten o'clock the following morning the majority reassembled to breakfast when all complained more or less of headache or slight sickness, except the gay young Captain De Lancy,[4] who protested he never was better in his life, and had slept uninterruptedly from which "he was sure the wines were sterling". "A hair of the same dog" on the 5th set all the complainers to rights, and the scene of the preceding day was renewed. The 6th the whole party dined with the Dutch Governor, Mr. Van Citters, who gave us a most splendid entertainment, with a Ball at night, where all the beauties of the Settlement were present, the merry dance being continued until near daylight in the morning. On the 7th we returned to Calcutta. . . .'

Hickey met Wellesley through his friendship with Colonel John Sherbrooke, also of the 33rd Foot, who frequently invited Hickey to dine with him at the Regimental Mess, 'where either he or Colonel Wellesley made a point of being present five or six times a week. They lived inimitably well, always sending their guests away with a liberal quantity of the best claret. They generally entertained from five to ten guests daily at their table. But the most dangerous parties in point of success were those that took place at Colonel Sherbrooke's country residence, a small mansion at the pretty village of Alypore, three miles from Calcutta, where I witnessed some extreme hard drinking. . . .'[5]

---

[1] Major Barrington Bradshaw, formerly of the Horse Guards.
[2] Captain Arthur Forrest, an Engineer officer.
[3] Richard Conryns Birch and his brother John.
[4] At this time General St. Leger's aide-de-camp, William De Lancy of the 16th Light Dragoons became a colonel, served in the Peninsula as Assistant Quartermaster-General, was knighted and died of wounds received at Waterloo.
[5] *Memoirs of William Hickey*, edited by Alfred Spencer, vol. iv, pp. 160-1, 190.

When Colonel Wellesley first reached India — at Fort William, Calcutta, on February 17th, 1797 — the Governor-General was Sir John Shore, afterwards Lord Teignmouth, whom Wellesley termed 'a good man, but cold as a greyhound's nose'. In pursuance of Pitt's policy of attacking enemies through their colonial possessions, Shore was contemplating an expedition against Manilla, capital of the Spanish settlements in the Philippines — since the previous October Spain had been allied with France in the war against Great Britain. Wellesley's task was to organise this expedition, and he was soon urging Sir John Shore to allow the force to seize the Dutch colony of Batavia on Java in passing. In August the expedition sailed from Calcutta, Wellesley commanding the 33rd, and the troops landed at Penang; but at this juncture it was recalled, in part because the discovery that Tippoo Sahib, ruler of Mysore, had been in correspondence with the French in Mauritius, known at the time as the Ile-de-France, made any distant foreign venture too hazardous.

In January 1798, on his return from Penang, Wellesley saw the 33rd settled into Calcutta and then took leave to visit his friend Lord Hobart, who was on the point of relinquishing the Governorship of Madras. At the request of General Harris, commanding the East India Company's troops in that Presidency, he remained at Fort St. George to assist the new Governor, the second Lord Clive. Wellesley was still with Lord Clive when the 33rd Regiment was transferred from the Bengal establishment to that of Madras.

2

TO THE EARL OF MORNINGTON

Fort William,[1] 12th July, 1797

My dear Mornington,

No opportunity of sending letters to England has offered lately; but even if any had offered, so little has passed which could interest anybody at a distance from this country, that it would not have been worth while to write. Everybody has been taken up with making preparations for the expedition, which is at last to sail from hence in the beginning of August, and from Madras in the middle of that month. Such is the strength and goodness of the army, that I have little doubt of its success, whether the attack be made upon Manilla, Mauritius, or Batavia. The Admiral [2] and the Governments say that their intentions are upon the former; and as their preparations, such as ordering

---

[1] Fort William, on the Hooghly River at Calcutta, was completed in 1773.
[2] Vice-Admiral Peter Rainier (1741 ?–1808) was Commander-in-Chief in the East Indies from 1793 to 1804.

refreshments at Prince of Wales' Island,[1] at Malacca, &c., are upon the road to it, I believe them. They have, however, been guilty of great neglect in suffering a ship under Danish colours to go out of the Ganges about six weeks ago, avowedly bound to Manilla; and of great oversight in not fitting out the expedition in time to attack and destroy the Dutch settlements upon Java with the same force which is to attack Manilla. If they had been ready early in this month, they would have arrived at Batavia early in the next, when the climate is not as unwholesome as at other periods of the year; and such is the weakness of the Dutch, that it is universally believed by those who are best acquainted with their situation, that our objects there, whether of destruction or of making permanent establishments, would have been accomplished the moment we appeared; whereas if we go after we shall have been at Manilla (which we must do now or not go to Manilla at all), although we shall meet with the same success, yet it will be with such loss from the unwholesomeness of the climate at that season of the year as this country cannot well bear. The destruction of Batavia would ruin the Dutch; but it may be a question whether it would be right completely to annihilate them, and it is probably that consideration which has prevented us from attacking them at this moment. Mauritius ought to be taken. As long as the French have an establishment there, Great Britain cannot call herself safe in India. They must be particularly guarded against after the war, as it may be depended upon that swarms of them (aristocrats, democrats, modérés, &c. &c.) will come here to seek service in the armies of the Native princes, and all Frenchmen in such a situation are equally dangerous. They would shortly discipline their numerous armies in the new mode which they have adopted in Europe, than which nothing can be more formidable to the small body of fighting men of which the Company's armies in general consist; and in the end they would force us to increase our armies and of course our expense to such a degree, that the country could not be kept, or indeed would not be worth keeping. At present the country powers are quiet. People say that Tippoo Sahib[2] has an army on foot, which I don't believe, as I have observed since my arrival here that he is a constant object of

---

[1] Also called Penang Island, off the west coast of Malaya.
[2] Tippoo Sultan (1753–99), son of Hyder Ali, founder of the Muslim Kingdom of Mysore.

fear to the English, and whenever they want to add a little colouring to a statement of danger, they find out that he has an army in motion. . . .

. . . I have not heard from England since I left it, which is extraordinary, considering that that was in June '96. I hope to receive some account that can be depended upon of the Irish invasion; [1] old John Latouche [2] must have made a good orderly dragoon. The confusion must have been comical.

The success at sea is astonishing.[3]

Excepting a slight fever, which I had about a month ago at the cantonment at Moorshedabad,[4] I have been perfectly well ever since my arrival in this country. We have got through the hot weather, as it is called, and are now in the midst of the rains; but I have not found either so oppressive as people in general have represented them. It is, however, a miserable country to live in, and I now begin to think that a man well deserves some of the wealth which is sometimes brought home, for having spent his life here.

The natives, as far as I have observed, are much misrepresented. They are the most mischievous, deceitful race of people I have seen or read of. I have not yet met with a Hindoo who had one good quality, even for the state of society in his own country, and the Mussulmans are worse than they are. Their meekness and mildness do not exist. It is true that the feats which have been performed by Europeans have made them objects of fear; but wherever the disproportion of numbers is greater than usual, they uniformly destroy them if they can, and in their dealings and conduct among themselves they are the most atrociously cruel people I ever heard of. There are two circumstances in this country which must occasion cruelty, and deceit, and falsehood wherever they exist. First, there is a contempt of death in the natives, high and low, occasioned by some of the tenets of the religion of both sects, which makes that punishment a joke, and I may say an honour, instead of what it is in our country. All our punishments almost are the same, excepting imprisonment and whipping, which occasion loss of caste, and are, therefore, reckoned too severe for the common

[1] A French expedition to invade Ireland had failed in December 1796 after reaching Bantry Bay.

[2] John Latouche was a banker in Dublin and became M.P. for Leitrim.

[3] This probably refers to Jervis's victory over the Spanish fleet off Cape St. Vincent on February 14th, 1797.

[4] A Bengal town a little over 100 miles north of Calcutta.

crimes for which we inflict them at home. The punishments of the Mussulman Governments are precisely in the same state. The Hindoos don't care for them, excepting they occasion loss of caste; and the Mussulmans are now so nearly Hindoos, that they have not a better effect upon them. Secondly, there is no punishment for perjury either in the Hindoo or Mussulman law. Their learned say that God punishes that crime, and therefore man ought not; and as oaths are notwithstanding administered and believed in evidence, no man is safe in his person or property, let the Government be ever so good. The consequence of all is, that there is more perjury in the town of Calcutta alone than there is in all Europe taken together, and in every other great town it is the same.

Notwithstanding all this, being here for a few years would place you in so high a situation for the remainder of your life, that I should like to see you in that of Governor-General.

I have no time to write to anybody else, and I wish you would let my mother, &c., know that I am well.

Believe me, &c.,

Arthur Wesley [1]

3

TO THE EARL OF MORNINGTON

Fort William, 27th July, 1797

My dear Mornington,

I have received your letters of the 5th and 21st of March. You will have seen before now what my sentiments were respecting your coming to this country. In a letter which I wrote to you, I believe in the month of March, I pressed you to look to the Government of this country, and you may easily conceive that I am glad to find that there is so near a prospect of my wishes upon that subject being accomplished. I am convinced that you will retain your health; nay, it is possible that its general state may be mended; and you will have the fairest opportunities of rendering material services to the public, and of doing yourself credit, which, exclusive of other personal considerations, should induce you to come out. I acknowledge that I am a bad judge of the pain a man feels upon parting from his

---

[1] *Supplementary Despatches*, i, 12-17.

family ; [1] but in this case it is to be considered that it is impossible to bring them with you without doing each of them, according to their respective ages, a very material injury ; nay, that you might lose some of them : and, on the other hand, if for the sake of remaining with them in England you refuse this offer, you forego both for yourself and them what will certainly be a material and a lasting advantage. I shall be happy to be of service to you in your Government ; but such are the rules respecting the disposal of all patronage in this country, that I can't expect to derive any advantage from it which I should not obtain if any other person were Governor-General. You may nevertheless be certain that I shall do everything in my power to serve you. I have written you several letters, in all of which I have delivered opinions upon military and political subjects as they occurred to me : probably upon reconsidering some of them I should not think them well founded, but in general I believe they are so. As I am going to Manilla, I probably shall not hear of your appointment as Governor-General [2] as soon as it takes place ; but as soon as I do hear of it I will write you a letter, which will be delivered to you upon your arrival, in which you shall have my opinion of the principal men in this country, as far as from the short acquaintance with them I have been able to form it. At present, to leave it here would betray your secret, which I shall take care to avoid ; and to write you a letter upon that subject to England would be useless, as probably you will sail before it would reach you. If you should not have sailed before this reaches you, I shall have returned from the expedition before your arrival, in which case I shall be able to give you opinions in person better founded of course than those I have now upon the different subjects which you have desired me to consider.

I am obliged to you for your applications to Lord Camden,[3] and respecting the 33rd Regiment I don't think the letter you

---

[1] In November 1794 Mornington had married Mademoiselle Hyacinthe Gabrielle Roland, with whom he had been living for some years and who had borne him five children. In the circumstances, and because of the risk to health, he decided to leave her at home to bring up the children.

[2] Mornington sailed from England as Governor-General on November 7th.

[3] John Jeffreys Pratt, 2nd Earl of Camden (1759–1840), was appointed Lord-Lieutenant of Ireland in 1794, after serving as M.P. for Bath and as a Lord of the Admiralty and of the Treasury. When rebellion broke out in Ireland in 1798, Lord Camden asked to be succeeded by a military commander, whereupon Lord Cornwallis was appointed. Camden was Secretary of State for War in 1804–5, and twice President of the Council. In 1812 he was created first Marquess of Camden.

sent gives any reason to hope for any thing from his Excellency. However, I have long determined to be silent, and if possible not to think upon that subject, and I shall at present adhere to that determination. I have received the papers, &c., &c. They make me to a certain degree *au fait* of what has been going on since my departure from Europe.

Believe me, &c.,

Arthur Wesley [1]

[1] *Supplementary Despatches*, i, 17-18.

PART TWO

INDIA: THE SETTLEMENT OF MYSORE

INTRODUCTION TO PART TWO

THE thirty-eight-year-old Earl of Mornington accepted the post of Governor-General and arrived in Calcutta on May 17th, 1798, bringing as Secretary one of his brothers, Henry Wellesley. Responsible alike to the British Government, to a Board of Control composed of Cabinet Ministers and to the Court of Directors of the Honorable East India Company, Mornington soon made his mark by extravagant pomp and splendour as well as by proconsular zeal and a measure of autocracy which led one of his staff to write that the Governor-General 'is his own Secretary at War, his own minister of foreign relations, his own Master General of Ordnance, and his own Chancellor of the Exchequer'.

When he reached India the land possessed by the East India Company comprised parts of Bengal, held since the days of Clive and governed from Fort William in Calcutta, and two distant and widely separated enclaves round Madras and Bombay. Occupation of these, which included a 200-mile stretch of the Malabar coast, dated back no further than the defeat in 1792 of Tippoo, Sultan of Mysore, who had ever since been waiting upon a chance to avenge his failure, and looked to France to furnish the opportunity and requisite power.

Lord Mornington had scarcely installed himself in Calcutta when a crisis occurred. The French Governor of Mauritius issued a proclamation calling for volunteers to go to the aid of Tippoo who, he claimed, 'only awaits the moment when the French shall come to his assistance to declare war against the English, whom he ardently desires to expel from India'. It appeared that some French officers had actually landed from Mauritius and joined Tippoo in Seringapatam. The Governor's premature proclamation served to warn the British authorities of obvious dangers, and Lord Mornington was for declaring war at once on Tippoo in order to forestall his designs. He was induced to defer so precipitate a step by his brother Arthur, on the grounds that the army, dispersed, and short alike of money and of bullocks, was not ready for such a campaign, nor was the season appropriate. Campaigns in India had to be timed so as to avoid the monsoons, which, by flooding rivers and turning roads to mud, would render almost impossible an advance requiring the support of thousands of beasts of burden and the crossing of a score of waterways. In any case, Arthur and others advised keeping peace with Tippoo, being willing to give him the benefit of the doubt and overlook bad faith in negotiation, even when it became patent that the Sultan was in fact conspiring against the British.

Meanwhile the Nizam of Hyderabad was well disposed towards the

17

Company's representatives, but his army of fourteen thousand being officered by the French, he could barely stand out against Tippoo's French-backed plans. Accordingly, Colonel Wellesley, who had been at Fort St. George to co-operate with General Harris, commanding all troops in the Madras Presidency, in keeping the new Governor, Lord Clive, on the right road, advised a *coup de main* to disarm this force. Accordingly, six thousand men were sent to Hyderabad in October, but the job was largely done for them by a mutiny against the French officers, who surrendered and were shipped to England. The Nizam was also persuaded to enter into a subsidiary treaty of alliance with the East India Company, to place his army under British officers, and to maintain six thousand of the Company's soldiers at Hyderabad for the security of his dominions, these being in some danger from Tippoo's Muslim Mysore in the south and, to the north and west, from the warlike Hindu chiefs of the Mahratta Confederacy.

Negotiations with Tippoo were being drawn out, for the Sultan, made bold and hopeful by Napoleon's promise from Egypt of an invincible army on its way to his support — a promise frustrated by Nelson's victory at the Nile — was playing a waiting game. In the face of this procrastination, Arthur Wellesley was still against driving the ruler of Mysore too far : 'I would confine the demand to his receiving an ambassador from us'. But Lord Mornington was impatient of Indian delaying courtesies, and on January 9th, 1799, he set a time limit, adding the caution that 'dangerous consequences result from the delay of arduous affairs'.

Early in February he ordered the army to advance into Mysore. Since November a force had been assembling inland from Madras under the temporary command of Colonel Harvey Aston ; but when this senior officer was killed in a duel, the command devolved upon Colonel Wellesley until such time as General Harris arrived to take charge. When he did so he found the twenty-one thousand troops in an excellent state, largely thanks to the efforts of the Colonel, who was now placed in command of the Nizam of Hyderabad's contingent — some sixteen thousand strong. He also had his own 33rd Regiment of Foot.

The campaign began when Tippoo, having decided under persuasion from his French officers to resist invasion, attacked the small Bombay army which, under Major-General James Stuart, had landed at Cannanore and was moving up the Western Ghauts. Finding himself thus threatened from both east and west, the Sultan hoped to defeat Stuart before he had a chance to join Harris. At Sedaseer, some thirty miles from Seringapatam, Colonel John Montresor's brigade of native infantry was moving through thick jungle, isolated from the rest of the force, when it was attacked. Montresor's men held out long enough to allow Stuart to hurry up two British regiments and not only rescue the brigade but also to defeat and scatter Tippoo's army.

Meantime Harris's columns, eager as they were to reach Seringapatam before the monsoon floods made the Cauvery impassable, had been harassed by native light horse. Grappling with problems of forage, and encumbered by a vast amount of baggage, a host of followers and 120,000 bullocks, besides camels and elephants, they had made slow progress — twenty-five miles in five days — on their route past Bangalore and over the Maddoor river. On March 27th they encountered the enemy on the ridge of Mallavelly. Five hours' stiff fighting, then Tippoo's men yielded their strong positions and escaped pursuit. Harris crossed the Cauvery unopposed by troops or floods, and on arrival outside the Sultan's capital, set to besiege Seringapatam. When, after a month, the town was stormed on May 4th, Tippoo's corpse was found among the fallen.

Mysore was now annexed and partitioned by the East India Company, who reinstated the original dynasty which had been supplanted many years before by Tippoo's father, Hyder Ali. The extreme youth of the new rajah, a boy of five, meant that Arthur Wellesley, as Governor of Seringapatam and commander of the forces in Mysore, together with the Political Resident, Colonel Barry Close (see page 40), had virtual charge of the kingdom. Their administration was on the whole moderate, merciful and scrupulous in regard for native rights and customs.

4

TO THE HON. HENRY WELLESLEY

Fort St. George,[1] 14th Oct., 1798

My dear Henry,

As I think it probable that we shall take the field, and as in that case I shall be obliged to keep a table, I must get some plate, which is the only certain method of having anything to eat off, and in the end it comes cheapest. If Mornington has bought that plate of Hunt's,[2] and does not want it, I shall be glad to have the soup-tureen and dishes at the price which he paid for them; and I shall be obliged to you if you will order for me at Raitt's[3] as many dishes of the same pattern, in addition thereto, as Lamette[4] will think necessary for a camp dinner for twelve people. If Mornington wants Hunt's plate, order for me, at Raitt's, a soup-tureen and dishes for twelve people, and desire him to make them of the pattern of the two plates which I got from him before I left Bengal.

Send them to me by the first ship. I shall not want plates,

[1] In Madras.
[2] Mr. J. Hunt was clerk to Hippolitus Poignand, a Calcutta jeweller.
[3] Alexander Raitt was another Calcutta jeweller.
[4] Lamette was *maître d'hôtel* to the Governor-General.

knives, forks, nor spoons, as everybody in an Indian camp brings those articles for himself: the host finds eatables and dishes only. . . .

Believe me, &c.,

Arthur Wellesley [1]

5

TO THE HON. HENRY WELLESLEY

Camp near Wallajah-Nuggur, 2nd Jan., 1799

My dear Henry,

What I have to say respecting the propositions I shall state very shortly, as I really have not time to write much.

Your propositions to Tippoo ought to be moderate, at least so much so as to make it probable that he will acquiesce in them, because I am of opinion that our war cannot be successful in one campaign. First, there is a general scarcity of grain in the country, which will greatly impede our military operations. Secondly, there is a want of money, which must be fatal. Thirdly, there is a chance that the Nizam's troops will not join us in time to enable us to advance together to the siege of Seringapatam. Fourthly, preparations do not appear to be sufficiently advanced on the Malabar side of India to make it certain that we shall have the co-operation of the Bombay army. Fifthly, we have no General.[2] I have repeated some of these objections to hostilities so frequently, that I am afraid I shall be accused of boring Mornington; but some of them are new, and have been occasioned by the circumstances of the present time.

There are three demands which can be made upon Tippoo. First, that he should receive an ambassador. Secondly, that he should dismiss his Frenchmen, taken into his service under his offensive treaty. Thirdly, that he should give up to us his sea coast. I think still that the first would give security, but I see that preparations are very forward, and I know that our war must in the end be successful, and therefore, I would demand

---

[1] *Supplementary Despatches*, i, 107. His elder brother Richard having decided to change the spelling of the family name from Wesley to Wellesley, Arthur did the same, in May 1798.

[2] Lieut.-General George Harris (1746–1829) had not yet arrived to assume command. After service in America, where he was wounded at Bunker Hill, in the West Indies, and in the first campaign against Tippoo Sahib, Harris commanded the Madras army from 1796 to 1800. He was created a baron in 1815. In his *Reminiscences*, the 2nd Lord Teignmouth wrote: 'General Harris wore a gold plate on his head, having been trepanned at Bunker Hill'.

the second. As to the third : first, I don't think it absolutely
necessary for our security, as, in consequence of having a resident with him, we shall be able to watch his transactions with
the French, and can guard his coast by our cruisers when we
find it necessary to prevent his communication by sea with
European powers. But I think it will be difficult hereafter to
prevail upon any French to adventure in this country when it
will be known that Tippoo has sent away those whom he took
into his service under the terms of the most solemn treaty. In
the next place, I don't think that we have any right to expect that
he should give up territory without a war, which even the most
successful war might not enable us to gain. If that be true, we
must give him something in exchange, and I don't see anything
that we can give him to lose which would not be a greater disadvantage than we can possibly reap benefit from the acquisition.
If the Allies would give up a portion of their territory for what
we now demand, and would take compensation from us in
peshcush ¹ or remission of subsidy for our troops they have in
their service, it might answer ; but I imagine it will be as difficult
to persuade them to do that as to persuade Tippoo to give up
his coast.

Thirdly, there is another view of the question which relates
to the Allies. How are we to divide with them what we may
acquire ? The fairness of the division in the last war ² is the
cause of the ease with which they are prevailed upon to join us
at present ; and no division at all, which must be the case if we
get the sea coast, or a division disadvantageous to them, may
occasion jealousies which will eventually do us more harm than
anything we can gain will do us good.

I have written this in a hurry, and there are many people
waiting for me in my tent, and probably I have not paid so much
attention to the subject as I ought. You have, however, the
result of my reflections upon the subject for some time past, and
if you'll come here we can talk it over.

Believe me, &c.,

Arthur Wellesley

You may give what interest you please, but you will get no
money at Madras.³

¹ *Peshkash*=a quit-rent paid to Government as an acknowledgment of any
tenure.
² The war against Tippoo Sahib of 1790–2.
³ *Supplementary Despatches*, i, 152-9.

6

TO THE HON. HENRY WELLESLEY

Camp near Wallajah-Nuggur, 7th Jan., 1799

My dear Henry,

. . . When I left Madras to take the command of the troops, which, with their followers are above 30,000 men, I had not even a servant with me, and I came away at an hour's notice. There was not a grain of rice to be got in the bazaar at Arcot, and, after bullying and writing day and night, I have got plenty in my camp, and have been able to go on for a fortnight without drawing upon the public stores, contrary to the expectation of everybody, and without putting the public to the expense of a single shilling. This I shall continue to do as long as the army may remain here. I asked for assistance, and he sent me two Company's officers; one of them, a brother of ——, so stupid that I can make no use of him, and the other such a rascal that half of my occupation consists in watching him, lest under the authority of my name he should play tricks in the country. At all events, they are not my personal staff; they have their own duties, and can't assist me in doing mine; and if they had not, I cannot trust them even to copy a letter for me, as they would reveal its contents. Besides this, they neither of them understand one syllable of the language; have never been even in a camp, much less on service; and I may say of them, as I do of ——, that they are an incumbrance.

I mention these circumstances to you in order that if —— complains to Mornington, you may know what to say to him. There is no officer in the army excepting myself to whom he would dare to behave as he has done to me; and if I did not believe that he would be glad to seize an opportunity of sending me away from hence, and if I had not particular reasons for wishing not to appear to hang back upon the present occasion, I should desire to join my regiment. I assure you that during two nights, whilst Colonel Aston's [1] court of inquiry was sitting,

---

[1] Lieut.-Colonel Henry Hervey Aston commanded the 12th Regiment of Foot. In his *Twelve Years' Military Adventure*, Lieutenant Blakiston writes of Aston : 'He had seen a good deal of the world before he came out to India, had been a great fox-hunter, a patron of the fancy, and a leading member in the sporting circles. He had many good points about him ; was generous and brave, but he had a most inveterate disposition to quizzing, which involved him in many personal encounters, whereby he obtained the reputation of a professed duellist.' He was killed in December 1798 in a duel with a major of the 12th.

I was in bed only two hours; and had black grain merchants teasing me almost the whole time that I was employed upon other business.

Believe me, &c.,

Arthur Wellesley

I have opened this, as I forgot to put up the letters.[1]

7

TO THE EARL OF MORNINGTON

Camp near Vellore, 29th Jan., 1799

My dear Mornington,

I have just received a letter from Henry, in which he has desired that I should give you my opinion respecting the propriety and utility of your joining the army and accompanying it during the campaign.

I am entirely ignorant of the objects which you may have in view in coming, which may certainly counterbalance the objections I have to the measure; but it appears to me that your presence in camp, instead of giving confidence to the General [Harris], would in fact deprive him of the command of the army, and that scene would be acted over again, probably in the presence of the enemy, which, to my annoyance, I have so often witnessed at Madras. Every thing which the General might think necessary will be thwarted and canvassed, not by you probably, but by those whom you will naturally wish to consult; the General's own staff, and the principal officers of his army, who ought to think of nothing excepting how his orders are to be carried into execution, instead of their propriety, and in what manner they shall thwart them if they should not approve of them. All I can say upon the subject is, that if I were in General Harris's situation, and you joined the army, I should quit it.

In my opinion he is at present awkwardly situated, and he will require all the powers which can be given to him to keep in order the officers who will be in his army. Your presence will diminish his powers, at the same time that as it is impossible you can know any thing of military matters, your powers will

[1] *Supplementary Despatches*, i, 166-7.

not answer the purpose, which even those which he has at present may, if you [1] or Lord Clive [2] are not in the army.

Believe me, &c.,

Arthur Wellesley

The General arrived in camp this morning.[3]

8

DRAFT OF A LETTER TO MAJOR JOHN SHEE

Camp, 21st March, 1799

I received your letter at so late an hour last night that it was impossible then to answer it.

If I had passed a censure upon your conduct for a circumstance which no exertion of yours could have prevented, I should probably have been as unreasonable as you have represented me in the epithets which you have applied to it ; but the fact is, I passed no censure. I sent you directions ; and if Mr. Gaff [4] told you otherwise, he is not fit for the situation to which I have provisionally appointed him. There is no necessity for referring to the authorities which you have quoted upon the subject. I saw and spoke to the men at a distance in front of their regiment on the forming flank of the line, at the distance of about 200 yards from it. Some of them had arms, others had not ; and I sent them all back, with orders not to quit their regiment again ; and in the evening I sent you directions to prevent it if you possibly could : but in the most distant manner I never alluded to the manner of marching of the regiment, excepting in approbation of it, as so many men were brought under arms every day when it took up its ground.

I conceive that I have a right, and that it is my duty, to interfere in any matter of detail in which the 33rd are concerned ;

[1] On February 2nd Mornington replied : 'I entirely concur in your opinion respecting the impropriety of my taking the field with the army ; my judgment was always the same as yours ; but certain persons made such clamour on the subject, that I wished to learn how you thought upon it'.

[2] Edward, 2nd Lord Clive (1754–1839), had arrived in August as Governor of Madras. Arthur Wellesley described him thus to Mornington : 'He is a mild, moderate man, remarkably reserved, having a bad delivery, and apparently a heavy understanding. He certainly has been unaccustomed to consider questions of the magnitude of that now before him, but I doubt whether he is so dull as he appears, or as people here imagine he is.'

[3] *Supplementary Despatches*, i, 187.

[4] Lieutenant, afterwards Captain, George Gaff, of Wellesley's 33rd Regiment.

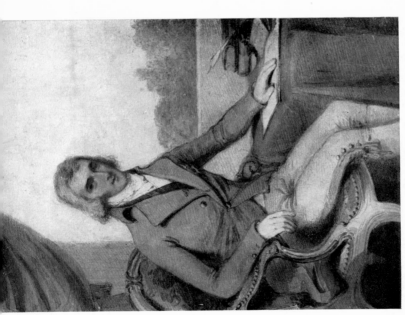

RICHARD, MARQUESS WELLESLEY

From the drawing by Henry Edridge at Windsor Castle

MAJOR-GENERAL SIR HENRY TORRENS

*From a mezzotint by C. Turner after the portrait
by Sir Thomas Lawrence*

and that being the case, it was my duty to send to you when I thought something had escaped your notice.

This is not the first time that I have had occasion to observe, that, under the forms of private correspondence, you have written me letters upon public duty, couched in terms to which I have not been accustomed. It is impossible to believe that you mean to use those terms; and yet I cannot but reflect that no sensible man ever writes a letter in a passion; that he inquires and considers, and, in the end, finds, as you would have done in this instance, that he had no reason to be displeased. However, it is necessary that I should inform you, that the next letter of that kind that I receive I shall send to the Commander-in-Chief, and leave it to him to give such answer to it as he may think fit.

It will be much better, and it will make both your situation and mine more comfortable to both, if you will understand one thing, that I have no intention whatever of doing anything which can have any effect unpleasant to your feelings, and that the best method of coming to such an understanding as we ought to live upon is, to inquire before you act in consequence of anything that passes. Of this you may be certain, that however my attention may be engaged by other objects, whenever I find it necessary I shall interfere in everything which concerns the 33rd. I have written more than I intended; and in hopes that I shall hear no more of it,

I remain, &c.,

Arthur Wellesley [1]

9

TO THE EARL OF MORNINGTON

Camp near Allagoor, 25th March, 1799

My dear Mornington,

An opportunity of sending a letter having offered, I write to inform you that we are going on now as well as you could wish. There is not *now* a doubt but that we shall bring that monstrous equipment [2] to Seringapatam, and, in that case, we shall certainly take the place. The whole army will be across

---

[1] *Supplementary Despatches*, i, 202-3.
[2] He referred to the host of camp followers, the cart-loads of baggage, the droves of bullocks which accompanied and encumbered the army on the march. 'When we were together, there was a multitude in motion which covered about eighteen square miles.'

the Maddoor river to-morrow. Tippoo was on the other side of it yesterday, but quitted a strong position on our approach, and is now gone towards Seringapatam. I write such good news that I don't put my letter in cypher. You will have heard many reports about us, but you may depend upon what I have above mentioned.

Believe me, &c.,

Arthur Wellesley

I am very well, but not a little fagged.[1]

✻

[Though we have no precise description of one of Colonel Wellesley's camps, we can readily picture the scene, as an army on the march settles into camp, from this account by Major William Thorn of the 25th Light Dragoons, writing from General Lake's army in 1803 :

'The power of the imagination can scarcely figure to itself the sudden transformation that takes place on these occasions, when an Indian camp exhibits with the effect of enchantment, the appearance of a lively and populous city amidst the wilds of solitude, and on a dreary plain. . . . Throughout long and regular streets of shops, like the booths at an English fair, may be seen in every direction all the bustling variety of trade, the relaxation of enjoyment, and the pursuits of pleasure. Here, sheroffs, or money changers, are ready with their coin to accomodate those who are unprovided with the currency requisite for the purchase of the necessaries or luxuries of life. In such a situation, where nothing more could be well expected than what serves to alleviate the present cravings of nature, every kind of luxury abounds ; and while some shops allure the hungry passenger with boiled or parched rice, others exhibit a profusion of rich viands, with spices, curry-materials, and confectionary, for the indulgence of a voluptuous appetite. European merchants here, called sadawkers, either by themselves or their native agents, are busily employed in vending wines, liquors, and groceries ; while other traders exhibit for sale fine cloths, muslins, and rich cashmerian shawls. Here also are to be found goldsmiths and jewellers exercising their occupations, and endeavouring to attract the fancy by a display of elegant ornaments, as though war had been deprived of its austerity, or that victory had already been decided. Besides these and various other traffickers, the camp exhibits the singular spectacle of female quacks, who practise cupping, sell drugs, and profess to cure disorders by charms. Nearly allied to these are the jugglers, shewing their dexterity by numerous arts of deception ; and, to complete the motley assemblage, groups of dancing girls have their allotted station in the bazaar. . . .

[1] *Supplementary Despatches*, i, 206.

'. . . Of the camp itself, and its grotesque appearance, something remains to be observed. Excepting the tents of the military, which are all of an uniform description, and pitched in regular lines, the collection of coverings used by the followers to screen them from the heat of the sun by day and the dews by night, exhibit a motley variety of colours, materials and figures, according to the taste or circumstance of individuals. Thus, in some places, ragged cloths or blankets are stretched over sticks or branches of trees, and in others, palm leaves are hastily spread out upon similar supports ; while handsome tents and splendid canopies are intermixed with asses, oxen, tattoos,[1] or ponies ; which ludicrous contrast becomes more striking, from the throngs of camels and elephants making a tinkling sound with the bells which are hung about their necks or legs ; to complete which confusion, an endless variety of tongues is heard, English, Hindoostanee, Persian, Arabic, and a number of provincial dialects, altogether forming a scene that may well be compared to the migration from Babel.' [2]]

10

TO THE EARL OF MORNINGTON

Camp, 2 miles west of Seringapatam,
5th April, 1799

My dear Mornington,

We arrived here this morning, and I take the opportunity of writing to you which is offered by General Floyd[3] going to meet General Stewart.[4] I wrote you two letters before : one to inform you that we should cross the Maddoor on the 26th ; the other to let you know that we had had an action with Tippoo, in which his troops had been driven and defeated by ours.

We had much difficulty to contend with after the army entered the Mysore country. The bullocks in the department of the Commissary of Stores failed almost entirely, notwithstanding that there were quantities of forage in the country, of which they might have had their share. This failure of the bullocks increased in so alarming a manner by the time that we

[1] From the Hindi word *tattu*, a pony.
[2] *Memoir of the War in India*, pp. 88–91.
[3] Major-General, afterwards General Sir John, Floyd (1748–1818) was second-in-command to General Harris and led the cavalry during this second war against Tippoo Sultan. Floyd had served in the Seven Years' War, being a riding-master at the age of fifteen ; he had first come to Madras in 1781 in command of a light dragoon regiment.
[4] This should be Major-General James Stuart (1741–1815), who had served in India under Sir Eyre Coote and Lord Cornwallis, and in 1796 had commanded the expedition sent to capture Ceylon.

got in the neighbourhood of Bangalore, particularly on the last march towards that place, that I had serious apprehensions that we should have been obliged to take post there, and defer our further operations to an ensuing season. However, upon inquiry it was found that the root of the evil lay in a parcel of absurd, impracticable, shopkeeping regulations which had been made for the bullock department, under which no great undertaking could ever prosper, and the first step taken was to abolish them all. The spirit and zeal of the army were then called forth with the greatest success. Many stores (absolutely useless excepting as lumber, and which I had pressed the General to leave behind him at Vellore) were destroyed; and, in short, we have contrived to bring on the largest useful equipment that ever was known in this country. We have plenty to take this place, which appears to me at present to be strong only from its situation. I have great satisfaction in informing you that the Nizam's sirdars [1] exerted themselves, as well as the rest of the army, in carrying stores. Above eight thousand shot have been brought here from the neighbourhood of Bangalore by Meer Allum [2] and the people immediately belonging to the Nizam alone, without counting what have been brought by the Company's servants.

We shall commence all our preparatory operations to-morrow, and probably we shall break ground before General Stewart arrives. It is the General's intention to attack, from both sides of the river, the western angle, and I think that we shall contrive to have such a fire upon it as will make it impossible for the Sultaun's [3] troops to remain long in the place.

I reckon that we have forty days before us from this time, and even more, if we can contrive a passage over the river when it swells. However, five days will make a breach for us after we once begin to batter, out of which his troops will not be able to keep ours.

In the action of the 27th of March, at Mallavelly, his troops behaved better than they have ever been known to behave. His infantry advanced, and almost stood the charge of bayonets of the 33rd, and his cavalry rode at General Baird's European brigade.[4] He did not support them as he ought, having drawn

---

[1] *Sirdars* (or *sardars*): native chiefs, headmen.
[2] The Nizam's Prime Minister. He commanded the Nizam's cavalry in this campaign.
[3] Tippoo.
[4] Major-General David Baird (1757–1829) had the 12th and 74th Regiments of

off his guns at the moment we made our attack, and even pushed forward these troops to cover the retreat of his guns. This is the cause of the total destruction of the troops he left behind him, without loss to us, and of the panic with which we have reason to believe all his troops are now affected. His light cavalry, looties,[1] and others, are the best of the kind in the world. They have hung upon us, night and day, from the moment we entered his country to this. Some of them have always had sight of us, and have been prepared to cut off any persons venturing out of the reach of our camp-guards. We came by a road so unfrequented that it was not possible to destroy all the forage, which would have distressed us much; but they did as much, even in that way, as could be expected from them. If Tippoo had had sense and spirit sufficient to use his cavalry and infantry as he might have done, I have no hesitation in saying that we should not now be here, and probably should not be out of the jungles near Bangalore.

We have had much blundering and *puzzling*, and I have been present at many strong and violent discussions in the cabinet. However, all parties are apparently well together, and we are now here with a strong, a healthy, and a brave army, with plenty of stores, guns, &c., &c., and we shall be masters of his place before much more time passes over our heads.

The fatigue and heat of the weather (which is greater here than even at Calcutta) and bad water had given me a bowel complaint, which did not confine me, but teased me much. I have nearly got the better of it, and I hope to be quite well in a few days.

Believe me, &c.,

Arthur Wellesley

I omitted to mention to you that we have thirty-three days' rice for thirty thousand men at full allowance, besides what the brinjarries [2] have, so that there is no danger of our feeling want.

Foot and the Scotch Brigade. Baird had very personal motives in this war, because for nearly four years until his release in 1784 he had been a prisoner in Seringapatam. Then in 1792 he had helped to defeat Tippoo. His last battle was to be in 1809 at Corunna, where, as Sir John Moore's second-in-command, he was severely wounded and lost an arm.

[1] Mounted mercenaries.

[2] Dealers who supplied the army with grain and rice. Wellesley defined them as 'a class of carriers who gain a livelihood by transporting grain or other commodities from one part of the country to another. They attend armies, and trade nearly in the same manner as they do in common times of peace.' See page 30.

General Harris does not write, trusting to my giving you an account of our state.[1]

�֎

[Of brinjarries Lieutenant John Blakiston of the Engineers wrote in his memoirs : 'To my European readers, the best description I can give of their habits and appearance, is to compare them to a gypsy muleteer, if such a thing can be imagined. They possess a distinct costume — that of the women is extremely fantastic ; and they adorn their bullocks with bells. . . . They are in general armed with a sword and buckler, which they well know how to use in self-defence ; live constantly in tents, carrying the whole of their families with them ; and are employed as the general carriers throughout India. They are remarkable for their punctuality and honesty in their engagements, and it is as much good policy as good faith, to be just and liberal towards them. In fact, there was no carrying on the war without them.' [2]

By contrast with this eulogy, we find Wellesley expressing a firmly adverse opinion of their honesty. 'To give them money or grain in advance will not answer. They are notoriously dishonest, and they would run away with the former, and would sell the latter in any place at which they could find a more ready or a more advantageous market than the camp.' Yet he gave an altered view to the Rev. G. R. Gleig, one of his biographers, many years afterwards : 'Pay them well, and you may almost always depend upon them. I never found them fail me. If I had endeavoured in that war to carry about with me stores of grain sufficient for the consumption of the sepoys and the animals, I should have done nothing. It was difficult enough to transport my ammunition, and supplies of meat and rum and bread for the Europeans.' [3]]

II

TO LIEUT.-GENERAL GEORGE HARRIS

Seringapatam, 6th May, 1799

My dear Sir,

Plunder is stopped, the fires are all extinguished, and the inhabitants are returning to their houses fast. I am now employed in burying the dead, which I hope will be completed this day, particularly if you send me all the pioneers.

It is absolutely necessary that you should immediately appoint a permanent garrison, and a commanding officer to the place ; till that is done, the people will have no confidence in us,

---

[1] *Supplementary Despatches*, i, 206-8.
[2] *Twelve Years' Military Adventure*, vol. i, pp. 191-2.
[3] *The Life of Arthur, Duke of Wellington*, p. 40.

and every thing must be in confusion. That which I arrange this day, my successor may alter to-morrow, and his the next day; and nothing will ever be settled. A garrison which would be likely to remain here, would soon make themselves comfortable, although it might be found convenient hereafter to change some of the corps sent in: but these daily reliefs create much confusion and distrust in the inhabitants; and the camp is at such a distance, that it is impossible for the officers or soldiers, or sepoys to get down their dinners.

I shall be obliged to you, if you will order an extra dram and biscuit for the 12th, 33rd, and 73rd [1] regiments, who got nothing to eat yesterday, and were wet last night.

In hopes that you will attend to my recommendation to send a garrison in to-morrow, I shall look out for a place to accommodate one or two battalions of Europeans, and three or four of sepoys.

I am, my dear Sir, &c.

Arthur Wellesley

❋

[That Colonel Wellesley should have been appointed by General Harris to command Seringapatam after its capture exacerbated Major-General Baird's already sore feelings towards the Governor-General's brother. There was an exchange over breakfast, and Baird wrote: 'Before the sweat was dry on my brow, I was superseded by an inferior officer'. Over thirty years afterwards, the Duke of Wellington set down his thoughts about Baird, in the following letter to Mr. Croker.]

12

TO JOHN WILSON CROKER [2]

London, 24th January, 1831

My dear Croker,

I have received your note, and shall be happy to see you on the day that you have fixed.

I have often heard of Sir D. Baird's dissatisfaction on my appointment to take command at Seringapatam when he had commanded the successful storm of the town, on which I was not even employed, having been appointed to command the

---

[1] The 12th (East Suffolk), the 33rd (1st Yorkshire West Riding) and 73rd (Highland) Regiments.

[2] Croker (1780–1857), who was temporarily Chief Secretary for Ireland in 1808, served for many years as Secretary to the Admiralty.

reserve in the trenches. Of course I had nothing, I could have nothing to say to the selection of myself, as I was in the trenches, or rather in the town, when I received the order to take the command of it, and instructions to endeavour to restore order.

Baird was a gallant, hard-headed, lion-hearted officer, but he had no talent, no *tact*; had strong prejudices against the natives; and he was peculiarly disqualified from his manners, habits, &c., and it was supposed his temper, for the management of them. He had been Tippoo's prisoner for years. He had a strong feeling of the bad usage which he had received during his captivity, and it is not impossible that the knowledge of this feeling might have induced Lord Harris, and those who advised his Lordship, to lay him aside.

However, of course I never inquired the reason of my appointment, or of Baird being laid aside. There were many other candidates besides Baird and myself, all senior to me, some to Baird. But I must say that I was the *fit person* to be selected. I had commanded the Nizam's army during the campaign, and had given universal satisfaction. I was liked by the natives.

It is certainly true that this command afforded me the opportunity for distinction, and thus opened the road to fame, which poor Baird always thought was, by the same act, closed upon him. Notwithstanding this, he and I were always on the best terms, and I don't believe that there was any man who rejoiced more sincerely than he did in my success.[1]

Believe me, &c.,

Wellington [2]

❃

[Describing the people of Mysore, near Hurryhur, in his unpublished manuscript journal, Lieutenant William Lambton of the 33rd Regiment of Foot wrote on Monday, August 5th, 1799:

'The inhabitants appear to be intelligent & curious, distinguished like all hindoos by a simplicity and gentleness of manners. Their stature is but small, but they are much more active & industrious than the Natives

---

[1] In a letter dated November 21st, 1832, Sir John Malcolm (see pp. 93-4) wrote: 'I never saw Baird from 1803, when he spoke thus sorely about Wellesley being so often, as he called it, "put over his head", until ten years afterwards, when I met him in Hyde Park. He then came up with open hand and heart, saying: "Times are changed; no one knows so well as you how severely I felt the preference given on several occasions to your friend Wellesley. But now I see all these things from a different point of view. It is the highest pride of my life that anybody should ever have dreamed of my being put in the balance with him. His fame is now to me joy, and I may also say glory, and his kindness to me and mine has all along been most distinguished."'

[2] *The Correspondence and Diaries of the Right Hon. J. W. Croker*, vol. ii, p. 102.

of the Carnatic. Their Villages are extremely neat, being laid out in streets, & their habitations white washed, or coloured, & swept clean within. Having never before seen an European face, they were struck with astonishment at the sight of our complexions, & wondered to see hair of any other colour than that of black. They had been taught to consider the English as Monsters, & at first approach were timid and cautious, but smiles & gentleness soon gained their confidence. They were delighted at our admiration of their implements of husbandry, but to convince them that Europeans were not entirely ignorant of arts, we shewed them a watch & a Spy-Glass — the ticking of the former excited much wonder among the old men, which was encreased beyond description when they saw the Machinery. But the most amusing part of the exhibition was their viewing a horse through the Spy-Glass reversed. To see a large animal transformed in a moment to a great distance by looking through a Tube, excited such a degree of surprize and good humour, that the impatience they all had to see so rare a sight, made them seize it with such eagerness, that two got hold of it at the same time, & peeping in at each end of it, they afforded us much amusement.' [1]

Lambton relates how, on September 14th, 1799, the 74th Regiment crossed the River Toom near Hoolinore where the Toom and the Budrah join. 'The men were carried over by the Elephant (and so were men of the 73rd Regiment), the baggage in boats — many of the followers made rafts by fixing a number of the pots (chatties) together, lashing them fast with Bamboos. These pots are narrow at the top and swell out into a globular form, holding 7 or 8 Quarts — nine or ten of these fastened with the tops through the openings of the bamboo raft will sustain a great weight. The plan is simple and excellent. Five men are as many as can conveniently pass upon an Elephant — there is not room for more to sit.' [2]

Wellington himself, many years later in October 1825, told Samuel Rogers how he had used elephants in India for the conveyance of stores or artillery. 'I had once occasion to send my men through a river upon some. A drunken soldier fell off and was carried down by the torrent till he scrambled up a rock in the middle of the stream. I sent the elephant after him, and with large strides he obeyed his driver. When arrived he could not get near the rock, and he stiffened his tail to serve as a plank. The man was too drunk to avail himself of it, and the elephant seized him with his trunk, and, notwithstanding the resistance he made, and the many cuffs he gave that sensitive part, placed him on his back.' [3]

Lambton of the 33rd also records in his diary how on November 7th, 1799, Colonel Wellesley and Barry Close, the Resident, received a visit from the Anngundah Rajah on the tableland beyond the Rahhully pass.

'That personage being descended from the oldest Rajahs in the Deccan, conceives it incumbent to keep up all the antient state and formality of the East. He never makes a Salam to any one, nor does he

---

[1] B.M. Add. MSS. 13664, ff. 21-2.   [2] *Ibid.* f. 83.
[3] *Recollections by Samuel Rogers.*

deign to speak, unless he be spoken to, and even then but seldom, as he is attended by a person through whom he conveys his meaning and his orders. His arrival was nearly two hours after the appointed time and his approach was notified by the clamours of the crowd, which preceded him. When he was within a short distance of the great Tent, his Palenkeen [1] was placed on the ground, and he there remained motionless till he was handed out by the two Gentlemen to whom the visit was intended ; and by them conducted into the Tent where a carpet was spread for him ; but in this instance, and I suppose for the first time in his life, he took his seat on a chair, and remained for a considerable time sullen in silence receiving and returning compliments, through the person who was the vehicle of his thoughts ; at length some few words passed between him and Purneah, and that was all that dropped from this *man* of *Cast*. During the whole time of this fantastical visit, one of his people continued to proclaim aloud the catalogue of his titles, and the dignities annexed to them. Two other attendants stood behind him, with huge bunches of Peacocks feathers, preventing the flies from insulting his turban.

'After this solemn ceremony had continued near half an hour, his servants brought him otto of roses, and Beetle nut. A large silver turin contained the former, and it was sprinkled over his head and garments by the Resident who sat at his right. The Beetle was introduced, and handed in silver dishes.

'After this service was performed this mighty man took his departure with all the state and pageantry that dignified his entrance, and after being handed into his Palenkeen, amidst the acclamations of his creatures, he was then hoisted away, preceded by his Pikemen, and followed by a mob.

'He appears to be upwards of sixty years of age, and we were told that his Mother is still living & is near ninety. His person is tall and straight, and his visage thin and long, but by no means devoid of expression ; and were he not burthened with his antient dignity, his countenance would carry the marks of intelligence.' [2]]

13

TO LIEUT.-COLONEL JOHN DOVETON [3]

Seringapatam, 24th Dec., 1799

My dear Sir,

Within these few days I have received an application from a very respectable man (Père Dubois [4]) to have returned to their

---

[1] See note to letter no. 29.   [2] B.M. Add. MSS. 13664, ff. 90-2.

[3] Afterwards General Sir John Doveton (1768–1847), he was at this time paymaster of the stipends at Vellore.

[4] The Abbé J. A. Dubois (*c.* 1770–1848), author of *Mœurs, institutions, et cérémonies des peuples de l'Inde,* translated as *Hindu Manners, Customs and Ceremonies.*

husbands the wives of about 200 Christians, and other unmarried Christian women, whom Tippoo had carried off from their husbands and friends upon different occasions when he visited the Malabar coast and Canara, and who were placed, and are now supposed to be, in his Zenana.[1] I have refused to comply with this request, although the refusal is unjust, because, the Company having taken this family under its protection, it is not proper that anything should be done which can disgrace it in the eyes of the Indian world, or which can in the most remote degree cast a shade upon the dead, or violate the feelings of those who are alive. Le Père Dubois has made another request upon this subject which can do neither, and he places it upon such strong grounds that it does not appear to me to be possible to refuse compliance.

He says that the husbands of these women, who were taken from them in the most indecent and tyrannical manner accompanied by acts of cruelty which it is unnecessary here to detail, are desirous of marrying again ; and he says that he cannot perform the marriage ceremony unless he ascertains whether their former wives are really dead. The means of ascertaining this fact are possible, and, therefore, until they are resorted to, he will not perform the ceremony. This appears to me so reasonable that I have not thought it proper to refuse compliance ; and I have accordingly desired to have a list of the names of the Christian women still alive in the Mahal.[2] Some difficulty has been made in giving it, and I have not received it yet, but I hope to get it in a day or two.

I understand that many of these women went to Vellore with the Princes, and I shall be obliged to you if you will endeavour to procure a list of the names of those who are still alive. I make no doubt but that, upon representing the cause of the request, and upon giving an assurance that it is not intended to ask for a single woman, the good sense of the young men will induce them to grant what we are obliged to ask. I must observe that, although I have given this assurance here, and press you to give it at Vellore, I am by no means certain that if the matter came before Government they would not be obliged to give up every woman of them. Justice and all our prejudices and passions are on the side of the Christians, and there is nothing which can induce the Government to refrain from doing what is just except-

[1] Female apartments ; seraglio.   Seraglio.

ing the consideration which I have above mentioned has weight with me, which after all is only one of policy, and that not of a very urgent nature. If the Princes and the family here carry *their* prejudices so far as to refuse compliance with the reasonable request of Père Dubois, the granting of which will enable him to remove much of the inconvenience and grievance suffered in consequence of Tippoo's tyranny and injustice in this instance, I shall be under the necessity of forwarding to Government the whole that has passed upon this subject, and the result will then be most probably, that Government will give orders not only that every Christian woman, but every woman detained in the Zenana against her consent, may be allowed to depart. I don't wish to hint this idea, much less hold it out as a threat; but I mention it to you, as I know your wishes for the ease, honour, and satisfaction of this family, as an inducement to you to urge them most seriously to give the information required, and to allow no vain prejudices to affect their conduct upon an occasion so interesting to a large number of people.

I enclose you a letter which I have received from Père Dubois. You perceive that he asks information only about a few; but he has repeatedly told me that the husbands of others are coming from the coast upon the same errand, and I have therefore determined at once to procure a list of all those still alive.

Believe me, &c.,

Arthur Wellesley [1]

[One consequence of Tippoo's defeat in May 1799 had been the disbandment of his army, whereupon many restless, loot-lusting malcontents found themselves an able, daring leader in Dhoondiah Waugh. This experienced freebooter, who had escaped from prison a day before the fall of Seringapatam, had in the general confusion been able without much trouble to capture several fortresses, and being as well imbued with ambition as he was supplied with artillery and lesser weapons, he proclaimed himself 'King of the Two Worlds'. So formidable a threat did he soon become that Wellesley had to take suppressive steps, and in July his two columns seized the fort of Chitteldroog, then overwhelmed six hundred of Dhoondiah's adherents, took two other strongholds, and at Shikapoor defeated fifteen hundred horsemen and infantry. Dhoondiah escaped into Mahratta territory and that seemed to be the end of his nuisance. But it was by no means so, for in the spring of 1800 he was back at his plundering, this time on the Carnatic and in the district of

[1] *Supplementary Despatches*, i, 419-21.

Darwar. When five thousand Mahratta cavalry sent to destroy Dhoondiah were defeated, the Governor-General ordered his brother to hunt down the freebooter and hang him. Accordingly the Colonel marched on May 21st from Seringapatam and assembled his force at Chitteldroog. He reached Hurryhur on June 16th, just one day too late to ford the Toombudra before the monsoon broke. Instead, the troops took a week to cross in boats. Then they stormed the fort of Ranny Bednore, and pursued Dhoondiah north-west towards Savanore, capturing garrisons but not Dhoondiah himself and being constantly hampered as much by rivers to cross as by lack of grain, problems of forage and shortage of bullocks. However, by the end of July Dhoondiah had lost all his strongholds in the Savanore and Darwar districts, as well as his baggage and guns. Yet he was still elusive, and the chase had to be renewed. To thwart his opponent's doubling to and fro by the Malpurba river, Arthur Wellesley sent off columns to drive Dhoondiah into a corner where two flooded rivers converged, but even here he failed. Not until September 10th did he come to battle with Dhoondiah's five thousand and kill the robber and disperse his surviving followers.

The successful conclusion of Wellesley's first campaign in sole command elicited from a gratified Governor-General the declaration that 'we have now proved (a perfect novelty in India) that we can hunt down the lightest footed and most rapid armies as well as we can destroy heavy troops and storm strong fortifications'.]

14

TO MAJOR THOMAS MUNRO [1]

Seringapatam, 7th May, 1800

Dear Munro,

I am glad to find that your people in Canara are so free from the foul crime of rebellion. We shall not be able, in this year, to make an impression on Kisnapah Naig,[2] which will keep him entirely quiet; but on the 30th of last month he received a beating from Colonel Montressor,[3] who took from him his post of Arakeery, which will, at least, give him reason to believe that it is not easy to keep our troops out of any place into which they are ordered to enter. The entire subjection of him depends

---

[1] Munro, afterwards Sir Thomas (1761–1827), went to India at the age of eighteen, fought against Hyder Ali in 1780–3 and then against Tippoo Sahib in 1790–2. He spent seven years administering some of the lands acquired from Tippoo, and after the Sultan's death at Seringapatam he spent a similar period in charge of the northern districts ceded by the Nizam of Hyderabad. In 1820 Munro was appointed Governor of Madras; he died of cholera in 1827.

[2] The Rajah of Bullum.

[3] John Montresor, 80th Regiment. He died in 1804.

upon the destruction of his strong holds; and for that, as we cannot expect much more fair weather, we have not at present a sufficiency of time. . . .

I think that upon the whole we are not in the most thriving condition in this country. Polygars,[1] nairs,[2] and moplas[3] in arms on all sides of us; an army full of disaffection and discontent, amounting to Lord knows what, on the northern frontier, which increases as it advances like a snowball in snow. To oppose this, we have nothing that ought to be taken from the necessary garrisons, and the corps we have in them are incomplete in men and without officers. If we go to war in earnest, however, (and if we take the field at all, it ought to be in earnest), I will collect every thing that can be brought together from all sides, and we ought not to quit the field as long as there is a discontented or unsubdued polygar in the country.

Believe me, &c.,

Arthur Wellesley

15

TO THE EARL OF MORNINGTON

Camp at Curruh, 29th May, 1800

My dear M.,

I have received your letter of the 13th instant, and I am very much obliged to you for the offer which you make me of sending me with the Admiral [Rainier] to Batavia.[4]

I do not deny that I should like much to go; but you will have learned, before you receive this, that my troops are in the field, and it is therefore probable that Lord Clive will be desirous that I should remain in this country until its tranquillity is ensured, and the troops can be sent back to their different garrisons. I have written to him upon the subject, and I have desired him to accept your offer for me or not, as he may find it most convenient for the public service, after having ascertained from the

---

[1] Polygars: natives who thought themselves independent and, armed with pikes and matchlocks, lived in hills, woods and forts.

[2] Nairs: a warlike race living in the mountains and jungles of Malabar. 'Nairs, I am informed, are gentlemen', wrote Wellesley, 'and probably the idlest of that character.' See letter no. 19.

[3] Moplahs: another Malabar race, descended from the Arabs who colonised that coast.

[4] Wellesley had been offered command of a force to be sent to capture Batavia from the Dutch. Lord Clive decided against its acceptance and Wellesley was instructed to enter the Mahratta country and hunt down Dhoondiah.

Admiral at what time he proposes to depart from the coast on this service. If he should not depart until late in the year, I think it more than probable that I shall be able to go with him. I do not know which of the services will answer best; but I am certain that it will be more easy to spare troops from the Carnatic and Mysore, towards the end of the year, than it is at this moment.

Dhoondiah is certainly a despicable enemy; but, from circumstances, he is one against whom we have been obliged to make a formidable preparation. It is absolutely necessary to the peace of this country of Canara and Malabar, that that man should be given up to us; and I doubt not that before now you will have made a demand for him upon the government of Poonah. If we do not get him, we must expect a general insurrection of all the discontented and disaffected of these countries. I have information that letters have been received by most of them, either from him, or from others written in his name, calling upon them to take the opportunity to rebel against the Company's government, or that of their allies; and his invasion of our territory is looked to as a circumstance favourable to their views.

The destruction of this man, therefore, is absolutely necessary for our tranquillity; and nothing will be more easy, if the Mahrattas are really disposed to enter into the plan. If they are not, it will be a matter of difficulty, and it may become a question whether the whole power of the Company ought not to be turned to this object. I was aware that this was the case before the troops were collected; and although I was certain that it was the only mode of saving this country from being plundered, I did not like to put it in execution without Lord Clive's orders.

It was clear that when an army should be collected to oppose a man who had an asylum in the Mahratta country, and who may therefore be reckoned a part of the Mahratta state, the government would be committed with that of the Mahrattas, and our honor would require that we should go through with the business until that man should be given up to us, or that we should have some adequate security for his good behaviour.

If, then, the government of Poonah is inclined to give this man up to us, or to co-operate with us in his destruction, it may be possible for me to go to Batavia. If they should not, matters here will take a very serious turn, and no prospect of advantage or of credit to be gained shall induce me to quit this country.

Besides the destruction of this Dhoondiah, there are other objects, which comparatively, however, are of a trifling nature. The attainment of these might be given in charge to other people, if it should be thought desirable to postpone the expedition to Batavia until matters are settled on the Mahratta frontier.

Ever yours most affectionately,

Arthur Wellesley

❊

[The next letter is addressed to one of the most distinguished of Arthur Wellesley's associates in India : Colonel Barry Close. Born in December 1756, the third son of Maxwell Close of Drumbanagher, Co. Armagh, he had begun his Indian service as a cadet in Madras back in 1771. By 1799 he was adjutant-general of Harris's army, and soon afterwards he took up the post of Resident at Mysore, moving in 1801 to a similar appointment at Poona.

That Close was among Wellesley's most frequent and welcome correspondents is shown by the fact that between December 8th, 1799, and December 9th, 1800, Wellesley wrote him at least 145 letters. He held Barry Close in high esteem, describing him to his brother Henry as 'by far the ablest man in the Company's army' and 'the ablest man in the diplomatic line in India'. To Lord Mornington he wrote of Close : 'he is the only man I have seen yet who manages the natives properly, and that merely from his perfect knowledge of their language' ; and again, in August 1802 : 'Close is a great authority, and I would submit to his decision upon most occasions'.

Wellesley had in Close the utmost confidence, and their degree of co-operation when faced with a variety of harassing problems was unusually effective. 'It is impossible for two men to go on better than he and I, notwithstanding that his temper is not of the best, and his mode of enforcing his reasonings not the most agreeable. But he is able and zealous to a degree in the public cause, and it is always pleasant to act with such a man, whatever may be his temper.'

Colonel James Welsh describes Close as 'a short swarthy looking man, and rather inclined to fat, though he was as hardy and active in body as in mind ; and even when far advanced in life, he would ride thirty or forty miles a day, and chase a hare, an antelope, or a fox, with all the fire and vigour of youth'.[1] His appearance conjured up in the mind of Sir James Mackintosh, Recorder of Bombay, a taller and less unwieldy version of Charles James Fox. 'He is without accomplishment or show, plain, cautious, and with a degree of mildness that forms a singular contrast with the firmness, and even sternness which he has shown on trying occasions. He has a calm understanding, wholly employed in practice, united to a strength of nerve, which qualifies him equally for a cautious

---

[1] *Military Reminiscences*, vol. i, p. 209.

COLONEL SIR JOHN MALCOLM

COLONEL BARRY CLOSE IN 1794

or a vigorous policy. He is a very superior man, who might easily pass among common observers for a very common man.' [1]

When Barry Close returned to England in 1811 he was created a baronet, but long service in India having impaired his health, he died within two years. On learning of his death, another great figure in that period of Indian history, Mountstuart Elphinstone, wrote this tribute in his journal : 'I doubt whether such an assemblage of manly virtues remains behind him. A strong and hardy frame, a clear head, and vigorous understanding, fixed principles, unshaken courage, contempt for pomp and pleasure, entire devotion to the public service, joined to the utmost modesty and simplicity, formed the character of Sir Barry Close — a character such as one would rather think imagined in ancient Rome than met with in our own age and nation.' [2]]

16
TO LIEUT.-COLONEL BARRY CLOSE

Camp at Ranny Bednore,[3]
June 30th, 1800

My dear Colonel,

... What a pity it is that I can't move on for want of Grain : My troops are in high health, order, and spirits ; but the unfortunate defect of arrangement in the poor man at Chittledroog, previous to my arrival, has ruined every thing.

I had at one time nearly 4000 loads in Camp ; if I had been able to reach the river one day sooner, I should have been across before it filled : the delay in crossing was one of about ten days, during that time we were feeding upon the Brinjarries, as we did not draw a grain from the country, which reduced the full bags in Camp to about 2000, and about as many more they say on the road. Then comes the delay in filling, travelling, passing the river, &c., and it becomes absolutely impossible to say at what time we shall have a sufficiency to cross the Werdah,[4] although the Brinjarries swear that there are large quantities of Rice coming on to us.

All this delay would have been avoided if when I wrote on the 10th of May, measures had been taken to make them all fill, and to collect them together ; but instead of that, until I wrote on the 5th of June to know what had been done, no steps were

---

[1] *Life of Sir James Mackintosh*, vol. i, p. 458.
[2] *The Life of the Honourable Mountstuart Elphinstone*, vol. i, p. 270.
[3] Ranibennur.   [4] The Varada river.

taken, and I was four days at Chitteldroog before I could even see one of the Naigs.[1] How true it is that in military operations time is every thing. . . .

> Believe me, Your's most sincerely,
> Arthur Wellesley [2]

17

TO LIEUT.-COLONEL BARRY CLOSE

> Camp near Luckmaseer,
> July 23rd, 1800

My dear Colonel,

In two days at Savanore I was entirely destroyed. I lost upon a moderate calculation about half my cattle.

I have however contrived to crawl here, I am in the midst of large villages full of Cattle, which I am now employed in seizing and arranging to departments, and I hope to be able to move on to-morrow. Never surely was there any thing so unfortunate, but I hope to remedy it in some degree. There is nothing so faulty as our Bullock system, and its effects are now most severely felt.

I assure you that we have never wanted forage; at Savanore it is true the Cavalry in the first two days used all there was in the fort, notwithstanding the orders to cut grass for the Horses, but still forage was plentiful at the distance of two or three miles. There is however clearly so little interest in the preservation of the Bullocks, in the breast of the Bullock men, that they could not be prevailed upon to go out these two or three miles to bring in forage; in some instances they were driven out; the weather became severe to a degree, and the consequence has been that we have lost half our Cattle. We lost only 4 Gun Bullocks, and from yesterday's march I should imagine that the private Cattle of the Army, and those belonging to the Bazaar people, are as well if not better than they were on the last day's march.

I have some suspicion of Dubash [3] tricks, such as fictitious owners and Maistries [4] in Camp, the real owners being Conaco-

---

[1] The title of the chiefs of the Bheels, wild people living in mountainous districts.
[2] *The Mysore Letters and Dispatches of the Duke of Wellington*, pp. 107-8.
[3] Agent ; interpreter.
[4] Head men in charge of draught cattle.

polies [1] in the Office at Seringapatam; and if I find a real and clear proof of that transaction I shall send the whole of it to Madras.

Believe me,
Your's most sincerely,
Arthur Wellesley

I have got bullocks, and am able to get on again once more.[2]

18

TO LIEUT.-COLONEL BARRY CLOSE

Camp at Yepalpervy,
11th September, 1800

My dear Colonel,

I have the pleasure to inform you that I gained a complete victory yesterday in an action with Doondiah's Army, in which he was killed. His body was found and recognized, and was brought into Camp on one of the Guns attached to the 19th Dragoons.

I had before informed you of my plan of operations in the Dooab.[3] I marched from Konna Gerry on the 8th, left my Infantry at Nowly, and proceeded on with the Cavalry only. I arrived here on the 9th, and the Infantry at Shinnoor about 15 miles in my rear. On the 9th Doondiah marched from Malgerry about 25 miles on this side of Rachore, towards the Kistna : but he saw Col. Stevenson's [4] Camp, turned back immediately, and encamped on that night about 9 miles from hence, between this place and Bunnoo. The night was so bad, and my horses were so much fatigued, that I could not move till morning, although I had intelligence of the place at which he was encamped; after passing a most anxious night between the 9th and 10th, I moved yesterday morning, and met the whole of the enemy's army at Cona Gull about six miles from hence, and three from the ground on which he had been encamped. He

---

[1] Store clerks.
[2] *The Mysore Letters and Dispatches of the Duke of Wellington*, pp. 122-3.
[3] The word *Doab* means 'the country between two rivers'.
[4] Colonel James Stevenson, a distinguished cavalry officer on the East India Company's Military Establishment at Fort St. George. In September 1798 his daughter Elizabeth had died there, aged two months, seventeen days.

had not heard of my being near him, was on his march with an intention of passing to the Westward, between my detachment which he supposed to be at Shinnoor, and the Mogul and Mahratta Cavalry at Moorky Belganoor. He however drew up in a remarkably strong position when he saw me, and his people, whom I think to have been 5000 in number, stood with apparent firmness. I charged them with the 19th and 25th Dragoons, and the 1st and 2nd Regiments of Native Cavalry, and drove them till they dispersed, and were scattered over all parts of the country. I then returned to the Camp, and got possession of Elephants, Camels, Baggage, &c. &c. which were still upon the ground. If the Mogul and Mahratta Cavalry had marched in decent time, the whole body must have been dead, as they fled in the line on which they must have met them; but I imagine they did not march till after they had heard that I had moved, and of course were late; they have been employed in the pursuit since yesterday evening, and I expect will destroy the whole body.

The troops behaved admirably, and I assure you that if they had not done so, not a man of us would have quitted the field. . . .

Believe me, Your's most sincerely,

Arthur Wellesley [1]

19

TO LIEUT.-COLONEL JOHN CONRAD SARTORIUS [2]

Camp at Kanna Gerry, 18th Sept., 1800

My dear Sir,

I have had the pleasure of receiving your letter of the 6th instant. The first object of your attention must be to throw into Montana such a supply of provisions as will secure that garrison from a probability of want. To that everything else must give way. To weaken Coti-angurry or any other post in the country which has heretofore been reckoned of importance is a matter of immaterial consequence when compared with the necessity of getting the better of, or, I may say, of defending yourself against the Pyche Rajah.[3] When he shall have been subdued, everything

---

[1] *The Mysore Letters and Dispatches of the Duke of Wellington*, pp. 143-4.
[2] Colonel Sartorius, of the Bombay Engineers, died at Cannanore on December 10th, 1801.
[3] The Pyche Rajah, who derived his name from the town of Pyche, north-east of Tellicherry, had seized the Wynaad district in the south-west corner of Mysore.

else will be quiet, and probably the numerous posts now out in Malabar will be found to be of no use. The Rajah presses you now upon Montana; you must relieve that post in the first instance by all means and at all events, and it will be time enough afterwards to consider in what mode we shall carry on the war.

The result of my observations and considerations upon the mode of carrying on war in jungly countries is just this, that as long as the jungle is thick, as the enemy can conceal himself in it, and from his concealment attack the troops, their followers, and their baggage, the operations must be unsuccessful on our side. You propose, as a remedy, to move in small compact bodies in different directions, in order that the enemy might have no mark, might be in constant fear of falling in with some party, and might lose confidence. I agree in opinion with you that your remedy might answer some purposes for a body of troops which could move without baggage or incumbrances of any kind; I say only some purposes, because their success would not be complete; our troops cannot move to all parts of the jungle as the Nairs [1] can, and it might always be expected that at some place or other our detachment would get into a scrape. But as we know that no troops can move without baggage so as to answer any purpose for which an operation might be undertaken, and as that mode of carrying on the war will avowedly not answer where there is baggage, we must look for some system the adoption of which will enable us to bring on in safety that necessary evil. I know of no mode of doing this excepting to deprive the enemy of his concealment by cutting away the lower part of the jungle to a considerable distance from the road. This, you say, is a work of time: it is true it is so, but it must be recollected that the labour of every man turns to account, that the operations, however long, must in the end be successful, and we shall not have to regret, after a great expense of blood and treasure, that the whole has been thrown away, and the same desultory operations are to be recommenced in the following season, as has been the case hitherto, and as will always be the case until some such mode of carrying on the war with security to the followers is adopted.

We will suppose that my principle is conceded, and that it is agreed that in order to be successful we must secure those who supply us with all we want, and that the best mode of doing this is to cut away the jungle in order to deprive the enemy of his

[1] See note on page 38.

concealment ; I proceed to state in what manner I should carry on my operations in Cotiote.

I would assemble my troops at Cotaparamba, and begin by laying open the country back to Tellicherry lest when I should move on towards Montana the enemy should take advantage of the close jungles between Cotaparamba and Tellicherry in order to interrupt my communication with the latter, which must be secure before I can hope for success. After having done this I should push forward my advanced posts, well strengthened in different directions, as you propose in your letter of the 6th instant. Under their cover strong working-parties should be employed in clearing the jungle. When they should have cleared forward to the distance of two or three miles, I would move the camp that distance, and remain in that new position till more road and country should have been cleared for me. By degrees I should get forward to the most advanced of my posts, and the result of my labours would be, that no Nair would venture into a country where I had deprived him of his advantage, viz. his concealment. But even if he should venture in my rear, tempted by the prospect of interrupting my communication and distressing me for provisions, he could not do so without my knowledge, and a very small body of troops would answer to protect my convoys when the country will have been opened, and I should be thus enabled to derive all the advantage of the discipline of my troops.

After having thus got myself well forward in the country, my posts well established and supplied, and my communication with my rear well secured, as well as that between one post and another, I would begin to carry on the war on a more active plan, and I would send out light detachments in all directions in order to hunt out every Nair who should be in the country. If at the same time another body of troops were carrying on operations on a similar system in Wynaad, I would endeavour to open a secure communication with that country. In the end you may depend upon it that neither the Pyche Rajah, nor any other man, could hold out ; he would be deserted by his people, and probably at last would fall into the hands of one of my detachments, as Dhoondiah did a few days ago.

Depend upon it, my dear Sir, that the success of military operations in India depends upon supplies ; there is no difficulty in fighting, and in finding the means of beating your enemy either without or with loss : but to gain your object you must feed, and you can feed only by communication with the sea, and you can secure that communication only by the operations which I have above described.

In the meantime, however, many modes of distressing the Pyche Rajah might be adopted. Nairs, I am informed, are gentlemen, and probably the idlest of that character. The Wynaad country, which is in their possession, is almost a desert, and certainly does not produce a sufficiency for their consumption. They live there upon what is sent to them from the coast, and they pay for what they get by sandal-wood, pepper, &c. I am informed that the Company's servants buy these articles from the Nairs of Wynaad. In the first place, you should call upon the Commissioners publicly (and do so in my name, if you like it) to put a stop to all communication between Wynaad and Malabar, and particularly to stop the trade from the latter in rice.

There is a fellow, by the name of Mousa, at Tellicherry, who supplies the Rajah with rice to my certain knowledge. A hint might be given to him that I am in the habit of hanging those whom I find living under the protection of the Company and dealing treacherously towards their interests ; that I spare neither rank nor riches ; but that, on the contrary, I punish severely those who, by their example, create the evils for which the unfortunate people suffer.

I have written you this letter in a private form, but I beg that you will hand it over to your successor, if you should think of going to Bombay, as containing my sentiments on the operations to be carried on in Cotiote, and the grounds upon which I have formed them.

Believe me, &c.,

Arthur Wellesley [1]

20

TO LIEUT.-COLONEL HARVEY CHARLES PALMER [2]

Camp at Kopul, 20th Sept., 1800

Sir,

I have had the honour to receive your letter of the 1st instant, and I lose not a moment to reply to that part of it in which you

---

[1] *Supplementary Despatches*, ii, 165-8.
[2] British Resident at Poona.

mention that complaints had been made to the Peshwah [1] of the violence committed by my soldiers on numbers of Mahratta women, the wives of Brahmins. I received particular directions from the government of Fort St. George upon this subject, and had therefore every inducement of duty, as well as of inclination, to prevent the excesses of which the Peshwah complains. I am happy to say that I have found my soldiers as orderly and as obedient as they are brave; I have stormed the enemy's camps twice, and I have had the misfortune of being under the necessity of taking three fortified places (besides two taken by one of my detachments) by storm. I have never heard a complaint of such a thing as you mention, excepting at Dummul. Two women, not Brahmins or Mahrattas, were taken out from that fort, but were restored to a person who claimed them in less than an hour after they were taken out.

Ball Kishen Bhow [2] has been with my army since I entered the Mahratta country, must have heard of those complaints if any grounds for them had been given, and of course would not conceal what he had heard from the Peshwah. I have the honour to enclose you a paper written by him upon this subject. Not only have no excesses been committed by my troops, but I have the satisfaction of knowing that the inhabitants of the country have uniformly looked up to me for protection against the violence and oppression of the Mahratta chiefs; I have always been obliged to protect those in the neighbourhood of my camp by safeguards, and I have frequently been under the necessity of remonstrating with the different chiefs regarding the manner in which they treated the unfortunate inhabitants. In justice to my army I must also state one fact, which will prove in the clearest manner their good conduct. It has seldom happened to me to halt a day at any place excepting to make preparations for crossing one of the rivers; but I have never halted anywhere that a bazaar has not been opened, and that the inhabitants did not continue in the pursuit of their different occupations.

[1] The Peshwah Bajee Rao Ragonaut Rao Pundit Purdhaun Behauder. Arthur Wellesley wrote in 1804 that he was 'callous to every thing but money and revenge'. And many years later: 'A shocking fellow ! — impossible to get on with him. He said afterwards that he had only three friends in the world — Malcolm, Colonel Close, and myself !' The word *Peshwa*, 'leader' or 'guide', was the title of a Mahratta minister.
[2] One of the lesser Mahratta chiefs, he commanded 500 horse and had entered the service of the Peshwah.

I have been thus particular in my answer to this part of your letter because I received the most positive orders from the government which I have the honour to serve upon this subject; and I had flattered myself that the conduct of my troops had been such as to give universal satisfaction.

I have the honour to be, &c.,

Arthur Wellesley [1]

21

TO CAPTAIN JAMES ACHILLES KIRKPATRICK [2]

Camp at Mayoondie, 10th Nov., 1800

Sir,

. . . I am obliged to you for the communication of your sentiments regarding the situation of our affairs with the Mahrattas. I agree entirely in your opinion that it is most desirable that they should be speedily brought to an issue; that the present period appears favourable to bring them to a crisis; and that, particularly at this moment, there is no reason to apprehend the consequences even of an appeal to arms for that purpose.

The only questions then are the propriety and justice of commencing a war to obtain our ends. I can give no opinion upon this point, as I am unacquainted with the particulars of the late unsuccessful negotiations; but if war should be determined on, I am convinced that we shall suffer no inconvenience from my having withdrawn from the Mahratta territory; if we are not to go to war, you appear to be of opinion that it is proper that I should withdraw without loss of time.

As to the justice of such an appeal; our governments in India are strongly prohibited from commencing wars excepting in case of attack, or preparation for an attack, by one of the Native

---

[1] *Supplementary Despatches*, ii, 168.
[2] He had succeeded his brother, Colonel William Kirkpatrick, as Resident at the Court of the Nizam of Hyderabad. Nicknamed 'Hushmut Jung' ('Pomp of War'), he was described by Mountstuart Elphinstone as 'a semi-Indianised Englishman who had married the daughter of the Nizam's Persian Prime Minister, and led a half-Oriental life. . . . He is a good-looking man ; seems about thirty, is really about thirty-five. He wears mustachios ; his hair is cropped very short, and his fingers are dyed with henna. In other respects he is like an Englishman. He is very communicative, and very desirous to please ; but he tells long stories about himself, and practises all the affectations of which the face and eyes are capable.' Kirkpatrick, born in 1764, died as a lieutenant-colonel in October 1805.

powers. The refusal of the Mahrattas to accede to our terms of closer alliance cannot be deemed an attack, and I have not heard of any circumstances in their late conduct which can be deemed one. Hostility then on our part might be thought a breach of the laws for the government of this empire.

But not only might it be considered in that light, but as an act of great political injustice. In fact, one country has no right to commence a war upon another because at some time or other that other may form an alliance with its enemy prejudicial to its interests, and because it refuses to draw closer the terms of its alliance with the country which proposes it. The question of peace or war is not, and cannot be, only the probability of success, but must depend upon other circumstances, and in this country must depend upon the prospect of being attacked by the power with which it is proposed to go to war.

These general principles are certain, and must be familiar to you, who are more in the habit of considering these questions. I mention them only as the groundwork of my opinion that it is proper that I should withdraw from the Mahratta territory. From these principles I conclude that we shall not go to war with the Mahrattas; and in that case you are of opinion that I ought not to maintain my position within the territories of the Peshwah. If from any circumstances in our situation it is inexpedient that we should have recourse to arms, the more plain that we make the real moderation of our views, the more we conciliate the Peshwah's government, the less likely will he be to throw himself into the hands of the French to curb our influence.

In truth, the conduct of our government in withdrawing from the Mahratta territory, after having had possession of a great part of it, is unexampled, and will be a lasting argument to those about the Peshwah who, however disinclined they may be to a closer connexion with us, may be still more so to see the French established in the centre of the Mahratta empire. We ought, therefore, to withdraw as soon as possible.

If, however, the wisdom of government should decide that it is proper to go to war, I am fully prepared.

I don't see any reason why Lieutenant-Colonel Bowser [1]

---

[1] Thomas Bowser, 18th Regiment of Native Infantry, had commanded a brigade under Wellesley in the 1799 campaign against Tippoo Sahib; and had led 1000 of the Nizam of Hyderabad's cavalry in the operations against Dhoondiah.

should remain any longer in the Dooab.   There is not now an
ember of Dhoondiah's rebellion remaining.
The Killadar [1] of Moodgul has given up all our property.
I have, &c.,

Arthur Wellesley [2]

✼

[At the end of 1800 the Governor-General took his brother from
Mysore and appointed him to command five thousand troops in Ceylon.
They were to embark and either attack the French in Mauritius — a haunt
of privateers and, to quote Lord Wellesley, 'a prolific source of intrigue in
peace, and of piracy and buccaneering in war' — or else go to the support
of Sir Ralph Abercromby's expedition to Egypt by attacking the French
in the rear from the Red Sea.   Colonel Wellesley went to Trincomalee
and made intensive and most competent arrangements for equipping,
provisioning and transporting his force, but the ships failed to arrive
because Admiral Rainier, perhaps jealous of receiving orders from an East
India Company Governor, refused to attack Mauritius on the grounds
that as a naval officer he could not do so unless he had a direct order from
King George III.   In any case the plan for Mauritius was shelved in
favour of Egypt, and the Earl of Mornington, now elevated to be the
Marquess Wellesley, found himself obliged, partly under pressure from
angry senior officers, to supersede his brother by Major-General David
Baird, with whom Arthur's relations at Seringapatam had not been happy.
When he had first given his brother the Ceylon post, the Governor-General
had foreseen that 'great trouble will arise among the general officers in
consequence of my employing you ; but I employ you because I rely on
your good sense, discretion, activity, and spirit ; and I cannot find all these
qualities united in any other officer who could take such a command '.
    Before he heard that Baird was to supersede him, Wellesley had been
informed by Lord Clive of the decision to send his force to Egypt, so to
facilitate this he had embarked the troops and sailed round to Bombay.
Baird was not at all pleased when he reached Trincomalee to find the
force gone — a thousand miles nearer to their destination.   He himself
did not arrive in Bombay until March 26th.   If Baird was angry, Wellesley
was chagrined and indignant at his brother's treatment and apparent lack
of confidence, especially after all his drudgery in preparing for the expedition.   In the end he went down with fever and contracted the Malabar
itch, which made it impossible for him to accompany Baird to the Red
Sea.   Instead he returned to his post in Seringapatam, on May 7th.   The
breach with the Governor-General took many months to heal, and in the
meantime they corresponded by intermediaries.]

[1] Killadar : commandant of a fort (*kila*).
[2] *Supplementary Despatches*, ii, 254-6.

22

TO THE HON. HENRY WELLESLEY

Bombay, 23rd March, 1801

My dear Henry,

I have received your note of the 3rd of March, but none of your other letters which you say that you have written to me. I hope that you received those which I wrote to you while you were in England,[1] giving an account of how we were going on in this country. I enclosed them to the Doctor,[2] and desired him to destroy those which should arrive subsequent to your departure, on your return to this country ; so that some of them written lately you will probably never see. I was very anxious about you, as you must have come from the Cape in the track of the French privateers homeward bound ; and you were longer on your passage than we had reason to expect you would be.

I have written a long letter to Government this day, about my departure from Ceylon, which I hope will explain everything. Whether it does or not, I shall always consider these expeditions as the most unfortunate circumstances for me, in every point of view, that could have occurred ; and, as such, I shall always lament them.

I was at the top of the tree in this country ; the governments of Forts St. George and Bombay, which I had served, placed unlimited confidence in me, and I had received from both strong and repeated marks of their approbation. Before I quitted the Mysore country, I arranged the plan for taking possession of the Ceded Districts, which was done without striking a blow ; and another plan for conquering Wynaad and re-conquering Malabar, which I am informed has succeeded without loss on our side. But this supercession has ruined all my prospects, founded upon any service that I may have rendered. Upon this point I must refer you to the letters written to me and to the Governor of Fort St. George in May last, when an expedition to Batavia was in contemplation ; and to those written to the governments of Fort St. George, Bombay, and Ceylon ; and to the Admiral [Rainier], Colonel [Forbes] Champagné, and myself, when the troops were assembled in Ceylon. I then ask you, has

---

[1] Henry Wellesley had been sent home with despatches, and with the Partition Treaty of Mysore and the Subsidiary Treaty of Seringapatam. He set off back to India at the end of August 1800.

[2] The Hon. Dr. Gerald Valerian Wellesley, born on December 7th, 1770, became Prebendary of Durham and Chaplain to Queen Victoria. He died in 1848.

there been any change whatever of circumstances that was not expected when I was appointed to the command ? If there has not, (and no one can say there has, without doing injustice to the Governor General's foresight), my supercession must have been occasioned, either by my own misconduct, or by an alteration of the sentiments of the Governor General.

I have not been guilty of robbery or murder, and he has certainly changed his mind ; but the world, which is always good-natured towards those whose affairs do not exactly prosper, will not, or rather does not, fail to suspect that both, or worse, have been the occasion of my being banished, like General Kray,[1] to my estate in Hungary. I did not look, and did not wish, for the appointment which was given to me ; and I say that it would probably have been more proper to give it to some body else ; but when it was given to me, and a circular written to the governments upon the subject, it would have been fair to allow me to hold it till I did some thing to deserve to lose it.

I put private considerations out of the question, as they ought and have had no weight in causing either my original appointment or my supercession. I am not quite satisfied with the manner in which I have been treated by Government upon the occasion. However, I have lost neither my health, spirits, nor temper in consequence thereof.

But it is useless to write any more upon a subject of which I wish to retain no remembrance whatever. . . .

Yours most affectionately,

Arthur Wellesley

23

TO THE HON. FREDERICK NORTH [2]

Bombay, 30th March, 1801

My dear Sir,

I have received your letters of the 20th and 27th February, for which I am much obliged to you.

[1] Paul Kray, Freiherr von Krajova (1735–1804), commanded the Allied advance guard in France in 1793, and was a corps commander on the Rhine and Danube in 1796. He defeated Kléber at Wetzlar, but in June 1800 his Austrian army on the Danube sustained a severe defeat at Hochstadt. He was relieved of his command.

[2] Frederick North (1766–1827), younger son of the 2nd Earl of Guilford, was Governor of Ceylon from 1798 to 1805. Before that he had been Comptroller of Customs in the Port of London. He succeeded his brother as 5th Earl in 1817. All his life he was philhellene in sympathy and in 1824 became the first Chancellor of the Ionian University of Corfu, which he had done much to promote.

Our passage to this place was extremely tedious, particularly the first part of it; but our delay here has been short, as some of the ships which came in first, sail this night. In fact, it would have been impossible to go on without calling at some port, as ballast was wanting for the ships as well as water and provisions. However, I have strong hopes that before a month is over our heads the greatest part of the fleet will be off Cosseir, and higher I conceive that it will neither be possible nor proper to go. Upper Egypt must be the seat of the operations of this army, which, it appears, are intended to distract the enemy.

I am by no means desirous that any part of our correspondence regarding my coming to Bombay should appear upon the records of your government. By Lord Wellesley's last letters it appears that he is not pleased at my having quitted Ceylon without his orders; although I believe that, however we may have differed as to the propriety of coming to Bombay, you thought that I ought to quit Ceylon immediately; it was the opinion of the government of Fort St. George, and it was expected by that of Bombay.

I have written to the Governor-General to explain to him the grounds on which I decided to quit Ceylon as soon as I heard of the call for the troops in the Red Sea, and those on which I determined to come to Bombay. In my opinion, his instructions required that I should sail as soon as I received the copy of the despatches from the Secretary of State of the 6th of October; and if that opinion should be acquiesced in, the displeasure which he has shown in consequence of my having departed on the service without his orders justifies me sufficiently for having come here, if only to receive them. But when I consider that ballast, provisions, water, refreshments, were absolutely necessary; when one corps only, the 10th regiment,[1] has lost above twenty men since it left Ceylon, and will leave near one hundred in the hospital at Bombay; when there are one hundred and twenty of the 88th on the sick list; I believe it will be allowed that a shilling has not been unnecessarily thrown away.

In deciding upon conduct in these points, it is necessary that the person who forms the decision should, for a moment, put himself in the place of him of whose conduct he is to judge, and, if that be done in my case, I may make my mind easy as to the

[1] The 10th (North Lincolnshire) Regiment.

result. If a man is to sit down at Calcutta to judge of my conduct, and is to be decided in his opinion of my actions by his *own knowledge* of what he was doing at the time, and not by any which I had or could have; if it be remembered that a letter from Calcutta does not arrive at Ceylon for nearly a month; and if he imagine that as soon as a letter is written the person to whom it is addressed knows its contents, I have good reason for all the uneasiness which I feel upon this occasion.

You see, my dear Sir, that I have taken the liberty of writing to you upon this subject as to an old acquaintance; and I hope that you will keep to yourself what I have said to you.

I had determined not to go upon the expedition, but despatches recently received make it probable that Sir Ralph Abercromby has attacked Alexandria.[1] I then determined to go immediately with all the troops then ready, and to commence the operations without loss of time; but I have been prevented from going by an attack of fever, which has kept me in bed for three days.

Believe me, &c.,

Arthur Wellesley [2]

24

TO THE HON. HENRY WELLESLEY

Bombay, 8th April, 1801

My dear Henry,

My fever has left me, but I am still weak, and I have got another disorder, of which it appears the medical men here do not know the nature, and which, I think it probable, will oblige me to go to a cold climate. This circumstance, and the great probability held out by the late dispatches from Europe, that Sir Ralph Abercromby's attack upon Lower Egypt will be postponed, or rather will never take place, and, therefore, that the operations proposed in the Red Sea will likewise be relinquished, have induced me to determine not to go. I shall write to the Governor General upon this subject as soon as I am able.

In the meantime, it is but justice to General Baird to say,

---

[1] General Sir Ralph Abercromby (1734-1801), commanding the British force in Egypt, was mortally wounded on March 21st, 1801, during a battle outside Alexandria, and died a week later. Alexandria did not surrender until September 1st.

[2] *Supplementary Despatches*, ii, 344-7.

that his conduct towards me has by no means occasioned this determination, but that it has been perfectly satisfactory. He offered Colonel Coleman [1] to appoint him Deputy Quarter Master General, which the latter declined.

I hope that if the service goes on, matters will be conducted satisfactorily. I have been a slave to it till this moment, notwithstanding I was sick; and now they have only to take care of what they have got, till the operations on shore commence. I have given the General my opinion fully in writing upon this part of the subject.

The ships are all gone, excepting one which came in only yesterday, having sprung a leak at sea. Arrangements were immediately made to move the troops to other ships, and they will go to-morrow. From what I have seen of the state of the ships, the troops, the water casks, &c., I am convinced that if we had not come here, the expedition would have been obliged to quit the Red Sea before they would have been there one month. The 10th regiment have to a man got the scurvy, and lost above twenty men on their passage from Ceylon.

Affectionately your's,

Arthur Wellesley

25

TO MAJOR-GENERAL DAVID BAIRD

Bombay, 9th April, 1801

Dear General,

The first circumstance I have to detail to you is the state of my health, which is indeed the cause of this letter. I have had no fever since I saw you; but I am sorry to say that the breaking out of which I complained is worse than it was; and has become so bad as to induce Mr. Scott [2] to order me to begin a course of nitrous baths.[3] This remedy, exclusive of the disease itself, is

[1] Lieut.-Colonel Edward Edwin Coleman, 84th Regiment, to whom Wellesley wrote on September 26th, 1803 : 'My dear Colonel, we shall get on very well, but it will be better when you have a fit of bile to keep it to yourself, and not give it me in a letter'.

[2] Helenus Scott (1760–1821) was a physician on the medical staff of the East India Company at Bombay.

[3] On October 16th, 1837, Wellington said to Lord Mahon : 'What I had then was the Malabar itch — a much worse kind of itch than ours — it would not yield to brimstone. I caught it on shipboard at Madras — in a man's bed that was given up to me. Dr. Scott, the same who invented nitric acid, cured me at last by baths of that nitric acid : they were so strong that the towels which dried me on coming out were quite burnt.'

ARTHUR WELLESLEY TO JOSIAH WEBBE
FACSIMILE OF A LETTER DATED MARCH 22ND, 1800

sufficient to induce me to be desirous to wait, at least rather longer than the Susannah ¹ will; if not to give over all thoughts of joining you.

I do this, I assure you, with reluctance, notwithstanding I think it very probable that I shall soon hear of your being recalled; however, considering that circumstance, and the bad state of my body, and the remedy which I am obliged to use, I should be mad if I were to think of going at this moment.

As I am writing upon this subject, I will freely acknowledge that my regret at being prevented from accompanying you has been greatly increased by the kind, candid, and handsome manner in which you have behaved towards me; and I will confess as freely, not only that I did not expect such treatment, but that my wishes before you arrived, regarding going upon the expedition, were directly the reverse of what they are at this moment.

I need not enter further upon this subject, than to entreat you will not attribute my stay to any other motive than that to which I have above assigned it; and to inform you, that as I know what has been said and expected by the world in general, I propose, as well for my own credit as for yours, to make known to my friends and to yours, not only the distinguished manner in which you have behaved towards me, but the causes which have prevented my demonstrating my gratitude, by giving you every assistance in the arduous service which you have to conduct.

I shall stay here as long as the season will permit, and then I propose to go round to Madras; and if I cannot get well, I believe I must try a cold climate. . . .

Believe me, &c.,

Arthur Wellesley

26

TO THE MARQUESS WELLESLEY ²

Bombay, 16th April, 1801

My dear Mornington,

The letters which I have written to you lately will have shown you that nothing could be more agreeable to me than the

---

¹ The *Susanna* transport, in which Wellesley was to have travelled, was lost on the voyage; so probably the fever saved his life.

² The Earl of Mornington had been created Marquess Wellesley on December 20th, 1800, in recognition of his services in the conquest and resettlement of Mysore. He was bitterly disappointed at being still an Irish peer.

permission which I received yesterday to return to the Mysore country. But the first paragraph of the letter contains a reason for my original removal from thence, and my appointment to the chief command of the troops assembled at Ceylon, which indeed I read once before in the despatch to Sir Ralph Abercromby, and I wish to trouble you with a few lines upon it.

To avail yourself of my knowledge and experience in the equipment of the expedition to be employed on the shores of the Red Sea, is said to have been your inducement to call me away from Mysore; but, if this were the case, it was never so stated to me, and, if it had been, I should have requested you to employ in the drudgery that person who it was intended should reap all the honour of the service; and at least I should have refrained from incurring expense, and from taking officers from their situations to put them under the command of a man they all dislike.

The fact was, that in the month of October you were carried away, by some fortunate circumstances that had occurred, and by your partiality for me, to appoint me to the chief command of the troops to be employed at the Mauritius, in the Red Sea, or, eventually, in India, and the governments were ordered to furnish me with any additional troops that I might require. On the 21st December you first announce your intention to appoint Sir James Craig [1] or General Baird to the command. I don't deny that I conceive that they had reason to complain when I was appointed to this command, and I believe they did complain; but, in order to do justice to them, why should a greater injury and injustice than they complained of be done to me, and why should reasons for my appointment be publicly given to the whole world, which at least tend to show that you conceived I was fit for the equipment of the expedition, but not to conduct it after it was equipped?

You have repeatedly stated to me an opinion directly the contrary. But the reason of the change stands now publicly unexplained, excepting in the manner above mentioned (I don't know what is the reason of it, excepting it be that you thought you had done an injustice to General Baird, and were desirous

---

[1] Lieut.-General Sir James Henry Craig (1748–1812) had been Governor of Cape Colony for two years before his arrival in India in 1797. Between 1807 and 1811 he was Governor of Canada.

to repair it); and as your success in this country, and your character, must give to your opinions the fullest weight, I stand publicly convicted of incapacity to conduct more of a service than its equipment. I need not represent how injurious that opinion must be to my future prospects; particularly so as the public in general, and those who are to judge of my conduct, know well that your partiality to me would have induced you to refrain from delivering it, if the incapacity had not been manifest upon experiment.

If the change in the command were made only because I had not sufficient rank, and because others had the rank required, and complained of the preference shown to me at that time, it would have been fair towards me to state it (although, by the bye, I don't conceive those to be any good reasons for superseding a man when he has been appointed to a command). The next best thing would have been to give no reason at all for my appointment or my supersession. In either of these cases I should have lamented only that the impropriety of the appointment had not been found out before it was made, the expense which I had unnecessarily incurred, and that I had been induced to remove officers from a situation which they did like to one they do not. But I have a right to complain when I am superseded, and the reason stated for the supersession amounts to a charge of incapacity.

I don't want to trouble you with my private feelings or concerns, when I know that you have enough to think of; and, whatever I might have felt, I should never have said or written another word upon the subject if I had not received yesterday your letter of the 28th March.

The supersession has astonished, and is the conversation of, the whole army and of all India, and numbers of my friends have urged and written to me to request that I would have it explained. Let Henry ask any indifferent man what is his opinion of it. After all this, if the same circumstances could have happened under any other government, although I am fully aware of the right of government to change officers as they may think proper, I should certainly have asked whether any misconduct or incapacity of mine had occasioned my supersession.

The Admiral [Rainier] arrived yesterday, and I shall take an opportunity of talking to him respecting your views upon the Mauritius and Batavia.

I had two fits of fever upon the return of the spring-tides, and I therefore propose to quit this place as soon as I can.

Believe me, &c.,

Arthur Wellesley [1]

✻

[On his arrival in Seringapatam, Captain George Elers, 12th Regiment, records an impression of Colonel Wellesley at this period. 'When the dinner-hour arrived he placed me on his left hand, and said : "That is your place" ; and there I sat every day for the next three months. We sat in the centre of the table, his A.D.C., Captain West,[2] at the top of the table, and Captain Barclay, the Deputy Adjutant-General, at the bottom. This comprised the family, but there were always other officers, guests, altogether from eight to a dozen, every day. Colonel Wellesley kept a plain but good table. He had a very good appetite, and his favourite dish was a roast saddle of mutton and salad. This dish was placed opposite to him, and he generally made his dinner off it. He was very abstemious with wine ; drank four or five glasses with people at dinner, and about a pint of claret after.

'He was very even in his temper, laughing and joking with those he liked, speaking in his quick way, and dwelling particularly upon the few (*at that time*) situations he had been placed in before the enemy, the arrangements he had made, and their fortunate results, all of which were applauded by his staff, who had shared in the glory and peril. This generally formed the topic of conversation after dinner. He was particularly severe upon any neglect of the commissariat department, and openly declared that, if he commanded an army, he should not hesitate to hang a *Commissary* for any dereliction of duty. He was very apprehensive of being superseded in his command of Mysore; and when a General Frazer[3] of the King's service had at that time just landed in India, he was apprehensive he might take his command from him. He said : "We want no Major-Generals in Mysore."

'I remember one day, on our march from Cannanore, he received an overland despatch from England. The chief item of intelligence was that the Earl of Mornington had received a pension of £5,000 a year for his services and judicious arrangements with respect to the war with Tippoo Sahib. The next was a brevet giving the old Colonels the step of Major-Generals. He was all hope and animation. "Do you happen to have an Army List, Elers ?" I said "Yes", and I ran to my tent and fetched it for him, saying : "I am sorry to tell you, Colonel, it does not include you as a Major-General. You are within about five or six of it." He said sorrowfully : "*My highest ambition* is to be a *Major-General* in His Majesty's service." This was uttered to me in May, 1801.'

---

[1] *Supplementary Despatches*, ii, 362-5.
[2] Captain Francis Ralph West, 33rd Regiment.
[3] See note to letter no. 55.

Wellesley was not promoted until April 29th, 1802.

Elers also tells us that Colonel Wellesley's health was poor at this time. 'He had had a touch of the jungle fever in the Bullum country, and I believe at Bombay a violent eruption came out all over his body, but when I saw him he was getting convalescent, but was rather subject to slight touches of fever and ague. No one but those who have experienced these attacks are sensible how they undermine the constitution. They will turn a young man's hair gray very soon. . . . Colonel Wellesley was just thirty-two, and I saw some gray hairs about his temples mixed with his fine crop of light-brown hair. . . . He never wore powder, though it was at that time the regulation to do so. His hair was cropped close. I have heard him say he was convinced the wearing of hair powder was very prejudicial to health as impeding the perspiration, and he was doubtless right.

'. . . His dress consisted of a *long coat*, the uniform of the 33rd Regiment, a *cocked hat*, white pantaloons, Hessian boots and spurs, and a large sabre, the handle solid silver, and the mounting of the scabbard of the same metal, but all gilt.' [1]]

27

TO THE HON. HENRY WELLESLEY

Seringapatam, 4th June, 1801

My dear Henry,

My last letter will have shown you that I had no desire whatever that the letter should be recorded in which I had endeavoured to justify my conduct in proceeding to Bombay, as it appeared, by letters which I received after it was written, that that step was never disapproved of.

In regard to your reasoning upon the letter, in which it is said that I was appointed to prepare the equipment of the expedition which another man was to command, I have only to appeal to the fact in answer to it. I was appointed to command a body of troops, which it was expected might go to Egypt, to which country they have gone, and it was also expected that it might be necessary to reinforce them to a great extent. Still when I was appointed to the command, and for two or three months afterwards, not a word was said of appointing any other person, or of my being employed solely to prepare the equipments ; and as the Governor-General did not mention it in his private letters, I have reason to believe that the idea of superseding me never

---

[1] *The Memoirs of George Elers*, pp. 116–17, 124.

occurred to him till a late period. If I should agree with your reasoning upon the subject, abstracted from all its circumstances, which I am not inclined to do ; if I should think that it does not lower a man in the opinion of the world in general, to employ him in the equipment only of an expedition which it is intended that another should command. I never could agree with your reasoning upon the subject when the circumstances of my case are to be taken into consideration. Is not an officer lowered, does he not receive a mark of the disapprobation of the government which he serves, when he is superseded in the command which was given to him absolutely and without reserve, and is told that it was never intended to employ him in more than the preparations ? All I wish is, that no more should be said than what is the fact, and I conceive that then I shall have but little reason to complain.

I am concerned that Mornington should be annoyed by any thing that I have written to him on this subject, as I certainly never intended to annoy him by my private grievances. He cannot expect, however, that I should have no feeling regarding what has happened : if he does, he must suppose that I feel differently from what he does upon these occasions. I only ask what would he have felt and have said if such a thing had happened to him ?

I am indifferent regarding the promotion ; it must come soon.

Believe me, &c.,

Arthur Wellesley [1]

28

TO THE HON. HENRY WELLESLEY

Seringapatam, 10th Oct., 1801

My dear Henry,

. . . I regret exceedingly Close's departure.[2] Although there is no doubt whatever but that he is the ablest man in the diplomatic line in India, and that his knowledge of the languages is so extraordinary, and so superior to that of any other European in India, that that alone renders him the most fit for a diplomatic situation ; and besides that qualification, he has others in an

---

[1] *Supplementary Despatches*, ii, 424-5.
[2] Close had been transferred from the Residency in Mysore to that at Poona.

equal, if not a superior, degree to other candidates for those situations. Nevertheless, I consider that his presence in Mysore for a few years longer would have been of great benefit, and would have established the new government on so firm a foundation that nothing could hereafter shake it. The great want in this country is of money. There is plenty of everything to bring it into the country; but as it is entirely cut off from the sea, and has no navigable streams, there is no commerce, and accordingly in many parts of the country the revenue is paid in kind and the common purchases are made by barter. As the Company will take nothing but money in payment of the subsidy, I am always afraid that the government will, at some time or other, be reduced to borrow upon the crops from the Madras sharks, and the first time they do that they take a stride towards their downfall, which will soon be followed by others. Close had a thorough knowledge of this evil, and, by his care and management, I think that he would have prevented its bad effects.

I have been lately employed upon a very pleasant service, that of prosecuting three rascals at a court martial for robbing the stores and selling them during the different times that I was absent in the field.[1] I believe that I have convicted them all. . . .

I have still thoughts of going home, particularly if there be a peace; but I won't leave this country at all events till Malcolm [2] arrives.

Believe me, &c.,

Arthur Wellesley [3]

29

TO JOSIAH WEBBE [4]

Seringapatam, 22nd March, 1802

My dear Webbe,

I am very glad to find that the King's ministers are likely again to take the power over this country into their own hands, and make use of the control which they have over the gentry in

---

[1] The store department at Seringapatam. A colonel, a captain and a local agent were involved in what Wellesley termed 'a scene of villainy and peculation which has never been surpassed, and seldom equalled, in this country'.
[2] Major John Malcolm. See pp. 93-4.
[3] *Supplementary Despatches*, ii, 570-5.
[4] Josiah Webbe was Chief Secretary at Madras and Resident with Scindiah. Malcolm described him as 'the most virtuous and ablest man I had ever known . . . the story of his life, one which cannot be heard without stimulating the coldest

Leadenhall-street.[1]   I do not know exactly the points upon
which Lord Wellesley is at issue with them, but I judge from
Malcolm's account of the letters which he has received from
England, that whatever they may be, he will be supported by
the Board of Control, particularly as he appears disposed to
make every reduction in the military expenses which is at all
practicable.

I agree with you entirely about the peace.   It establishes the
French power over Europe, and when we shall have disarmed
we shall have no security excepting in our own abjectness.
There is a report that the finances were in a very embarrassed
state, which I am afraid is true, as there could have been no
other inducement to make such a peace.

I look upon the question of reduction in this country to stand
upon grounds entirely independent of peace or war in Europe.
We have carried on no offensive operations in this quarter, and
we have long ceased to fear an attack from the French.   The size
of our army is to be attributed to the demands for its services
existing in India, and is by no means occasioned by the war in
Europe.   The question is, whether those demands are likely to
be lessened or to cease upon the conclusion of the peace.   I rather
believe that as that event will be accompanied by the return of
the French and Dutch to their settlements in India, it might be
concluded with more truth that the army ought to be increased
rather than diminished.

The people of England, however, will not willingly hear of
the existence of our large military establishments in India in
time of profound peace in Europe.   They will not easily believe
that there is a necessity for them in India in the most peaceable
times, and some reduction is therefore absolutely necessary.   On
this ground only does the peace influence the question of reduction.   But it is very clear that the army ought to be reduced as
little as possible, particularly that its effective strength ought to
be kept entire.

If there is to be any reduction of numbers below what they

to exertions in the cause of humanity and his country'.   In the dining-room at
Strathfieldsaye a lady visitor was attracted by a print of Webbe's portrait.   She
asked the Duke of Wellington who the man was.   The Duke replied : 'That man
was one of the ablest I ever knew, and, what is more, one of the honestest'.   Lord
Wellesley wrote of him : 'I consider Mr. Webbe to be the most distinguished
public servant in a subordinate situation in India'.   Webbe died on November 9th,
1804, aged thirty-seven.

[1] The Court of Directors of the East India Company had their headquarters
in East India House, Leadenhall Street, London.

will be after the supernumeraries are struck off, I think the best mode will undoubtedly be to decrease the number of men in each battalion, rather than to disband any of the regiments. By this mode it will be more easy at all times to increase the army to its present numbers; and as by either mode the officers must still be in the service, on the establishment, and in the receipt of their pay and batta,[1] it will be equally economical for the present. Hereafter, however, when the number of officers will have decreased, to disband some of the regiments will be the more economical mode; but it will be attended with the disadvantage of great difficulty in increasing the numbers of the army again.

I am glad to hear that your commission goes on so well. It would certainly have been impossible to make the arrangements for the perpetual settlement by means of a board of revenue composed of such discordant materials as that at Madras is at present.

I return Malcolm's letter.

Let me know on what day you propose to leave Madras, and on what day you will be at Bangalore, in order that I may have my palanquin [2] boys posted in time.

Believe me, &c.,

Arthur Wellesley [3]

30

TO MAJOR JAMES ACHILLES KIRKPATRICK

Seringapatam, 19th June, 1802

Sir,

I have had the honour of receiving your letter of the 7th instant, and I shall lose no time in procuring and sending to Hyderabad the bark [4] which you require, if the tree can be found. I wish that it may be beneficial to the health of his Highness the Nizam, but I acknowledge that I fear the only

---

[1] *Bhatta*: an extra allowance for troops on the march.
[2] A long box, with sliding sides, in which a person was carried on the shoulders of four or six men. In 1804 Wellesley wrote to the Governor-General's private secretary: 'Give orders that a palanquin may be made for me; let it be very light, with the panels made of canvass, instead of wood, and the poles fixed, as for a doley. Your Bengally palanquins are so heavy, that they cannot be used out of Calcutta.' *Supplementary Despatches*, iii, 119-20.
[3] *Supplementary Despatches*, iii, 119-20.
[4] The bark referred to was recommended by the Nizam's physicians as a remedy for the palsy.

benefit he will derive from the prescription will be that which a person who has long been afflicted with sickness derives from the hope of a cure.

I have, &c.,

Arthur Wellesley [1]

31

TO MAJOR JAMES ACHILLES KIRKPATRICK

Seringapatam, 1st July, 1802

Sir,

I have this day sent off two camel hircarrahs [2] with the bark of the only tree remaining at Kope of the kind described in your letter to me, and some more of the bark of the tree at Chinroy-patam : leaves, &c., accompany both parcels. I hope that they will be beneficial to the Nizam. They will, at least, prove the desire which I have, and which, I am convinced, every British officer has, to do what can be gratifying to his Highness.

I have, &c.,

Arthur Wellesley [3]

32

TO HIS HIGHNESS THE NIZAM OF HYDERABAD [4]

21st Sept., 1802

After the assurance of devoted submission, the representative of the sincere well wisher, Colonel Wellesley, has the honour to state to the attendants on the Presence, the treasury of bounty, of the unsullied Nabob of exalted titles, whose turrets are the

---

[1] *Supplementary Despatches*, iii, 205-6.
[2] Blakiston, in *Twelve Years' Military Adventure*, writes : 'The persons employed in carrying dispatches in India are called hircarrahs, and are generally mounted on fleet camels, which will travel a great distance at the rate of fifteen miles an hour. But where great secrecy is required, footmen are generally employed ; they go disguised as peasants, and have the most ingenious modes of concealing the papers with which they are intrusted.'
[3] *Supplementary Despatches*, iii, 217.
[4] Translated from a letter in Persian, on the records of the Residency at Hyderabad.

heavens, and whose origin is celestial, (be his dignified shade extended!) that two purses, containing the illustrious enayet-namahs, replete with kindness, the one vouchsafing the acknowledgment of the bark of the Maumyah trees, and the other communicating the extensive benefit which had been effected by it, with an order for the transmission of some bark from the trunks of both the trees, sealed, and under the charge of the camel hircarrah of the prosperous Sircar,[1] honoured and elevated me by the grandeur of their approach and the dignity of their arrival.

On learning the circumstance of the benefit which had been experienced by the brilliant constitution, from the attendants on the Presence, from the application of the aforesaid bark, I derived the utmost happiness.

In compliance with the exalted order, two bundles of the desired bark, the one from the trunk of the tree at Chinroypatam, and the other from the trunk of that at the village of Kope, have been delivered, sealed, to the camel hircarrahs of the Sircar, abounding in kindness, and are despatched to the exalted Presence. They will pass, no doubt, under the noble inspection.

In consequence of the length of the journey from Seringapatam to the village of Kope, which is situated at the distance of 400 miles, and of the incessant rain in the vicinity of Nuggur, the passing and repassing on the road is very dilatory and difficult, and the procrastination and delay of some days have, therefore, occurred in obeying the orders of the unsullied Presence. I hope that the medicine which is transmitted, having attained the honour of application, may be beneficial in its effects on the constitution, replete with purity.

The desire of my heart, the seat of constancy, is that the exalted attendant will confidently regard and esteem the aforesaid bark as a memorable instance of the loyalty of the well wisher, and as a testimony of the anxiety of British officers to effect all arrangements which may be desired by, or beneficial to, the noble Presence.

May the God of his slaves grant that the orb of your Prosperity may shine and glitter from the eternal horizon, like the sun in the zenith!

Arthur Wellesley [2]

---

[1] Sircar: head of a government; here, the British Government.
[2] *Supplementary Despatches*, iii, 309-10.

33

TO MAJOR WILLIAM MACLEOD [1]

Seringapatam, 14th Nov., 1802

My dear Macleod,

I cannot express to you how much annoyed I am to observe not only that you have omitted to answer the private letters which I have written to you upon the subject of Wynaad, but that your public letter is written in a style of coldness to which I am but little accustomed, particularly from you. We have been long acquainted, and have long and frequently communicated upon public subjects; and however we may differ in opinion upon certain topics, I know that I have always done you the justice to believe you to be zealous, active, able, and honest in the public cause, and I don't see any reason which has occurred lately for an alteration in the style of our correspondence. If I have done anything which has made you feel uncomfortable, I beg that you will let me know it, and you will find me disposed to make you amends. I declare that I never should have written a line publicly upon this subject, or one which any body else would have seen, if it had not been in answer to your first letter. . . .

. . . I cannot conclude this letter without adverting to your letter of the 9th to Lieutenant-Colonel [Burnaby] Boles. You will permit me as a friend to tell you that I don't think it was called for by his letter to you, to which it is a reply; and I hope that when you consider of it you will do something to soften it.

My wish is to see all matters go on quietly, and that persons in authority should refrain from writing these violent epistles to one another; but if in a moment of warmth they should do so, it is best that they should settle matters amicably.

Believe me, &c.,

Arthur Wellesley [2]

[1] Macleod was Principal Collector in Malabar.
[2] *Supplementary Despatches*, iii, 395-7.

INDIA: THE MAHRATTA WAR

INTRODUCTION TO PART THREE

THE Marquess Wellesley now set about the extension of British influence into the great robber confederacy of the Mahrattas to the north-west of Mysore. To do so was made easier by the quarrelling which went on among the five semi-independent Mahratta chiefs : Bajee Rao, the Peshwah of Poona and titular head of the Confederacy ; Dowlut Rao Scindiah ; Jeswunt Rao Holkar ; the Gaikwar of Baroda, with whom a defensive treaty had already been concluded ; and, to the east, Ragojee Bhoonslah, the Rajah of Berar.

Prominent among these princes was Scindiah, whose armies had for years been organised, trained and largely officered by the French. Holkar, his rival, had been induced by jealousy to follow this model ; and after two years of causing serious depredations to his neighbours, he attacked and utterly defeated the combined armies of Scindiah and the Peshwah outside Poona. The Peshwah thereupon fled to the British for protection, was taken by ship to Bassein near Bombay, and there on the last day of the year signed a treaty by which he entered into an alliance, agreed to retain in his service no Europeans whose countries might be at war with Britain, to engage in neither hostilities nor negotiations without British consent and to receive within his territory a suitable number of the East India Company's soldiers. In return he was to be restored to his throne.

Judging that this Treaty of Bassein was a first step towards curtailing his own independence, Scindiah made overtures to Holkar and then, having allied himself with the Rajah of Berar, took up a position which threatened the Deccan. Ten thousand troops under Arthur Wellesley were assembled at Hurryhur on the northern borders of Mysore to prevent any hostile Mahratta thrust and to escort the Peshwah back to Poona. After long preparations they crossed the Toombudra on March 12th and a month later joined up with the Nizam of Hyderabad's contingent commanded by Colonel James Stevenson. Holkar, meanwhile, had retired more than a hundred miles north of Poona, leaving there a garrison which departed on Wellesley's hurried approach. On May 13th the Peshwah was ceremonially restored to his throne.

That summer of 1803 a Wellesley hopeful of maintaining peace involved himself in a web of negotiations with procrastinating Mahratta chiefs in his desire to keep them either friendly or neutral. For two months the armies of Scindiah and the Rajah, numbering some fifty thousand, had been encamped on the Nizam's north-western frontier, rejecting every representation that they should withdraw. The Major-General grew increasingly impatient, and at the beginning of August the

71

rebuff of yet another request for withdrawal brought matters to a crisis, Scindiah declining to move unless the British withdrew into Mysore. In his reply Wellesley declared : 'I offered you peace on terms of equality, and honourable to all parties : you have chosen war and are responsible for all consequences'.

War it was. While one army under General Gerard Lake marched up the Ganges from Cawnpore towards Delhi to fight a strong Mahratta force under French leadership, Arthur Wellesley moved forward on August 8th to nearby Ahmednuggur, and by capturing this fort and walled town provided for the campaign a secure advanced base. Then his troops crossed the wide, rain-swollen Godavery in basket boats, aiming to keep the enemy on the move and thus to tire him out. The Mahratta army, having on September 2nd lost Jalnapur to Stevenson's division which had meanwhile been advancing on its own, was in retreat northwards to the Adjuntee Ghaut. Wellesley, planning to attack on the 24th with his united force, had taken the considerable risk of splitting his strength and sending Stevenson by another route. A day sooner than anticipated he came upon the enemy strongly entrenched in a position of their own choice — 'confoundedly strong and difficult of access' — between two rivers at Assaye (also spelt Assye). Rather than wait for Stevenson to come up, he judged it wiser to attack at once on his own with seven thousand men, even though against heavy odds ; the alternative was to retreat and thereby expose his small force to the swarms of Mahratta horsemen in the offing. After a fierce battle in which his own casualties were severe, he gained the victory. Scindiah and the Rajah both fled early in the fight, and their armies, leaving 102 guns and twelve hundred soldiers on the field, retreated to the north.

Here, meantime, Agra and Delhi had fallen to Lake's men, who on the last day of October defeated Scindiah in the desperate battle of Laswaree, where the Mahrattas fought, to quote Lake : 'like devils, or rather like heroes. . . . I never was in so severe a business in my life or anything like it.'

On Wellesley's front two months went by in marching and in negotiation, in the capture by Stevenson of the fortresses of Burhampur and Asseerghur, before Scindiah and the Rajah of Berar sued for peace. On November 22nd a suspension of hostilities was agreed, but Scindiah did not keep to the conditions which required a short withdrawal. So a second battle was fought, this time on the plain of Argaum, where, on November 29th, the Mahrattas were routed after a precarious opening when Wellesley had personally to check and re-deploy two native battalions, who marred their splendid behaviour at Assye by breaking away in panic. 'I am convinced that if I had not been near them to rally them and restore the battle, we should have lost the day.' The final stage in the war was the storming on December 15th of the Rajah's mountain stronghold at Gawilghur, largely garrisoned by infantry defeated at Argaum. That month two treaties of 'perpetual peace and friendship' rounded off a year of decisive achievement.

34

TO —— ——

Seringapatam, 20th Jan., 1803

I have the honour of receiving your letter of the 15th this day, and I lose no time in replying to that part of it in which you inform me that the Rajah, or Dessaye,[1] of Kittoor has expressed a wish to be taken under the protection of the British government, and has offered to pay a tribute to the Company, and to give you a bribe of 4000 pagodas,[2] and me one of 10,000 pagodas, provided this point is arranged according to his wishes. I cannot conceive what could have induced the Rajah of Kittoor to imagine that I was capable of receiving that, or any other sum of money, as an inducement to do that which he must think improper, or he would not have offered it.

. . . In respect to the bribe offered to you and myself, I am surprised that any man, in the character of a British officer, should not have given the Rajah to understand that the offer would be considered as an insult, and should not rather have forbidden its renewal than have encouraged it, and even have offered to receive a quarter of the sum proposed to be given to him for prompt payment. I can attribute your conduct upon this occasion to nothing excepting the most inconsiderate indiscretion, and to a wish to benefit yourself, which got the better of your prudence. I desire, however, that you will refrain from a renewal of the subject with the Rajah of Kittoor at all; and that, if he should renew it, you will inform him that I and all British officers consider such offers as insults on the part of those by whom they are made. . . .

Arthur Wellesley

※

[Lieutenant Blakiston of the Engineers affords us a glimpse of Major-General Wellesley during March.

'The tract of country between the Toombudra and Poonah has long been under the dominion of the Mahrattas, although divided among a number of chiefs, each assuming supremacy in his own petty dominions; in fact, exhibiting a kind of feudal system. Some of these viewed us with a degree of suspicion, keeping aloof, and shutting the gates of their fortresses against us; but the majority, who were attached to the Peishwah,

[1] Appa Dessaye (or Desai), a Mahratta chief.
[2] A pagoda was a gold coin, then worth about 8s.

manifested a friendly disposition, and exchanged civilities with the General. These consisted chiefly in ceremonial visits, on which occasions the native chieftains were accompanied by their principal officers and a considerable train of followers. . . .

'From the intermixture of howdaed elephants, led horses in gay trappings, Hircarrah camels, ornamental kettle-drums, &c. these cavalcades, or souwarrees, had a most picturesque appearance ; while the sound of instruments, more martial than musical, joined to the stentorian voice of the person who runs before proclaiming the title of the chief, afforded the ear its full share in the amusement.

'On our part, these chiefs were received with military honours, having a salute of artillery fired for them, according to their rank. During the conference, the usual ceremonies of handing betel-leaf, sprinkling rose-water, &c were gone through ; and presents, generally consisting of an elephant, and some ornament of jewellery for the turban of the chief, with shawls and *kinkaubs* to some of the principal officers, were distributed. On the occasion of the visit being returned by our commander, a squadron of cavalry generally formed his escort, and he was accompanied by the staff, brigadiers, and heads of departments, who received presents nearly corresponding with those presented by our chief. On one of these occasions I was not a little astonished to hear a fat fellow of a chieftain give vent to a savoury, sonorous eructation, right in our General's face, and was equally surprised to witness the apparent composure with which it was taken ; till a brother officer, more conversant with Indian customs, explained to me that it was the greatest compliment which could be paid by a native.' [1]]

35

MEMORANDUM RESPECTING BASKET BOATS

Camp, 27th March, 1803

1. The size best calculated for strength and use is 10 feet diameter in the clear, and 2 feet 3 inches high.

2. It is indispensable that the covering of leather should come over the gunwale of the boat, to be lashed to the framework within : most accidents that happen to this kind of boats arise from a neglect of this precaution. There ought to be a double covering of leather, to add to their security and strength ; but this is of less importance than that any part of the gunwale should be left uncovered. It may be useful to notice that the hides should be sewed with leather.

3. The materials that are required for basket boats are bam-

---

[1] *Twelve Years' Military Adventure*, vol. i, pp. 88-90.

boo lath; jungle wood (the best is called souri, a tough thorn); country rope; leather.

4. A framework should be made of three of these laths together, and worked with others, about 4 inches apart, in a succession of triangles, until it allows the diameter required, 10 feet. In this state it is fixed in uprights driven in a circle of 10 feet diameter, the ends bent upwards and worked close with single lath for 2 feet 3 inches, which forms the sides of the boat; the remaining ends are then twisted in with the small parts of souri, or pliable jungle wood, and this forms the gunwale, which should be well lashed with country rope. This is the mode of making the boats, with which the Natives are as well acquainted as we are.

5. In this state it is taken from the uprights, and the centre of the boat fixed in a little mound of earth (say 6 inches), when it is lined with the toughest jungle wood that can be procured, and lashed to the frame within it; these should cross each other, so that the pressure may be equal on every part of the boat. Eight pieces are sufficient, about the thickness of $2\frac{1}{2}$ or 3 inch rope, made long enough, with the ends pointed, to run into the bottom of the gunwale, and secured with country rope.

6. It is absolutely necessary that a frame to fit, made exactly as the bottom of the boat, should be then fixed within it, the smooth part of the bamboo uppermost. This is laid over the lining of the jungle, to which it is lashed by the same wood within to the sides of the boat.

7. This is the general mode of making boats: the great error is in preparing the lath too thick, whereas it can scarcely be made too thin. The strength of the boat depends upon the goodness of the jungle wood for lining, and its being equally crossed, in order that it may sustain an equal pressure in all its parts.

8. It is desirable that there should be a second frame, worked close in a circular manner, and lashed within; for, on the transporting of baggage, it prevents a pressure on the leather from bamboos, feet of cots, and tables, that pass through the triangle bamboo work of the boat. It preserves the leather, and adds but little to the weight.[1]

Arthur Wellesley [2]

[1] On November 24th, 1840, Wellington told Samuel Rogers: 'I had Caesar's Commentaries with me in India, and learnt much from them, fortifying my camp every night as he did. I passed over the rivers as he did, by means of baskets and boats of basket-work; only I think I improved upon him, constructing them into bridges, and always fortifying them, and leaving them guarded, to return to them if necessary.'   [2] *Supplementary Despatches*, iv, 55-6.

36

TO THE MARQUESS WELLESLEY

Camp at Ahmednuggur, 12th August, 1803

My Lord,

The weather cleared up so much on the 7th instant, as to allow me to march to this place on the 8th. I had in the morning dispatched a messenger to the killadar of Ahmednuggur, to require him to surrender his fort; and, on my arrival in the neighbourhood of the pettah,[1] I offered cowle [2] to the inhabitants. This was refused, as the pettah was held by a body of Arabs, who were supported by a battalion of Scindiah's regular infantry, and a body of horse encamped in an open space between the pettah and the fort.

I immediately attacked the pettah with the piquets of the infantry, reinforced by the flank companies of the 78th regiment, under the command of Lieut. Colonel Harness; [3] in another place with the 74th regiment and 1st battalion of the 8th, under the command of Lieut. Colonel [William] Wallace; and in a third with the flank companies of the 74th, and the 1st battalion 3rd regiment, under the command of Captain [P. H.] Vesey. The pettah wall was very lofty, and defended by towers, and had no rampart; so that when the troops had ascended to the attack, they had no ground on which they could stand; and the Arabs who occupied the towers defended their posts with the utmost obstinacy.

At length they were obliged to quit the wall and fled to the houses, from which they continued a destructive fire upon the troops. Scindiah's regular infantry also attacked our troops after they had entered the pettah. In a short time, however, after a brisk and gallant contest, we were completely masters of it; but with the loss of some brave officers and soldiers, as your Excellency will perceive by the enclosed return. The enemy's loss was, from the nature of the contest, necessarily much greater than ours; and on the night of the 8th, all that part of their force, which was not required for the defence of the fort, went off to the northward; including all the Arabs who survived

---

[1] The outwork of a fortified place, with wall and ditch.
[2] Mercy, protection.
[3] Colonel William Harness died at Ellichpur on January 1st, 1804. The 74th and 78th were both Highland Regiments.

the contest in the pettah, excepting a small number who attended one of their wounded chiefs, who could not be removed farther than the fort.

On the 9th, I reconnoitred the ground in the neighbourhood of the fort; and on that evening Lieut. Colonel Wallace, with five companies of the 74th regiment and the 2nd battalion 12th regiment, seized a position within four hundred yards of it; on which, in the course of that night, a battery was constructed for four guns, to take off the defences on the side on which I proposed to make my attack. This opened at daylight on the 10th; and it was so advantageously placed, and fired with such effect, as to induce the killadar to desire that I should cease firing, in order that he might send a person to treat for his surrender. In my answer I told him, that I should not cease firing till I should have taken the fort, or he should have surrendered it; but that I would listen to whatever he was desirous to communicate.

Yesterday morning he sent out two vakeels [1] to propose to surrender the fort, on condition that he should be allowed to depart with his garrison, and that he should have his private property.

Although I consented to this proposal, it was five in the evening before the hostages arrived in camp, without whose presence I refused to stop the fire from the British batteries. According to his engagement, however, the killadar marched out of the fort this morning, with a garrison consisting of 1400 men, and the troops under my command took possession of it.

In this manner has this fort fallen into our hands: [2] our loss since the 8th has been trifling, which I attribute much to the spirit with which our attacks on that day were carried on. . . .

I have the honor to be, &c.,

Arthur Wellesley

✻

[Colonel James Welsh has this to say about the capture of Ahmednuggur. 'It was a matter of little wonder that they gave up the fort so early, when our ally, Gokliah, a Mahrattah chief residing in our camp, with a body of horse, wrote thus to his friends at Poonah : "These English are a strange people, and their General a wonderful man : they came here

---

[1] Vakeel: envoy or ambassador.
[2] Murray's *A Handbook for Travellers in India, Burma and Ceylon* (1909) states that a tamarind tree, under which Wellesley is said to have lunched, is pointed out on the south-west side of the fort.

in the morning, looked at the Pettah wall, walked over it, killed all the garrison and returned to breakfast ! what can withstand them ?"

'. . . In the fort we found the Palace of Scindiah and several old buildings, which must originally have been houses of some consequence. In the former, which had a large garden attached to it, was a profusion of valuable articles, over which as prize property, I had European sentries immediately placed : but the spirit of plunder suddenly overcame discipline ; for all hands, even the sentries not excepted, speedily turned to, and when the General [Wellesley] arrived, he found an indiscriminate crowd in the house, each helping himself to what came first to hand : for which two of our Native soldiers were instantly seized and hanged, in the only gateway, *in terrorem* ; though the Europeans escaped. It is difficult to describe the articles which were thus suddenly exposed to view. On entering with the General, I observed, in two apartments only, several dozens of large handsome pier glasses, two electrifying machines, an organ, a piano-forte, lustres, chandeliers, globes, and many other similar luxuries : in others, the richest stuffs of India, gold and silver cloths, splendid armour, silks, satins, velvets, furs, shawls, plate, cash, &c. &c ; all of which were undergoing the close examination of our unfortunate looties, who, however, were generally forced to relinquish their plunder before they quitted the place.' [1]]

37

TO LIEUT.-COLONEL JOHN COLLINS [2]

Camp at Ahmednuggur, 15th August, 1803

Sir,

. . . The Mahrattas have long boasted that they would carry on a predatory war against us : they will find that mode of warfare not very practicable at the present moment. At all events, supposing that they can carry their design into execution, unless they find the British officers and soldiers to be in the same corrupted, enervated state in which their predecessors found the Mussulmann in the last century, they cannot expect much success from it. A system of predatory war must have some foundation in strength of some kind or other. But when the Chiefs avow that they cannot meet us in the field ; when they are obliged to send the principal strength of their armies upon which the remainder depend to a distance, lest it should fall into our hands, they must have little knowledge of human nature if they suppose that their lighter bodies will act, and still less of the British officers, if they imagine that, with impunity, they can do the

---

[1] *Military Reminiscences*, vol. i, pp. 164-5.
[2] Resident with Scindiah. He died in 1807.

smallest injury, provided only that the allies, who are to be first exposed to their attacks, are true to their own interests.

I have the honor to be, &c.,

Arthur Wellesley

38

TO LIEUT.-COLONEL JOHN COLLINS

Camp North of the Nimderrah Ghaut,
18th Aug., 1803

My dear Colonel,

I have received your letter of the 16th. I am sincerely desirous of peace, and will certainly conclude one when I can; but we must proceed with caution, because I am afraid that we shall miss our object if we should appear too desirous to attain it. If any overtures should be made to you, let them know that you will communicate them to me, but that you are convinced that more pacific professions, unaccompanied by facts, will not persuade me that their intentions are sincere.

If any such overtures should be made to you, favour me with your opinion regarding them at the time you will communicate them.

You see the advantage which we derive from the commencement of hostilities during the season in which the rivers are full.

We have got possession of Scindiah's only hold in the Deccan; he cannot receive assistance from Holkar, supposing that chief to be inclined to assist him; and he is confined by the Godavery in the execution of his plan of predatory war, supposing him capable of carrying it into execution. In the mean time I shall fill Ahmednuggur with provisions; and when that is completed, all the Mahrattas in India would not be able to drive me from my position. I believe also that although Colonel Stevenson in particular has suffered much in his equipments lately, and we have all suffered more or less from the severity of the weather, it has done more harm in Scindiah's army, and he is more crippled by it, than any of us.

Believe me, &c.,

Arthur Wellesley

❋

[Blakiston describes a meeting between Wellesley and this Colonel Collins at Aurangabad, on August 29th, 1803.

'On reaching the tent of the Resident we were unexpectedly received with a salute of artillery, for such was the state maintained by this representative of John Company (known in Bengal by the nickname of King Collins), that he had a brigade of field-pieces, worked by native artillerymen, attached to his escort. In front of a noble suite of tents, which might have served for the Great Mogul, we were received by an insignificant, little, old-looking man, dressed in an old-fashioned military coat, white breeches, sky-blue silk stockings, and large glaring buckles to his shoes, having his highly powdered wig, from which depended a pig-tail of no ordinary dimensions, surmounted by a small round black silk hat, ornamented with a single black ostrich feather, looking altogether not unlike a monkey dressed up for Bartholomew fair. There was, however, a fire in his small black eye, shooting out from beneath a large, shaggy, pent-house brow, which more than counterbalanced the ridicule that his first appearance naturally excited. After the usual compliments, the principals retired into an inner tent, where matters not to be entrusted to vulgar ears were discussed. But the last words uttered by the little man, as they came forth from the tent, I well recollect. "I tell you, General, as to their cavalry, you may ride over them wherever you meet them ; but their infantry and guns will astonish you." As, in riding homewards we amused ourselves, the General among the rest, in cutting jokes at the expence of "little King Collins", we little thought how true his words would prove.' [1]

The next letter, no. 39, is addressed to Major Merrick Shawe, secretary and trusted confidant of Lord Wellesley. Born in Ireland in the early 1770's, Shawe had first come out to India in 1790 as an ensign in the 76th Foot, and had soon found himself fighting in the Mysore War of 1791–2, being badly wounded at the victory of Seringapatam, where he received a bullet in his shoulder which stayed there for the rest of his life. Seven years of garrison duty in Calcutta found him a captain, but he was then appointed to the Governor-General's staff, and remained with Lord Wellesley until they both sailed for England in 1805. Shawe served with the army for a year or two in Ireland before commanding the 76th Regiment in the Walcheren expedition of 1809, and he retired in May of the following year. But we find him on the Duke of York's staff at the Horse Guards until 1819, when he was appointed a Commissioner of Stamps, a post he only gave up in order to rejoin his old chief, Lord Wellesley, who had become Lord-Lieutenant of Ireland.

Himself a bachelor, Shawe became, through the marriage of one of his half-brothers, an uncle to William Makepeace Thackeray. The novelist, who first got to know 'the dear old gentleman' in London during 1836, used Major Shawe as the original for Major Pendennis in his novel *Pendennis*. Merrick Shawe died in November 1843.[2]]

[1] *Twelve Years' Military Adventure*, vol. i, pp. 144-5.
[2] *The Buried Life: A Study of the Relation between Thackeray's Fiction and his Personal History*, by Gordon N. Ray, Professor of English in the University of Illinois.

39

TO MAJOR MERRICK SHAWE

Camp at Assye, 24th September, 1803

My dear Sir,

I attacked the united armies of Scindiah and the Rajah of Berar yesterday with my division, and the result is, that I have taken about sixty pieces of cannon. The action was very brisk indeed, the fire from the enemy's cannon the hottest that has been known in this country for some time; and our loss in officers and men has been very great. Among others, your brother [1] in the 74th is wounded; Colonel Maxwell [2] was killed; Colonel Harness, Colonel Wallace, and I, and I believe every officer of the staff, had horses shot under us.[3]

Scindiah's infantry behaved remarkably well, and stood to their guns to the last; but their execution was with them only, I do not believe that they carried away more than two, and I doubt whether they have got even that number.

I will write to the Governor General in detail upon the subject of this action, as soon as I can get accurate returns of the killed and wounded, and of the ordnance taken.

Believe me, &c.,

Arthur Wellesley

The enemy fled towards the Adjuntee ghaut, and I believe have descended it.

✻

[On October 20th, 1825, at Stratfieldsaye, Wellington gave John Wilson Croker an instance of the importance of a very ordinary degree of common sense.

'He described his very critical position on the march before the battle of Assaye, when his small force was threatened by an overwhelming deluge of native cavalry, and his only chance, not of victory only, but of safety, was his getting to the other bank of the river (Kistna), which was a few miles on his right. He had some of the best native guides that could be had, and he made every possible effort to ascertain whether the river was

---

[1] His half-brother Matthew. See note to letter no. 42.
[2] Maxwell, 19th Dragoons, commanded a cavalry brigade.
[3] In *The Nineteenth and their Times* Colonel John Biddulph quotes a MS. note in the India Office Library : 'The General was so overcome by his great and gallant exertions throughout the day, so overpowered both in mind and body, that during the greater part or whole of the following night he sat on the ground with his head bent down between his knees, and said not a word to anyone.'

anywhere passable, and all his informants assured him that it was not. He himself could not see the river, and the enemy's cavalry was in such force that he could not send out to reconnoitre. At last, in extreme anxiety, he resolved to see the river himself, and accordingly, with his most intelligent guides, and an escort of, I think he said, all his cavalry, he pushed forward in sight of the river in the neighbourhood of Assaye, which stood on the bank of another stream that ran nearly parallel to that which he wished to cross. When they came there he again questioned his guides about a passage, which they still asserted not to exist ; but he saw through his glass, for the enemy's cavalry were so strong that he could not venture to get closer, one village on the right, or near bank of the river, and another village exactly opposite on the other bank, and "I immediately said to myself that men could not have built two villages so close to one another on opposite sides of a stream without some habitual means of communication, either by boats or a ford — most probably by the latter. On that conjecture, or rather reasoning, in defiance of all my guides and informants, I took the desperate resolution, as it seemed, of marching for the river, and I was right. I found a passage, crossed my army over, had no more to fear from the enemy's cloud of cavalry, and my army, small as it was, was just enough to fill the space between the two streams, so that both my flanks were secure, and there I fought and won the battle of Assaye, the bloodiest, for numbers, that I ever saw ; and this was all from my having the common sense to guess that men did not build villages on opposite sides of a stream without some means of communication between them. If I had not taken that sudden resolution, we were, I assure you, in a most dangerous predicament." [1]

In November 1840 Wellington remarked to Croker : 'Strange impressions come now and then after a battle ; and such came to me after the battle of Assaye in India. I slept in a farm yard, and whenever I awakened, it struck me that I had lost all my friends, so many had I lost in that battle. Again and again, as often as I awakened, did it disturb me. In the morning I enquired anxiously after one and another ; nor was I convinced that they were living till I saw them.'

Fifteen years after the battle, John Malcolm [2] wrote the following to Wellington, on September 25th, 1818 : 'The day before yesterday the whole of the officers in camp dined with me to celebrate the anniversary of the battle of Assye ; and it was celebrated with proper enthusiasm by men who were sensible of all the advantages the Indian army derives from having its fame associated with your history. . . . Our Assye festival did not finish with my dinner. My native aide-de-camp, Subadar Syud Hussein, a gallant soldier, owes his rise to that day. He was the leading havildar of the Fourth Cavalry in the charge ; and he afterwards dashed into the centre of a party of the enemy's horse, and bore off their standard. His commanding officer, Floyer, brought him and the standard to you ;

---

[1] *The Croker Papers*, vol. i, pp. 353-4.   [2] See page 93.

and upon the story being told, you patted him upon the back, and with that eloquent and correct knowledge in the native language for which you were celebrated, said, "Acha havildar ; jemadar". A jemadar he was made ; and though the anecdote has no doubt been expelled from your memory to make room for others of more interest, it holds an important place in Syud Hussein's ; and amid all his subsequent successes in Persia and in India, which have raised him to medals, pensions, and a palanquin from Government, his pride is the pat on the back he received at Assye ; and he told me the other day with great *naïveté* that he felt raised by your actions, as your increasing fame gave increasing value to the notice you had once taken of him. This grateful soldier followed my feast by one on the 24th to two hundred subadars, jemadars, havildars, and naicks of my division ; and a grand nautch which he gave in the evening to about four hundred spectators was attended by all the English officers in camp. A very good transparency of your head, with the word Assye, which had ornamented my bungalow, was put up by him in a large tent, and the Persian name of Wellesley Sahib Bahadur, in Persian characters, announced to those who had not seen the light of your countenance in the original, for whom the picture was intended. The subadar was pressed to call you the Duke of Wellington ; but he said (and I think very justly) that was your European name, but your Indian name was Wellesley Bahadur.' [1]]

40

TO LIEUT.-COLONEL THOMAS MUNRO

Camp, 1st October, 1803

My dear Munro,

. . . I entirely agree in the opinions expressed in your letter, upon the subject of offensive and defensive war ; however, I think that you are mistaken respecting the possibility of checking, by defensive measures, a predatory war, carried on by horse only ; indeed, I have done it already in this campaign. The fact is, that a predatory war is not to be carried on now as it was formerly. All the principal villages in the country are fortified (excepting in our happy country, in which our wise men have found out that fortifications are of no use) ; a few peons [2] keep the horse out ; and it is consequently necessary that they should have a camp and a bazaar to resort to for subsistence, in which every thing they get is very dear ; besides, this necessity of seeking subsistence in the camp prevents them from extending

---

[1] *The Life and Correspondence of Major-General Sir John Malcolm*, vol ii, pp. 278-9. Bahadur is a courtesy title, literally meaning 'invincible'.
[2] Irregular infantry used mainly for the defence of forts.

their excursions so far as they ought, to do any material injury.

The camp, on the resources of which an army of this kind must subsist, must be rather heavy; besides, there are great personages in it. They must have tents, elephants, and other sewary; [1] and must have with them a sufficient body of troops to guard their persons. The number of cavalry retained in such a camp must consequently be very large.

Large bodies move slowly, and it is not difficult to gain intelligence of their motions. A few rapid and well-contrived movements, made not directly upon them, but with a view to prevent the execution of any favorite design, or its mischievous consequences, soon bring them to their bearings; they stop, look about them, begin to feel restless, and are obliged to go off.

In this manner I lately stopped the march of the enemy upon Hyderabad, which they certainly intended; they were obliged to return, and bring up and join their infantry: and you will have heard that, in a most furious action which I had with their whole army, with one division only, on the 23rd of September, I completely defeated them, taking about one hundred pieces of cannon, all their ammunition, &c. They fled in the greatest confusion to Burhampoor. Take my word for it, that a body of light troops will not act, unless supported by a heavy body that will fight; and what is more, they cannot act, because they cannot subsist in the greater part of India at the present day. . . .

Believe me, &c.,

Arthur Wellesley

41

TO THE HON. HENRY WELLESLEY

Camp 50 miles North of Aurungabad,
3rd Oct., 1803

My dear Henry,

I wrote to you on the 17th of September, and since that time I have completely defeated the enemy, and have taken from them ninety eight pieces of cannon, with their ammunition, &c. I enclose a copy of my letter to the Governor General on this subject, which will give you an idea of the action.

I have little to add thereto, excepting to tell you, that Scindiah's French infantry were far better than Tippoo's, his artillery

---

[1] *Sawari* : equipage, especially riding.

excellent, and his ordnance so good, and so well equipped, that it answers for our service. We never could use Tippoo's. Our loss is great, but the action, I believe, was the most severe that ever was fought in this country; and I believe such a quantity of cannon, and such advantages have seldom been gained by any single victory in any part of the world.

The enemy had twelve hundred men killed on the field of battle, and I suppose about four times that number wounded. They plundered one another after the action, and many of their troops have deserted—the whole have fled to Burhampoor, about eighty miles from hence, in the greatest confusion.

I lost two horses. Diomed (Colonel Aston's horse, who has carried me in so many campaigns) piked, and another horse shot under me.[1] Almost all the staff had their horses either killed or wounded, or were struck in some place or other.

In the enclosed letter, I only report ninety pieces of cannon taken; but when I dispatched it, I did not know the extent of our gains. In fact, I believe we took one hundred and two, but we destroyed some, and there is a mistake respecting the number; I know there are ninety eight.

Holkar has hitherto taken no part in the war, and I fancy that he will now remain neutral.

I intend to move forward immediately. I have been detained hitherto by the difficulty of providing a secure place for my wounded soldiers; but I have got one at last; Colonel Stevenson, with the Nizam's army, is pushing the enemy forward.

I am well supplied with every thing. I have already got some of the enemy's supplies, and I have great hopes that I shall get more.

Ever your's affectionately,

Arthur Wellesley

[1] On September 26th he wrote to Malcolm : 'The bay horse was shot under me, and Diomed was kicked, so that I am not now sufficiently mounted. Will you let me have the grey Arab? I must also request you to get for me two good saddles and bridles.' In February 1804 Malcolm found Diomed and after hard bargaining bought him back for 250 rupees. 'The old horse is in sad condition', he told Wellesley, 'but he shall be treated like a prince till I have the pleasure of restoring him to you.' Diomed, a very fine grey Arab, had been left to Wellesley by Aston just before his last and fatal duel.

42

TO MAJOR MERRICK SHAWE

Camp at Pahlood, 26th October, 1803

My dear Sir,

I have received your letter of the 4th, and Sydenham's report of the campaign to the northward, up to the 17th September. Every thing appears to prosper, and I hope we shall soon bring the war to a conclusion.

Since the battle of Assye, I have been like a man who fights with one hand and defends himself with the other. With Colonel Stevenson's [1] corps I have acted offensively, and have taken Asseerghur; and with my own, I have covered his operations, and defended the territories of the Nizam and the Peshwah. In doing this, I have made some terrible marches, but I have been remarkably fortunate: first, in stopping the enemy when they intended to pass to the southward, through the Casserbarry ghaut; and afterwards, by a rapid march to the northward, in stopping Scindiah, when he was moving to interrupt Colonel Stevenson's operations against Asseerghur; in which he would otherwise undoubtedly have succeeded.

I moved up the ghaut as soon as Colonel Stevenson got possession of Asseerghur; and I think that, in a day or two, I shall turn Ragojee Bhoonslah, who has passed through to the southward. At all events, I am in time to prevent him doing any mischief.

I think that we are in great style to be able to act on the offensive at all in this quarter; but it is only done by the celerity of our movements, and by acting on the offensive or defensive with either corps, according to their situation, and that of the enemy. . . .

I saw your brother [2] yesterday, and he is doing well: indeed, all the wounded officers and men are fast recovering.

Believe me, &c.,

Arthur Wellesley

---

[1] See note to letter no. 18.
[2] One of Merrick Shawe's half-brothers, Henry, a lieutenant in the 74th Foot, had been killed in India in 1799. Another, Charles Fielding Shawe, was killed in the Pyrenees in 1813, while serving as a captain with the 6th Foot. A third brother, Mathew, Lieut.-Colonel of the 59th Regiment, married Isabella Creagh, and their eldest daughter, Isabella Gethin Shawe, married William Makepeace Thackeray.

Pray do not forget to send us money round to Bombay, as that presidency is in great distress. That is the only want which I now fear; for I believe I have settled the rice concern, but that very settlement creates a want of money.

[That October Captain Jasper Nicolls, 45th Regiment, then on Wellesley's staff, wrote in his journal after the capture of Asseerghur: 'Visiting the sick officers and wounded, we heard of General Wellesley's liberality to them. The evening we left Asseerghur, he sent in to every one a dozen of Madeira from his stock, and that wine is neither cheap nor plentiful; to-day he was in amongst them before the camp was pitched, making inquiries that are as honourable to his feelings as they are agreeable and gratifying to the poor invalids. The men have every comfort which can be afforded from the camp, or procured here, which I fear are not very numerous; indeed, the refugees from the adjoining parts, and Scindiah's wounded men, are dying here every day in want of the commonest and coarsest food.' [1]

Colonel Welsh describes how on November 7th an envoy arrived at General Wellesley's camp from Scindiah. The Vakeel, Jeswunt Rao Goorparah, had an elephant, two camels, a number of led horses and an escort of ninety of his master's best cavalry. The 7th being deemed a day of ill omen, he was not brought to General Wellesley until the next morning.

'Having passed at a canter to the Mahratta lines on our left, and there meeting the Vakeel, who with his friends had dismounted to receive the General, we all alighted, when a *gullehmillow*, or hugging scene, commenced among the great folks, which lasted some minutes; after which the ambassador and General Wellesley again mounted, followed by the rest, and the cavalcade returned by torchlight to head quarters, where the band of his Majesty's 78th regiment and a company were drawn up, who saluted the Vakeel as he dismounted. The General's tent, a large square single-poled one of about thirty feet, although half the officers had retired, could hardly contain the genteel crowd which remained.

'Taking a particular interest in the scene, I contrived to get close to the General's chair. He first handed the Vakeel in, and seated him on his right hand, and Gocklah, our head ally, on his left, and so on with the rest, according to their rank. A silver salver with betel was then brought in, which the General distributed to all the seven natives on his right and left entitled to such a compliment. He then gave them rich dresses and shawls, and, lastly, presented the Vakeel in particular with two superb jewels, and a rich gold chain, which were immediately fastened round his turban, and several more beautiful shawls and dresses were added to that donation; during which time the band of the 78th played " God save the

[1] Stoqueler, i, 21.

King". The great men conversed on common topics, till the last present, when the Vakeel told General Wellesley, in very good Hindoostanee, that "the Maharajah, his master, wished for nothing so ardently as his friendship and amity" ; and rising to take leave, was conducted to the door by the General. As a great concourse had assembled at the entrance, it was with difficulty the guard could make way for a very large elephant and beautiful horse to be brought up, and presented to the Vakeel, who, mounted on a superb white charger, most richly caparisoned, galloped off in great style, followed by his presents and escort ; — and thus ended the visit." [1]

On November 15th, 1803, in a Camp at Deotanna, Mountstuart Elphinstone wrote to his friend Edward Strachey : 'Here is Camp day. General at half-past four. Tent-pins rattle, and I rise and dress while they are striking my tent. Go to the front, and to the Quarter-master-General's tent, and drink a cup of tea. Talk with the *état-major*, who collect there till it grows light. The assembly beats and the General comes out. We go to his breakfast table in front of his tent and breakfast ; talk all the time. It is bitter cold, and we have our greatcoats on. At half after six, or earlier, or later, mount and ride, or, when there is no hunt, we do not mind one another. The General generally rides on the dusty flank, and so nobody stays with him. Now we always join Colonel Wallace, and have such coursing a mile or so out on the flank, and when we get to our ground from ten to twelve we all sit, if our chairs have come up, or lie on the ground. The General mostly lies down. When the tent is pitched we move in, and he lies on the carpet, and we all talk, &c., till breakfast is ready. Then we breakfast off fried mutton, mutton chops, curries, &c., and from eleven to two get to our tents, and I arrange my hircarras, write my journals, read Puffendorf,[2] Lysias,[3] and write you and Adam, and sometimes translate, and sometimes talk politics and other privitie with the General ; and then at two or three I eat a loaf and drink two glasses of port and water ; and when it grows dark, unless I am writing, as I am now, I get shaved and walk about head-quarters line till it is pitch dark, and then dress, go to dinner, and we all talk about the march, &c., and they about their former wars, and about this war, and Indian Courts, and politics, &c. At nine we break up, and the Quarter-master-General and Major of Brigade and I hold a committee and settle whether we march next day, and then I go to palankeen. All this is very pleasant." [4]]

[1] *Military Reminiscences*, vol. i, pp. 186-7.
[2] Samuel von Pufendorf (1632–94) was a German legal and historical writer who devised a system of universal law — *Elementorum Jurisprudentiae Universalis libri* (1660). He also published *De Jure Naturae et Gentium* (1672) and a history of Sweden, having been appointed Historiographer Royal in Stockholm.
[3] Lysias (*c*. 458–378 B.C.), an Athenian orator.
[4] *The Life of the Honourable Mountstuart Elphinstone*, vol. i, pp. 84-5.

43

TO THE MARQUESS WELLESLEY

Camp at Paterly, 30th November, 1803

My Lord,

I have the honor to inform you that I attacked the armies of Dowlut Rao Scindiah and the Rajah of Berar yesterday afternoon, on the plains of Argaum in this neighbourhood, with the divisions of the army under my immediate command, and the subsidiary force serving with the Soubah[1] of the Deccan, under Colonel Stevenson, and completely defeated the enemy, having taken from them their cannon, ammunition, &c., and destroyed vast numbers of them.

I have reason to believe that the loss which I have sustained upon this occasion has not been great. No officer has been killed, and but few wounded. I will forward to your Excellency a detailed account of this action, as well as of the circumstances which led to it, as soon as I shall receive a return of the killed and wounded.

I have the honor to be, &c.,

Arthur Wellesley

44

TO MAJOR MERRICK SHAWE

Camp at Akote, 2nd Dec., 1803

My dear Sir,

I have but little to add to my letter of the 30th to the Governor General respecting the battle of Argaum. The number of the enemy destroyed is very great. Vittell Punt, who commanded the cavalry of the Rajah of Berar, was killed ; and Gopal Bhow, who commanded Scindiah's cavalry that fought, was wounded. If we had had daylight one hour more, not a man would have escaped.

We should have had that time, if my native infantry had not been panic struck, and got into confusion when the cannonade commenced. What do you think of nearly three entire battalions, who behaved so admirably in the battle of Assye, being broke and running off, when the cannonade commenced at Argaum,

---

[1] Suba : a province or large division of the Mogul empire ; also a governor.

which was not to be compared to that at Assye ? Luckily, I happened to be at no great distance from them, and I was able to rally them and re-establish the battle. If I had not been there, I am convinced we should have lost the day. But as it was, so much time elapsed before I could form them again, that we had not daylight enough for every thing that we should certainly have performed.

The troops were under arms, and I was on horseback, from six in the morning until twelve at night.

Nothing could have been more fortunate than my return to the northward. I just arrived in time. Colonel Stevenson [1] was not delayed for me more than one day ; and it is a curious circumstance, that, after having been so long separated, and such a distance between us, we should have joined at a moment so critical. . . .

Believe me, &c.,

Arthur Wellesley

❦

[While Wellesley and Stevenson were defeating the Mahrattas at Assaye and Argaum, General Gerard Lake, the Commander-in-Chief, had been campaigning hundreds of miles to the north-west against Scindiah's French-trained forces. Lake left his headquarters at Cawnpore on August 7th, stormed the fortress of Aligarh, and moved on Delhi, which he entered on September 12th after a battle outside. The enemy retired upon Agra, which city was carried by assault. Scindiah next reinforced his remnant army by sending fourteen battalions and many guns from the Deccan, but although Lake was now outnumbered by at least two to one, he pursued the enemy with his cavalry and light troops, came up with them at Laswaree and there on November 1st won a protracted and very hard fought battle. He thereby destroyed Scindiah's influence and French power in northern India.

It was Holkar who next occupied Lake's attention. He drove the Mahratta army west in the spring of 1804, then withdrew to frontier cantonments until the end of the rainy season allowed him to conduct a decisive campaign against the freebooter. Two hundred miles in advance of the main army he left Colonel William Monson with twelve thousand men and fifteen guns. The imprudent Colonel moved forward through mountain passes into Holkar's territory and assaulted a fortress, whereupon Holkar turned upon him with forty thousand troops.

Had Monson, notwithstanding the disparity of numbers, attacked Holkar, especially when the latter was involved in crossing a swollen river, he might well have carried the day. Instead he delayed, then retreated

---

[1] Blakiston says that Stevenson was so weak from ill health that he could not mount a horse, but, seated on an elephant, brought his division into action at Argaum in excellent style.

early in July. His cavalry were overwhelmed, his guns were abandoned. In heavy rain his soldiers struggled through the passes, harassed by Mahratta horsemen, faced with rivers to cross, weakened by serious desertions. Barely one thousand of Monson's force reached Agra.

Arthur Wellesley referred to Monson's 'retreats, defeats, disgraces and disasters' as 'the greatest and most disgraceful to our military character that have ever occurred'. That was written in September. The Major-General, whose wish to return to England had been deferred in response to his brother Richard's anxieties, had been busy but not a little bored with writing military and political memoranda. However, when Lake, now Lord Lake of Laswaree and Delhi, crushed Holkar on November 17th, 1804, at Farukhabad and also at Deeg, Wellesley felt the way clear for him to depart. He booked a passage early in 1805 and sailed in March.

On October 12th, 1839, Lord Mahon rode out with the Duke of Wellington hunting, and mention of the probable results of the projected penny postage led to an account of the post in India. 'It is called the *Dawk* in some districts; the *Tappal* in others. It is always carried by a man on foot, who travels prodigious distances, going at the rate of five or six miles an hour, and bearing a kind of rattle whose sound scares away the snakes and other dangerous animals from his path as he moves along. His loins are very tightly girded.

'So sure and certain is this mode of conveyance, even through very unsettled countries, that the Duke, after having been separated from Colonel Stevenson for several months and along hundreds of miles — one on each side of the Taptee — was able to combine his movements with his so accurately, that they met in the appointed field and time just before the battle of Argaum. "I saw the dust raised by his march in the distance, and I desired an officer near me to ride off to him and tell him to move to a particular village which I pointed out, and that there he should have further orders. But, said the officer, what am I to do if it should not be Colonel Stevenson? Why, then, I answered, you are mounted on a damned good horse, and you have eyes in your head — and you must ride off as hard as you can.

'"The Mahrattas near me were much surprised at my message. How, they said, can you possibly tell Colonel Stevenson's dust from anybody else's dust ?"'[1]

45

TO THE MARQUESS WELLESLEY

Camp, 21st January, 1804

My dear Mornington,

I have only this day received your letter of the 23rd of December, which had been transmitted by the Soubah's dawk

[1] *Notes of Conversations with the Duke of Wellington*, pp. 181-2.

to Ellichpoor, and I am delighted to find that you are pleased with our battle of Argaum.

I do not know whether I detailed the causes of the departure from the armistice, in that instance, in any of my public or private letters; but they appear fully on the minutes of the conferences. The fact was, that Scindiah complied with none of the conditions of the armistice, which he had not ratified at that time, and I attacked him, as I gave notice to his vakeels that I should on the preceding day. They thought he was at too great a distance from me, and the intention of both Scindiah and Vincajee Bhoonslah, in drawing up their army and apparently offering battle, was to impose upon the troops, and induce them to believe that we wanted confidence in our own strength. They would have drawn off at night, and we should have been obliged to fight a more desperate battle, in a position more favorable to the enemy, under the guns of Gawilghur.

You will see, by one of the dispatches which I have written to you this day, that I have arranged to send a regiment of European infantry to Fort William, and that I have provided an efficient disposable corps for Guzerat, and an European garrison for Bombay.

I have written to Colonel Close to have his opinion upon some points relative to the subsidiary force with the Peshwah, and as soon as I receive his answer, I shall issue orders for the establishment of it. I propose to appoint Colonel Wallace [1] to command it till your orders shall be received. He is a brave soldier in whom the troops have confidence. I shall leave the remains of the 74th with the subsidiary force for some time, till we see how affairs settle at Scindiah's durbar.

I am much annoyed by the lumbago, a disorder to which, I believe, all persons in camp are liable; and if I do not go into a house soon, I am afraid I shall walk like old Pomeroy [2] for the remainder of my life. I do not propose, however, to break up till I shall receive the ratification of the treaty of peace; although I shall have all the preparatory arrangements made, such as subsidiary force established, &c. &c.

I am now going across the Godavery, to try if I cannot

[1] Lieut.-Colonel William Wallace, 74th Foot, had commanded a brigade at Assaye.
[2] Arthur Pomeroy was in 1783 elevated to the peerage of Ireland as Baron Harberton of Carbery, Co. Kildare, and in 1791 was advanced to Viscount. He had died in 1798. His wife was a niece of Richard, 1st Lord Mornington.

surprise and cut up the banditti upon the Nizam's frontier. At all events, I shall disperse them. . . .

. . . I have allowed Colonel Stevenson to go to Madras for his health. He must go to England soon, or he will not live. Colonel Halyburton [1] now commands the Nizam's subsidiary force, in Colonel Stevenson's absence, and I recommend him as his successor, if Colonel Stevenson should go to England. He has been long at Hyderabad, and has served well during the campaign.

I have generally written to Major Shawe for two reasons: first, because it was probable I should get an answer from him; secondly, it was probable that this answer would contain intelligence of matters in Bengal which it was desirable that I should have.

Ever yours, most affectionately,
Arthur Wellesley

Malcolm writes from Scindiah's camp, that at the first meeting Scindiah received him with great gravity, which he had intended to preserve throughout the visit. It rained violently; and an officer of the escort, Mr. Pepper,[2] an Irishman, (a nephew of old Bective's,[3] by the by), sat under a flat part of the tent which received a great part of the rain that fell. At length, it burst through the tent upon the head of Mr. Pepper, who was concealed by the torrent that fell, and was discovered after some time by an " Oh Jasus! " and an hideous yell. Scindiah laughed violently, as did all the others present; and the gravity and dignity of the durbar degenerated into a Malcolm riot—after which they all parted upon the best terms.

The Malcolm referred to in the last letter was one of Wellesley's closest friends and a brilliant colleague in the affairs of India. One day younger than Arthur Wellesley, Malcolm had arrived there in the spring of 1783. A fine shot, athlete and scholar, the young Scot had a gaiety and playful humour which endeared him to all and gained him the nickname of 'Boy' Malcolm. As he put it to his sister in 1797: 'You know that I can be the most serious man on earth when I assume that character. I have not found that necessary for more than five hours of my life, and

[1] Lieut.-Colonel John Haliburton, 7th Regiment of Native Infantry.
[2] Lieutenant George John Pepper, 2nd Regiment of Native Infantry.
[3] Thomas, Lord Bective, succeeded his father as 2nd Marquess of Headfort in 1829.

I hope that I may laugh through the remainder as happily. Laughing or crying, I always am your affectionate brother.'

In the words of one contemporary, 'his overflowing spirits made him riotous'; but these did not vitiate his rare abilities and capacity for hard and effective work. 'Malcolm is indefatigable,' wrote Wellesley in an expressive phrase, 'and leads the life of a canister at a dog's tail.'

After serving as Persian interpreter to the Nizam of the Deccan and then as secretary to two successive commanders-in-chief, he was in September 1798 appointed assistant to Captain Kirkpatrick at the Hyderabad Residency and remained there until in the following August Lord Mornington sent him as special envoy to Persia. On his successful return in 1801 Malcolm became private secretary to the Governor-General and two years later he joined Arthur Wellesley as his political agent during the Mahratta War.

In later life Sir John Malcolm, as he became, was Governor of Bombay. He wrote several historical works, among them *A Political History of India* (1811), *A History of Persia* (1818), *The Administration of India* in 1833, the year of his death, and posthumously in 1836 *The Life of Robert Lord Clive*, the three volumes of which were reviewed by Lord Macaulay in the *Edinburgh Review* of January 1840, and formed the starting-point for his famous essay on Clive.

In 1824 Malcolm was paid a handsome tribute by the Duke of Wellington, who wrote to his old friend : 'I can answer for it that from the year 1796 no great transaction has taken place in the East in which you have not played a principal, most useful, conspicuous, and honorable part ; and you have in many services, diplomatic as well as military, been distinguished by successes, any one of which in ordinary circumstances would have been deemed sufficient for the life of a man, and would have recommended him to the notice of his superiors'.

After his presentation to Dowlut Rao Scindiah in the Mahratta camp on January 12th, Malcolm had written to Arthur Wellesley :

'We were well received by the Maharajah, who is a good-looking young man. He preserved great gravity when we first went in ; and probably we might have left him without seeing that his gravity was affected, had not a ridiculous incident moved his muscles. A severe shower took place whilst we were in his tent. The water lodged on the flat part of the tent, under which Mr. Pepper was seated, and all at once burst in a torrent upon his head. From the midst of the torrent we heard a voice exclaim, "*Jesus !*" [1] — and soon after poor Pepper emerged. The Maharajah laughed loud, and we all joined chorus. A shower of hail followed the rain, and hailstones were brought in and presented in all quarters. My hands were soon filled with them by the politeness of Dowlut Rao and his Ministers ; and all began to eat, or rather to drink them. For ten minutes the scene more resembled a school at the moment when the boys have got

[1] Malcolm adds the footnote : 'Mister Pepper begs permission to deny the "Jesus", though he is free to confess the sousing'.

to play than an Eastern Durbar. We parted in great good humour ; and, as far as I can judge from physiognomy, every one in Camp is rejoiced at the termination of hostilities.' [1]

46

TO COLONEL JOHN MURRAY [2]

Camp, 26th January, 1804

Sir,

. . . I have now only to recommend to your attention the discipline of the troops under your command, and a determined resistance to every thing like an abuse in the service, which can tend to substract from the efficiency of the corps in the field. I have lately written to Mr. Duncan,[3] to propose an alteration in the plans which I submitted to him on the 2nd of August last, according to which, if he should adopt it, your strength in European troops will be diminished, but that of native troops will be increased by two battalions. This arrangement is advisable, and indeed necessary, for many reasons not necessary at present to discuss ; but if troops in Guzerat are kept in a proper state of discipline and efficiency, I do not apprehend any inconvenience from it.

Upon this subject I have to observe, that there is a tendency in the service in this country to admit abuses beyond any other that I have met with. I cannot say whether this is to be attributed to former habits and example, or to the laxity which must attend all distant establishments. But of this I am very certain, that it is the first duty of a commanding officer to resist every thing of the kind in a most determined manner. The want of discipline among troops is very bad, and renders them useless : but the want of efficiency, which is the result of the application to private purposes or profit of the persons paid by the public as troops, or as the necessary attendants or equipments of these troops, is worse, as it may exist with a certain degree and appear-

---

[1] *The Life and Correspondence of Major-General Sir John Malcolm*, vol. i, pp. 245-6.

[2] Colonel, afterwards General Sir John, Murray (? 1768–1827) had served in the Red Sea before going to India in 1801. He was Quartermaster-General of the army there till his promotion to major-general in 1805. He campaigned in the Peninsula and in 1815 was court-martialled for having abandoned guns and stores at Tarragona two years before.

[3] Jonathan Duncan (1756–1811) was Governor of Bombay for sixteen years.

ance of discipline, and Government may be misled by the notion that they have an army, whereas they have nothing but paper.

The troops under your command are in a distant country, and they can come but seldom under the view or inspection of the Government; it is therefore particularly incumbent on you to take care that no practice or custom shall exist which may destroy their discipline or lessen their efficiency; and I beg leave to assure you, that without the most constant vigilance on your part, you will not be able to avert these evils.

I have the honor to be, &c.,

Arthur Wellesley

47

TO COLONEL JOHN MURRAY

Munkaiseer, 7th February, 1804

Sir,

. . . On the day before yesterday I destroyed a band of free-booters, who had for some time plundered the Nizam's terri-tories, and had become very formidable, had beaten his High-ness's troops, and taken from them four guns.

I marched on the morning of the 4th, twenty miles; at night, twenty-four miles, and arrived here at nine o'clock on the morning of the 5th. Some of our faithful allies in my camp had given them intelligence of my march, and they had struck tents and were going off. But I pursued them, cut up many, took all their baggage, bazaars, guns, ammunition, &c., and entirely dispersed them.

The 74th regiment, one battalion of native infantry, and five hundred men from the other corps in camp were up in the pursuit. The whole was over by twelve o'clock on the 5th. I think that by that time the troops had marched sixty miles, from six in the morning of the 4th, in which time they halted ten hours, from twelve at noon to ten at night of the 4th.[1]

If the night had not been very dark, and the road very bad, I should have been in their camp at daylight, and should have taken the whole party.

---

[1] Wellesley later assured his brother Henry: 'This was the greatest exertion I ever saw troops make in any country'.

I think we now begin to beat the Mahrattas in the celerity of our movements.[1]

I have the honor to be, &c.,

Arthur Wellesley

❋

[Two days later, on February 9th, Wellesley wrote to Major Kirk-patrick : 'I do not propose at present to follow the remains of the free-booters towards the Solapoor country. In the first place, it has now become a matter of the utmost importance to give some rest to the division under my command, who have been marching since February, 1803 ; and who, since the battle of Assye in September, have not halted more than one day in any place, excepting during the siege of Gawilghur.'

He brought up the subject of swift movement when, on November 11th, 1831, he said to Lord Mahon, afterwards Earl Stanhope : 'The most surprising march, I believe, ever made was one of mine in India — seventy-two miles from five one morning to twelve the next ; — and all fair marching ; nor could there be any mistake as to distance, for in India we always marched with measuring wheels. The country was not very flat — a few hills, but however no *ghaut* or mountain pass to get over.'[2]

The Duke of Wellington also told William, Baron de Ros, that his troops in India always marched by the wheel or perambulator. 'The men who had charge of these wheels attained such extraordinary correctness of judging distance that they could be depended upon almost as completely without the wheel as with it. The soldiers were in messes of six or eight ; each mess had its own native cook and a bullock which carried the men's knapsacks and their cooking materials, etc. The native soldiers, however, at that time carried their knapsacks on their backs, but I believe they no longer do so. An army in good order in India would march very near three miles an hour. Everything depended on finding halting stations at convenient distances, 16 or 18 miles, where there was water. Generally the villages were by the bank of what in winter was a river, but in summer was to all outward appearance perfectly dry and a mere bed of sand. The water, however, though unseen, was always flowing at a depth of from one to three feet below this bed of sand. Scouts were always sent forward to look for these dry rivers, and on the arrival of the army a great number of small wells were excavated the first thing. A few days afterwards the sand would blow into these holes, and after a short time no vestige of wells or excavations would remain.'[3]]

[1] In January 1800 he had written : 'In the wars which we may expect in India in future, we must look to light and quick movements ; and we ought always to be in that state to be able to strike a blow as soon as a war might become evidently necessary'.

[2] *Notes of Conversations with the Duke of Wellington*, p. 16.

[3] Quoted from the De Ros. MS. by Sir Herbert Maxwell in *The Life of Welling-ton*, vol. i, pp. 72-3.

48

TO MAJOR MERRICK SHAWE

Camp, 26th February, 1804

My dear Sir,

. . . The reform of the army is the point upon which I am not of the same opinion with the Governor General, and I think it very possible that my opinion may be biassed by the inconveniences which I have experienced during the war from the extreme weakness of the Government of the Soubah of the Deccan. However, on the other hand, I do not think that sufficient weight is given in Bengal to the necessity that the army should be employed in all these native governments, in the administration of the civil government and in the collection of the revenue.

Bengal, " the paradise of nations," enjoys the advantage of a civil government, and requires its military force only for its protection against foreign enemies. All the other barbarous establishments called governments, without excepting even that of Fort St. George, have no power beyond that of the sword. Take from them the exercise of that power, and they have no other; and can collect no revenue, can give no protection, and can exercise no government. The native governments, I mean those of the Nizam and the Peshwah, are fifty times worse than ours in this respect. They do not choose to keep armies themselves, their territories are overrun by a race of armed men, who are ready to enlist with any body who will lead them to plunder; and there is no power in the country to support the government and give protection to the industrious classes of the inhabitants, excepting the British troops.

Upon this subject two questions occur for consideration: one is, whether the subsidiary British troops, now with the Peshwah and the Nizam, are sufficiently strong to be able to give the requisite support to the civil government in all parts. As far as I am able to form a judgment, I am of opinion that they are not; and that if the Peshwah and the Soubah of the Deccan are not to entertain armies for the support of their own authority, the number of troops supplied to each ought to be doubled. I am clearly of opinion that each force is fully equal to any particular service in which they may be employed; but their services are required in so many places at the same time, in these extensive countries, that the number of troops are not sufficient for the demands upon them.

The next question is, whether the Soubah of the Deccan or the Peshwah will pay for an increase of the forces subsidized. It must not be expected that the Soubah of the Deccan will do any such thing. The Peshwah, indeed, may be induced to grant land in Bundelcund, or in any other province of which he has not possession, to increase his subsidiary force, if at any time he should be disappointed in the execution of any favorite plan, from its weakness; but not otherwise. In fact, excepting in Bundelcund, the Peshwah has nothing to give; and the Soubah of the Deccan will not give any thing.

I have no apprehension of any future foreign wars. Indeed no foreign powers now remain; even if Scindiah should not come into the defensive alliance, we have got such a hold in his durbar, by the treaty of peace, that if ever he goes to war with the Company, one half of his chiefs and of his army will be on our side. But I think that we run a great risk from the free-booter system.

It is not known to the Governor General, and you can have no idea of the extent to which it has gone; and it increases daily. I could state facts on this subject, which would prove the extraordinary weakness of the allied governments, and would show the necessity of strengthening them. But a letter is not the proper place for them. Conceive a country, in every village of which there are from twenty to thirty horsemen, who have been dismissed from the service of the state, and who have no means of living excepting by plunder. In this country there is no law, no civil government, and no army to keep these plunderers in order; and no revenue can be collected,—indeed no inhabitant can, nor will remain to cultivate, unless he is protected by an armed force stationed in his village.

This is the outline of the state of the countries of the Peshwah and the Nizam.

The extension of our arms and influence certainly increases this evil; because, wherever we go, it is soon found out that we are always ready and willing to fight; money is always wanted for the expenses of luxury and debauchery, and armies are discharged to procure it. The danger of the evil is also increased by the extension of our arms, our influence, and our protection:

first, by the increase of the number of the people, who must and will subsist by plunder; secondly, by narrowing the scene in which the freebooters may plunder with impunity. The first requires no illustration. In respect to the second, I have to observe, that after having stood still nearly forty years, (with the exception of the small acquisitions made by Lord Cornwallis [1] from Tippoo,) we have, within the last five years, extended ourselves by our policy and our bravery over the whole of India, excepting the territories of Holkar and the Rajah of Berar; supposing that Scindiah should come into the defensive alliance. In this vast extent of country, in which the numbers of the people, with arms in their hands, who have no means of living excepting by plunder, are so much increased, no man can venture to plunder without incurring the risk, at least, of being destroyed by a British army. Habits of industry are out of the question; they must plunder for subsistence, or be destroyed, or starve, or be taken into the service of some of the allied powers. As we have now narrowed the scene so much, we must not expect that our own territories will be entirely free from their depredations. In fact, if they are to meet the Company's troops in all countries, they have no choice excepting the richest and best cultivated; and those in which they are likely to meet the smallest number of these formidable troops. The Company's territories answer the description in every respect; and there, I think, is the danger of our present exalted situation.

The Governor General has never had this picture before him. No man has ever had so many opportunities of contemplating the subject in all its parts as I have; and possibly no man has ever adverted to it. The remedy is clear, viz., to force the allies to keep up their military establishments. This is the first step; I would then give them no assistance in carrying on their internal government, excepting to oppose formidable rebellions. After this is done, by degrees a regulation may be introduced, which I recommended in 1800, in Mysore, viz., that no horse be kept that is not registered, and that no horseman should be allowed to travel through the country without a passport from the Government. In this manner the breed will, by degrees, be diminished.

[1] Charles, Marquess Cornwallis (1738–1805), who had fought in America and had capitulated at Yorktown, defeated Tippoo Sahib in 1792, was Viceroy in Ireland in 1798, negotiated the Treaty of Amiens in 1801. In 1805 he went to India again, as Governor-General, but died soon afterwards.

But Mr. Edmonstone [1] says, in his dispatch, that to put the military establishments of the allies in a state of efficiency is inconsistent with the fundamental principles on which all the treaties of defensive alliance have been framed, which were to make the powers dependent upon the British Government. In the first place, the military establishments can never be made so efficient as to place the native powers in any other excepting a state of dependence on the British Government, in respect to all their foreign concerns. In the second place, the measure which I propose goes no further than to insist upon having that body of troops ready, which the treaties require they should have. In the third place, if, after all that has happened, I could suppose it possible that any of our allies would rebel against us (for I think that the breach of the defensive alliance ought with propriety to be called rebellion) I should say, that they have in their hands at this moment a most formidable weapon against us, in the numerous horse which reside in their countries; every one of whom would join their standard, if it were raised to collect a body for the invasion of the Company's territories, by any chief, no matter by whom. This weapon, the strength of which my system would go to destroy, is far more formidable in the hands of any one of them, than the regular military establishments of all of them put together.

I see clearly that the Governor General has never contemplated this state of the question; indeed he could not contemplate it, for it has never been brought before him in any shape. The gentlemen at the Residences see nothing excepting what passes in the durbars,[2] and therefore could not report it; and it could not reach the Governor General in any other manner. I have had many opportunities of seeing and feeling the effects of the evil. . . .

Believe me, &c.,

Arthur Wellesley

I shall be at Poonah to-morrow.

[1] Neil Benjamin Edmonstone (1765-1841) began as a writer to the East India Company, and in 1794 was appointed Persian translator to the Government. In 1801 he became Political Secretary in succession to Colonel Kirkpatrick. From 1812 to 1817 he was a member of the Supreme Council in Calcutta.

[2] The court of an independent prince.

49

TO MAJOR GRAHAM [1]

Poonah, 2nd March, 1804

My dear Sir,

I have received your letter of the 1st instant. It is necessary for a man who fills a public situation, and who has great public interests in charge, to lay aside all private considerations, whether on his own account or that of other persons. I imagine that you must feel on this subject as I do.

I am very much distressed on account of the inconveniences which your family suffer in your absence from Madras; and equally so, that it is not in my power to relieve their distress, by allowing you to quit your situation. But, under present circumstances, it is not in my power to grant your request to go to Madras, consistently with the duty which both you and I owe to the public, as public men.

I shall be much obliged to you if you will not urge me again upon this subject.

Believe me, &c.,

Arthur Wellesley

50

TO GENERAL GERARD LAKE [2]

27th May, 1804

Sir,

... The account you give of the state of Holkar's army is very satisfactory. I have served a good deal in this part of India against this description of freebooter; and I think that the best mode of operating, is to press him with one or two corps capable of moving with tolerable celerity, and of such strength as to render the result of an action by no means doubtful, if he should venture to risk one. There is but little hope, it is true, that he will risk an action, or that any one of these corps will come up with him. The effect to be produced by this mode of operation is to oblige him to move constantly and with great celerity.

[1] Graham was Collector at Ahmednuggur.
[2] Lake (1744–1808), who was M.P. for Aylesbury from 1790 to 1802, became Commander-in-Chief in India in 1800. He was created a baron in 1804 and advanced to a viscountcy three years later, soon after his final return from India.

When reduced to this necessity, he cannot venture to stop to plunder the country, and he does comparatively but little mischief : at all events the subsistence of his army becomes difficult and precarious, the horsemen become dissatisfied, they perceive that their situation is hopeless, and they desert in numbers daily : the freebooter ends by having with him only a few adherents ; and he is reduced to such a state as to be liable to be taken by any small body of country horse, which are the fittest troops to be then employed against him.

In proportion as the body of our troops, to be employed against a freebooter of this description, have the power of moving with celerity, will such freebooter be distressed. Whenever the largest and most formidable bodies of them are hard pressed by our troops, the village people attack them upon their rear and flanks, cut off stragglers, and will not allow a man to enter their villages ; because their villages being in some degree fortified, they know well that the freebooters dare not wait the time which would be necessary to reduce them. When this is the case, all their means of subsistence vanish, no resource remains excepting to separate ; and even this resource is attended by risk, as the village people cut them off on their way to their homes. . . .

I have the honor to be, &c.,

Arthur Wellesley

51

TO MAJOR MERRICK SHAWE

Camp at Chinchore, 8th June, 1804

My dear Sir,

I wish you to take an opportunity of mentioning to the Governor General, that having a very strong desire to return to Europe, I applied lately to the Commander in Chief for leave to quit this country when circumstances will permit it ; and General Lake has given me his permission to go whenever I may think proper.

My principal reason for wishing to go is, that I think I have served as long in India as any man ought, who can serve any where else ; and I think that there appears a prospect of service in Europe, in which I should be more likely to get forward.

Another reason is, that I have been a good deal annoyed by

the rheumatism in my back, for which living in a tent during another monsoon is not a very good remedy; and a third is, that I do not think I have been very well treated by the King's government.

It is now about two years since I have been a Major General, and nearly as much since I was appointed to the staff at Fort St. George, by General Stuart. Since that time, it has been perfectly well known that I had led a body of British troops into the Mahratta territories; and supposing that I had no other pretensions to be placed on the staff, I might have expected a confirmation of General Stuart's act, under those circumstances. The staff in India had been under consideration, and another officer had been appointed to it.

This last reason for wishing to go to Europe is the only one which I have stated to General Lake, although it is the least strong; as I am very certain that I shall have been appointed to the staff, as soon as it was known in England that I had reached Poonah with the army; and General Lake has consented to my departure.

If the war with Holkar had not broken out, there would have been no difficulty in the business; and I should have been able to go in October, being the first period at which I could sail. As affairs are situated, I think it probable that the Governor General will have no objection to my departure, and this is the principal reason for which I trouble you.

In the present state of affairs, I can do but little in the Deccan, and that little may as well be done by any body else. The siege of Chandore, when it can be undertaken, is a military operation of but little importance; and the operations of the troops from Guzerat are already beyond my guidance.

Under these circumstances, I wish that the Governor General would allow me to relinquish the command in the Deccan. If I should be able to go to England in October, it must be supposed that I have money matters to arrange in Mysore, and at Madras; particularly at the latter: my accounts of the late war, which, although sent up regularly every month, have not yet been passed.

I am, therefore, very anxious to receive your answer to this letter, at an early period, in order that I may arrive at Madras, if possible, early in September.

I need scarcely add, that, if the Governor General should

have any desire that I should remain in this country, or should think that I can be of the smallest use to his plans, I shall remain with pleasure.

Believe me, &c.,

Arthur Wellesley

52

TO LIEUT.-COLONEL WILLIAM WALLACE

Camp at Niggeree, 28th June, 1804

My dear Wallace,

I have not yet been able to send you the copies of my letters to the Resident, which I promised you, but I shall send them as soon as I shall have a leisure moment.

I have got on well; but nothing can be more erroneous than Captain Johnson's [1] route. He was wrong eight miles between Poonah and Kichaire, and between that place and this about twenty miles!!! He did not even measure the route correctly from his own map. The road is very good, and Hill [2] will get on well.

I beg you to let me hear any reports that may reach you about your own situation. You need be under no apprehension. You may depend upon it that I will take care that you shall not lose it.

I believe that in my public dispatches I have alluded to every point to which I should wish to draw your attention, excepting one, which I will mention to you—that is, the secrecy of all your proceedings.

There is nothing more certain than that, of one hundred affairs, ninety-nine might be posted up at the market-cross, without injury to the public interests; but the misfortune is that, where the public business is the subject of general conversation, and is not kept secret, as a matter of course, upon every occasion, it is very difficult to keep it secret upon that occasion on which it is necessary. There is an awkwardness in a secret which enables discerning men (of which description there are always plenty in an army) invariably to find it out; and it may be depended upon that, whenever the public business ought to

---

[1] Captain J. Johnson was an officer in the Bombay Engineers.
[2] Major Thomas Hill was First Assistant Secretary in the Military Department.

be kept secret, it always suffers when it is exposed to public view.

For this reason secrecy is always best, and those who have been long trusted with the conduct of public affairs are in the habit of never making public business of any description, that it is not necessary that the public should know. The consequence is that secrecy becomes natural to them, and as much a habit as it is to others to talk of public matters; and they have it in their power to keep things secret or not, as they may think proper.

I mention this subject to you because, in fact, I have been the means of throwing the public affairs into your hands, and I am anxious that you should conduct them as you ought. This is a matter which would never occur to you, but it is essentially necessary.

Remember, that what I recommend to you is far removed from mystery: in fact, I recommend silence upon the public business upon all occasions, in order to avoid the necessity of mystery upon any.

Believe me, &c.,

Arthur Wellesley

53

TO LIEUT.-GENERAL JAMES STUART

Fort St. George, 2nd August, 1804

Sir,

I have the honor to inform you, that if you should have no objection to the measure, I propose recommending to the Governor General, to give a gratuity of one month's pay to the persons belonging to the public bullock department, who served with the troops under my command, during the late war. These persons marched from Seringapatam with the troops; they served throughout the war in a country in which grain, when cheapest, was in the proportion of twelve to one dearer than in Mysore; they always did their duty without grumbling; and I do not recollect an instance of desertion. They were necessarily present in the actions which were fought; some of them were killed, and others desperately wounded.

Upon the occasion of laying before you my intention to recommend this description of the public servants of the army to the favor of his Excellency the Governor General, I cannot avoid drawing your notice to the benefits which have resulted from the establishment to which they belonged.

It must be recollected, that in former wars, the utmost exertion which it was possible for the army to make, was to draw its train of artillery to Seringapatam. It was not possible and never was expected, that the guns and carriages which were drawn there, should be brought away again; and accordingly, notwithstanding the undoubted talents, and the great reputation of the officers, who have at different times led British armies to that place, it has invariably happened, that by far the greater part of the train and carriages have been left behind when the army marched away.

Those who have seen the mode in which those armies made their marches, and were acquainted with the system under which cattle were, and must necessarily be, procured for the service, will not hesitate to allow, that the slowness of all our operations, and the necessity to which I have above alluded, of leaving our guns after they had been drawn about three hundred miles, were to be attributed entirely to the faults of the system under which the cattle were procured for the service.

But although I am addressing myself to an officer whose experience reaches beyond the times to which I have alluded, it is only necessary that I should advert, in proof of my assertion, to the circumstances of the late war. From a variety of causes, it was necessary, at the commencement of the war, to hire cattle to draw the train from Madras to the frontiers of Mysore; and you will recollect the difficulties under which you labored; and that in fact you could not have brought your carriages to the frontier without the assistance of the public cattle sent to join you; and that if the circumstances of the times had required that the whole army should have advanced to Poonah, you would probably have thought it proper to have taken with you those carriages only for which you might have had a sufficient number of the public draught cattle.

All the carriages attached to the division under my command, were drawn by the public cattle; and I shall advert to a few facts, to point out the difference between this part of the equipment of the troops in the late and in former wars.

We marched to Poonah from Seringapatam, the distance being nearly six hundred miles, in the worst season of the year, through a country which had been destroyed by Holkar's army, with heavy guns, at the rate, upon an average, of thirteen and a half miles a day ; and if the twelve days on which we halted upon the Toombuddra for orders be included, we arrived at Poonah in two months from the time we marched. On this march we lost no draught cattle. I remained in the neighbourhood of Poonah, in a country which deserves the name of a desert, for six weeks ; and then marched again with the train, in the same state, as to numbers, as when it left Seringapatam, and the troops and cattle were in the field during the monsoon.

It is needless to advert to the distance marched during the war, or to recapitulate the events, all of which must show the efficient state of the equipments ; but it has been frequently necessary for the troops to march for many days together ; a distance from fifteen to twenty miles daily ; the heavy artillery always accompanied them, and I always found that the cattle could go as far as the troops. Upon one occasion, I found it necessary to march a detachment sixty miles in thirty hours, and the ordnance and provision carriages, drawn by the Company's bullocks, accompanied this detachment.

Instead of being obliged, as the Commanders in Chief of armies in former wars have been, to leave guns and carriages behind, such was the state of efficiency of this department throughout this severe service, that I was able, with but little assistance, to draw away the guns which the troops took.

After all this service, in which so much country has been marched over, the number of cattle which have died is, I believe, really not greater than it would have been at the grazing ground ; and the department is at this moment in a state of great efficiency.

It would not be difficult to prove, that in point of actual expense, this establishment is cheaper to the public, than to hire cattle in the old mode ; but the consideration respecting a public establishment of this description, is not referable entirely to cheapness.

It must be obvious to every man, that in a war, such as the late war, there could be no success, unless the officer commanding the troops was able to move, at all times, with the utmost celerity of which the troops were capable, and to continue his movements so long as was necessary. Rapid movements with guns and carriages cannot be made without good cattle, well driven, and well taken care of ; and without adverting to what passed subsequently, it is more than probable, that if I had had the service of such cattle only, as served Lord Cornwallis and General Harris in former wars, I should never have reached Poonah, and that I should have been obliged to find my way back without the wheel carriages, in the best manner I could.

I therefore take the liberty of recommending this establishment of cattle to your protection. It is founded upon the most efficient and most economical principles, and will never fail the army, so long as it is superintended and conducted, as it has been hitherto.

I have the honor to be, &c.,

Arthur Wellesley

54

TO MAJOR JOHN MALCOLM

Fort William, Sept. 14, 1804

My dear Malcolm,

I have just received your letter of the 4th. You are already acquainted with my intentions to go into the Deccan again, and I shall stay there as long as it may appear that my presence is necessary, owing to the state of affairs in Hindostan, and the consequences of Monson's defeat.[1] But I acknowledge that I don't exactly see the necessity that I should stay several years in India in order to settle affairs which, if I had been permitted, I should have settled long ago, or any reason for which I should involve myself in fresh troubles and difficulties with which I have hitherto had no concern. I look to England, and I conceive that my views in life will be advanced by returning there. I don't conceive that any man has a right to call upon me to remain in a subordinate situation in this country, contrary to my inclination, only because it will suit his views, and will forward objects for which he has been laboring. If an officer in my situation is the proper person to be entrusted with the execution of the measures to secure those objects, there will be many equally capable with myself of performing those duties. If they are duties which require extraordinary qualifications in the person who is to perform them, let General Lake, or the Commander in Chief at Fort St. George, or anybody else, be charged with

---

[1] Lieut.-Colonel William Monson (1760–1807), son of the 2nd Baron Monson, first went to India with his regiment in 1780. See pages 90–1.

them. But surely it is not exactly reasonable to expect that I should remain in a subordinate situation, contrary to my inclination, only to involve myself in fresh troubles and difficulties. I am positively determined that, whether the Governor General goes or stays, I quit India as soon as Holkar will be defeated. . . .

Ever, my dear Malcolm,[1]

Yours most inscerely,

Arthur Wellesley

❋

[Early in December Wellesley wrote to Close : 'I have had an attack not very unlike a fever and ague. I am induced to think it is nothing more than the increase of rheumatism, which I have had hanging about me for the last eighteen months ; but it is attended by all the symptoms and inconveniences, and requires the same remedies, as fever.'

When, three years before, his brother Henry had been most unwell, Arthur Wellesley had told him : 'I know but one receipt for good health in this country, and that is to live moderately, to drink little or no wine, to use exercise, to keep the mind employed, and, if possible, to keep in humour with the world. The last is the most difficult, for, as you have often observed, there is scarcely a good tempered man in India.'

Many years later, according to the Earl of Ellesmere, the Duke of Wellington, temperate in his diet, 'was fond of telling of the uniform good health which he enjoyed in India, where for three years he lived under canvas, eating little but rice, and drinking little or no wine. His Indian habits as to rice continued through life ; he ate it with meat, and almost everything, and those who knew his habits had it in readiness where he dined out.'

Though the Duke seems to have forgotten the heavy drinking at William Hickey's, the Malabar itch which kept him from the expedition to Egypt, and the rheumatism, his years in India did not harm his constitution ; indeed, almost alone of all the senior officers in Spain and Portugal, he went through the war there without being obliged to go home with some illness.]

55

TO MAJOR MERRICK SHAWE

Seringapatam, 4th January, 1805

My dear Shawe,

When I left Calcutta, the objects of my journey into the Deccan were to prevent Scindiah and the Rajah of Berar from becoming parties in the war against the Company; and, if

---

[1] A week later Malcolm obtained his lieutenant-colonelcy.

110

possible, to march a corps of cavalry to join the troops acting in Malwa,[1] under the orders of Colonel Murray. It appeared to me possible, that before I could arrive in the Deccan, some event might occur which would render my presence in the Deccan unnecessary, and I asked the Governor General his opinion upon that subject. He answered, that he conceived that the defeat of Holkar's army would render it unnecessary for me to go there ; or to stay, if I should hear of its defeat after my arrival.

Under these circumstances, and having had an attack of fever on the day before that fixed for my departure, I determined to delay my march to the northward as soon as I heard of Holkar's defeat, until I should see the impression which that defeat had made upon the durbars of Scindiah and the Rajah of Berar.

I believe that Malcolm apprized you in due course of this determination ; but should he not have so done, I mention it now, in order that you may be informed of the cause of my delay to march.

The latest intelligence gives reason to believe that Scindiah and the Rajah of Berar will remain at peace ; and therefore I consider that one of the objects in view in sending me into the Deccan is accomplished. In regard to the other, to endeavor to march a corps of cavalry from the Deccan into Malwa, I have to observe,

First, That as the troops are only now ready in the ceded districts, the season is too far advanced to make the attempt.

Secondly, I see that Colonel Murray is running, the Lord knows where, away from General Jones [2] and all his supplies, in obedience to orders which he says he has received from the Commander in Chief.

Thirdly, Holkar's army having been defeated, the necessity of a corps of cavalry in Malwa is no longer so pressing ; and the difficulties and dangers attending the undertaking, (the latter as affecting both the corps of cavalry which should make the attempt, and the Deccan,) exist to as great a degree as ever.

Upon the whole, therefore, I conceive that I am justified in not going into the Deccan, by the accomplishment of one object in view in sending me there ; by a concurrence of circumstances,

---

[1] Malwa, a district lying near Indore, between Baroda and Bhopal.
[2] Colonel Murray, to the annoyance and apprehension of Sir Arthur, left Gujerat ' to its fate', and fled north to Kotah, leaving two forts in enemy hands. Major-General Jones commanded a force which pursued one of Holkar's allies and then joined General Lake. Wellesley's knighthood dated from September 1st, 1804.

which render another impracticable, useless, and dangerous; and by the sentiments of the Governor General.

I acknowledge, however, that I have determined not to go into the Deccan without a considerable degree of doubt and hesitation. I know that all classes of the people look up to me, and it will be difficult for another officer to take my place. I also know that my presence there would be useful in the settlement of many points which remain unsettled, and which probably will require time and peace to bring to a conclusion. But these circumstances are not momentary; whenever I should depart, the same inconveniences would be felt even in an increased degree, and very possibly the same state of affairs which now renders my presence in the Deccan desirable, will exist for the next seven years. I certainly do not propose to spend my life in the Deccan; and I should not think it necessary, in any event, to stay there one moment longer than the Governor General should stay in India. I conclude that he intends to go in February, as he proposed when I left Calcutta, in case Holkar should be defeated, and the peace should be certain; and upon this point, having considered whether my presence in the Deccan for one, two, or three months would answer any purpose whatever, I am decidedly of opinion that it would not.

In regard to staying longer, the question is exactly whether the Court of Directors or the King's Ministers have any claim upon me, strong enough to induce me to do any thing so disagreeable to my feelings (leaving health out of the question) as to remain for a great length of time in this country.

I have served the Company in important situations for many years, and have never received any thing but injury from the Court of Directors, although I am a singular instance of an officer who has served under all the governments, and in communication with all the Political Residents, and many civil authorities; and there is not an instance on record, or in any private correspondence, of disapprobation of any one of my acts, or a single complaint, or even a symptom of ill temper from any one of the political or civil authorities in communication with whom I have acted.

The King's ministers have as little claim upon me as the Court of Directors. I am not very ambitious; and I acknowledge that I never have been very sanguine in my expectations that military services in India would be considered in the scale in which are considered similar services in other parts of the world. But I might have expected to be placed on the Staff in India; and yet if it had not been for the lamented death of General Fraser,[1] General Smith's arrival [2] would have made me supernumerary. This is perfectly well known to the army, and is the subject of a good deal of conversation.

If my services were absolutely necessary for the security of the British empire, or to ensure its peace, I should not hesitate a moment about staying, even for years; but these men or the public have no right to ask me to stay in India, merely because my presence, in a particular quarter, may be attended with convenience.

But this is not the only point in which this question ought to be viewed. I have considered whether, in the situation of affairs in India at present, my arrival in England is not a desirable object? Is it not necessary to take some steps to explain the causes of the late increase of the military establishments, and to endeavor to explode some erroneous notions which have been entertained, and circulated upon this subject? Are there not now a variety of subjects in discussion, relating to this country, upon which some verbal explanation is absolutely necessary? I conceive, therefore, that in determining not to go into the Deccan, and to sail by the first opportunity for England, I consult the public interests not less than I do my own private convenience and wishes.

I have now detailed the grounds upon which I have formed my plans and determination to go home; however, I must inform you, that I am not in a hurry to carry them into execution. I am prepared for every thing, and in five days I can be at Madras; and on the other hand, if I should see any solid necessity for going into the Deccan, I shall not be remiss in my duty. But I can tell you that I shall not be drawn there by mere suspicions and unfounded surmises.

Believe me, &c.,

Arthur Wellesley

[1] Major-General J. H. Fraser died of wounds on November 24th, 1804, during Lake's pursuit of Holkar, north-west of Agra.

[2] Major-General John Smith arrived in Calcutta from England with his wife and son in November 1804, set off in a palenkeen to go 900 miles to join the army and within a few months he died of fever and was buried at Muttra near Fraser's grave.

56

TO MAJOR MERRICK SHAWE

Seringapatam, 3rd Feb., 1805

My dear Shawe,

Your letters of the 14th of January have removed from my mind a load of anxiety upon the subject of my remaining at this place; and I observe from those documents, and the Governor General's dispatch of the 9th of January, that I have acted in conformity with his wishes and intentions. I now feel an anxiety only about my departure for England, the extent of which I cannot describe.

I have no confidence in my own judgment in any case in which my own wishes are involved. This is the cause of the great anxiety which I have felt, and still feel, upon these subjects.

I know that my presence in England would be useful, and I am certainly very anxious to go there. The peace appears to be established in India: we are certain that the Rajah of Berar will remain at peace; and as for Scindiah, he has crossed the Nerbudda, and, by a letter from Colonel Close of the 21st of January received this day, and written from the neighbourhood of Colonel Hallyburton's [1] camp, I see that, up to that period, he had received no intelligence from Mr. Jenkins.[2] I conclude, therefore, that all is right, particularly as the Rajah of Berar offered to my acceptance. In respect to the latter, however, I believe that my opinion is not incorrect; and I have determined not to accept it if it should be offered.

Many local considerations, into which it is impossible to enter in a letter, have induced me to come to this determination; and when I shall have an opportunity of explaining them to you, I think that you will be of my opinion.

I shall now observe upon our difference of opinion upon this subject, that you think about my staying in India like a man who has just come out, and I like one who has been here for seven years involved in perpetual troubles. I acknowledge that I am anxious to a degree which I cannot express to see my friends again; and even if I were certain that I should not be employed

[1] Lieut.-Colonel John Haliburton.
[2] Sir Richard Jenkins (1785–1853) was acting Resident at the court of Scindiah, 1804–5. Later he was Resident at Nagpur and in 1839 became Chairman of the East India Company. He was twice M.P. for Shrewsbury.

in England at all, there is no situation in India which would induce me to stay here.

I am not rich in comparison with other people, but very much so in comparison with my former situation, and quite sufficiently so for my own wants. I got a great deal of prize money in the last war; which with what I got before, and a sum of money which the Court of Directors gave me for a service rendered to them in this country, and the accumulation of the interest upon those sums, have rendered me independent of all office or employment.

Believe me, &c.,

Arthur Wellesley [1]

57

TO COLONEL BARRY CLOSE

Fort St. George, 4th March, 1805

My dear Colonel,

. . . In regard to myself, I before informed you, that with the consent of the Governor General, founded upon his hopes that the peace would be uninterrupted in the Deccan, I was going home. From a letter which I received from Major Shawe, dated the 18th of February, since I began this letter, I judge that the Governor General is of opinion, that the late transactions in Scindiah's camp, of which he had received a tolerably accurate report, through hircarrahs, would not lead to war, and he is determined to preserve the peace, if it can be preserved.

Under the circumstances I do not see any thing to alter my determination. But at all events, supposing it were desirable that I should return to the Deccan, three months must elapse before I could join the army; the season for operations would be over; and the expectation of my return, as it would check all decided measures, would be more injurious than my presence would be beneficial; therefore, I still propose to embark with the Admiral.

I acknowledge that I wish that affairs were in a more settled state; but I do not conceive that my presence will make any alteration in them. We must expect that, for a time, the affairs of the Mahratta empire will be unsettled; and I do not consider that the late events in Scindiah's camp have, in any degree,

<hr>

[1] *Supplementary Despatches*, iv, 483-4.

altered the grounds on which I determined to go home; more particularly as, supposing that war should be the consequence of them, the scene of operations will be in Hindustan.

I leave in this country some valuable friends, with whom I have been intimately connected in friendship, and in constant communication on public affairs for some years; and I part from them with regret. I consider you as one of them, and I assure you that it will give me the greatest satisfaction to meet you again.

Believe me, your's most sincerely,

Arthur Wellesley

INTERIM: 1805–1807

INTRODUCTION TO PART FOUR

SIR ARTHUR WELLESLEY'S journey home from India by way of St. Helena lasted six months. Sir Jonah Barrington, a Judge of the High Court of Admiralty in Ireland, had described Wellesley in 1793 as 'ruddy faced and juvenile in appearance'. Now he found him 'looking so sallow and wan, and with every mark of what is called a worn out man'.

For some time after Wellesley's return the Government consulted him about various expeditions to the Continent, and he talked and wrote memoranda to such good effect that Pitt was induced to observe : 'I never met a military officer with whom it is so satisfactory to converse. He states every difficulty before he undertakes any service, but never after he has undertaken it.' He was asked to undertake a service in December 1805, when he was given command of a brigade to go to Hanover. His three battalions spent a rough week at sea, landed near Bremen, waited there for six dull weeks and then came back. By now it was February, and Wellesley, gratified by his appointment to the colonelcy of his old Regiment, the 33rd Foot, took command of a brigade at Hastings, guarding a stretch of coast which, since Trafalgar, was in scant danger of invasion.

On April 10th he married the Hon. Catherine Pakenham in Dublin [see page 122] and two days later was returned to Parliament as Member for Rye. He joined his brother William Wellesley-Pole in the House of Commons, not because he wanted to but in order to defend his brother Richard's administration in India. The Marquess Wellesley, who had resigned after a dispute with the East India Company, was accused of tyranny, fraud and extravagance, of 'high crimes and misdemeanours', and even impeachment was threatened. Arthur Wellesley pressed for specific charges to be brought, he opposed the frequent postponement of the motion of censure, he spoke on the Indian budget and he travelled to and fro between Hastings and London. All the while he grew restless, wanting employment abroad on active service, where other generals were being sent. The Cabinet now consulted him about ventures to South America — he evaded one proposed expedition to Mexico by way of Singapore. But as he later declared to John Wilson Croker, he owed nothing to the Horse Guards. 'In the first place, they thought very little of any one who had served in India. An Indian victory was not only no ground of confidence, but it was actually a cause of suspicion. Then because I was in Parliament, and connected with people in office, I was a politician, and a politician can never be a soldier. Moreover, they looked upon me with a kind of jealousy, because I was a lord's son, "*a sprig of nobility*", who came into the army more for ornament than use.'

The New Year 1807 saw his election to Parliament for a Cornish borough, and, on February 7th, the birth of his elder son, Arthur. The dismissal from office of the Whigs in March led to Wellesley being offered the post of Chief Secretary for Ireland, under the Duke of Richmond as Lord-Lieutenant. He first consulted the Duke of York, Commander-in-Chief, who did not consider that acceptance of the civil post would prejudice the Major-General's professional career. He was assured by Ministers that he would be free to relinquish his office in Dublin should an opportunity of employing him in a military command occur. On this condition Wellesley accepted.

A decade had passed since he had been in Ireland as aide-de-camp and Member of Parliament : since the Act of Union there had been no separate Irish Parliament, but now he gave up his Cornish seat and in May 1807 was returned for both Newport and Tralee, and of the two chose to represent the Isle of Wight.

Dublin Castle found him dealing with the threat of invasion from without and of insurrection from within, organising for the one a system of coastal defence and, for the other, a police force in the capital. He advocated equal education for Roman Catholic and Protestant children, refused endless applications for pensions, favours and promotion, disposed of bishoprics and lesser posts and manipulated skilfully the Irish constituencies to Government advantage during the elections of 1807. Busy as he was, Wellesley kept his eyes open for the chance of active service, and on hearing of a proposed expedition to the Baltic that summer, pressed Lord Castlereagh to release him for a command. Sir Arthur was given a division under Lord Cathcart, and leaving his wife in Dublin he crossed to London and then sailed from Sheerness at the end of July.

One of the secret clauses of the Treaty of Tilsit, by which Napoleon and the Tsar of Russia made peace, had been that the French were to seize the Danish fleet. To this end thirty thousand troops under Bernadotte had been assembled to invade Denmark. Canning, however, was informed of these plans and he acted swiftly to foil the plot. When the francophile ruler of Denmark rejected Britain's demand to surrender the fleet into safe keeping on terms of hire, Cathcart's expeditionary force landed on the island of Zealand and soon defeated the Danish army. Despite Wellesley's protests, Copenhagen was bombarded on September 2nd, the Danes surrendered five days later and the fleet was removed from French reach.

The expedition succeeded in its purpose, but was neither glorious nor ethical : indeed, the timely but high-handed action aroused indignation not only in Europe but also among the Whig opposition in Parliament. Wellesley, on learning that he had not meantime been replaced as Chief Secretary for Ireland, obtained permission to return to Dublin, where he was soon immersed in the network of tithes, jobbery, regulations for barracks, frauds in the Excise, arrangements for militia and yeomanry units, and Church administration.

As none of Sir Arthur Wellesley's many letters about Irish affairs is included in this volume, one could quote two declarations of policy and principle which guided him in his task as Chief Secretary. On January 14th, 1808, for example, he wrote as follows : 'The misfortune of Ireland is that the existing evils are so great and so obvious that everybody sees them ; and it is easy to find out how things ought to be by adverting to England. The difficulty is to bring them from the state in which they are in this country to that in which they are in England, and I have not yet seen any practical solution for this difficulty.

'I am convinced that all sudden and hurried reforms fail, and I think I could prove, by adverting to the history of the last twenty years in this country, that they have invariably ended by making matters worse than they were. This is, however, no reason for not making a beginning to reform abuses, and I hope that we have not only made a beginning in that good work, but some effectual progress in every department of the state.'

And again on the same theme, on Christmas Day of 1807 : 'Ireland is not a country on which the experiment of sudden and rapid reforms can be tried. However enormous the latter may be, they are too inveterate and of too long standing to bear the sudden application of the former ; but I know that neither the abuses which exist, nor the reforms which can be applied to them, have been lost sight of since I have been in this country.'

58

MEMORANDUM ON BRITISH TROOPS IN INDIA

[During the sea voyage from St. Helena to England Sir Arthur Wellesley wrote a lengthy memorandum on a plan proposed for an exchange of native troops of India and the Negro Corps of the West Indies, a topic which had already exercised the minds of Lord Castlereagh and the Marquess Wellesley. The following extract is both relevant and of importance.]

The English soldiers are the main foundation of the British power in Asia. They are a body with habits, manners, and qualities peculiar to them in the East Indies.

Bravery is the characteristic of the British army in all quarters of the world ; but no other quarter has afforded such striking examples of the existence of this quality in the soldiers as the East Indies. An instance of their misbehavior in the field has never been known ; and particularly those who have been for some time in that country cannot be ordered upon any service, however dangerous or arduous, that they will not effect, not only with bravery, but a degree of skill not often witnessed in persons of their description in other parts of the world.

I attribute these qualities, which are peculiar to them in the East Indies, to the distinctness of their class in that country from all others existing in it. They feel that they are a distinct and superior class to the rest of the world which surrounds them ; and their actions correspond with their high notions of their own superiority. Add to these qualities that their bodies are inured to climate, hardship, and fatigue, by long residence, habit, and exercise, to such a degree, that I have seen them for years together in the field without suffering any material sickness ; that I have made them march 60 miles in 30 hours, and afterwards engage the enemy ; and it will not be surprising that they should be respected, as they are, throughout India. Their weaknesses and vices, however repugnant to the feelings and prejudices of the Natives, are passed over in the contemplation of their excellent qualities as soldiers, of which no nation has hitherto given such extraordinary instances. These qualities are the foundation of the British strength in Asia, and of that opinion by which it is generally supposed that the British empire has been gained and upheld. These qualities show in what manner nations, consisting of millions, are governed by 30,000 strangers. . . .

[On April 10th, 1806, Sir Arthur Wellesley married Miss Kitty Pakenham, the girl whom he had loved a decade before, but with whom he had never exchanged letters during his long absence abroad — Miss Pakenham confessed to the Queen that she had often thought of him but had never written ; however, some contact was maintained through their mutual friend, Olivia Sparrow. The marriage took place in St. George's Church, Hill Street, Dublin, and after only a week General Wellesley returned to his duties in England, leaving Kitty to follow later with his brother Gerald.

Though she bore him two sons, the marriage was not a happy one, for all her pride and loyalty. Frances, Lady Shelley, who came to know them well, was told by Mrs. Arbuthnot, afterwards Wellington's intimate friend for many years, that it would have been easy for his wife to have made him happy. 'He only asked for repose from the turmoil of public affairs, for absolute truth, and the absence of little-mindedness. Alas ! the Duchess had precisely those faults which annoyed him most. Under the mistaken impression that she was smoothing family difficulties, she made the Duke's children as afraid of speaking openly to him as she was herself. The words "Don't tell your father" were ever on her lips.

'It seemed to be the one object of her life to pose as a cruelly neglected wife. Unfortunately, she succeeded in making that impression upon her eldest son.

'The Duchess was the slave of her boys when they came home for the holidays. I have seen her carrying their fishing-nets, their bats, balls, and stumps, apparently not perceiving how bad it was for them to regard a woman, far less their mother, as a simple drudge, fit only to minister to their pleasures. In consequence, her sons pitied without respecting her.' [1]

Frances, Lady Shelley also records that Dr. Gerald Wellesley told her husband that he would never be able to forget Arthur Wellesley's face when he first saw his future bride after their long separation. He turned to Gerald and whispered : 'She is grown damned ugly, by Jove !' This alteration in Kitty Pakenham's looks is confirmed by Mrs. Frances Calvert, who met Sir Arthur's new wife in London on May 5th, 1806. 'He must have found her sadly altered, for she was a very pretty little girl, with a round face and fine complexion. She is now very thin and withered (I believe pining in his absence helped to make her more so). I think she looks in a consumption, which idea a short cough increases, and I know Sir Walter Farquhar [2] has desired her to take great care of herself. She is gentle and amiable. I hear that when someone told Sir Arthur he would find her much altered, he answered that he did not care ; it was her mind he was in love with, and that could not alter.' [3]]

59

TO LIEUT.-COLONEL JOHN MALCOLM

London, 25th February, 1806

My dear Malcolm,

I returned from the Continent only a few days ago, and have not yet had leisure to read the Indian papers which have come into my hands, in order to enable me to form an opinion of the state of affairs up to the latest period. I think it possible, however, that you will have peace ; and that may be permanent, or otherwise, in proportion to our own firmness, and the means of the enemy of disturbing our tranquillity. So many principles, however, have been abandoned or overturned, that we must look for peace from a course of accidental circumstances, and not from the steady adherence to any settled system of policy.

[1] *The Diary of Frances Lady Shelley*, vol. ii, pp. 311-12.
[2] Sir Walter Farquhar (1738–1819) was Physician in Ordinary to the Prince of Wales.
[3] *An Irish Beauty of the Regency*, pp. 66-7.

I will try to get a living for your brother,[1] but you see that a revolution (commonly called a change) has taken place in the government of this country. *We* are not actually in opposition, but we have no power; and if I get anything for your brother, it must be by the influence of private friendship.

I don't think that this government can last very long.[2] You can have no idea of the disgust created by the harshness of their measures, by the avidity with which they have sought for office, and by the indecency with which they have dismissed every man supposed to have been connected with Pitt.[3] His friends will, I think, remain connected, and will act together as a body, and a most formidable one they will be to any government on account of their numbers.

I am tolerably well in health, and I shall be quite well if I can continue to spend a few weeks at Cheltenham in this summer. The regiment which they have given me, and the Staff, have made me rich.

As soon as I shall have read all the Indian papers, which I have got, I will sit down and write to you a long despatch upon them.

Believe me, yours most sincerely and affectionately,
Arthur Wellesley

There is a report about London, which I cannot bring myself to give credit to, that you had been kicked by a horse, and that your leg had, in consequence, been amputated. I was employed for two days ascertaining the truth of this report, and at last I found that you had been bit by a horse in the arm: I only hope not by *Sultan*.[4]

✳

[On July 31st, 1806, he wrote to John Malcolm from Hastings: 'I am here now in command of a force — stationed in this part of the coast — the old landing-place of William the Conqueror. You will have seen that I am in Parliament, and a most difficult and unpleasant game I have had to play in the present extraordinary state of parties.'

A friend asked Wellesley at Hastings how, having commanded armies

---

[1] This is Gilbert, the sixth of the ten Malcolm brothers, and a country clergyman.
[2] On Pitt's death Lord Grenville formed a national administration 'of all the talents', with Fox as Secretary of State for Foreign Affairs. Pitt's friends were omitted. The Government lasted barely a year.
[3] William Pitt had died on January 23rd.
[4] *Supplementary Despatches*, xiii, 278-9.

of forty thousand men in the field and having been made a Knight of the Bath for his services, he could submit to be reduced to the command of a mere brigade of infantry. Sir Arthur replied as follows : ' For this plain reason. I am *nimmukwallah*,[1] as we say in the East ; that is, I have ate of the King's salt, and, therefore, I conceive it to be my duty to serve with unhesitating zeal and cheerfulness when and wherever the King or his Government may think proper to employ me.']

60

TO THE MARQUESS WELLESLEY

Hastings, October 26, 1806

My dear Mornington,

Another of my regts has received orders to march to Deal, where I suppose it is to embark for the Continent. If troops are to be sent into Germany, of course all other views must for the present be abandoned ; & I hope that as four out of five regts have now been taken from my Command to be sent on Service, I shall now be sent ; & I don't care in what situation. I am only afraid that Lord Grenville [2] does not understand that I don't want a Chief Command if it cannot be given to me ; & that I should be very sorry to stay at home when others go abroad, only because I cannot command in Chief.

Ever yours most affectionately

Arthur Wellesley [3]

61

TO VISCOUNT CASTLEREAGH [4]

Dublin Castle, 1st June, 1807

My dear Lord,

By all accounts you are advancing the preparations for your expedition to the Continent, which I now conclude will be sent. I hope that you recollect what I said to you upon this subject. It may happen that you have it not in your power to employ me

[1] *Nimmuk* means 'salt' in Hindustani.
[2] William Wyndham Grenville, Baron Grenville (1759–1834), was Foreign Secretary between 1791 and 1801, and led the 'Ministry of all the Talents' in 1806–7.
[3] B.M. Add. MSS. 37415, f. 23.
[4] Robert Stewart, Viscount Castlereagh, and in 1821 2nd Marquess of London-derry (1769–1822), was Secretary of State for War from 1807 to 1809 and Foreign Secretary from 1812 until his death by suicide.

as I wish, and it might have happened that I should not have been so employed if I had not been appointed to the office which I fill in this country. But that will not be believed; and it will be understood and said that I had avoided or had not sought for an opportunity of serving abroad in order to hold a large civil office.

As I am determined not to give up the military profession, and as I know that I can be of no service in it unless I have the confidence and esteem of the officers and soldiers of the army, I must shape my course in such a manner as to avoid this imputation. If, therefore, you send the expedition, I wish you would urge Lord Hawkesbury [1] to fix upon a successor for me, as I positively cannot stay here whether I am to be employed with it or not.

When you will urge this request upon him, I beg you to tell him that the zeal and anxiety for the success of the present government, which induced me to come here, are by no means diminished. I would do anything to serve them; but I am convinced they will all see that I should lose half the power of being of use to them if any imputation could be cast upon me. I have also to observe that they will have no difficulty in finding a successor for me, and that this wish of mine must have been expected.

Believe me, my dear Lord,
Ever yours most sincerely,
Arthur Wellesley

62

TO THE DUKE OF RICHMOND [2]

London, 24th July, 1807

My dear Duke,

You will have heard of the intended expedition from this country, the object of which is to attack the Danish island of Zealand [3] and to endeavour to obtain possession of the Danish fleet. The success depends in my opinion in a great measure

[1] Robert Banks Jenkinson, Lord Hawkesbury (1770–1828), was Home Secretary. In 1808 he succeeded his father as Earl of Liverpool, and was Secretary for War and the Colonies and, from 1812 to 1827, Prime Minister.
[2] Charles, 4th Duke of Richmond and Lennox (1764–1819), was Lord-Lieutenant of Ireland from 1807 to 1813. In 1818 he was appointed Governor of Canada, and died there of hydrophobia, after being bitten by a fox. The Duke and his family were among Wellington's closest friends.
[3] Zealand, the eastern Danish island on which lies Copenhagen.

upon the possibility of bringing the Danish army over from Holstein. If that should be possible, I think the success very problematical, as it may be depended upon that the Danes will be joined and assisted by the French; and if the first can pass unmolested by our ships, the last will find no difficulty in passing.

However, whatever may be the chance of success of the expedition, it would not answer for me to allow it to go on without expressing a desire to be employed upon it. I accepted my office in Ireland solely on the condition that it should not preclude me from such service when an opportunity should offer; and I am convinced that, although you may feel some inconvenience from my temporary absence, supposing that it is intended that I should return to you, or from the loss of the assistance of an old friend, supposing that it is not, you would be the last man to desire or to wish that I should do anything with which I should not be satisfied myself. And I acknowledge that I should not be satisfied if I allowed any opportunity of service to pass by without offering myself. Under these circumstances, I have desired to be employed; and I understand that if the expedition should go on, I am to go with it. I don't know, and I have not asked, whether I am to return to my office when this coup-de-main will have been struck or will have failed. All that I can tell you is, that nothing will give me greater satisfaction than to assist you as long as I can be useful to you, and that I have been desired by Lord Hawkesbury and Lord Castlereagh to settle with Long [1] to take charge of my business in parliament while I shall be absent.

I will write you the particulars of everything I shall hear or learn upon the subject. In the mean time I tell you that I heard a piece of news this morning which looks very like a stop to the expedition, viz., that the Danes had already begun to move their troops out of Holstein. If that be the case, probably we shall not go.

In this state of uncertainty I have not written to Lady Wellesley upon this subject; and it is as well not to say anything to her about it till it will be positively settled that we are to go.

Ever, my dear Duke, yours most sincerely,
Arthur Wellesley

---

[1] Charles Long (1761–1838), M.P. for Haslemere, 1806–26. He was Secretary of State for Ireland in 1806, and for many years Paymaster-General. In 1820 he was created Baron Farnborough.

63

TO LIEUT.-GENERAL LORD CATHCART [1]

Braesenborg, 14th Sept, 1807

My Lord,

There is every appearance at present of perfect tranquillity in the country. I hear from Copenhagen that the work in the dockyards is advancing with rapidity, and there is reasonable ground for a belief that it will be brought to a conclusion far within the space of time allotted for it in the capitulation. Under these circumstances I am induced to lay before your Lordship the situation in which I stand in respect to my office. When I left England Mr. Long undertook to carry through the business which remained unfinished in the House of Commons, and I acknowledge that I was very uncertain and very indifferent whether I should continue to hold the office. I find, however, that I am still in it, and your Lordship will readily believe there is much to do in Ireland. The *long nights* are approaching fast, and if I am to have any concern in the government of that country, it is desirable that I should be there. If, therefore, your Lordship should think that you can give any officer leave of absence, or that you can spare me in consequence of the tranquillity of the country, or the general situation of our affairs in Zealand, I shall be very much obliged to you if you will allow me to return home. But if you should think that I can be of the smallest use in any way in bringing matters to the termination which you wish, I should be sorry to go, and I am ready of course and willing to stay as long as a man will remain.

I have, &c.,

Arthur Wellesley

64

TO LIEUT.-COLONEL JOHN MALCOLM

Dublin Castle, 15th October, 1807

My dear Malcolm,

I received your letters, written in March, a few days ago upon my return from Zealand; and I took care to communicate

---

[1] William Schaw Cathcart (1755–1843), 10th baron, was created a viscount in 1807 and an earl in 1814. He became Ambassador to Russia, like his father before him.

to Mr. Dundas [1] your sentiments on the state of the army and on the causes which have led to the unpleasant temper which appears to exist in it. I agree with you entirely in some of your opinions on the causes which have produced this temper, particularly among the officers; and I also agree in your opinions on the remedies which ought to be adopted. Firmness of temper and uniformity and good sense in conduct by the government would soon bring all about; and I have no doubt whatever that if it should please the government here to send me to India again, I should have it in my power to re-establish the temper and spirit of the army in the manner in which it existed in our better times. I acknowledge, however, that I have not much fear for the safety of India, even if things should remain some time longer as they are. No country was ever lost by the mutiny, much less by the discontent, of its troops; and I am not quite certain that in order to produce radical good, it is not requisite to show the necessity of a complete change in respect to Indian manners and opinions, and to let matters continue for some time longer in the unpleasant state in which they are. But I have no inclination to refuse my services in that country, if they should be called for at present, or to do anything here to serve those for whom I must ever retain the strongest sentiments of gratitude and affection.

I don't think it probable that I shall be called upon to go to India. The fact is that men in power in England think very little of that country, and those who do think of it feel very little inclination that I should go there. Besides that, I have got pretty high upon the tree since I came home, and those in power think that I cannot well be spared from objects nearer home. At the same time the Indians in London are crying out for my return.

I shall not pretend to give you any news. You will see the accounts of our Zealand expedition, which has had great effect in London, and has added to the popularity and strength of the ministry. The Danes did not defend themselves very well, and I think we might have taken the capital with greater ease than we forced them to the capitulation which I settled with them. I am now come here in consequence of the disturbed state of this country, and I shall stay here until the meeting of Parliament. I strongly recommend you not to return home as long as your

[1] Mr. Robert Dundas was President of the India Board.

health will permit you to remain in India, and as you can retain office. Take my word for it, you are not yet sufficiently rich ; you will have to return there, and you may possibly find it difficult to get employment in the line to which you are so well suited, and to which you have always been accustomed.[1]

Remember me most kindly to Wilks,[2] Close, Barclay,[3] and all friends, and believe me, my dear Malcolm,

Ever yours most affectionately,

Arthur Wellesley[4]

[1] On February 23rd, 1807, Wellesley had written in the same strain to Malcolm : 'I do not recommend you to be in a hurry to come to England. Expenses here are very heavy, and fortunes very large. Notwithstanding all the taxes, and the rise in price of every article in life, there is more luxury than ever, more appearance of riches in the country, and more persons with large fortunes of moderate extent, than there were formerly. You could not exist in the way you would like under a much larger fortune than you possess ; and, take my word for it, you will lose nothing by staying away from England a little longer.'

[2] Major Mark Wilks (1760 ?–1831) had been military and then private Secretary to Lord Clive in Madras. He was the author of *Historical Sketches of the South of India*, 1810–14, and was Governor of St. Helena.

[3] Barclay had been Adjutant-General at Assaye and elsewhere.

[4] *Supplementary Despatches*, xiii, 288-9.

PART FIVE

THE PENINSULAR WAR: 1808–1813

THE YEAR 1808

In the latter part of 1807 Napoleon, furious at being thwarted in Denmark, turned against Britain's ally Portugal in the hope of capturing the fleet in Lisbon. He recalled the French Ambassador and assembled an army under General Junot at Bayonne. Manuel Godoy, the first minister of Spain, signed the secret Treaty of Fontainebleau on October 29th, whereby he agreed to French soldiers crossing his territory in order to invade Portugal, which country was to be split into three. Britain urged the Portuguese Regent, Prince John, to stand by her oldest ally, and to make war on France from Brazil if the need should arise, but the Regent hesitated, as well he might, and then made up his mind to side with France. But too late, for on February 1st Napoleon proclaimed that the House of Braganza had ceased to reign. Junot's troops hurried across Spain, seeking to capture the Portuguese fleet before Britain could remove it. As at Copenhagen they were forestalled, and reached Lisbon to find that Prince John, with the mad Queen Maria and his two sons, was already bound for Rio de Janeiro under British naval escort.

A hundred thousand French soldiers, having deceitfully seized important towns south of the Pyrenees, marched across Spain to be welcomed as liberators by a nation which had long deplored the corrupt and inefficient rule of King Charles IV. This monarch was obliged to abdicate in favour of his son Ferdinand, but no sooner had the young man been proclaimed king than he was kidnapped and taken to a French prison, while Napoleon transferred his brother Joseph Bonaparte from Naples to the throne of Spain. An insurrection in Madrid on May 2nd was ruthlessly subdued, yet patriotic feeling surged through the country, town governors known to support the French were killed, and the province of Asturias in the north formed an army and declared war on France.

Although Spain was still officially at war with Britain, emissaries travelled to London early in June and appealed for help. Their enthusiastic reception by the crowds in London and elsewhere was backed with Government promises of money, arms and ammunition ; and peace was made between the two nations. A British squadron aided the inhabitants of Cadiz to seize French naval ships at anchor in the bay.

In Portugal, meanwhile, Junot had occupied the whole country without much trouble, and had been well enough received by the Portuguese, who resented the departure of their Regent. But soon they came to resent far more bitterly the oppression exercised by French generals, and Oporto, declaring itself independent of France, elected a Junta, or Government, headed by the Bishop. Isolated risings occurred all over Portugal, and Junot found himself reduced to holding the Lisbon area and the principal fortresses. However, as the French had astutely sent most of the best Portuguese troops to northern Europe, the Junta had to rely upon ill-trained militia who were no match for French regular soldiers, and so they too appealed to Britain for aid in the struggle.

In July 1808 ten thousand troops sailed from Cork under Sir Arthur Wellesley, charged with aiding the Spanish and Portuguese nations to throw off the yoke of France. A further contingent under Sir Brent Spencer was to join Wellesley from Gibraltar, while Sir John Moore's corps, just back from a strange and abortive venture to Sweden, were also to land in Portugal. Sir Arthur had orders to attack the French if he did not find them in overwhelming strength, to gain control of the Tagus, and then to secure Cadiz and destroy the enemy's force in southern Spain.

A dispute between the Cabinet and the Duke of York over a ministerial wish to supersede Sir John Moore by the junior Wellesley led to the appointment of a senior general, Sir Hew Dalrymple, to the over-all command, and another elderly general, Sir Harry Burrard, as second-in-command. Meanwhile Wellesley had beaten the French at Roliça and on August 21st his men defeated Junot's at the battle of Vimeiro, which victory Burrard was just in time to witness ; he then held up pursuit of the enemy until Moore's force had come ashore. On the next day Dalrymple arrived on the scene, in time to frustrate yet again the exploitation of success, and to infuriate Wellesley, the victor, to such an extent that he wished heartily that he had never left Ireland.

When the French sent in a flag of truce so that terms might be negotiated for the evacuation of Portugal, the generals allowed the prospect of gaining Lisbon without a fight and of thus freeing their troops for a campaign in support of Spanish independence to outweigh the chance of defeating Junot's army entirely. By the Convention of Cintra, signed on August 30th, the French secured most favourable terms : they would not be treated as prisoners ; on arrival in France in British ships they would be free to fight again ; and their cavalry, artillery, equipment and baggage, not to mention private plunder which they smuggled aboard, would accompany them. British troops occupied Lisbon on September 10th, and the French sailed for home three days later. Within a week Sir Arthur Wellesley, superseded and with little to do, had obtained leave to return to England and resume his duties as Chief Secretary for Ireland.

When the details of the Convention reached Britain, public indignation was loudly voiced. Prints announcing and denouncing the Convention carried a black border, the three generals deemed to have thrown away a victory were abused as traitors and cowards, while cartoons, pamphlets and public meetings bore witness to the widespread sense of humiliation and dismay. The British Government, realising that nothing less than a court of enquiry into the causes, circumstances and conditions of the Convention would appease the popular feeling, recalled Dalrymple and Burrard. In due course the court, which assembled on November 14th, adjudged that no one was to blame, that zeal and firmness had been displayed throughout and that there was no case for a court-martial. Dalrymple was publicly rebuked, both he and Burrard were relegated to the unemployed list and Wellesley, supported by Castlereagh and other friends, was spared this fate. Indeed, his victories at Roliça and Vimeiro received a vote of thanks in both Houses of Parliament. Meanwhile, command of the King's army in the Peninsula had been entrusted to Sir John Moore.

Leaving ten thousand troops for the defence of Portugal, Moore was to enter northern Spain with the remainder of his force, link up with Sir David Baird, who was being sent direct to Corunna with eighteen thousand men, and then to aid the Spanish armies in expelling the French. Three such armies were in position, but as the enemy received strong reinforcement, so one by one they were defeated. Moore, hampered by lack of information on Spanish plans, by delays once Baird reached Spain, by poor local co-operation and by having his force dangerously scattered, found himself up against Napoleon in person, disposing of some 120,000 troops. Sir John stayed as long as he dared to help the Spaniards if opportunity allowed, but thrice he had to change his plans, and eventually to avoid being cut off and overwhelmed he ordered a retreat through the mountainous country of Galicia to Corunna and Vigo, where he expected ships to embark the army.

The story of that terrible winter retreat, of the successful battle fought outside Corunna, of Moore's death does not concern us here. The British effort, though to many it appeared an utter failure, did in fact compel Napoleon to call off his advance on Lisbon ; it diverted his forces to the north-west corner of the Peninsula ; and it gave time for the Spaniards to regroup their beaten armies and for the Government in London to organise a new expeditionary force which it would support with more knowledge and zeal and which could restart the Peninsular War on a new footing.

65

TO THE HON. WILLIAM WELLESLEY-POLE [1]

Head Quarters at Vimieiro.
August 19th, 1808

My dear William,

You will see the account of our Action on the 17th. of which you will form your own judgement. Three mistakes prevented

[1] William Wellesley-Pole (1763–1845), second son of the 1st Earl of Mornington, took the additional name of Pole in 1778 on succeeding to the estates of a cousin. He was M.P. for East Looe from 1790 to 1794, and for Queen's County from 1801 to 1821. In 1807 he was Secretary to the Admiralty, and in 1809 he succeeded his brother Arthur as Chief Secretary for Ireland, where he served for three years. Later he joined Lord Liverpool' cabinet as Master of the Mint (1814–23). He was Postmaster-General from 1834 to 1835. In 1821 he was created Baron Maryborough and in 1843 succeeded as 3rd Earl of Mornington in the Irish peerage.

it from producing the entire destruction of La Borde's [1] Corps. The first that General Ferguson [2] was ordered to descend the heights instead of continuing his march to turn the Enemy's left in the Mountains. This was not committed by me. The second was that Lake [3] went up the wrong pass; he ought to have gone up that on his right; he hurried his Men, did not clear the pass of the Enemy by his Light Infantry before he entered with his column; & he hurried his attack before the 5th regt. or any of the other troops ascended the other passes to support him.

This I did all I could to prevent; & if I had succeeded we should still have taken or destroyed the whole of La Borde's Corps. The third was a misfortune rather than a fault. We could not find the road by which to bring up our Artillery & a body of regularly formed Infantry. If we had had them early La Borde could not have retreated & in fact he ceased his attacks as soon as he saw our Guns & fresh Infantry advance. But it was then too late to do any thing; the day was worn out; & he had got a start of three miles which I should never have recovered. As it is the French have lost 1500 Men; & I understand that they say they never were so attacked before; & I never saw troops behave so well as they did.

We shall have another brush with them in a day or two; & if we should be successful we shall get hold of Lisbon.

I don't know what Govt. propose to do with me. I shall be the junior of all the Lt. Generals; & of all the awkward situations in the world that which is most so is, to serve in a subordinate capacity in an Army which one has commanded. However I will do whatever they please. I think they had better order me home.

I think Lord Chatham [4] will repent that he did not allow me to have Artillery Horses. Those we have are very fair, & very good of their kind. But marching as we do every day we ought to have the best horses the Army could afford, instead of the worst; & likewise a regt. of Mounted Cavalry.

[1] Henri François, Comte de Laborde (1764–1833), a French general who afterwards fought in Russia.
[2] Major-General, afterwards General Sir Ronald Craufurd, Ferguson (1773–1841) commanded a brigade. He went home in 1810 because of a liver complaint.
[3] Major George Augustus Frederick Lake, commanding the 29th Foot, was killed in the battle. He was the second son of General Lord Lake, who had died in the previous February.
[4] General Sir John Pitt, 2nd Earl of Chatham (1756–1835), was the inept commander of the Walcheren expedition in 1809. He spent the last fifteen years of his life as Governor of Gibraltar.

As for Lord Wellesley I am convinced that his fornication has kept him out of Office. In spite of his Idleness he would have been in Office before now, if he had not taken to Whoring.[1]

William [2] is very well. Give my best love to Mrs Pole & the Girls [3] &

Believe me ever Yours most affectionately,

Arthur Wellesley

I beg that you will not communicate to any body the remarks which I have made upon the action of the 17th. because as all did their duty I do not wish to hint that there was blame any where.[4]

66

TO VISCOUNT CASTLEREAGH

Vimieiro, 22nd Aug., 1808

My dear Lord,

After I wrote to you yesterday morning, we were attacked by the whole of the French army, Sir Harry Burrard [5] being still on board ship, and I gained a complete victory. It was impossible for troops to behave better than ours did ; we only wanted a few hundred more cavalry to annihilate the French army.

I have sent my report upon this action to Sir Harry Burrard, who will send it home. You will see in it that I have mentioned Colonel Burne [6] of the 36th regiment [7] in a very particular manner ; and I assure you that there is nothing that will give me so much satisfaction as to learn that something has been done for this old and meritorious soldier. The 36th regiment are an example to this army.

Sir Harry did not land till late in the day in the midst of the attack, and he desired me to continue my own operations ; and as far as I am personally concerned in the action, I was amply rewarded for any disappointment I might have felt in not having

---

[1] See also the letter No. 100 dated April 6th, 1810.

[2] This is Wellesley-Pole's eldest son, born in 1788 and later 4th Earl of Mornington.

[3] Katherine Elizabeth, eldest daughter of Admiral the Hon. John Forbes. The three girls were Mary Charlotte Anne, Emily Harriet and Priscilla Anne.

[4] *Camden Miscellany*, vol. xviii.

[5] Lieut.-General Sir Harry Burrard (1755–1813) had served in America and in Flanders, and in 1807 on the Copenhagen expedition.

[6] Lieut.-Colonel Robert Burne.

[7] The Herefordshire Regiment.

had an opportunity of bringing the service to a close, by the satisfaction expressed by the army that the second and more important victory had been gained by their old General. I have also the pleasure to add, that it has had more effect than all the arguments I could use to induce the General to move on, and I believe he will march to-morrow. Indeed, if he does not, we shall be poisoned here by the stench of the dead and wounded; or we shall starve, every thing in the neighbourhood being already eaten up.

From the number of dead Frenchmen about the ground, and the number of prisoners and wounded, I should think their loss could not be far short of 3000 men. The force which attacked us was very respectable, and probably not short of 14,000 men, including 1300 dragoons and artillery, and 300 chasseurs à cheval.

Sir Hew Dalrymple [1] arrived last night, and will land this morning.

> Believe me, my dear Lord,
> Ever yours most sincerely,
> Arthur Wellesley

67

TO THE HON. WILLIAM WELLESLEY-POLE

Camp at Vimieiro.
August 22nd, 1808

My dear William,

We gave the French an unmerciful beating yesterday. Sir Harry Burrard arrived on the evening of the 20th., & I did every thing in my power to induce him to march on; which he resisted till he should be reinforced by Moore; a decision with which I was not pleased any more than I was with the manner in which it was made. Sir Harry did not come on shore that night; & as I am the 'Child of Fortune' & Sir Harry did not chuse to march towards the Enemy, the Enemy came to us with his whole force & attacked us in our position; & we gained a most compleat Victory; Sir Harry not being in the field till one of the attacks was compleatly beaten off, & the other begun & all

---

[1] Lieut.-General Sir Hew Dalrymple (1750–1830) had been Lieutenant-Governor of Guernsey, 1796–1801, and commanded at Gibraltar from 1806 until he went to Portugal to assume chief command.

the dispositions made for defeating it. The French have lost not less than 3000 Men I should think.

The army are delighted that they gained this second Victory under the Command of their Old General.

I have desired Campbell [1] who is going home to tell you that I am by no means satisfied with the way in which I see things will go on here; & I should be glad to be called home to my Office, or any thing else in which I could be useful.

Sir Hew Dalrymple arrived this morning; but I have not seen him.

I still command the Army; as all the Heads of Department won't go to anybody else for orders.

Ever Yours most affectionately
Arthur Wellesley

Give my best love to Mrs. Pole & the Girls. [2]

68

TO THE HON. WILLIAM WELLESLEY-POLE

Camp at Ramalhal.
August 24th, 1808

My dear William,

I have received your letter transmitted by Charles Stewart, [3] & you will have learnt by my letters to you, my messages by Campbell, & my dispatches to Lord Castlereagh the state of affairs. Matters have gone worse since Campbell went away. Sir Hew has agreed to a suspension of hostilities which he made me sign. I inclose you a copy of a letter which I have written to Lord Castlereagh upon this subject; & I authorize you to say that although I approve of allowing the French to withdraw from Portugal, because Sir Harry Burrard & Sir Hew Dalrymple would not, or could not carry into execution the plan of

---

[1] Captain, afterwards General Sir Colin, Campbell (1776–1847) was the aide-de-camp sent to England with Wellesley's Vimeiro despatch. He had served in India at Ahmednuggur and Assaye, and had also been with Wellesley in Denmark.

[2] *Camden Miscellany*, vol. xviii.

[3] Brigadier-General the Hon. Charles Stewart, afterwards 3rd Marquess of Londonderry (1778–1854), half-brother to Lord Castlereagh, commanded the cavalry brigade in Wellesley's force. He was for three years Adjutant-General in the Peninsula, and then had a distinguished career in diplomacy.

operations for Sir John Moore's corps which I had proposed to Sir Harry, according to which it would have been placed at Santarem & would have cut off the retreat of the French to Elvas; & therefore the convention is necessary in order to set the British troops at liberty to go into Spain at an early period of the year; I entirely disapprove of the indefinite term given to the suspension of Hostilities. But although I think it may be right to give to the Russians the advantage of the neutrality of the Port of Lisbon, I entirely disapprove of the Insertion of any thing in the convention for the suspension of hostilities or in that for the evacuation of Portugal which has any thing to do with the Russians. I also think that some measures must be adopted to force the French Generals to disgorge some of the Church Plate which they have stolen.

I wish that I was away from this Army. Things will not flourish as we are situated, & organized; & I am much afraid that my friends in England will consider me responsible for many things over which I have no power. There is no more confidence in me on the part of the Chiefs than if I had been unsuccessful; & I am the only person in whom the Army have any. The Chiefs ask my opinion about every thing, & never act according to it; & Sir Burrard by his Interference after the Battle of the 21st. prevented me from marching in pursuit of the Enemy, by which he saved them from total destruction. He came determined to think that I had not a sufficient force; & notwithstanding my remonstrances against delay he wrote for Moore's Corps to come down & be disembarked at Maceira; & *at all events to come himself with any part of it he should be enabled to bring*; which letter he had the folly & the impudence to shew to me. Then Sir Hew landed on the day after the Battle of the 21st., & I did every thing in my power to prevail upon him to march, in which I failed entirely, & was going away; when one of his Staff who had been in Portugal only two days took him aside, & settled in a few words that we should march. Is this the confidence in the opinion of a Man who has conducted the service successfully to the present moment, which is to make him responsible to his friends in the Govt. for the events which will occur here? I knew what would be the consequence of the new measures in England, when I heard of them; &, when Moore comes & new fuel will be added to the Flame, matters will be much worse. At the same time it is quite ridiculous ; but there is not one of them capable of commanding the Army, & at this moment it rests with me ; the Departments look to me alone, & I give what orders I please not only referring to matters of discipline, but to those of general regulation ; & the people of the Country will communicate with nobody else.

August 26th

Since I wrote the Above the Admiral [1] has relieved us from the difficulty in which [we] were involved by the Article in the agreement respecting the Russians, by refusing to agree to it. I prevailed upon the General therefore to send Murray [2] to Junot [3] yesterday to inform him, that that stipulation could not be agreed to, & that as Kellerman [4] had urged it in the manner of a sine quâ non, the agreement for suspending hostilities must be put an end to at the end of 48 hours from this day at twelve o'clock. If Junot should express a desire to negotiate the convention for the evacuation on the basis of the remaining Articles of the agreement Murray is authorized to settle it, according to the terms of a Memm. inclosed in my letter to Lord Castlereagh of which you have a copy inclosed.

In the mean time we are going to Hell by another Road. The French are fortifying trenches at Cabeça de Montechique, & we shall have to conquer them again ; & it is said this morning that the Russians have joined them. The General has no plan, or even an idea of a plan, nor do I believe he knows the meaning of the Word *Plan*. I entered fully into a discussion upon the situation of the Army the day before yesterday ; in which I pointed out the inutility of augmenting his Army here, & the danger of the measure if he should not (and he could not) augment his means of supply ; & I gave him papers to read upon the subject of his future operations. He has not uttered one word to me upon that subject from that time to this ; & Moore told me last night that he had said to him, ' you may either land your Corps or not as you think proper ' ; as if it was a matter of perfect Indifference whether this Army should have 10,000 Men

---

[1] Vice-Admiral Sir Charles Cotton, Bart. (1753–1823), held command in the Tagus in 1807–8, and afterwards in the Mediterranean and the Channel.

[2] Colonel, afterwards General Sir George, Murray (1772–1846) was the great Quartermaster-General of the Peninsular War. He was less successful as Colonial Secretary, 1828–30.

[3] General Andoche Junot, Duc d'Abrantès (1771–1813), commanded the French troops in Portugal. He later served in the Russian campaign, and died by his own hand. His widow wrote a famous series of Memoirs.

[4] General François Étienne Kellermann, Duc de Valmy (1735–1820).

in addition, or whether 15000 additional Mouths should be fed by means calculated for half the number. These People are really more stupid & incapable than any I have yet met with; & if things go on in this disgraceful manner I must quit them.

August 27th, 1808

I have reason to believe that the negotiation for the convention is going on well; at the same time an arrangement is made for a March upon Lisbon tomorrow morning if it should not answer. I shall therefore close this letter. Ever Yours most affectionately A.W.[1]

69

TO CAPTAIN PULTENEY MALCOLM, R.N.[2]

Torres Vedras, 29th Aug., 1808
half past 5, P.M.

My dear Malcolm,

Captain Dalrymple arrived this morning with the Convention, signed by General Kellerman and Colonel Murray; but it was so objectionable in many parts, that a meeting of the General Officers was called to deliberate upon and settle the alterations to be made in it, which meeting I attended. The result of the meeting was a proposal to make certain alterations, which I acknowledge I do not think sufficient, although the treaty will answer in its amended form. In the mean time the army remains on its present ground, very much against my opinion.

I am afraid that I am so much connected with the credit of this army, that I cannot remain with it without falling, as it will fall. If I could be of any use to men who have served me so well, I would stay with them for ever; but as matters are situated, I am sure that I can be of no use to them: I am convinced they cannot render any service, and I have determined to go home immediately.

At the same time I must say that I approve of allowing the French to evacuate Portugal, because I see clearly that we cannot

---

[1] *Camden Miscellany*, vol. xviii.
[2] Captain, afterwards Admiral Sir Pulteney, Malcolm (1768–1838), a brother of Wellesley's friend in India, John Malcolm, commanded H.M.S. *Donegal* and the convoy which had brought the troops to Portugal.

get them out of Portugal otherwise, under existing circumstances, without such an arrangement; and we should be employed in the blockade or siege of the places which they would occupy during the season in which we ought and might be advantageously employed against the French in Spain. But the convention, by which they should be allowed to evacuate Portugal, ought to be settled in the most honorable manner to the army by which they have been beaten; and we ought not to be kept for ten days on our field of battle, before the enemy (who sued on the day after the action) is brought to terms.

I am quite annoyed on this subject.

Believe me, &c.,

Arthur Wellesley

70

TO VISCOUNT CASTLEREAGH

Camp, North of Torres Vedras,
30th Aug., 1808

My dear Lord,

A convention, signed by General Kellerman and Colonel Murray, for the evacuation of Portugal by the French troops, was brought here yesterday morning; but it was not ratified by the General, in consequence of his finding some fault with it. It was altered, but not as I thought as it ought to have been, and was returned to Junot yesterday afternoon. In the mean time, the army has halted its position; with the only difference, that we have a corps in Torres Vedras, instead of three miles from that town. In short, in ten days after the action of the 21st, we are not farther advanced; or, indeed, as I believe, so far advanced as we should and ought to have been on the night of the 21st.

I assure you, my dear Lord, matters are not prospering here; and I feel an earnest desire to quit the army.[1] I have been too successful with this army ever to serve with it in a subordinate

---

[1] On September 5th he wrote again to Lord Castlereagh : 'It is quite impossible for me to continue any longer with this army; and I wish, therefore, that you would allow me to return home and resume the duties of my office, if I should still be in office, and it is convenient to the Government that I should retain it; or, if not, that I should remain upon the staff in England; or, if that should not be practicable, that I should remain without employment'.

situation, with satisfaction to the person who shall command it, and of course not to myself. However, I shall do whatever the Government may wish.

Believe me, my dear Lord,
Ever yours most sincerely,
Arthur Wellesley

71

TO THE DUKE OF RICHMOND

Zambujal, 9th Sept., 1808

My dear Duke,

Nothing particular has occurred since I wrote to you last: the French are about to evacuate Lisbon, under the Convention, as soon as the transports shall be ready; and the Russians have concluded a convention with the Admiral from their fleet, under which they are to be taken to a British port.[1] I have neither seen one nor the other of these conventions, and I cannot tell you their contents; but I am convinced that neither are what they ought to be, considering the success of the army. The country has, however, acquired the honour of reconquering Portugal, and of restoring the rightful ruler to this government; and with these advantages I hope they will be satisfied.

I have only to regret that I signed the agreement for the suspension of hostilities without having negotiated. I have already told you the reasons why I did so, but I doubt whether good nature, and a deference to the opinion of an officer appointed Commander-in-Chief on the day of his taking the command, and to his orders, and a desire to avoid being considered the head of a party against his authority, will be deemed sufficient excuses for an act which, on other grounds, I cannot justify. I have had nothing to do, however, with any subsequent transaction, excepting to advise stronger measures, and that the Commander-in-Chief should insist on better terms.

I am sick of all that is going on here,[2] and I heartily wish I

[1] A Russian fleet lay in the Tagus, but remained neutral in the contest. The French proposed that the Russians should be allowed to return to the Baltic unmolested. The British Admiral, Sir Charles Cotton, refused this. Wellesley thought the best plan would have been to leave the Russian ships in the port of Lisbon on the ground of its neutrality.

[2] On the 6th he had written to William Wellesley-Pole : 'I am sick of the state of publick affairs here, of which I shall say nothing except to tell you that I don't know what they are about at Head Quarters ; I have not seen their Convention ; & I have no communication with them'.

had never come away from Ireland, and that I was back again with you. Remember me kindly to the Duchess.[1]

Believe me, &c.,

Arthur Wellesley [2].

72

TO THE HON. WILLIAM WELLESLEY-POLE

Lumiar.
September 16th, 1808

My dear William,

I am much obliged to you for your letter of the 4th. which I received last night. In respect to rewards I have never allowed myself to think about them; much less to write to any body or to make any application. I consider them valuable only as they are granted spontaneously, & from a conviction in the minds of those who have the power of granting them, & from the sense of the publick that they are deserved. In any other case they are favours which I feel no inclination to sollicit. Under the circumstances I regret that Wellesley's affection & zeal for whatever can tend to my advantage should have induced him even to talk upon the subject with Lord Castlereagh; but as I am convinced that he meant well, & as Lord Castlereagh understands that I never wrote one Line, or said one word to any body on the subject, I beg that you will not tell Wellesley that I feel any regret upon what has passed.

I shall here drop the subject; & I only beg that no friend of mine will ever even talk upon it with the Ministers, or those connected with them.

In respect to the other part of your letter I acknowledge that in general a Man ought not judge for himself; & there are no persons to whose judgement I would more willingly defer than

[1] The Duke had married in 1789 Charlotte, daughter of the 4th Duke of Gordon. Catherine, Countess of Charleville, wrote on October 18th, 1809, of the Richmonds :

'the night we sat to please the Duke,
the morning rose to please the Dss.

who is sawcy & ill tempered to a degree that my pen cannot do justice to. She is jealous not only of his attentions to ladies, but of his being amused, & a walk, a ride, a dance is treasonable ! ! ! he did all those things with the sweetest good temper & really seems of a most delightful character to please in society, condescending & affable, with great dignity to all about him — and tho' she was very civil, yet I confess her tantrums to him made me think her disagreeable.' (*The Marlay Letters*, p. 129.)

[2] *Supplementary Despatches*, vi, 132-3.

to your's & Lord Castlereagh's. But I think that you are not aware of the circumstances of my situation; & you have not considered many points which I think bear materially upon the question. I admit that I owe the situation in which I stand, in a great degree to the Willingness I have always manifested to serve in any capacity civil or Military in which I could be useful. The question is whether it will be believed that I am unwilling to serve in a subordinate military capacity if under existing circumstances I quit the Army? Those who know what has passed here; those who have seen the manner in which I & all those belonging to me from the General Officers down to the Common Soldiers have been treated will not believe that because I have again commanded an Army, & have again been successful, I am unwilling to serve under the Command of any body else. To serve in an Army is a very honorable situation, & I have always been of opinion & continue of the same that provided the troops are British, there is no great choice among them; & that without reference to the number or quality of the Troops under the Command of Individual General Officers, they were generally classed on Service according to their respective talents & merits. But these opinions are true only in the ordinary cases of the Service; they are not true, & an Officer cannot serve with satisfaction, & possibly not with Honor, when he sees in the Comr. in Chief & in those who surround him, not a want of confidence, for they can't help feeling that I alone in Army can overcome their difficulties, & put them in the right road; but a determination not to confide, & to pull me down from the situation in which I stand with the Army. What do you think of my having now 4 Battalions under my Command, there being two Major Generals with six & a Brigadier General with four in the Army? What do you think of their having deprived my General officers of their Brigades, broken them up, separated the regts., which they had led to Victory, some of which they had had under their command for years, separated their Staff Officers from them, deprived two of them of their Brigades entirely? They have annoyed the Soldiers too as much as they could; & have put themselves to an inconvenience to detach the regts. which were under my Command to distant Garrisons, the Soldiers from the marches they had already made having no shoes to their feet, & feeling a very natural desire to see the place for which they had fought.

Then my orders & regulations in respect to the discipline & supply of the Army are treated as so much waste paper; contradicting orders are issued without even a reference to them; & there never was such a state of confusion as we are now in in this respect. To this add that they have illegally broken the contract which was made under my authority for the supply of Meat to the troops; & the consequence is that a great proportion of the Army is now fed upon Salt provisions. Then the tricks they have played me personally are no bad symptom of their feelings towards me. Sir Hew Dalrymple the other day offered to send me on a mission to Madrid; & as soon as I accepted it, & pointed out the view in which I thought such a mission would be useful, & the nature of the Instructions I ought to receive, he writes me a letter of which no Man can comprehend the meaning; & sends Lord William Bentinck [1] upon the mission, to whom I knew he had offered it, before he offered it to me. To this add the stupid incapacity of these poor creatures for the situation in which they have been placed, that they are the Laughing stock not only of ours but of the French Army, that every Individual from Sir Harry Burrard down is dissatisfied; & I ask you will it be believed by those who consider fairly the conduct of other Men that I have altered my ways of thinking & of acting in respect to serving the publick, since I have had these last successes?

I am aware that there is a party which will run me down for coming away; but I have never cared much for what people say of me without cause; & I shall care less for it than ever I believe now. In short I have determined to quit the Army if these Gentlemen continue in the Command of it; & I never was more convinced of any thing than that I judge right in making this determination.

In respect to the situation in which I shall be when I shall have quitted the Army I am entirely indifferent. I'll return to Ireland if the Ministers wish it; if they don't, I don't desire it. If I should not return to Ireland I'll remain upon the Staff in England; or, if that is impossible, I'll do nothing, and amuse myself with hunting and shooting.

I have already in more than one letter explained the part I

---

[1] He was sent to arrange a plan of co-operation with the Spanish generals, of whose strength, positions and intentions all too little was known. See note to letter no. 120.

had in the agreement for suspending hostilities; & I consider that as the only act of mine since I have been in Portugal which requires explanation. I sacrificed my own opinion & probably my reputation to a Man in whom Govt. had confided the Command of the Army; who neither deserved their confidence, or such a sacrifice on my part. My refusal to sign the Agreement could not have prevented it; & would have placed me at the Head of a party against the Comr. in Chief who was but just arrived; & created a breach between us; the refusal therefore not only would have been attended by no publick advantage but would have injured the publick inasmuch as it was desirable that he & I should be on good terms, & that I should support & not oppose his authority & Influence among the troops. There was a sacrifice however; but it was of a personal nature; viz my own opinion & my reputation which will not stand clear till the circumstances are explained; which sacrifice I should always be ready to make to answer a publick object; & I now regret it only because the person for whom I made it is unworthy of any sacrifice. I did every thing I could to prevail upon him not to agree to the objectionable parts of the agreement, but in vain; & my refusal to sign would have had no effect excepting to save me personally from the share of the odium which must attend the transaction whenever it is known. Believe me ever Yours most affectionately

Arthur Wellesley[1]

73

TO LIEUT.-GENERAL SIR JOHN MOORE

Lumiar, 17th Sept., 1808

My dear General,

I write to you on the subject to which this letter relates with the same freedom with which I hope you would write to me on any point in which you might think the public interests concerned.

It appears to me to be quite impossible that we can go on as we are now constituted; the Commander in Chief must be changed, and the country and the army naturally turn their eyes to you as their commander. I understand, however, that you have lately had some unpleasant discussions with the King's

[1] *Camden Miscellany*, vol. xviii.

Ministers, the effect of which might be to prevent the adoption of an arrangement for the command of this army, which, in my opinion, would be the best, and would enable you to render those services at this moment for which you are peculiarly qualified.

I wish you would allow me to talk to you respecting the discussions to which I have adverted, in order that I may endeavor to remove any trace which they may have left on the minds of the King's Ministers, having the effect which I have supposed.

Although I hold a high office under Government, I am no party man; but have long been connected in friendship with many of those persons who are now at the head of affairs in England; and I think I have sufficient influence over them, that they may listen to me upon a point of this description, more particularly as I am convinced that they must be as desirous as I can be to adopt the arrangement for the command of this army which all are agreed is the best.

In these times, my dear General, a man like you should not preclude himself from rendering the services of which he is capable by any idle point of form. Circumstances may have occurred, and might have justified the discussions to which I have referred; but none can justify the continuance of the temper in which they are carried on: and yet, till there is evidence that it is changed, it appears to be impossible for the King's Ministers to employ you in the high situation for which you are the most fit, because during the continuance of this temper of mind there can be no cordial or confidential intercourse.

In writing thus much I have perhaps gone too far, and have taken the permission for which it was the intention of this letter to ask; but I shall send it, as it may be convenient for you to be apprized of the view which I have already taken of these discussions, as far as I have any knowledge of them, in deciding whether you will allow me to talk to you any further about them. If you should do so, it would probably be most convenient to us both to meet at Lisbon, or I can go over to you, if that should suit you better.[1]

Believe me, &c.,

Arthur Wellesley

[1] Wellesley called on Moore at Queluz on September 18th.

74

TO THE MARQUESS WELLESLEY

London, October 5th 1808

My dear Wellesley,

I arrived here this day, & I don't know whether I am to be hanged drawn & quartered; or roasted alive. However I shall not allow the Mob of London to deprive me of my temper or my spirits; or the satisfaction which I feel in the consciousness that I acted right.

Ever yours most affectionately

Arthur Wellesley [1]

75

TO THE MARQUESS OF BUCKINGHAM [2]

London, 11th Oct., 1808

My dear Lord,

I assure you that I am most sensible of the friendship and kindness of Lord Temple [3] and yourself, of which I hope to prove myself worthy. My situation is a very awkward one, and I can relieve myself from it only by the result of an inquiry.

I am accused of being the adviser of persons over whom I had no control and who refused to follow my advice, and am made responsible for the acts of others. The real share which I have had in the transactions — which in my opinion have deservedly incurred the displeasure of the public — cannot be known till they will be inquired into; and in the mean time Sir Hew Dalrymple has left the Government and the public so completely in the dark respecting the military expediency of allowing the French to evacuate Portugal, that that part of the question, which is the only one in which I am involved, is as little understood as the rest. I know of no immediate remedy for these difficulties of my situation excepting patience and temper, and I thank God that the undeserved abuse which has been heaped upon me has not altered the latter.

[1] B.M. Add. MSS. 37415, f. 47.
[2] George Nugent-Temple Grenville, 1st Marquess of Buckingham (1753–1813), had been Lord-Lieutenant of Ireland in 1782–3 and from 1787 to 1789.
[3] Richard Lord Temple, afterwards 2nd Marquess of Buckingham, born in 1776.

In respect to the conduct of my case, I have determined that I will publish nothing, nor will authorize the publication of anything by others. This forbearance is particularly incumbent upon me, as the whole subject must be inquired into. I have also determined that I will not involve others in scrapes because they differed in opinion with me previously to the 22nd August, notwithstanding that difference of opinion and the alteration of system were the cause of the military expediency of allowing the French to withdraw from Portugal. I am afraid that I shall experience some difficulty in carrying this intention into execution, because the truth must come out; but I will endeavor not to bring others (viz. Sir Harry Burrard) into a scrape, not only out of regard to him, but because I think it fatal to the public service to expose officers to the treatment which I have received, and to punishment for acting upon their own military opinions, which opinions they may fairly entertain. I have also determined to stand singly. There is nothing in common between Sir Hew Dalrymple and me, or between the Government and me, if the Government are supposed to be involved in the question, and I shall act accordingly. . . .

Believe me, my dear Lord,
Ever your most affectionate and faithful humble servant,
Arthur Wellesley [1]

[1] Quoted in *The Life of Arthur Duke of Wellington*, by G. R. Gleig, pp. 81-2.

THE YEAR 1809

On January 9th Britain concluded a treaty of alliance with Spain's provisional government, and a new and larger expedition was set on foot. In the Cabinet Lord Castlereagh prevailed upon his colleagues to submit Sir Arthur Wellesley's name to the King for the command of this expedition. Wellesley was appointed at the end of March, whereupon he resigned his post in Ireland and sailed for Portugal — for the second time. Including the ten thousand troops left in Lisbon by Moore, he disposed of twenty-one thousand men. Within two days of landing in Lisbon he declared his intentions : first, to attack Marshal Soult, who had seized Oporto on March 29th, and then to join forces with General Cuesta, Captain-General of Extremadura, in operations against the French in central Spain, where two Spanish armies had been driven into the mountains.

The army of British and raw Portuguese troops was assembled and reviewed at Coimbra before marching north to the Douro. Here the over-confident enemy's failure to guard the river bank and the fortunate discovery of four barges enabled the British regiments to cross and drive the French from Oporto on May 12th. They left behind wagons, stores and guns, and retreated in hungry disorder over mountainous country into Galicia. Thus, within less than a month, Wellesley had cleared Portugal.

Now he turned against Marshal Victor. But co-operation with his Spanish allies under the elderly, ailing and incompetent Cuesta proved a severe strain upon his patience and equanimity, which were equally tried by shortage of supplies, lack of money and the propensity of his troops to plunder.

On July 3rd the allied armies crossed into Spain from Abrantes and gathered at Plasencia. Wellesley, disquieted no less by Cuesta's obstinacy, pride, impracticability and decrepitude than by the unpromising appearance of the Spanish army at a torch-light inspection, moved as far as Talavera, but refused to go further when the impulsive Cuesta, who had earlier thrown away a splendid chance of attacking an inferior French corps, hustled his thirty-five thousand troops into a dangerous pursuit towards Madrid. This reckless advance was short-lived, and on encountering forty thousand Frenchmen commanded by Napoleon's brother, King Joseph, and Marshal Jourdan, the Spaniards streamed in retreat.

Wellesley concentrated his own force at Talavera, and throughout a sweltering July 28th the French attacked his positions in vain. The battle was fierce, the errors were costly, but victory was achieved. Sir Arthur then prepared to advance to Madrid, but being threatened alike by Soult's move from the north to cut his road back to Portugal and by the failure of the Spanish authorities to help him with supplies, he felt obliged to withdraw his starving soldiers to the frontier near Badajoz and the unhealthy, mosquito-ridden Guadiana valley.

The military *débâcle* of Austria at Wagram, the inept and fever-laden fiasco at Walcheren, and the infuriating unreliability of Spanish promises of food and transport were scarcely offset by Wellesley's personal elevation as Baron Douro of Wellesley and Viscount Wellington of Talavera, honours which roused the Whig Opposition to passionate criticism. No less passionate, and infinitely more justified, was Wellington's denunciation of the ill-judged autumn campaign which led the Spanish armies into a series of defeats of which the most disastrous, Ocaña in November, cost them fourteen thousand prisoners, four thousand casualties and fifty guns.

The new Viscount, planning a defence line which would enable him to hold the French without being cut off from his base as might well happen if he tried to defend the long frontier between Portugal and Spain, examined the hills above Torres Vedras and instructed his engineers to prepare fortifications and other obstacles to a French advance upon Lisbon.

76

TO VISCOUNT CASTLEREAGH

Abrantes, 17th June, 1809

My dear Lord,

I cannot, with propriety, omit to draw your attention again to the state of discipline of the army, which is a subject of serious concern to me, and well deserves the consideration of His Majesty's ministers.

It is impossible to describe to you the irregularities and outrages committed by the troops. They are never out of the sight of their officers, I may almost say never out of the sight of the Commanding officers of their regiments, and the General officers of the army, that outrages are not committed ; and notwithstanding the pains which I take, of which there will be ample evidence in my orderly books, not a post or a courier comes in, not an officer arrives from the rear of the army, that does not bring me accounts of outrages committed by the soldiers who have been left behind on the march, having been sick, or having straggled from their regiments, or who have been left in hospitals.

We have a Provost marshal, and no less than 4 assistants. I never allow a man to march with the baggage. I never leave an hospital without a number of officers and non-commissioned officers proportionable to the number of soldiers; and never allow a detachment to march, unless under the command of an officer; and yet there is not an outrage of any description which has not been committed on a people who have uniformly received us as friends, by soldiers who never yet, for one moment, suffered the slightest want, or the smallest privation. In the first place, I am convinced that the law is not strong enough to maintain discipline in an army upon service. It is most difficult to convict any prisoner before a regimental Court Martial, for I am sorry to say that soldiers have little regard to the oath administered to them; and the officers who are sworn ' well and truly to try and determine, *according to the evidence*, the matter before them', have too much regard to the strict letter of that administered to them. This oath, to the members of a regimental Court Martial, has altered the principle of the proceedings of that tribunal. It is no longer a court of honor, at the hands of which a soldier was certain of receiving punishment if he deserved it; but it is a court of law, whose decisions are to be formed according to the evidence, principally of those on whose actions it is constituted as a restraint. But, admitting the regimental or detachment Court Martial, as now constituted, to be a control upon the soldiers equally efficient with that which existed under the old constitution of a Court Martial, which my experience tells me it is not, I should wish to know whether any British army (this army in particular, which is composed of 2nd battalions, and therefore but ill provided with officers) can afford to leave with every hospital, or with every detachment, 2 captains and 4 subalterns, in order to be enabled to hold a detachment Court Martial. The law in this respect ought to be amended; and when the army is on service in a foreign country, any one, 2 or 3 officers ought to have the power of trying criminals, and punishing them *instanter*; taking down all proceedings in writing, and reporting them for the information of the Commander in Chief on their joining the army. Besides this improvement of the law, there ought to be in the British army a regular provost establishment, of which a proportion should be attached to every army sent abroad. All the foreign armies have such an establishment: the French *gendarmerie nationale*, to the amount of 30 or 40 with each of their corps; the Spaniards their *policia militar*, to a still larger amount; while we, who require such an aid more, I am sorry to say, than any of the other nations of Europe, have nothing of the kind, excepting a few serjeants, who are taken from the Line for the occasion, and who are probably not very fit for the duties which they are to perform.

The authority and duties of the Provost ought, in some manner, to be recognized by the law. By the custom of British armies, the Provost has been in the habit of punishing on the spot (even with death, under the orders of the Commander in Chief) soldiers found in the act of disobedience of orders, of plunder, or of outrage. There is no authority for this practice excepting custom, which I conceive would hardly warrant it; and yet I declare that I do not know in what manner the army is to be commanded at all, unless the practice is not only continued, but an additional number of Provosts appointed.

There is another branch of this subject which deserves serious consideration. We all know that the discipline and regularity of all armies must depend upon the diligence of the regimental officers, particularly the subalterns. I may order what I please; but if they do not execute what I order, or if they execute it with negligence, I cannot expect that British soldiers will be orderly or regular.

There are two incitements to men of this description to do their duty as they ought; the fear of punishment, and the hope of reward. As for the first, it cannot be given individually; for I believe I should find it very difficult to convict any officer of doing this description of duty with negligence, more particularly as he is to be tried by others probably guilty of the same offence. But these evils of which I complain are committed by whole corps; and the only way in which they can be punished is by disgracing them, by sending them into garrison and reporting them to His Majesty. I may and shall do this by one or two battalions, but I cannot venture to do it by more; and then there is an end to the fear of this punishment, even if those who received it were considered in England as disgraced persons rather than martyrs.

As for the other incitement to officers to do their duty zealously, there is no such thing. We who command the armies of the country, and who are expected to make exertions greater than those made by the French armies, to march, to fight, and to keep our troops in health and in discipline, have not the power of rewarding, or promising a reward, for a single officer of the army; and we deceive ourselves, and those who are placed under us, if we imagine we have that power, or if we hold out to them that they shall derive any advantage from the exertion of it in their favor.

You will say, probably, in answer to all this, that British armies have been in the field before, and that these complaints, at least to the same extent, have not existed; to which I answer: 1st, that the armies are now larger, their operations more extended, and the exertions required greater than they were in former periods; and that the mode of carrying on war is different from what it was; 2ndly, that our law, instead of being strong in proportion to the temptation and means for indiscipline and irregularity, has been weakened, and that we have not adopted the additional means of restraint and punishment practised by other nations, and our enemies, although we have imitated them in those particulars which have increased and aggravated our irregularities. And, finally, that it is only within late years that the Commanders in Chief abroad have been deprived of all patronage, and, of course, of all power of incitement to the officers under their command.

It may be supposed that I wish for this patronage to gratify my own favorites; but I declare most solemnly that, if I had it to-morrow, there is not a soul in the army whom I should wish to promote, excepting for services performed.

I have thought it proper to draw your attention to these subjects, which I assure you deserve the serious consideration of the King's ministers. We are an excellent army on parade, an excellent one to fight; but we are worse than an enemy in a country; and take my word for it, that either defeat or success would dissolve us.

> Believe me, my dear Lord,
> Ever yours most sincerely,
> Arthur Wellesley

77

TO JOHN HOOKHAM FRERE [1]

Talavera de la Reyna, 24th July, 1809

My dear Sir,

. . . Although my troops have been on forced marches, engaged in operations with the enemy, the success of which I must

---

[1] Frere (1769–1846) was British envoy to the Junta of Spain. He was soon to be replaced by the Marquess Wellesley.

say depended upon them, they have had nothing to eat, while the Spanish army have had plenty; notwithstanding that I have returns of engagements made by the alcaldes of villages in the Vera de Plasencia [1] to furnish this army before the 24th of this month with 250,000 rations.

I certainly lament the necessity which obliges me to halt at present, and will oblige me to withdraw from Spain, if it should continue. There is no man that does not acknowledge, even Gen. Cuesta [2] himself acknowledges, the justice and propriety of my conduct in halting now, or in eventually withdrawing; and I can only say, that I have never seen an army so ill-treated in any country, or, considering that all depends upon its operations, one which deserved good treatment so much.

It is ridiculous to pretend that the country cannot supply our wants. The French army is well fed, and the soldiers who are taken in good health, and well supplied with bread, of which indeed they left a small magazine behind them. This is a rich country in corn, in comparison with Portugal, and yet, during the whole of my operations in that country, we never wanted bread but on one day on the frontiers of Galicia. In the Vera de Plasencia there are means to supply this army for four months, as I am informed, and yet the alcaldes have not performed their engagements with me. The Spanish army has plenty of every thing, and we alone, upon whom every thing depends, are actually starving.

I am aware of the important consequences which must attend the step which I shall take in withdrawing from Spain. It is certain that the people of England will never hear of another army entering Spain after they shall have received the accounts of the treatment we have met with; and it is equally certain that without the assistance, the example, and the countenance of a British army, the Spanish armies, however brave, will never effect their object. But no man can see his army perish by want without feeling for them, and most particularly must he feel for them when he knows that they have been brought into the country in which this want is felt by his own act, and on his own responsibility, and not by orders from any superior authority.

---

[1] The Alcalde was the Mayor. The valley of the Vera, a tributary of the Tagus, runs east from Plasencia below the Sierra de Vera.
[2] General Don Gregorio García de la Cuesta (1740–1812), commander of the Spanish armies in the Talavera campaign. He resigned soon afterwards, and died in retirement in Majorca.

I shall be obliged to you if you will make known to the government my sentiments upon this subject. . . .

Believe me, &c.,

Arthur Wellesley

78

TO JOHN CHARLES VILLIERS [1]

Talavera de la Reyna, 29th July, 1809

My dear Villiers,

The enemy having collected all the troops he had in this part of Spain, attacked us here on the 27th. The battle lasted till yesterday evening, when we beat him in all parts of our line ; and he retreated in the evening and night, leaving in our hands twenty pieces of cannon, ammunition waggons, prisoners, &c. The battle was a most desperate one. Our loss has been very great, that of the enemy larger. The attack was made principally upon the British, who were on the left ; and we had about two to one against us ; fearful odds ! but we maintained all our positions, and gave the enemy a terrible beating.[2]

The Spanish troops that were engaged behaved well ; but there were very few of them engaged, as the attack was made upon us. . . .

Believe me, &c.,

Arthur Wellesley

79

TO GENERAL DON GREGORIO CUESTA

Deleytosa, 11th August, 1809

Sir,

I have had the honor of receiving your Excellency's letter of the 10th instant, and I am concerned that you should conceive that you have any reason to complain of the conduct of the British troops ; but when troops are starving,[3] which those under

---

[1] Villiers (1751–1838) was Ambassador to Portugal from 1808 to 1810. He succeeded his brother as 3rd Earl of Clarendon in 1824.

[2] On August 1st he told William Wellesley-Pole : 'I was hit but not hurt & my coat shot through. Almost all the Staff are wounded or have had their horses shot. Never was there such a Murderous Battle ! !'

[3] On the 8th he told his brother William : 'We have suffered much from want of Provisions. The British Army is a bad one for a retreat or for any privations ; and I really believe that in every respect with the exception of the Guards & one or two other Corps this is the worst British Army that ever was in the field.'

my command have been, as I have repeatedly told your Excellency since I joined you on the 22nd of last month; and particularly had no bread whatever from the 3rd to the 8th instant, it is not astonishing that they should go to the villages, and even to the mountains, and look for food where they think they can get it.

The complaints of the inhabitants, however, should not have been confined to the conduct of the British troops : in this very village I have seen the Spanish soldiers, who ought to have been elsewhere, take the doors off the houses which were locked up, in order that they might plunder the houses, and they afterwards burnt the doors.

I absolutely and positively deny the assertion that any thing going to the Spanish army has been stopped by the British troops or Commissaries.

On the 7th, when the British troops were starving in the hills, I met a convoy of 350 mules, loaded with provisions for the Spanish army. I would not allow one of them to be touched, and they all passed on. General Sherbrooke,[1] on the following day, the 8th, gave a written order to another convoy, addressed to all British Officers, to allow them to pass through the army unmolested. Yesterday I met on the road and passed not less than 500 mules loaded with provisions for the Spanish army ; and no later than yesterday evening Major Campbell,[2] my aide de camp, gave an order to another large convoy, addressed to all British Officers and soldiers, not to impede its progress.

I also declare to your Excellency most positively, on the honor of a gentleman, that the British army has received no provisions since it has been at Deleytosa, excepting some sent from Truxillo by Señor Lozano de Torres ; [3] and I call upon the gentleman who has informed his friend that biscuit addressed to the Spanish army has been taken by my Commissaries to prove the truth of his assertion.

But this letter from your Excellency brings the question respecting provisions to a fair issue. I call upon your Excellency

---

[1] Lieut.-General, afterwards General Sir John Cope Sherbrooke (1764–1830), was Wellesley's second-in-command in the Peninsula until ill health obliged him to return to England in 1811. He was Governor-General of Canada from 1816 to 1818. Sherbrooke had commanded the 33rd Foot and served with Wellesley in India, notably at Seringapatam. See page 7.

[2] Colin Campbell. See note to letter no. 67.

[3] The Spanish superintendent attached to the British army and also a deputy from the Junta.

to state distinctly, whether it is understood by you that the Spanish army are to have not only all the provisions the country can afford, but all those which are sent from Seville, I believe, as much for the service of the one army as the other.

I beg you to let me know in reply to this letter whether any magazines of provisions have been formed, and from whence the British troops are to draw their provisions.

I hope that I shall receive satisfactory answers to these two questions to-morrow morning. If I should not, I beg that your Excellency will be prepared to occupy the post opposite Almaraz,[1] as it will be impossible for me to remain any longer in a country in which no arrangement has been made for the supply of provisions for the troops; and in which it is understood that all the provisions which are either found in the country, or are sent from Seville, as I have been informed, for the use of the British army, are to be supplied solely and exclusively to the use of the Spanish troops.

In regard to the assertion in your Excellency's letter that the British troops sell their bread to the Spanish soldiers, it is beneath the dignity of your Excellency's situation and character to notice such things, or for me to reply to them. I must observe, however, that the British troops could not sell that which they had not, and that the reverse of the statement of your Excellency upon this subject is the fact, at the time the armies were at Talavera; as I have myself witnessed in the streets of that town.

I have the honor to be, &c.,

Arthur Wellesley

P.S. I send Colonel O'Lalor [2] with this letter, who knows the truth of the facts stated in it respecting the convoys which have been forwarded, and respecting the supplies received here from Truxillo.

[1] Almaraz lies just north of the Tagus, some fifteen miles from Deleitosa and fifty from Talavera.

[2] An officer in the Spanish service.

Next day, August 12th, Wellesley wrote to Villiers: 'We are starving, and are ill treated by the Spaniards in every way. . . . It is useless to complain, but we are certainly not treated as friends, much less as the only prop on which the course in Spain can depend.'

And to his brother, the Marquess Wellesley: 'Either the British army must be fed and supplied with the necessaries which they require, or I shall march them back into Portugal'.

The Marquess told the Spanish Minister for Foreign Affairs that he would not trust 'the protection of a favourite dog to the whole Spanish army'.

80

GENERAL ORDER

Medellin, 23rd Aug., 1809

The women of the army must be prevented from purchasing bread in the villages within 2 leagues of the station of any division of the army; when any woman wants to purchase bread, she must ask the officer of the company to which she belongs for a passport, which must be countersigned by the Commanding officer of the regiment. Any woman found with bread in her possession, purchased at any place nearer than 2 leagues, will be deprived of the bread by the Provost or his assistants; as will any woman who goes out of camp to purchase bread without a passport. Women who will have been discovered disobeying this order will not be allowed to receive rations.

Arthur Wellesley

❀

[While on the subject of women with the army, it is relevant to quote a letter addressed in 1850 to the Marchioness of Salisbury, in which Wellington paints a vivid if melancholy picture of indiscipline and retribution in the Peninsula.]

81

TO THE MARCHIONESS OF SALISBURY [1]

Walmer, September 21, 1850

I am very much obliged to you, my dear Lady Salisbury, for your kindness in looking out and discovering the original charge against me for flogging women! You are very right, it was no less a personage than Sir Walter Scott the great novelist! and, what makes it worse, he was an intimate acquaintance and friend of me; and lived with me the whole time he was at Paris collecting these Lies.[2] But he was of a class not a little numerous in the

---

[1] Lady Mary Sackville-West, a daughter of the 5th Earl De la Warr, was born in 1824 and at the age of twenty-three became the second wife of James, 2nd Marquess of Salisbury. He died in 1870 and two years later she remarried, becoming Countess of Derby. She died in 1900.

[2] Sir Walter Scott visited Paris in the summer of 1815. See his *Paul's Letters to his Kinsfolk*. He told a friend: 'I have never felt awed or abashed except in the presence of one man — the Duke of Wellington, who possesses every one mighty quality of the mind in a higher degree than any other does, or has ever done'.

world ; of which the Individuals prefer fiction to fact upon military affairs and operations ! Accordingly when he came to Paris to enquire into details about the battle of Waterloo, instead of applying to me, as the principal of the Staff Officers of the Army with whom he was associating daily at night and in my house, he seeks out for a Highland Serjeant Corporal, or Serjeant, who crammed him with lies, not only about the Battle, but the details of his Military Life and Adventures.

I recollect such a fanciful man as Sir Walter Scott proposing to me to have a history written on the Battle of Talavera, by calling upon every individual who desired to write down his own account and refer these accounts to one Individual to make out a narration ! I answered that it would be as easy to write the account of a ball as of a Battle ! Who was the Partner of Who ? Who footed to each other ? Who danced down all the couples ? Which couples were started ? All such details would come into the details written by an Individual of a Battle.

In respect to the charge of flogging Women, the fact is there is in every Army in the field, particularly a British Army, an officer called the Provost Martial [*sic*]. I had one with seven assistant Provost Martials. The Duty of these Officers is to ride about with a Detachment of troops to prevent marauding and plundering by the Soldiers, and to inflict punishment on those whom he should find in the act of plundering. In truth, I believe these Officers punished but seldom ! The plunderers and marauders generally ran away as soon as they heard or saw the officer, who was titled the Bloody Provost. As I have stated, it was the Duty of the Provost Martial and his Assistants to punish those whom they should find in the act of Plundering or marauding. But no Officer in the Army was permitted to order one of these to punish anybody ! Of that I am quite certain ! and I do not think that I ever ventured myself to order that which I prevented others from ordering. Indeed, I recollect upon one occasion finding fault with one who had ordered a Provost to punish a man ! I stated that I could not give such an order myself. That the Provost could punish no man unless he found him in the act of Plundering.

Portugal, in which country we carried on operations for two or three campaigns, is a country producing everywhere Wine ! The wine is collected either in jars or in Casks amongst the most opulent of the Wine proprietors, in Cellars contiguous to the Houses in nearly every Village! The soldiers were in the habit of breaking into these Cellars. They bored holes in the Casks and set the Wine running; of which each partook and filled his Canteen, which every man carries! These were accompanied by their Women as usual, with their Children in their Arms! They were disturbed possibly by a fresh party and moved off, invariably leaving the Cask running! so that at last the Cellar itself became full of Wine up to their Middles, or even to their Chests! This went on, party of plunderers succeeding party of Plunderers, till the " Bloody Provost ", hearing of what was going on, in coming there upon his rounds interrupted the Sports! Being there up to the middle in Wine, and generally all drunk, they could not get away; and it was probably necessary that the Provost should exercise his authority and punish some in order to clear the Cellar! Mind, there were always Women in these Cellars as well as men! and it is not improbable that the women were the least capable of running!

As I said there was no order for punishing women! But there was certainly none for exempting Women from punishment! Such an order would have rendered the existence of such an institution entirely nugatory! It is well known that in all armies the Women are at least as bad, if not worse, than the men as Plunderers! and the exemption of the Ladies from punishment would have encouraged Plunder! This is the way in which this case stands; and I have availed myself of a Saturday to write you the details, as you took the trouble of searching for and informing me of the origin of the Report that Women were punished in the Army in which I commanded.

God bless you. I hope that you have had satisfactory accounts of Lord Salisbury's progress towards Home; with best wishes for your children believe me yours most affectionately

Wellington

We have a decided change of weather here. We shall certainly have a Southerly Equinox.

As I receive every morning numerous letters about this affair of flogging women I should not be surprised if I should be under the necessity of justifying myself, and I beg you to keep to yourself what I have written upon it.[1]

---

[1] *A Great Man's Friendship*, pp. 107-10.

[In this connection may be quoted a passage from John Scott's *Paris Revisited in 1815*. The author met several Highland soldiers in Péronne during July 1815 and enquired 'if the Duke of Wellington took severe measures of enforcing on his army that regard for the lives and property of the inhabitants of the seat of war, in maintaining which he has evidently placed the pride of his ambition, not less than in beating his armed adversaries ?

'"Na, sir, no here", was the reply, — "for the men ken him gailies now. But in Spain we aften had ugly jobs. He hung fifteen men in ae day, there, — after he had been ordering about it, God knows how long. And d——n me if he did'na ance gar the Provost Marshal flog mare than a dizen of the wimen — for the wimen thought themselves safe, and so they were war' than the men. They got sax and tharty lashes a piece on the bare doup, and it was lang afore it was forgotten on 'em."' [1]

Colonel Charles Leslie recorded in his *Military Journal* for July 4th, 1809, that when the 29th Regiment encamped at Zarza Maior, 'several of the soldiers' wives, having preceded the column, had taken the liberty of helping themselves to various articles in the shape of vegetables and other eatables. On complaint being made by the injured inhabitants, Lord Hill assigned the delinquents to the provost, *who exercised schoolboy discipline on a few as an example to the rest.*']

82

TO THE HON. WILLIAM WELLESLEY-POLE

Merida,
August 29th, 1809

My dear William,

. . . Since I have separated from the Spaniards I have received a letter from Lord Wellesley [2] in which he desires that I will remain in Spain ; & connect myself again with the Spanish Army in a plan to defend the Guadiana. I consider it however a question of a very different description, & one to be decided on grounds entirely different, whether I shall again enter into cooperation with the Spaniards having separated from them ; or being with them I should separate from them. . . .

My opinion is that in the existing state of their affairs we (the Army I mean) ought to have nothing to say to the Spaniards.

In fact they have not 80,000 Men they could put in the field, the French have 125,000 besides their Garrisons which are not

[1] Scott, 256–7.
[2] Richard, Marquess Wellesley, arrived soon after Talavera as British Ambassador to the Spanish Supreme Junta at Seville.

less than 25,000 more. The Spanish troops will not fight ; they are undisciplined, they have no Officers, no provisions, no magazines, no means of any description. If we enter into a cooperation with them the burthen of the war must fall upon us ; & with us will rest the disgrace of its certain & unavoidable failure. This is not an exaggerated picture. I was slow as every Man is to believe all the bad I had heard of the Spaniards,[1] but I assure you that there is nothing so bad in the Shape of troops ; & nothing so inefficient as the enthusiasm of which such a boast is made, & which such pains are taken to excite & keep up. At the same time the Spaniards really detest the French, and I believe it will be scarcely possible for Bonaparte to establish a Govt. in Spain. But the activity, excited by this detestation & the boasted enthusiasm of the people, is limited to great celerity in packing up all their goods, & running off to the Mountains as soon as they hear of the approach of a French Patrole. There are some instances of Couriers being cut off &c ; but when one sees the Country, & when one hears of the enthusiasm of the people, & their detestation of the French, it is a matter of astonishment that any Courier should ever reach his destination, and that any Small Patrole should ever get through the Country rather than that those we have heard of, have been cut off. To all this add that no Man even of ordinary talents has yet appeared among the Gentlemen of the Country to take the lead, & then tell me what can be expected in the Military Line from these people ? & what chance has a British Army of 25,000 Men even of safety by entering into any cooperation with them ? . . .

Give my best love to Mrs. Pole & Believe me Ever Yours most affectionately,

Arthur Wellesley [2]

83

GENERAL ORDER

Badajoz, 7th Sept. 1809

Notwithstanding the repeated orders given out upon the subject, the soldiers of the 4th division of infantry plundered

[1] On August 18th William Warre wrote to his mother : 'The character of the Spaniards is so selfish, jealous, and proud, with all the surliness of Englishmen and not a spark of their good qualities, that a foreign army in their country must always risk being abandoned'.
[2] *Camden Miscellany*, vol. xviii.

beehives [1] in the neighbourhood of Badajoz on the day before the division marched from that place : it is impossible these outrages can be committed daily, and that this last outrage in particular, could have been committed without the Officers obtaining some knowledge of it. The Officers with the army do not appear to be aware how much they suffer in the disgraceful and unmilitary practices of the soldiers, in marauding and plundering everything they lay their hands upon. The consequence is, the people of the country fly their habitations, no market is opened, and the Officers, as well as the soldiers, suffer in the privation of every comfort and every necessary, excepting their rations, from the neglect of the former and the criminal misconduct of the latter. The Commander of the Forces has done, and will continue to do, everything in his power to put an end to these disgraceful practices ; but it is obvious that all his efforts must be fruitless, unless the Officers of the army, generally and individually, exert themselves for the same object.

Arthur Wellesley

✳

[In this connection the Duke of Wellington told Lady de Ros, formerly Lady Georgiana Lennox, on May 29th, 1844 : 'There was a capital story told of me in Spain. I don't know that it was all quite true, but that don't signify. It was a fashion at one time for our men to plunder bee-hives. I met a fellow one day who had got one, and was carrying it off. I stopped him and asked him where he had got it. "Why, out there where the picket is, but if you don't make haste they will all be gone" was the soldier's reply ! A Spaniard caught one of our men plundering a bee-hive, and he took it and rammed it down on his head like a shako, with the bees and honey all in it !'

In his introduction to *The General Orders of Field Marshal the Duke of Wellington* Gurwood gives a similar version of the first story. 'Soon after the first order on "Beehives" was issued at Jaraicejo, Lord Wellington, in one of his rides, saw a man of the 88th, or Connaught Rangers, posting along as fast as his legs could carry him, with a beehive on his head. Lord Wellington, furious at so flagrant a disobedience of orders, which sapped all discipline, called out to him, "Hillo, sir ! Where did you get that beehive ?" Pat had enveloped his head and face in his greatcoat to prevent the bees stinging him, and thinking more of his prize than the tone of voice addressed to him, answered in pure Milesian, "Jist over the hill there ; and by Jasus, if ye don't make haste they'd be all gane." The blind good-nature of Pat stayed the Duke's anger, and it was reported at dinner as a good joke.']

[1] The 4th Division won for themselves the nickname of 'honey suckers'.

84

TO JOHN CHARLES VILLIERS

Badajoz, 8th Sept. 1809

My dear Villiers,

. . . The soldiers of the army have permission to go to mass, so far as this : they are forbidden to go into the churches during the performance of divine service, unless they go to assist in the performance of the service. I could not do more, for in point of fact, soldiers cannot by law attend the celebration of mass, excepting in Ireland. The thing now stands exactly as it ought ; any man may go to mass who chooses, and nobody makes any inquiry about it. The consequence is, that nobody goes to mass, and although we have whole regiments of Irishmen, and of course Roman Catholics, I have not seen one soldier perform any one act of religious worship in these Catholic countries, excepting making the sign of the cross to induce the people of the country to give them wine. Although, as you will observe, I have no objection, and they may go to mass if they choose it, I have great objections to the inquiries and interference of the priests of the country to induce them to go to mass. The orders were calculated to prevent all intrigue and interference of that description ; and I was very certain, that when the Irish soldiers were left to themselves either to go or not, they would do as their comrades did, and not one of them would be seen in a church.[1] I think it best that you should avoid having any further discussion with the priests on this subject ; but if you should have any, it would be best that you should tell them what our law is, and what the order of this army. Prudence may then induce them to refrain from taking any steps to induce the Roman Catholic soldiers to attend mass ; but if it should not, and their conduct should be guided by religious zeal, I acknowledge, that however indifferent I should have been at seeing the soldiers flock to the churches under my orders, I should not be very well satisfied to see them filled by the influence of the priests, taking advantage of the mildness and toleration which is the spirit of that order. . . .

Believe me, &c.,

Arthur Wellesley

[1] In his *Notes of Conversations with the Duke of Wellington*, the Earl Stanhope records on October 2nd, 1839 : 'The Duke told me that in Spain he had issued an order that no man of his army was to enter a place of worship except for the

85

TO THE HON. WILLIAM WELLESLEY-POLE

Badajoz,
Septr. 13th, 1809

My dear William,

I was certain there was something I had to write to you about this morning besides what I have written in the Inclosed, & that is the state of my affairs, respecting which the Ministers may make enquiries upon the Grant of the Peerage.

When I came from India I had 42 or 43,000 Pounds which I made as follows. I got 5,000 Prize money at Seringapatam; 25,000 £ Prize money in the Mahratta War; the Court of Directors gave me 4,000 £ for having been a Comr. in Mysore; & the Govt. paid me about 2,000 £ in one Sum the arrears of an Allowance as Comg. Officer at Seringapatam; & the remainder was Interest upon these Sums Savings &c during the time I was in India.

I believe I have about 40,000 £ remaining of the 43,000 £; of which 40,000, £ 20,000 £ & her own fortune 6,000 £ not included in the above are settled upon Lady Wellesley.

Of course I should not wish this statement to be made public; but it is right that you should know as well what I have, as how I got it, in case any of the King's Ministers should make enquiries respecting the state of my circumstances.

Unless I have spent it I have also 1700 Prize money for Copenhagen; but I fancy it is gone. Believe me Ever Yours most affectionately A.W.[1]

86

GENERAL ORDER

Badajoz, 16th Sept., 1809

The Commander of the Forces cannot avoid taking this opportunity of calling upon the field officers of the regiments in particular, and all the officers in general, to support and assist

purpose of joining in that worship, having found that many at first went into the churches only to stare and gape about them, as at a novelty.

'The Irish Catholic soldiers used to make use of their signs of the cross to get *aguardiente* in the villages; for the country people, seeing from this that they were brethren in faith, used to bring out their stores more readily.'

[1] *Camden Miscellany*, vol. xviii.

their Commanding officer in the maintenance of discipline, and in the preservation of order and regularity in their corps.

The officers of the army are much mistaken if they suppose that their duty is done when they have attended to the drill of their men, and to the parade duties of the regiment : the order and regularity of the troops in camp and quarters, the subsistence and comfort of the soldiers, the general subordination and obedience of the corps, afford constant subjects for the attention of the field officers in particular, in which, by their conduct in the assistance they will give their Commanding officer, they can manifest their zeal for the service, their ability and their fitness for promotion to the higher ranks, at least as much as by an attention to the drill and parade discipline of the corps. . . .

Arthur Wellesley [1]

87

TO SIR JOHN ANSTRUTHER [2]

Badajoz, 6th Oct., 1809

My dear Sir John,

I am very much obliged to you for your kind letter of the 2nd September, which I received the day before yesterday. We had certainly a most fierce contest at Talavera, and the victory which we gained, although from circumstances it has not been followed by all the good consequences which we might have expected from it, has at least added to the military reputation of the country, and has convinced the French that their title to be called the first military nation in Europe will be disputed, not unsuccessfully.

Nothing has occurred in this country deserving notice since the battle of Talavera ; and I believe that although the French are even in numbers stronger than the allies upon the Peninsula, they find they can do nothing without having another battle with us, which would be fatal to their operations, in the same manner as their strength, efficiency, and position must prevent us from succeeding in any offensive operation undertaken against them.

[1] Subsequent letters were signed 'Wellington', as since August 26th he had been Baron Douro of Wellesley and Viscount Wellington of Talavera, though the news of this elevation took three weeks to reach him.

[2] Born in 1753, Sir John took part in the impeachment of Warren Hastings, and served as Chief Justice of Bengal. He came home from England in 1806 and died five years later.

I fear that Lord Wellesley will not be able to do much with the Spaniards. Their government is a miserable one, deficient in every quality which a government ought to possess in these days. Their military establishment is very defective, and they have neither general nor inferior officers of any talents, nor sufficient numbers of troops; and these last appear to me to be worse as soldiers than their general officers are as Generals. The troops have neither arms, clothing, accoutrements, discipline, nor efficiency: there are no magazines, and no means of collecting from the country the supplies which all armies require. There is no plan of a campaign, either for carrying on the war, or for continuing the contest; and the efforts of the rulers appear to be directed, in the first instance, to keeping their own situations, and, in the second, to exciting and keeping up in the country a kind of false enthusiasm by which it is supposed that everything can be effected; and they endeavour to effect both these objects by the undertaking of little operations with little means, by the circulation of false intelligence, by the exaggeration of little successes and the concealment of great disasters. In this consists the secret of the government.

As to the enthusiasm, about which so much noise has been made even in our own country, I am convinced the world has entirely mistaken its effects. I believe that it only creates confusion where order ought to prevail, and disobedience of orders and indiscipline among the troops upon system, instead of obedience and discipline; and I fancy that, upon reflection, it will be discovered that what was deemed enthusiasm among the French, which enabled them successfully to resist all Europe at the commencement of the revolution, was force acting through the medium of popular societies and assuming the name of enthusiasm, and that force, in a different shape, has completed the conquest of Europe and keeps the continent in subjection. Really, when a Spaniard has cried out *vivat* and has put everything in confusion in his district or village, he sits down quietly and thinks he has done his duty till the first French patrol arrives, when he shows his activity in packing up his goods and running away, and there is no authority either to set them or keep them right. At the same time they are cordial haters of the French, and I think that whatever may be the result of the military contest in the Peninsula, much time will elapse before the French can establish a government in Spain, and still more time before they will derive such advantage from their influence in that country as they did before they invaded it.

Pray remember me most kindly to Lady Anstruther, and

Believe me, &c.,

Wellington [1]

88

TO BRIGADIER-GENERAL JOHN SLADE [2]

Lisbon, October 12th 1809

Sir,

I have perused the proceedings of the General Court Martial, of which you are President, on the trial of Lieut. Perse [3] of the 45th regt., for " most unofficerlike & ungentlemanlike conduct, in being concerned in an Affray which took place in the City of Lisbon on the night of the 3rd of March last, 1809," of which crime the Court have *honorably* acquitted him; and I request you to reassemble the General Court Martial, and to desire them to revise this Sentence.

It appears that the affray in which the Court have found that Lt. Perse was concerned originated in a Brothel, in which Lt. Perse was with other officers; and although his conduct in the affray might have been distinguished by his activity to quell it, & merits the acquittal which the Court have sentenced, I should not do my duty by them or by His Majesty who has entrusted me with the power of confirming their Sentence, if I did not draw their attention to the use of the term *Honorably* which it contains.

It is difficult & needless at present to define in what cases an honorable acquittal by a Court Martial is peculiarly applicable; but it must appear to all persons to be objectionable in a case in which any part of the Transaction, which has been the subject of Investigation before the Court Martial, is disgraceful to the character of the party under trial. A sentence of honorable acquittal by a Court Martial should be considered by the Officers & Soldiers of the Army as a subject of exultation; but no man

---

[1] *Supplementary Despatches*, vi, 387-9.

[2] Slade (1762–1859), who was created a baronet in 1831, commanded a cavalry brigade in the Peninsula until he was sent home in April 1813. His handling of the cavalry was often rash and inept. By his two marriages he had eleven sons and four daughters.

[3] Lieutenant William Pearse of the 45th (Nottingham) Regiment was killed at the top of the breach of Ciudad Rodrigo in January 1812.

can exult in the termination of any transaction, a part of which has been disgraceful to him; and although such a transaction may be terminated by an *honorable* acquittal by a Court Martial, it cannot be mentioned to the party without offence, or without exciting feelings of disgust in others. These are not the feelings which ought to be excited by the recollection and mention of a sentence of honorable acquittal.

I believe that there is no officer upon the General Court Martial who wishes to connect the term Honor with the act of going to a Brothel; the common practice forbids it; & there is no man who unfortunately commits this act who does not endeavor to conceal it from the world and his friends. But the honorable acquittal of Lt. Perse as recorded in this Sentence, which states that he was concerned in an affray which is known to have originated in a Brothel will have the effect of connecting with the act of going to a Brothel the honorable distinction which it is in the power of a Court Martial to bestow on those brought before them on charges of a very different nature, by the sentence which it may pass upon them. I therefore anxiously recommend to the General Court Martial to omit the word *Honorably* in their Sentence.[1]

I have the honor to be, Sir, your most obedient Hble. Servant

Wellington

89

TO THE HON. WILLIAM WELLESLEY-POLE

Lisbon, Oct 22nd 1809

My dear William,

I came down here a few days ago to arrange finally for the Defence of this Country, and I have received your letter of the 21st. Septr. . . .

---

[1] On another occasion in March 1813 Wellington wrote thus to a President of Court Martial: 'These three gentlemen were charged with a drunken riot at Coimbra, of the existence of which there is undoubted evidence on the face of the proceedings; and yet because none of the facts are proved against one of the three, the Court have thought proper *honorably* to acquit him! I should wish the Court to consider whether it is possible that there can be any honor in the conduct of any man in a riot by a drunken party of which he is one. His conduct may have been an exception to that of others, but it is quite impossible that it should be honorable.'

. . . As for my part my wishes are in favor of Perceval [1] & the Cabinet, and as far as I shall take any part in politicks I shall belong to them. But I don't conceive that I ought to embark in politicks to such an extent as to preclude my serving my Country under any administration that may employ me. In fact I have never felt any inclination to dive deeply in party Politicks; [2] I may be wrong but the conviction of my mind is that all the misfortunes of the present reign, the loss of America, the success of the French Revolution &c &c are to be attributed in a great degree to the Spirit of Party in England, & the feeling I have for a decided party politician is rather that of Contempt than any other. I am very certain that his wishes & efforts for his party very frequently prevent him from doing that which is best for the Country; & induce him to take up the cause of foreign powers against Great Britain, because the cause of Gt. Britain is managed by his party opponent. . . .

Ever Yours most affectionately W.

90

TO COLONEL WARREN PEACOCKE [3]

Lisbon, 26th Oct. 1809

My dear Sir,

I am concerned to be obliged to inform you, that it has been mentioned to me that the British officers who are in Lisbon are in the habit of going to the theatres, where some of them conduct themselves in a very improper manner, much to the annoyance of the public, and to the injury of the proprietors and of the performers. I cannot conceive for what reason the officers of the British army should conduct themselves at Lisbon in a manner which would not be permitted in their own country, is contrary to rule and custom in this country, and is permitted

[1] Spencer Perceval (1762–1812), after a distinguished legal career culminating in the posts of Attorney-General and Solicitor-General, became Chancellor of the Exchequer in 1807. He had recently succeeded the Duke of Portland as Prime Minister.

[2] On November 16th, 1809, he wrote to the Marquess of Buckingham : 'I am no party politician, but I wish that old friends would unite and form a strong government to carry the country through its difficulties, and I hope that the day is not very distant, on which people will find out that the best way of serving the country is not by forming parties to oppose or support particular men'.

[3] Peacocke of the Coldstream Guards was Governor of Lisbon during most of the Peninsular War. He became a major-general in 1811 and a Knight of the Tower and Sword (Portugal).

in none where there is any regulation or decency of behaviour. The officers commanding regiments, and the superior officers, must take measures to prevent a repetition of the conduct adverted to, and of the consequent complaints which I have received; or I must take measures which shall effectually prevent the character of the army and of the British nation from suffering by the misconduct of a few.

The officers of the army can have nothing to do behind the scenes, and it is very improper that they should appear upon the stage during the performance. They must be aware that the English public would not bear either the one or the other, and I see no reason why the Portuguese public should be worse treated. I have been concerned to see officers in uniform, with their hats on, upon the stage during the performance, and to hear of the riots and outrages which some of them have committed behind the scenes; and I can only repeat, that if this conduct should be continued, I shall be under the necessity of adopting measures to prevent it, for the credit of the army and of the country.

I beg you to communicate this letter to the commanding officers of the regiments in the garrison of Lisbon, and to the commanding officer of the detachments of convalescents, and desire them to communicate its contents to the officers under their command respectively.

Indeed, officers who are absent from their duty on account of sickness might as well not go to the playhouse, or at all events upon the stage, and behind the scenes. I beg you also to take such measures as may appear to you to be necessary to prevent a repetition of this conduct.

Believe me, &c.,

Wellington

91

TO THE HON. WILLIAM WELLESLEY-POLE

Badajoz.
Novr. 16th, 1809

My dear William,

Since I wrote to you last I have been to Seville & Cadiz to communicate with Wellesley. He went to England on the 11th. in high spirits, & determined to exert himself to make a strong Govt. for the King.

I have heard some most uncomfortable stories about Henry & Lady Charlotte [1] respecting which principally I write to you at the present moment.

I understand that she is already *under his protection*; & it is probable that they will soon come together again in some form or other.

I don't exactly understand however how her brother who I suspect has been the Instrument of bringing this about, can reconcile to his feelings & notions of Honour, to allow his sister to live & *perform* with a Man, from whom she has been divorced by the Church; & I conclude that Poor Henry will again be dragged through the Mire, & will marry this blooming Virgin again as soon as she will have been delivered of the consequences of her little amusements. Thus the World if not already apprized must eventually know of all these circumstances.

I believe I differ in opinion with you upon the line or rather the no line we ought to take upon these transactions. My opinion is that the Deed being done, that is to say Henry having taken her under his protection, & sent two of his Children to reside with her, we can & ought to avoid to give or even look an opinion upon the subject. We cannot be affected in any manner by this folly, excepting so far as we must be affected by his committing an act which must make him so unhappy; and we ought to avoid every thing which can add to his misfortunes. It is certain that nothing will make him more unhappy than to have any discussion with us upon this subject, or to perceive by our looks or our manner, that we are impressed with unfavourable Opinions upon his conduct.

We ought to consider this his folly as we did his first misfortune, a subject to be lamented, but not mentioned, & we should endeavour to alleviate it, & not to aggravate it by the communication of opinions which he must be certain that we entertain.

These are my sentiments & I hope & think that upon reflection they must agree with yours.

I have but little news for you. The Spanish Army of La Mancha has moved forward & is upon the eve of a General Action & I think of destruction.[2] . . .

Ever Yours most affectionately

Wellington [3]

---

[1] On September 20th, 1803, Henry Wellesley had married Charlotte, second daughter of the 1st Earl Cadogan. She was divorced in 1810 and married Henry, Lord Paget, afterwards Earl of Uxbridge and 1st Marquess of Anglesey.
[2] Wellington forecast correctly. Within three days the Spaniards had been crushed. See note to letter no. 93.   [3] *Camden Miscellany*, vol. xviii.

92

TO THE EARL OF LIVERPOOL [1]

Badajoz, 21st Nov. 1809

My Lord,

I beg to draw your Lordship's attention to the frequent paragraphs in the English newspapers, describing the position, the numbers, the objects, and the means of attaining them, possessed by the armies in Spain and Portugal. In some instances the English newspapers have accurately stated, not only the regiments occupying the position, but the number of men fit for duty of which each regiment was composed; and this intelligence must have reached the enemy at the same time it did me, at a moment at which it was most important that he should not receive it.

The newspapers have recently published an account of the defensive positions occupied by the different English and Portuguese corps, which certainly conveyed to the enemy the first knowledge he had of them; and I enclose a paragraph recently published, describing the line of operation which I should follow in case of the occurrence of a certain event, the preparations which I had made for that operation, and where I had formed my magazines. It is not necessary to inquire in what manner the newspapers acquire this description of information; but if the editors really feel an anxiety for the success of the military operations in the Peninsula, they will refrain from giving this information to the public, as they must know that their papers are read by the enemy, and that the information which they are desirous of conveying to their English readers is mischievous to the public, exactly in proportion as it is well founded and correct. Your Lordship will be the best judge whether any and what measures ought to be adopted to prevent the publication of this description of intelligence. I can only assure you that it will increase materially the difficulty of all operations in this country.

I have the honor to be, &c.,

Wellington

[1] Robert Banks Jenkinson, 2nd Earl of Liverpool (1770–1828), had recently become Secretary for War and the Colonies and thereby one of Wellington's most frequent correspondents.

93

TO THE EARL OF LIVERPOOL

Badajoz, 28th November, 1809

My dear Lord,

I have received your letter of the 1st instant, and I assure you that nothing can be more satisfactory to me than to renew my public communications with you. I am convinced that I shall always receive from you that fair protection, support, and assistance to which an officer is entitled when he acts fairly by the public, and all the friendship and kindness which I have been accustomed to receive from you in another situation.

I trust that my public and private letters on the subject of the war in the Peninsula, and of Portugal in particular, will have been satisfactory to you and to the Government. You see that I agree entirely in opinion with you, not only that we cannot in good policy give up the Peninsula, but that we may be able to continue the contest in Portugal with success, and that we shall finally bring off our army.

During the continuance of this contest, which must necessarily be defensive on our part, in which there may be no brilliant events, and in which, after all, I may fail, I shall be most confoundedly abused, and in the end I may lose the little character I have gained ; but I should not act fairly by the Government if I did not tell them my real opinion, which is, that they will betray the honor and interests of the country if they do not continue their efforts in the Peninsula, which, in my opinion, are by no means hopeless, notwithstanding the defeat of Areyzaga.[1]

Lord Castlereagh's misfortunes have given me the greatest concern. His kindness to me has been unbounded ;[2] and I shall always be happy to hear of any thing that can tend to his honor or satisfaction.

Believe me, &c.,

Wellington

[1] General Juan Carlos de Ariezaga, at the head of 50,000 Spanish troops, was routed at the battle of Ocaña, south of Aranjuez, on November 19th, 1809.

[2] As Secretary of State for the Colonies and War, Castlereagh had incurred much of the blame for the Walcheren expedition which he had instigated. Canning's intrigues among his Cabinet colleagues had led to the resignation of both men and a duel on Putney Heath on September 21st, in which Canning was wounded in the thigh. To Castlereagh Wellington had written on October 14th : 'I have experienced many acts of friendship and kindness from you. If I had been your brother you could not have been more careful of my interests than you have been in late instances.'

94

TO COLONEL JOHN MALCOLM

Badajoz, in Spain,
3rd December, 1809

My dear Malcolm,

. . . You will have heard of all that has passed in this country, and I will not, therefore, trouble you with a repetition of the story. The battle of Talavera was certainly the hardest fought of modern days, and the most glorious in its result to our troops.[1] Each side engaged lost a quarter of their numbers.

It is lamentable that, owing to the miserable inefficiency of the Spaniards, to their want of exertion, and the deficiency of numbers even of the allies, much more of discipline, and every other military quality, when compared with the enemy in the Peninsula, the glory of the action is the only benefit which we have derived from it. But that is a solid and substantial benefit, of which we have derived some good consequences already ; for, strange to say, I have contrived, with the little British army, to keep every thing in check since the month of August last ; and if the Spaniards had not contrived, by their own folly, and against my entreaties and remonstrances, to lose an army in La Mancha about a fortnight ago, I think we might have brought them through the contest. As it is, however, I do not despair. I have in hand a most difficult task, from which I may not extricate myself ; but I must not shrink from it. I command *an unanimous army* ; I draw well with all the authorities in Spain and Portugal, and I believe I have the good wishes of the whole world. In such circumstances one may fail, but it would be dishonorable to shrink from the task.

Pray remember me kindly to all friends in the East Indies. I do not mention names, as I do not know whom you have with you ; but I assure you that I have the most affectionate recollection of them all, and that nothing gives me greater pleasure than to hear of their prosperity.

Believe me, &c.,

Wellington

---

[1] To Major Barclay in India he wrote : 'The fire at Assye was heavier while it lasted ; but the battle of Talavera lasted for two days and a night'.

You will have seen that your father in law [1] distinguished himself in the battle of Talavera. He was wounded, and is gone to England; but he is now quite well, and I expect his early return to the army.

95

TO LORD BURGHERSH [2]

Badajoz, December 17th, 1809

My dear Burghersh,

. . . The Spanish people are like gunpowder — the least spark inflames them; and when inflamed there is no violence or outrage they do not commit, and nothing can stop their violence. They have already fired upon our people between this and Merida, and they killed a soldier in this town two nights ago, and I am obliged to stay, either to moderate and quiet the storm or to take a high tone, according to circumstances, upon the occurrence of these incidents. The fact is that these people have no reason to complain of us. We have spent and paid a million of money in this part of the country, and I never knew the British soldiers behave so regularly or so well; but the Spaniard is an undisciplined savage, who obeys no law, despises all authority, feels no gratitude for benefits conferred or favours received, and is always ready with his knife or his firelock to commit murder. At the same time, bad as they are, their vices and defects and the lamentable state of their country afford some hopes of the issue of the contest, and we cannot with honour withdraw from it till we shall be obliged to do so . . .

Ever yours most sincerely,

Wellington [3]

[1] Brig.-General Alexander Campbell, father-in-law of John Malcolm, had commanded the 4th Division at Talavera and had three horses shot under him.

[2] John Fane, Baron Burghersh, afterwards 10th Earl of Westmorland (1784-1859), was at this time travelling to Granada, Valencia, Alicante and other Spanish towns, and sending back detailed reports to Wellington. In 1811 he married Priscilla, one of Wellington's nieces.

[3] Printed in *Correspondence of Lord Burghersh*, page 39.

THE YEAR 1810

By the end of 1809 King Joseph, finding increasing difficulty in maintaining his court on the revenue from the Spanish provinces already under French control, turned covetous eyes on rich Andalusia; but not until Marshal Soult had beaten the main Spanish army at the battle of Ocaña was the way clear for an invasion of the south. Then, early in the new year, the cities of Seville, Cordova and Malaga were rapidly seized, and only Cadiz on its slender sea-girt isthmus of sand defied the French, who, without mastery of the Atlantic, set about blockading the white city — now temporary seat of the Spanish Government — from the land.

Meanwhile on January 15th Wellington, leaving General Hill with the 2nd Division at Abrantes to guard the line of the Tagus, had moved his troops across that river into cantonments extending from Guarda on the right towards the Douro, with his own headquarters at Viseu and the Light Division holding advanced posts along the Coa. The Portuguese were called upon to take up arms and by May they mustered thirty thousand regular soldiers, paid, armed and officered by the British.

In the same month of May Marshal André Masséna, Duke of Rivoli (1756–1817), took command of the French Armée de Portugal and drew up plans for capturing the vital frontier fortresses of Ciudad Rodrigo and Almeida. His object was to open the northern road for a cautious but none the less irresistible advance to Lisbon and the sea. Wellington, all too well aware that with his army outnumbered by more than two to one he could not permanently defend the frontier between Spain and Portugal, declined to go to the aid of the Spanish garrison when Ney invested Ciudad Rodrigo on July 2nd. For Wellington this decision, in the face of French taunts, Spanish accusations of indifference, appeals from the garrison and British uneasiness at such apparent apathy towards an ally, was a hard one, but he remained firm. The defenders held out for eight days and then surrendered.

After delays caused by the need to bring up supplies and by the rash skirmishing of Craufurd's Light Division on the far side of the Coa, the French turned against Almeida at the end of July. Here the Portuguese garrison might well have resisted for a long while had not a bomb exploded the main powder magazine and destroyed half the town. Bereft of ammunition, Almeida surrendered on August 28th.

When, in the middle of September, the French, numbering seventy-two thousand, advanced into Portugal along three routes, Wellington, reinforced by Hill from the south, withdrew his army of forty-nine thousand men, half British, half Portuguese. He withdrew despite bitter protests from the Regency in Lisbon, the restive grumbling of the public in Britain and the anxiety of the Government which supported him. Whereas the British tax-payers complained that they were compelled to pay out more and more money to keep abroad an army which did little but retreat, and whereas the Portuguese nobility suspected that the British Army was about to embark and leave the country to French occupation, the stoical peasants burned their crops and abandoned their homes in response to Wellington's appeals.

The Commander of the Forces, faced with these circumstances, determined, if he could gain a victory without incurring too serious a risk, to fight one battle before he finally withdrew to his winter defence line : success at this juncture might restore confidence in Portugal and help to maintain the hard-pressed Government at home. Accordingly he concentrated his divisions on the Mondego river and stood at bay along the ridge of Busaco. Here, on September 27th, he soundly defeated Masséna, but no sooner had he achieved this success, with meagre casualties, than he astonished his troops by resuming the southward retreat. While cavalry squadrons and the Light Division held off the pursuing French, and while Portuguese families cluttered the roads in their flight, Wellington's regiments marched through Coimbra and with ragged discipline covered another seventy miles.

On October 8th they reached the prepared defence lines by Torres Vedras — thirty miles of hills strengthened by forts, redoubts and other defence works which had been built in secret during the previous year. The Allies could retreat no further. Flanked by the sea and the Tagus estuary, they stood with their backs to the Lisbon base.

When Masséna arrived before the Lines, he was perturbed by their strength. He had no more suspected their existence than had most of his opponents. His troops faced the position for a month but never attacked. They came near to starving and on the night of November 14th retired upon Santarem and Thomar, where they remained, short of food and in great discomfort, throughout the winter. Wellington's army followed, and took up forward lines between Alcoentre and Villa Franca, with Headquarters at Cartaxo.

96

TO COLONEL WARREN PEACOCKE

Coimbra, 4th Jan. 1810

Sir,

I have been informed by the Sec. of State to the government of Portugal that certain officers in the garrison of Lisbon lately went in a masonic procession through the streets of the city, from the citadel to the British factory. I have no doubt but that this act was innocently committed by those concerned in it; but I have to inform you that the procession, the insignia, and the existence of Free-masonry, are contrary to the law in Portugal; and adverting to circumstances which have recently occurred at Lisbon, and to the reports in circulation of the causes of the confinement of different individuals by the government, I should have believed it impossible that it was not already known that these proceedings were illegal, if the persons concerned in them were not British officers. I am informed that this procession was most offensive to many persons in Lisbon, who are at least equally attached to the laws of the country as we are to those of our own; and that nothing prevented the expression of the general indignation by a riot, excepting the respect for the British character, and the hope entertained by the majority of the people that the violation of the law was to be attributed to ignorance of its provisions.

I beg of you to communicate the contents of this letter to the Commanding officers of regiments, and principal officers of the army at Lisbon, and that you will state to them my wish that the meeting of the masonic lodges in their corps, and the wearing of all masonic emblems, and all masonic processions, may be discontinued during the time they may be in Portugal.

I have the honor to be, &c.,

Wellington

97

TO THE EARL OF LIVERPOOL

Viseu, 24th Jan. 1810

My dear Lord,

. . . I am concerned to tell you, that, notwithstanding the pains taken by the General and other officers of the army, the conduct of the soldiers is infamous. They behave well generally when with their regiments, and under the inspection of their officers, and the General officers of the army; but when detached, and coming up from hospitals, although invariably under the command of an officer, and always well fed and taken care of, and received as children of the family by the housekeeper in Portugal, they commit every description of outrage. They have never brought up a convoy of money that they have not robbed the chest; nor of shoes, or any other article that could be of use to them, or could produce money, that they do not steal something. I have never halted the army for 2 days that I have not been obliged to assemble a General Court Martial; and a General Court Martial was assembled during the whole time the army was at Badajoz. At this moment there are 3 General Courts Martial sitting in Portugal for the trial of soldiers guilty of wanton murders, (no less than 4 people have been killed by them since we returned to Portugal,) robberies, thefts, robbing convoys under their charge, &c., &c. I assure you that the military law is not sufficiently strong to keep them in order; and the people of this country have almost universally such an affection for the British nation, that they are unwilling to prosecute these unworthy soldiers in cold blood for the injuries they have received from them, at the distance of time which must elapse before the soldier can be brought to trial; although ready enough to complain and prosecute when smarting under the injury. Then the truth can never be got from themselves. Perjury is as common as robbery and murder; and the consequence of swearing them to tell truth before a regimental Court Martial is, that they invariably commit perjury when examined before a General Court Martial, where formerly the sanction of an oath was seldom given to falsehood. But upon the whole of this important subject, I refer you to my letter to Lord Castlereagh of the 17th June last.

I certainly think the army are improved. They are a better army than they were some months ago. But still these terrible, continued outrages give me reason to apprehend that, notwithstanding all the precautions I have taken, and shall take, they will slip through my fingers, as they did through Sir J. Moore's, when I shall be involved in any nice operation with a powerful enemy in my front.

Believe me, &c.,

Wellington

98

TO THE HON. WILLIAM WELLESLEY-POLE

Viseu.
Jany. 26th, 1810

My dear William,

You will learn all the news from this quarter which affords but very little from my dispatches; as I conclude that before this letter will reach England you will have arrived from Ireland after your Election.

The object of my writing to you now is principally the state of our Naval concerns in Portugal. You have a general knowledge & so has Lord Mulgrave [1] I believe of the character of the Admiral [2] on this station but no general knowledge of Character can give either of you a notion of the difficulty of dealing with him in matters of Detail.

His activity is unbounded, the whole range of the business of the Country in which he is stationed, civil Military political Commercial, even ecclesiastical I believe as well as Naval are objects of his attention; & he interferes actively in every thing. In my life I never saw a Man who had had so good an education, & had been employed in publick station, & had had some communication with the world, whose understanding is so defective & who has such a passion for new invented modes of doing ordinary things & such a contempt for every thing that is practicable. I tremble when I think that I shall have to embark the Leopards [3] in front of Bonaparte aided by such a man, who has already twenty new invented modes of putting Leopards into Boats, & of getting boats off a coast to a ship besides new plans & inventions for the execution of all the ordinary Services that can occur. I am already & have been ever since I came to Portugal teazed to death by this Man with propositions for new modes of doing every thing in the Commissariat, the Artillery &c &c which coming from such an authority I cannot treat with the contempt they deserve. I am obliged to give answers, to reason, to temporize, to delay, & to get rid of this impracticable nonsense in the best & least offensive mode in my Power. But how is it to be when our decisions & execution must go hand in hand; when every thing to be done must be understood by those who are to execute, must be that which they have been taught to perform, is their daily business,

[1] Henry Phipps, 3rd Baron and afterwards 1st Earl Mulgrave (1755–1831), a general, was First Lord of the Admiralty from 1807 to 1810, when he resigned and became Master of the Ordnance.

[2] Vice-Admiral the Hon. George Cranfield Berkeley (1753–1818) had command of the British naval force in the Tagus and off the coast of Portugal from 1808 to 1812. He was a son of the 4th Earl of Berkeley.

[3] Wellington means the British Army. The three leopards passant were the ancient arms of the Kings of England. In September 1808 Napoleon had addressed reinforcements going to Spain as follows: 'Soldiers! I have need of you. The hideous presence of the leopard contaminates the peninsula of Spain and Portugal. In terror he must fly before you. Let us bear our triumphant eagles to the Pillars of Hercules.'

& must be performed immediately or cannot be performed at all ?

However I am aware of the reasons why this Gentleman was stationed here. & I know that the Duke of Richmond & Lord Bathurst [1] are most desirous that he should continue in command in a station in a Warm climate. I prefer to continue to go through what I endure from this Gentleman daily, & to risk all that we do risk by having him here at the moment we may be obliged to evacuate Portugal to his removal against their or his inclination.

I request you therefore if you think it proper to mention to Lord Mulgrave what I have said upon this subject, at the same time to tell him that I beg he will keep him in his station, if he cannot be otherwise employed, in a situation satisfactory to himself & his friends.

Ever Yours most affectionately W.[2]

99

TO THE EARL OF LIVERPOOL

Viseu, 2nd April, 1810

My dear Lord,

I have received your letter of the 13th March, and I am much obliged to you for the consideration you have given to our situation in this country, and your discussion of the subject.

The great disadvantage under which I labor is, that Sir John Moore, who was here before me, gave an opinion that this country could not be defended by the army under his command : and, although it is obvious that the country was in a very different situation at that time from what it is at present, that I am in a very different situation from that in which he found himself ; and that, moreover, it can be proved, from the marches and operations of the army under Sir John Moore, and his dispatches, that little was known of Portugal at that time ; yet persons, who ought to be acquainted with these facts, entertain a prejudice against the adoption of any plans for opposing the enemy, of which Portugal is to be the theatre, or its means the instrument, and will not even consider them.

---

[1] Henry, 3rd Earl Bathurst (1762–1834), was at this time President of the Board of Trade. He will play a prominent part later in this volume on becoming Secretary for War in 1812.

[2] *Camden Miscellany*, vol. xviii.

I have as much respect as any man can have for the opinion and judgment of Sir John Moore; and I should mistrust my own, if opposed to his, in a case which he had had an opportunity of knowing and considering. But he positively knew nothing of Portugal, and could know nothing of its existing state. Besides this prejudice, founded on Sir John Moore's opinion, there is another very general prejudice against any military operation in the Peninsula.

My opinion is, that as long as we shall remain in a state of activity in Portugal, the contest must continue in Spain; that the French are most desirous that we should withdraw from the country, but know that they must employ a very large force indeed in the operations which will render it necessary for us to go away; and I doubt whether they can bring that force to bear upon Portugal without abandoning other objects, and exposing their whole fabric in Spain to great risk. If they should be able to invade it, and should not succeed in obliging us to evacuate the country, they will be in a very dangerous situation; and the longer we can oppose them, and delay their success, the more likely are they to suffer materially in Spain.

All the preparations for embarking and carrying away the army, and every thing belonging to it, are already made; and my intention is to embark it, as soon as I find that a military necessity exists for so doing. I shall delay the embarkation as long as it is in my power, and shall do every thing in my power to avert the necessity of embarking at all.

If the enemy should invade this country with a force less than that which I should think so superior to ours as to create the necessity for embarking, I shall fight a battle to save the country, for which I have made the preparations; and if the result should not be successful, of which I have no doubt, I shall still be able to retire and embark the army.

In short, the whole of my conduct shall be guided by a fair and cool view of the circumstances of our situation at the moment, and a reference to your Lordship's instructions of the 27th February. . . .

. . . I am willing to be responsible for the evacuation of Portugal, under your Lordship's instructions of the 27th February. Depend upon it, whatever people may tell you, I am not so desirous as they imagine of fighting desperate battles; if I was, I might fight one any day I please. But I have kept the army for six months in two positions, notwithstanding their own desire, and that of the allies, that I should take advantage of many opportunities which the enemy apparently offered of striking a blow against them ; in some of which the single operation would certainly have been successful. But I have looked to the great result of our maintaining our position on the Peninsula ; and have not allowed myself to be diverted from it by the wishes of the allies, and probably of some of our own army, that I should interfere more actively in some partial affairs ; or by the opinion of others, that we ought to quit the country prematurely ; and I have not harassed my troops by marches and counter-marches, in conformity to the enemy's movements. I believe that the world in the Peninsula begin to believe that I am right.

I am convinced that, if the Spaniards had followed my advice, Spain would now have been out of danger, and that the conduct which I have pursued has given us at this moment an efficient army, which is the only hope of the Peninsula. I am perfectly aware of the risks which I incur personally, whatever may be the result of the operations in Portugal. All I beg is, that if I am to be responsible, I may be left to the exercise of my own judgment ; and I ask for the fair confidence of Government upon the measures which I am to adopt.

If Government take the opinions of others upon the situation of affairs here, and entertain doubts upon the measures which I propose to adopt, then let them give me their instructions in detail, and I will carry them strictly into execution. I may venture, however, to assure you, that, with the exception of Marshal Beresford,[1] who I believe concurs entirely in all my opinions respecting the state of the contest, and the measures to be adopted here, there is no man in the army who has taken half the pains upon the subject that I have.[2]

Believe me, &c.,

Wellington

---

[1] Lieut.-General Sir William Carr Beresford (1768–1854) had served at Toulon, in Corsica, the West Indies, India, Egypt, South America. He was with Moore at Corunna. He commanded and reorganized the Portuguese Army with British officers, and held the rank of Marshal.

[2] On September 18th, 1836, Wellington sent a memorandum to Lord Mahon, afterwards the 5th Earl Stanhope, in which he wrote : 'It is quite certain that my opinion alone was the cause of the continuance of the war in the Peninsula. My letters show that I encouraged, nay forced, the Government to persevere in it. The success of the operations of the army supported them in power. But it is not true that they did not, in every way in their power, as individuals, as Ministers, and as a Government, support me.'

100

TO THE HON. WILLIAM WELLESLEY-POLE

Viseu.
April 6th, 1810

My Dear William,
I have received your letter of the 9th. of March.

I doubt whether any offer has yet been made of the nature of that which you tell me was to be made to the Admiral [Berkeley]; as I have a letter from him of a very late date in which he does not mention it, & talks of our operations &c.

However I don't much care whether he goes or not, & I hope that Govt. understand me clearly; that I wish him not to go rather than that he should be removed against his wishes.

I think I have managed him rather better lately; & have explained to him more than once that I am responsible, & not he, for all the Military concerns in this Country. But still he bores me, & the Heads of all the Departments to death; & more than one of them has expressed a wish that the Admiral was not so great a General.

Your Admiral who has nothing to do in his own Department of the Service is a terrible bore in all countries!!

The account which you give of the state of affairs in England is not satisfactory. I wish that Wellesley was *castrated*; or that he would like other people attend to his business & perform too. It is lamentable to see Talents & character & advantages such as he possesses thrown away upon whoring.[1] Then the ruin to his Private Fortune which at his time of life is irretrievable is as certain as the loss of character, & the misuse of his Talents and the dereliction of his advantages; & the Injury which the Publick & his Party must suffer from this folly. This really gives me the greatest concern; & I really think that Sydenham &

---

[1] In November 1809 Samuel Taylor Coleridge wrote to Robert Southey about the Marquess Wellesley, 'who besides the delay from ministerial intrigue stayed a full month in town in consequence of a squabble about his taking out in great pomp — in a separate vessel hired for the purpose, a common whore called Sally Douglas whom he has in keeping — the King heard of it and expressed his displeasure and the Marquis took huff — at length, however, consented to take her more *clandestinely*, she went however and with a grand establishment, and is now with him in Spain — to the edification and that — O I am sick of my country. . . .' (*Unpublished Letters of Samuel Taylor Coleridge*, ed. Griggs (Constable, 1932), vol. ii, p. 24.)

Shaw [1] as they are the only persons who he allows to talk to him upon these subjects ought never to cease to represent to him the inevitable consequences of his perseverance in the system which he has adopted.

Things remain here in the same situation. I doubt whether the French are sufficiently strong to oblige us to quit the Peninsula. They are certainly confoundedly afraid of us. More so even than our Ministers are that I shall lose the Army. However I am in no scrape; [2] & if Mr. Pitt was alive, or if there was any thing like a Govt. in England, or any publick Sentiment remaining there, Bonaparte would yet repent his invasion of Spain. As it is I think they will not like to meddle with us, unless Bonaparte should come himself. At all events they will not touch us till towards the end of June, & then if we are not before destroyed for want of money which is now pinching us much, we shall be still stronger than we are now. I wish that the Govt. in England was half as stout in Heart & as strong as they ought to be for the circumstances of the moment. But it appears to me that we have lost our Spirit at the moment we most want it; & that we are thinking of our shillings & sixpences instead of opposing the Enemy as the circumstances of the World enable us to oppose him, & as we ought to oppose him.

Give my best love to Mrs. Pole & the Girls & believe me Ever Yours most affectionately W.[3]

IOI

TO BRIGADIER-GENERAL ROBERT CRAUFURD

Alverca, 23rd July, 1810

My dear General,

I received in the night your letter of the 22nd. I have been much annoyed by the foolish conversations and reports and private letters, about the 16th Light Dragoons. General Cotton

---

[1] Benjamin Sydenham and Merrick Shawe, who had been on his staff in India. Writing of the two men to the Duke of Richmond in February 1808, Sir Arthur Wellesley had said : 'They are both gentlemanlike men, well informed, and complete men of business as well as pleasant men in society, particularly Sydenham'.

[2] On April 7th he wrote to Vice-Admiral Berkeley : 'The Government are terribly afraid that I shall get them, and myself, into a scrape. But what can be expected from men who are beaten in the House of Commons three times a week ? A great deal might be done now, if there existed in England less party and more public sentiment, and if there was any Government.'

[3] *Camden Miscellany*, vol. xviii.

wrote to me shortly after the affair of the 11th,[1] to request that the conduct of that regiment might be inquired into; to which I replied, that in your report you had not made any charge against the 16th, and that it would not be just towards that regiment to make their conduct the object of inquiry, for a failure which appeared to me to have been produced by various unfortunate accidents, which could not be prevented. . . .

. . . I can only say that I have never seen an attack by our troops in which similar, if not greater, accidents and mistakes have not occurred, and in which orders have not been given, for which no authority had proceeded from the Commander, and in which there were not corresponding accidents and failures. This is to be attributed to the inexperience of our Officers, and I must add, to some good qualities in them, as well as in the troops.

All this would not much signify, if our Staff and other officers would mind their business, instead of writing news and keeping coffee houses. But as soon as an accident happens, every man who can write, and who has a friend who can read, sits down to write his account of what he does not know, and his comments on what he does not understand, and these are diligently circulated and exaggerated by the idle and malicious, of whom there are plenty in all armies. The consequence is that officers and whole regiments lose their reputation, a spirit of party, which is the bane of all armies, is engendered and fomented, a want of confidence ensues; and there is no character, however meritorious, and no action, however glorious, which can have justice done to it. I have hitherto been so fortunate as to keep down this spirit in this army, and I am determined to persevere.

In respect to the 16th Light Dragoons, they appear in this affair to have conducted themselves with the spirit and alacrity of soldiers. They failed in the intelligence, and coolness, and order, which can be acquired only by experience; but it would

---

[1] General Craufurd (1764–1812), commanding the Light Division north-west of Ciudad Rodrigo, ordered the 16th to pursue some French cavalry, which they did, taking 32 prisoners. But when the 14th Light Dragoons charged some 300 enemy infantry they failed and their colonel was killed. The 1st Hussars and 16th also had casualties in this engagement. Lieut. William Tomkinson of the 16th wrote: 'Never was a business so badly managed. In the first place, had we shown our force, their infantry would have laid down their arms; but from the hurry and confusion in which we attacked, had they surrendered, we must have ridden over them. . . . The charge was made in a scrambling manner. The French very justly made a flaming despatch. Their detachment should never have been allowed to go back to tell the story.' For General Cotton, see note to letter no. 126.

be too hard to impute to them, alone, the failure of complete success, which may be traced likewise to other accidental circumstances ; and it would be equally cruel to allow the reputation of this regiment to be whispered away by ignorance, idleness, and slander. You and I agree entirely upon the whole matter, and I have gone into this detail, just to explain to you what has passed here, and upon what principle I have acted.

Believe me, &c.,

Wellington

102

TO LIEUT.-COLONEL HENRY TORRENS [1]

Celorico, 4th Aug. 1810

My dear Torrens,

. . . I have never been able to understand the principle on which the claims of gentlemen of family, fortune, and influence in the country, to promotion in the army, founded on their military conduct, and character, and services, should be rejected, while the claims of others, not better founded on military pretensions, were invariably attended to. It would be desirable, certainly, that the only claim to promotion should be military merit ; but this is a degree of perfection to which the disposal of military patronage has never been, and cannot be, I believe, brought in any military establishment. The Commander in Chief must have friends, officers on the staff attached to him, &c., who will press him to promote their friends and relations, all doubtless very meritorious, and no man can at all times resist these applications ; but if there is to be any influence in the disposal of military patronage, in aid of military merit, can there be any in our army so legitimate as that of family connexion, fortune, and influence in the country ? I acknowledge, therefore, that I have been astonished at seeing Lloyd, with every claim that an officer can have to promotion, still a Captain ; [2] and others, connected with the officers of the staff, promoted as soon as their time of service had expired.

[1] Torrens (1779–1828), who had served in India, accompanied Sir Arthur Wellesley to Portugal in 1808 as Military Secretary. In 1809 he became Military Secretary to the Commander-in-Chief in London.

[2] Captain Thomas Lloyd, 43rd Regiment of Foot. In October 1810 he obtained the rank of major in the 94th, commanded that regiment at Salamanca and fell in the battle of the Nivelle in November 1813, as a thirty-year-old Lieut.-Colonel.

While writing upon this subject, I am also tempted to communicate to you my opinion upon another branch of it, viz., the disposal of the patronage of the troops when on foreign service. In all services, excepting that of Great Britain, and in former times in the service of Great Britain, the Commander in Chief of an army employed against the enemy in the field had the power of promoting officers, at least to vacancies occasioned by the service, in the troops under his own command; and in foreign services, the principle is carried so far, as that no person can venture to recommend an officer for promotion belonging to an army employed against the enemy in the field, excepting the commander of that army.

It was pretty nearly the case formerly in our own service; and I believe the greater number of the General officers of the higher ranks of the present day were made lieutenant colonels by Sir W. Howe, Sir H. Clinton, Lord Cornwallis, Gen. Burgoyne, Lord Dorchester,[1] &c. But how is it now? The form remains still in some degree the same; that is to say, my secretary keeps the register of the applications, memorials, and regimental recommendations, a trouble which, by the bye, might as well be saved; but the substance is entirely altered, and I, who command the largest British army that has been employed against the enemy for many years, and who have upon my hands certainly the most extensive and difficult concern that was ever imposed upon any British officer, have not the power of making even a corporal!!! It is impossible that this system can last. It will do very well for trifling expeditions and short services, &c.; but those who are to superintend the discipline, and to excite and regulate the exertions of the officers of the army, during a long continued service, must have the power of rewarding them by the only mode in which they can be rewarded, that is, by promotion. It is not known to the army and to strangers, and I am almost ashamed of acknowledging, the small degree (I ought to say nullity) of power of reward which belongs to my situation; and it is really extraordinary that I have got on so well hitherto without it; but the day must come when this system must be altered.

[1] General Sir William Howe, 1st Viscount Howe (1729–1814), was for a time Commander-in-Chief in the American War of Independence. So too was General Sir Henry Clinton (1738 ?–95) for three years till he quarrelled with his second-in-command, Charles, 1st Marquess Cornwallis (1738–1805). General John Burgoyne (1722–92) capitulated at Saratoga in 1777. General Sir Guy Carleton, 1st Baron Dorchester (1724–1808), was Commander-in-Chief in America, 1781–3.

I do not entertain these opinions, and communicate them to you, because there are any officers attached to me in the service for whom I desire promotion. All my aides de camp, respecting whom I do feel an interest, have been promoted in their turn in their regiments, or are to be promoted, for carrying home the accounts of victories. The only person, respecting whose promotion I ever interested myself personally, was that of Colin Campbell,[1] which the Duke of York had promised him, in consequence of his having brought home the accounts of two victories at the same time ; and the difficulty which I experienced in obtaining his promotion, notwithstanding that promise, is a strong practical proof of the effects of the system to which I have adverted. The consequence of the change of the system in respect to me would be only to give me the power of rewarding the services of those who have exerted, or should exert, themselves zealously in the service ; and thus to stimulate others to similar exertions.

Even admitting that the system of promotion by seniority, exploded in other armies, is the best for that of Great Britain, it would still be an advantage that those who become entitled to it should receive it immediately, and from the hand of the person who is obliged to expose them to danger, to enforce discipline, and to call for their exertions. I would also observe that this practice would be entirely consistent with the unvaried usage of the British Navy.

I admit that it may be urged with truth that a larger view may be taken of the interests of the public, in the mode of promoting officers of the army, than I am capable of taking ; and this view may have suggested the expediency of adopting and adhering to the mode now in use ; at the same time I must say that the public can have no greater interest than in the conduct and discipline of an army employed against the enemy in the field ; and I am thoroughly convinced, that whatever may be the result in my hands, a British army cannot be kept in the field for any length of time, unless the officers composing it have some hope that their exertions will certainly be rewarded by promotion ; and that to be abroad on service, and to do their duty with zeal and intelligence, afford prospects of promotion not afforded by the mere presence of an officer with his regiment, and his bearing the King's commission for a certain number of years.

---

[1] See note to letter no. 67. He took to England news of the battles of Roliça and Vimeiro.

I have been induced to communicate these opinions to you, from the consideration of the claims of those officers to which I have drawn your attention at the commencement [omitted] of this letter, from a strong conviction of their truth, and not, I assure you, from any interest I feel in the result. I would not give one pin to have the disposal of every commission in the army.

Believe me, &c.,

Wellington

103

GENERAL ORDER

Celorico, 10th Aug., 1810

. . . The Commander of the Forces will not make any inquiry to discover the writer of the letters which have occasioned this unnecessary alarm in a quarter in which it was most desirable it should not be created.[1] He has frequently lamented the ignorance which has appeared in the opinions communicated in letters written from the army, and the indiscretion with which those letters are published. It is impossible that many officers of the army can have a knowledge of facts to enable them to form opinions of the probable events of the campaign; but their opinions, however erroneous, must, when published, have mischievous effects.

The communication of that of which all officers have a knowledge, viz. the numbers and disposition of the different divisions of the army and of its magazines, is still more mischievous than the communication of opinions, as must be obvious to those who reflect that the army has been for months in the same position; and it is a fact come to the knowledge of the Commander of the Forces that the plans of the enemy have been founded on information of this description extracted from the English newspapers, which information must have been obtained through private letters from officers of the army.

Although the difficulties inseparable from the situation of every army engaged in operations in the field, particularly in those of a defensive nature, are much aggravated by communica-

[1] Wellington published to the army the extract of a letter conveying enclosures from the vice-consul in Oporto and from British officers of rank, exciting alarm in that city.

tions of this description, the Commander of the Forces only requests that the officers will, for the sake of their own reputations, avoid giving opinions upon which they cannot have a knowledge to enable them to form any; and that if they choose to communicate facts to their correspondents, regarding the positions of the army, its numbers, formation of its magazines, preparations for breaking bridges, &c., they will urge their correspondents not to publish their letters in the newspapers until it shall be certain that the publication of the intelligence will not be injurious to the army or to the public service.[1]

Wellington

104

TO DON JOSE PAES [2]

Alverca, 23rd August, 1810

Sir,

I have received your letter, containing a complaint against Major Marston,[3] of the QMG department, that he had ill-treated one of your servants, into which I shall make enquiry, and let you know the result.

It is impossible however for me to interfere in any manner with a Billet given by the Magistrate of Coimbra, for an officer & his family to be quartered in your house.

I must at the same time inform you that I am not a little surprized that a person of your rank & station & quality in the

---

[1] On the same day Wellington wrote to General Graham in Cadiz : 'I was astonished to see some time ago in the English newspapers an accurate account of the batteries and works erecting at Cadiz and on the Isla [de Leon], with the number of guns and of what calibre each was to contain, and their distance from each other and from the enemy's works. This information must have been extracted from the letter of an officer. If officers wish to give their friends this description of information they should request them not to publish their letters in the newspapers.'

Wellington often reverted to this subject. 'We are the most indefatigable writers of letters and of news that exist in the world, and the fashion and spirit of the times give encouragement to lies', he wrote on June 17th, 1810. And in a letter to the Earl of Liverpool dated March 16th, 1811, we find this : 'I am sure your Lordship does not expect that I, or any other officer in command of a British army, can pretend to prevent the correspondence of the officers with their friends. It could not be done if attempted, and the attempt would be considered an endeavor by an individual to deprive the British public of intelligence, of which the government and Parliament do not choose to deprive them. I have done every thing in my power by way of remonstrance, and have been very handsomely abused for it ; but I cannot think of preventing officers from writing to their friends.'

How far removed this all seems from the days of strict censorship of personal mail in modern wars !

[2] Inquisitor General of Coimbra.

[3] Molyneux Marston of the 48th (Northamptonshire) Regiment of Foot.

country should object to give accommodation in your house; & should make a complaint of this officer, that he had asked you for additional accommodation, when it appears by the letter which you enclosed & which I now return, that when you objected to give him this additional accommodation for which he had asked, he acquiesced in your objection & did not any longer require this accommodation.

The unfortunate situation in which Portugal is placed & the desire of the insatiable Enemy of Mankind to force this once happy and loyal people to submit to his Iron Yoke, to plunder them of their properties, to destroy their religion, & to deprive them of their Monarch, has rendered it necessary to collect in this country a large army in order if possible to defeat and frustrate the designs of the Enemy.

It is the duty of those whose Age, whose Sex or whose profession do not permit them to take an active part in the defence of their country, to assist those employed in its defence with provisions, lodgings for officers & troops, means of transport, &c., & at all events not to oppose themselves to the granting of this description of assistance. These duties are more peculiarly incumbent upon the rich & high in station, who would be the first victims of & greatest sufferers from the enemy's success; unless indeed they should be of the number of those traitors who are aiding to introduce the common enemy into the country to destroy its happiness & independence.

Under these circumstances, I am not a little astonished to receive these frivolous & manifestly unfounded complaints [1] from you; & that you should be the person to set the example of objecting to give quarters to an officer because he is married & has children.

It is not very agreeable to any body to have strangers quartered in his house; nor is it very agreeable to us strangers, who have good houses in our own country, to be obliged to seek for quarters here. We are not here for our pleasure; the situation of your country renders it necessary; & you, a man of family & fortune, who have much to lose, should not be the first to complain of the inconvenience of our presence in the country.

---

[1] In a letter dated August 12th, 1811, to the British Ambassador in Lisbon, Wellington wrote of the Portuguese: 'I am slaving like a negro for them; I have saved the people in Lisbon, particularly, from the enemy, and I take nothing from them, while they continually torment me with their frivolous complaints on subjects on which they ought to have no feeling'.

I do everything in my power to alleviate the inconvenience which all must suffer. We pay extravagant prices for every thing we receive with unparalleled punctuality; & I make it a rule to enquire into & redress every injury that is really done by the troops under my command, as I shall into that to which I have above referred of which you complain in the conduct of Major Marston towards your servant.

I have the honor to be, &c.,

Wellington

105

TO LIEUT.-COLONEL HENRY TORRENS

Celorico, 29th Aug., 1810

My dear Torrens,

I have received your letter announcing the appointment of Sir William Erskine, General Lumley, and General Hay [1] to this army. The first I have generally understood to be a madman: I believe it is your own opinion that the second is not very wise: the third will, I believe, be a useful man. But I should be glad to get rid of a few of the same description with Sir William Erskine and General Lumley; and there are some in this army whom it is disreputable and quite unsafe to keep. Colonel Sanders, whose memorial I enclose, who was sent away from Sicily by Sir John Moore for incapacity, and whom I was very glad to get rid of from hence last year, has lately come out again. I have been obliged to appoint him a Colonel on the Staff because he is senior to others; and I wished to keep him away, and prevent him from destroying a good regiment by joining it; and he remains at a distance till further orders, as perpetual President of General Courts-Martial.

Then there is General Lightburne,[1] whose conduct is really scandalous. I am not able to bring him before a court-martial as I should wish, but he is a disgrace to the army which can have such a man as a Major General.

[1] Major-General Erskine (1769–1813), who had been created a baronet in 1791, commanded the Light Division at Torres Vedras in Craufurd's absence, but was normally the cavalry commander with Hill's corps. His eyesight was poor and his mind unstable. He committed suicide in Lisbon. Major-General, afterwards General Sir William, Lumley (1769–1850) had served in Ireland, Egypt, Cape Colony and South America before coming to the Peninsula. From 1819 to 1825 he was Governor of Bermuda. Major-General Andrew Hay was killed outside Bayonne in 1814. Stafford Lightburne, 53rd Foot, had been a Major-General since 1808.

Really when I reflect upon the characters and attainments of some of the General Officers of this army, and consider that these are the persons on whom I am to rely to lead columns against the French Generals, and who are to carry my instructions into execution, I tremble; and, as Lord Chesterfield said of the Generals of his day, " I only hope that when the enemy reads the list of their names he trembles as I do." Sir William Erskine and General Hay will be a very nice addition to this list! However I pray God and the Horse Guards to deliver me from General Lightburne and Colonel Sanders.

Believe me, &c.,

Wellington [1]

106

TO THE HON. WILLIAM WELLESLEY-POLE

Gouveia, 5th Sept., 1810

My dear William,

. . . I have made all my dispositions for falling back, and collecting my army; and when that is done I shall act according to my own view of the circumstances of the moment. The enemy are exceedingly cautious; they risk nothing; and I think they are scarcely strong enough, even in their own opinion, for the attainment of their object. We have been now nearly in the same position since last January; and considering that almost with a touch they have overturned other powerful empires, our maintenance of this weakest country in Europe for so long is not discreditable, and I hope yet to save it.

I have, however, terrible disadvantages to contend with. The army was, and indeed is still, the worst British army that was ever sent from England. Then, between ourselves, the spirit of party and of the times prevails in some degree here as well as elsewhere. There is a despondency among some; a want of confidence in their own exertions; an extravagant notion of the power and resources of the French, and a distaste for the war in the Peninsula, which sentiments have been created and are kept up by correspondence with England, even with Ministers and those connected with them.

All this is uncomfortable. With the exception of Beresford, I have really no assistance; I am left to myself, to my own

[1] *Supplementary Despatches*, vi, 582.

exertions, to my own execution, the mode of execution, and even the superintendence of that mode : but still I don't despair. I am positively in no scrape ; and if the country can be saved, we shall save it. Government have behaved with their usual weakness and folly about reinforcements, and I shall get none of those which have been promised me, but the Duke of Brunswick's [1] infantry instead. . . .

Give my best love to Mrs. Pole and the girls, and the Duke and Duchess and all the little girls ; [2] and believe me

Ever yours most affectionately,

Wellington [3]

107

TO CHARLES STUART [4]

Gouveia, 11th September, 1810

My dear Sir,

. . . It appears that you have had a good smart contest with the Government respecting our plan of operations. They will end in forcing me to quit them, and then they will see how they will get on. They will then find that I alone keep things in their present state. Indeed, the temper of some of the officers of the British army gives me more concern than the folly of the Portuguese Government. I have always been accustomed to have the confidence and support of the officers of the armies which I have commanded ; but, for the first time, whether owing to the opposition in England, or whether the magnitude of the concern is too much for their minds and their nerves, or whether I am mistaken, and they are right, I cannot tell ; but there is a system of croaking in the army [5] which is highly injurious to the public

[1] Friederich Wilhelm, Duke of Brunswick-Oels (1771–1815), was to die at Quatre-Bras. The black-uniformed Brunswick-Oels Jäger served under Wellington from 1810 onwards.

[2] Wellesley-Pole was Chief Secretary for Ireland, where the Duke of Richmond was Lord-Lieutenant. The Duke and Duchess had seven daughters.

[3] *Supplementary Despatches*, vi, 588-9.

[4] In February 1810 Mr. Stuart (1779–1845) had succeeded Villiers as British Minister in Lisbon. From 1815 to 1830 he was Ambassador in Paris, and from 1841 to 1845 in St. Petersburg. He was created Lord Stuart de Rothesay in 1828.

[5] We find Lieut.-Colonel Frederick Ponsonby writing to his mother, Lady Bessborough, on February 21st, 1812 : 'We have our share of croakers and false prophets as well as you ; gentlemen who like their ease and comfort, and only find scarcity and a bivouacque, are apt to see things un peu en noire. They exaggerate the numbers of the French army and diminish our own, they would believe that the Emperor of China had landed 500 thousand men to assist the French, but

service, and which I must devise some means of putting an end to, or it will put an end to us. Officers have a right to form their own opinions upon events and transactions; but Officers of high rank or situation ought to keep their opinions to them-selves: if they do not approve of the system of operations of their commander, they ought to withdraw from the army. And this is the point to which I must bring some, if I should not find that their own good sense prevents them from going on as they have done lately. Believe me that if any body else, knowing what I do, had commanded the army, they would now have been at Lisbon, if not in their ships.

As for advancing into Spain the idea is ridiculous. I can only tell you that of which I am the most apprehensive, is that the enemy will raise the blockade of Cadiz.[1] Unless Heaven will perform a miracle, and give the Spaniards an army, arms, and equipments, we should be ruined by this measure, and then the cause is gone. . . .

Believe me, &c.,

Wellington

108

TO THE HON. WILLIAM WELLESLEY-POLE

Cartaxo, 8th Dec., 1810

My dear William,

I have received your letter of the 27th October, and I am glad that you approve of the battle of Busaco. I trust that you will approve equally of my subsequent proceedings. I am fully sensible of the situation of the world, and of the importance of every step which I may take. I feel that I must not lose a great battle; and I believe Masséna has very much the same feeling respecting his situation.

Including Spaniards and Portuguese, and supposing that Masséna has lost 20,000 men *hors de combat* since he entered Portugal, I have now 10,000 men more than he has; that is, I

they give no credit to a report of reinforcements landing for us. It makes one a little sick to be in a room with them; there are not however any great number of them. . . .'

Beresford was told by Wellington on September 8th: 'The croaking which already prevails in the army, and particularly about head quarters, is disgraceful to us as a nation, and does infinite mischief to the cause'.

[1] The French blockaded Cadiz from early in 1810 until August 25th, 1812.

have 60,000 men in their shoes, and he has 50,000. But this superiority of numbers is not sufficient to induce me to think it expedient to attack the French in a very strong position which they have got, which operation I should have to carry on under many disadvantages, of all of which they might and would avail themselves. It is wonderful that they have been able to remain in the country so long, and it is scarcely possible that they can remain much longer. If they go, and when they go, their losses will be very great, and mine nothing. If they stay, they must continue to lose men daily, as they do now; and I don't think that the troops engaged in the siege of Cadiz, in addition to the 9th corps, upon the frontiers of Portugal, joined to those now here, could enable them to beat me in our position between the Tagus and the sea.

Feeling, therefore, as I do, all the consequences which would ensue from the loss of a battle, and the risk which I must incur, in the existing situation of affairs, if I should fight one, I have determined to persevere in my cautious system, to operate upon the flanks and rear of the enemy with my small and light detachments, and thus force them out of Portugal by the distresses they will suffer, and do them all the mischief I can upon their retreat.

Masséna is an old fox, and is as cautious as I am: he risks nothing.[1] But it is astonishing what a superiority all our light detachments have assumed over the French.

From this statement you will see that, although I may not win a battle immediately, I shall not lose one; and you may depend upon it that we are safe, for the winter at all events.

. . . Give my best love to Mrs. Pole and the girls, and believe me

Ever yours most affectionately,

Wellington [2]

---

[1] In 1831 Wellington said: 'Soult was not the ablest general ever opposed to me; the ablest after Napoleon was, I think, Masséna'. He once told Samuel Rogers: 'When Masséna was opposed to me, and in the field, I never slept comfortably'. And to Lord de Ros he confided that Masséna 'gave me more trouble than any of them, because where I expected to find him weak, he generally contrived somehow that I should find him strong'.

[2] *Supplementary Despatches*, vii, 1-2.

109

TO JOHN WILSON CROKER

Cartaxo, December 20th, 1810

My dear Sir,

I am very much obliged to you for your notes to the 4th inst., and I am happy to learn that the King is doing so well.[1]

In regard to affairs here I must continue to do what I think will be good for the people of England under all the circumstances of the case, and not what I learn from this or from that print will please them.

The licentiousness of the press, and the presumption of the editors of the newspapers, which is one of the consequences of their licentiousness, have gone near to stultify the people of England; and it makes one sick to hear the statements of supposed facts, and the comments upon supposed transactions here, which have the effect only of keeping the minds of the people of England in a state of constant alarm and anxiety, and of expectation which must be disappointed.

In the early part of the campaign all was alarm and gloomy anxiety; the British army was doomed to destruction and I was to be well thought of if I could bring any part of it off the Peninsula without disgrace. Then came the battle of Busaco, and nothing would then suit the editors of the newspapers but that Masséna's army should be destroyed, although it was 20,000 men stronger than mine in that action; and, making a very large allowance for reinforcements to mine in the retreat, and for losses to the enemy in their advance, the numbers must have been nearly equal in the first days in October. Those who have seen or know anything of armies are aware that a combined army made up as mine is, and always has been, partly of recruits and in a great measure of soldiers in a state of convalescence, and composed of officers unaccustomed to the great operations of war, is not equal to a French army; and those who have been engaged with a French army know that it is not so very easily destroyed, even by one equal to contend with it. But nothing will suit editors (friends and foes are alike) but that the enemy

---

[1] This refers to King George III, whose health and recurring bouts of madness were for many years a source of anxiety and speculation. He became permanently deranged in 1811, and was also blind, but lived on till 1820.

should be swept from the face of the earth; and for a month they kept the people of England in trembling expectation of receiving the accounts of an action which was to relieve Europe from the yoke of the tyrant.

Then every word in a despatch is not only scrupulously weighed and canvassed, but synonymous terms are found out for, and false arguments are founded upon, expressions to which meanings are assigned which never entered into the contemplation of the writer. All this, I conclude, for the instruction of the people of England!

I really believe that, owing to the ignorance and presumption and licentiousness of the press, the most ignorant people in the world of military and political affairs (excepting the domestic politics of their own country) are the people of England; and I cannot but think that I act wisely and honestly towards them to do what I think is good for them, rather than what will please them. At the same time it is shameful to see the negligence of these same editors (who are so acute in respect to expressions and dates and reasonings in the despatches of a British officer) in respect to the lies of the ' Moniteur.' [1] In the last paper which I have received I see a letter of Masséna's, published in the ' Moniteur ' of the 23rd November, supposed to have been written on the 3rd of November, and to have been carried by General Foy.[2] A little reflection would show the editors that General Foy could not have gone the distance in the time. In fact he left Masséna on the 7th of October. But the letter which is published states that the paragraphs in the English newspapers about his distresses are falsehoods. It might have been expected that this attack upon their veracity might have attracted their attention! But what are the paragraphs alluded to, and when were they published?

They were the paragraphs published in consequence of the letters sent from here on the 13th and 19th October. Now I expect that Masséna has never seen either English or any other newspaper or letter (excepting those which I have sent him) since he entered Portugal in September; but unless he received these paragraphs by flying pigeons, and if he had had the best

---

[1] *Le Moniteur universel*, founded in 1789, was the official newspaper of the French Government.
[2] Maximilien Sébastien Foy (1775–1825), a French divisional commander in the Peninsula who later wrote an unfinished account of his campaigns, *La Guerre de la Péninsule*.

post in Europe, he could not have known on the 3rd of November at Alenquer ¹ of the paragraphs written in London in consequence of letters from Portugal of the 13th and 14th October. This despatch, therefore, of the 3rd of November is manifestly forged. But nobody in England could find it out ! !

Then the supposed statement of General Foy is as false evidently as the letter from Masséna is spurious. I don't appeal to my despatches for the truth of the fact, but to Masséna's intercepted despatches, the originals of which were sent home to Government and were published, and which contradict every word of it. But how interesting it is to the people of England and to the world to show them that the whole system in France is falsehood and fraud, and that not a word of truth is ever published in France, particularly respecting the affairs of the Peninsula ; and whatever proofs of these facts may have been drawn from these papers and from the circumstances known to the whole world, not an editor has taken the smallest notice of them. On the contrary, I understand that, when these publications reached England, notes were changed, and it was again supposed we were in a bad way. Even now it is represented, and with success, that England must pay the expense of feeding the people of Lisbon ! ! !

However grievous it is, and however injurious to the country, I cannot avoid laughing when I reflect upon all this folly ; and I don't know why I have taken the trouble of writing you so much upon it. I shall either fight a battle or not as I shall find it advantageous. The enemy have suffered enormously, and at this moment, including Spaniards, I have the inferior army by *ten thousand* men. But there is a great deal of difference (particularly in the blood to be spilt) between fighting in a position which I choose or in one in which the enemy choose to fight ! And the difference makes the question which the London editors and their readers cannot comprehend. There are, besides, some other considerations to be weighed upon which I will not trouble after having written you so long a letter about nothing, but to which it is obvious that these same wise gentlemen have never adverted.

Ever, my dear Sir,
Yours most faithfully,
Wellington

¹ Alenquer, a town some twenty miles north of Lisbon.

110

GENERAL ORDER

Cartaxo, 23rd Dec., 1810

The Commander of the Forces has frequently been obliged to request the officers of the army would not shoot the deer in the Royal or other parks without having leave to do so; but he is concerned to learn that the practice still continues in a great degree in the Duque de Lafões' park,[1] near the cantonments of the army.

The Commander of the Forces will avoid naming the regiments by the officers of which this has been done; but he requests those officers to reflect that their continuing to shoot the deer in these parks is not only a breach of military discipline, but shows an entire forgetfulness of the rights of property, which they would be obliged to respect in their own country, and which they ought to respect in this, where every individual of the British army has been so well treated.

The Commander of the Forces is not desirous of preventing the officers of the army from amusing themselves in any manner they may think proper, or which may be consistent with their duty, but he requests them to respect the parks and preserves of the Prince, and other inhabitants.

Wellington

[1] The Lafões' home, the Tapada da Torre Bela, with an extensive deerpark, lay a few miles west of Cartaxo, near Aveiras.

THE YEAR 1811

In March and early April the French retreated three hundred miles with skill and violence, covered by Marshal Ney's rearguard, which fought a series of actions with the British at Redinha beyond Pombal, at the bridge of Foz d'Aronce over the Ceira, by swollen rivers and in valleys where every town and village had been burnt by the French and where hundreds of Portuguese had died from starvation, bullets and outrage. Masséna, having reached Guarda, meant to halt and regroup his forces for a fresh advance on the capital, but Ney's blatant disobedience led to his dismissal. Meanwhile, Wellington, profiting by such dissension and by the arrival of reinforcements from Lisbon, drove the French off the heights of Guarda at the end of March, and on April 3rd, in the short but critical battle of Sabugal, spoilt Masséna's last attempt to hold a line in Portugal.

Once again the pendulum had swung, once again the scene changed to Spain. Yet so long as the French retained their grip on the vital fortress towns of Almeida, Badajoz and Ciudad Rodrigo, Wellington could not safely attack across the central plains to threaten the enemy's line of communication with France. To do so would be to leave wide open his own link with the south. When Masséna sought to relieve his garrison in Almeida, Wellington hurried north from before Badajoz and on May 5th defeated the French in a close-run struggle in the frontier village of Fuentes de Oñoro. Masséna withdrew to Salamanca again, and was superseded in the command by the thirty-six-year-old Marshal Marmont, Duke of Ragusa.

Wellington now left part of his force to guard the line of the Coa river and sent two divisions down to reinforce Beresford, who since May 4th had been besieging Badajoz without proper material or trained engineers. When Soult marched with eighteen thousand men and forty guns to relieve this town, Beresford raised the siege and took up positions to block the Frenchman's path. At Albuera on May 16th his soldiers won a desperate victory.

Several more assaults on Badajoz had failed when news came that Marmont was approaching Extremadura in order to join forces with Soult, which he did on June 15th. Wellington called off the siege and prepared to fight if attacked. However, the marshals were better commanders than colleagues and Soult soon went off to relieve Seville, while Marmont retired north of the Tagus. Wellington now decided against making another attempt to capture Badajoz. For one thing, the climate there was most unhealthy with fevers in midsummer. For another, he wished to avoid alarming Soult into abandoning once more his vain pursuit of guerrvillas among the Andalusian mountains and his equally fruitless blockade of Cadiz. Accordingly he marched his army of forty thousand to the Coa early in August and awaited a favourable opportunity of attacking Ciudad Rodrigo. He had doubts from the start as to whether he was strong enough for this enterprise, given what he called 'the facility with which the French march corps from one side of the Peninsula to the other'. In the event the arrival of some forty thousand French reinforcements enabled Marmont to move to the relief of the fortress town. The enemy approached on September 21st and three days afterwards escorted a large convoy of supplies to the garrison. Wellington had to withdraw to the Coa and the mountains of Beira from his positions near the town, but not before two sharp engagements at El Bodon and Aldea da Ponte and a further act of rash disobedience on the part of General Craufurd, whose Light Division was dangerously exposed, this time beyond the swollen Agueda.

Although the French had achieved little that year except the relief of Ciudad Rodrigo — and Wellington soon set preparations afoot for a siege early in 1812 — Napoleon would not bring himself to admit that the Allied army constituted a threat in the Peninsula. The reduction during the summer of Tarragona and Sagunto on the Mediterranean coast had suggested that organised resistance in eastern Spain would shortly be disposed of, since Valencia alone, defended by General Joachim Blake with thirty thousand Spanish troops and the British Navy, still held out. To hasten its fall the Emperor unwisely ordered Marmont to detach sixteen thousand of his troops facing Wellington. This error of judgment was typical of a Bonaparte who, though he left his Peninsular armies to look after themselves, continued from the long range of Paris to distract his jealous and bickering lieutenants with orders which too often arrived weeks out of date and bore little or no relation to the actual situation.

In fact, Napoleon was preoccupied with Russia. His alliance with the Czar had become so uneasy that when he proposed a joint effort to repress still more severely British trade, Alexander countered with the blunt suggestion that France should quit Prussia. This led Napoleon to mobilize the *Grande Armée* against Russia, to conscript another one hundred and twenty thousand men from the towns and villages of France, and to replace forty seasoned battalions in Spain with hurriedly trained recruits.

III

TO DR. ANDREW HALLIDAY [1]

Cartaxo, 15th January, 1811

Sir,

I have received your letter of the 13th instant, and I am highly flattered by your desire to write the history of the war in Portugal.

The events in this country of the three last years are fit subjects for the historian, and if well and truly related, may be deemed deserving the consideration of politicians and military men. But I am apprehensive that the time is not yet arrived in which either the facts themselves can be stated with accuracy or truth, or the motives for the different occurrences be stated.

I feel that I could not give an answer to many of the questions which it is probable you would be desirous of asking, without disclosing facts, opinions, and reasonings, which are not yet before the public, and which could not be disclosed by me without a breach of confidence. I would therefore recommend to you to postpone the execution of your design to some future period.

I have the honor to be, &c.,

Wellington

[Even as late as October 1821 we find Wellington writing to General Lord Hill : 'In respect to Mr. Southey, I have heard that he was writing a History of the War in the Peninsula, but I have never received an application from him, either directly or indirectly, for information on the subject. If I had received such an application, I would have told him what I have told others, that the subject was too serious to be trifled with ; for that if any real authenticated history of that war, by an author worthy of writing it, were given, it ought to convey to the public the real truth, and ought to show what nations really did when they put themselves in the situation the Spanish and Portuguese nations had placed themselves in ; and that I would give information and material to no author who would not undertake to write upon that principle. I think, however, that the period of the war is too near, and the character and reputation of nations as well as of individuals are too much involved in the discussion

---

[1] Halliday, who took his M.D. at Edinburgh in 1806, served with the Portuguese army in the Peninsula and with the British at Waterloo, of which campaign he later wrote an account. He was knighted in 1821, and two years afterwards became Inspector of Hospitals in the West Indies.

of these questions, for me to recommend or even encourage any author to write such a history as some, I fear, would encourage at the present moment. That is my opinion upon the subject in general, and I should have conveyed it to Mr. Southey if he or his friends had applied to me.'

Robert Southey produced a *History of the Peninsular War* between 1823 and 1832, while Sir William Napier's *History of the War in the Peninsula* appeared between 1828 and 1840.]

112

TO LIEUT.-COLONEL HENRY TORRENS

Cartaxo, 28th Jan. 1811

My dear Torrens,

. . . In respect to recruiting the army, my own opinion is that the government have never taken an enlarged view of the subject. It is expected that people will become soldiers in the line, and leave their families to starve, when, if they become soldiers in the militia, their families are provided for. This is an inconsistency that must strike the mind of even the least reflecting of mankind. What is the consequence ? That none but the worst description of men enter the regular service.

The omission to provide for the families of soldiers operates particularly upon the recruiting in Ireland. It is the custom in Ireland for the lower orders to marry when very young, and it will be found that in the Irish militia nearly every soldier is married. But when they volunteer from the militia to the line they lose the provision for their families ; the women, therefore, always object to the volunteering, and none but the worst members of society ever offer their services. This is one of the causes of the increase of desertion in the army on foreign service, and of the frequency and enormity of the crimes committed by the soldiers. Then what chance has the recruiting for the line in Ireland against the recruiting for the militia ? There is not much difference in the amount of bounty, and the family of the soldier in the militia is provided for, while that of the soldier in the line starves ! Who then but the worst member of society will become the soldier in the line ?

But it is said the state cannot afford the expense. In the first place, if the expense of double bounties is considered, the expense of bounties to deserters, and the enormous expense of bounties for substitutes, I doubt that the expense would be found to exceed that incurred at present. But why incur the expense for the families of militia men ? Why not stop that expense for all soldiers enlisted in the militia after a certain time, and incur it for the regular army ? Would not this saving go far to cover the expense to be incurred ?

But admitting the truth of the expense, I say that the country has not a choice between army and no army, between peace or war. They must have a large and efficient army, one capable of meeting the enemy abroad, or they must expect to meet him at home ; and then farewell to all considerations of measures of greater or lesser expense, and to the ease, the luxury, and happiness of England. God forbid that I should see the day on which hostile armies should contend within the United Kingdom ; but I am very certain that I shall not only see that day, but shall be a party in the contest, unless we alter our system, and the public feel in time the real nature of the contest in which we are at present engaged, and determine to meet its expense. I have gone a little beyond the question of recruiting ; but depend upon it that you will get men when you provide for the families of soldiers in the line and not in the militia, and not before. . . .

Believe me, &c.,

Wellington

I am much annoyed by the General and other officers of the army going home. They come to me to ask leave of absence, under pretence of business, which they say it is important to them to transact ; and indeed I go so far as to make them declare that it is paramount to every other consideration in life. At the same time, I know that many of them have no business, and that there is no business which cannot be, and that every business is, transacted by instruction and power of attorney. But how is leave to be refused upon such an application ?

I shall be very much obliged to you, however, if you will tell any General officer who may come out in future, to settle all his business before he comes out, for that he will get no leave to go home. The inconvenience of their going is terrible, and the detail it throws upon me greater than I can well manage ; for I am first to instruct one, then a second, and afterwards, upon his return, the first again, upon every duty. At this moment we have seven General officers gone or going home;[1] and excepting myself, there is not one in the country who came out with the army, excepting Gen. Alex. Campbell, who was all last winter in England.

113

TO LIEUT.-GENERAL HARRY CALVERT [2]

Cartaxo, 6th Feb. 1811

My dear General,

I believe that you have attended a good deal to the establishment of the Chaplains to the army, upon which I am now about to trouble you.

Notwithstanding all that has been done upon the subject, with a view to making these situations such as to induce respectable persons to accept of them, I fear that they are not yet sufficiently advantageous to insure the object. I believe the income, while they are employed abroad, to be sufficiently good, but that of retired Chaplains, after service, is not; and the period of service required of them is too long. You will observe that a man can scarcely be eligible to be an army Chaplain till he is 26 or 28, after an expensive education; and it can scarcely be said that the pay of a retired Chaplain, at 36 years of age, is what a respectable person would have acquired if he had followed any other line of the clerical profession besides the army. In my opinion, the period of service ought to be reduced from 10 to 6 years; but they ought to be years of service, without leave of absence, excepting on account of health; and the pay of the retired Chaplain ought to be augmented.

My reason for making these suggestions is, that really we do not get respectable men for the service. I have one excellent young man in this army, Mr. Briscall,[3] who is attached to head

---

[1] On March 9th Brigadier-General Robert Ballard Long wrote : 'Lord W. is exceedingly annoyed at the number of General Officers who have thought proper to go home on pleasure, and I do think we have reached a point beyond the mark of delicacy and high honor, when men of that rank persevere in such defection under a positive understanding that their requests for leave of absence had his *permission*, but *not his inclination*'. (*Peninsular Cavalry General*, p. 63.)

[2] Calvert (1763 ?–1826) was Adjutant-General of the Forces from 1799 to 1818.

[3] Rev. Samuel Briscall of Brasenose College, Oxford. In November 1820 Wellington wrote of him : 'By his admirable conduct and good sense I was enabled more than once to get the better of Methodism, which had appeared among the soldiers, and once among the officers'. And a year later he had this to say : 'He was chaplain at my headquarters from the year 1808 to the end of the year 1818, always conducted himself in the most exemplary manner, and I believe did more good and more for the cause of true religion than it ever fell to the lot of any person in his situation to do ; and he was respected by the whole army'.

quarters, who has never been one moment absent from his duty ; but I have not yet seen another who has not applied, and made a pitiable case, for leave of absence immediately after his arrival ; and, excepting Mr. Denis at Lisbon, who was absent all last year, I believe Mr. Briscall is the only Chaplain doing duty.

I am very anxious upon this subject, not only from the desire which every man must have, that so many persons as there are in this army should have the advantage of religious instruction, but from a knowledge that it is the greatest support and aid to military discipline and order.

It has besides come to my knowledge that Methodism is spreading very fast in the army. There are two, if not three, Methodist meetings in this town, of which one is in the Guards. The men meet in the evening, and sing psalms ; and I believe a serjeant (Stephens) now and then gives them a sermon. Mr. Briscall has his eye upon these transactions, and would give me notice were they growing into any thing which ought to be put a stop to ; and the respectability of his character and conduct has given him an influence over these people which will prevent them from going wrong.

These meetings likewise prevail in other parts of the army. In the 9th regt.[1] there is one, at which 2 officers attend, Lieut. —— and Dr. —— ; and the Commanding officer of the regiment has not yet been able to prevail upon them to discontinue this practice.[2] Here, and in similar circumstances, we want the assistance of a respectable clergyman. By his personal influence and advice, and by that of true religion, he would moderate the zeal and enthusiasm of these gentlemen, and would prevent their meetings from being mischievous, if he did not prevail upon them to discontinue them entirely.

This is the only mode in which, in my opinion, we can touch these meetings. The meeting of soldiers in their cantonments to sing psalms, or hear a sermon read by one of their comrades,

---

[1] The 9th (or the East Norfolk) Regiment of Foot. The Commanding Officer was Lieut.-Colonel John Cameron (see letter no. 162).

[2] In his unpublished journal for March 28th, 1811, Lieutenant Peter Le Mesurier of the 9th wrote : 'Whitley and Watson are the Officers that attempted to convert the men. Colonel Cameron told us it was quite laughable to hear the latter groaning. He tells the men and officers that he has cast the Devil from him. . . . They have attempted to make converts among the officers, but unfortunately their understandings are so confined, of the officers are so hardened, that they have not succeeded, and have drawn the contempt of all the Regiment on themselves. At the arrival of the Colonel, the Gentlemen will not be allowed to hold two situations at once — both Preachers & Officers, but the choice will be given them of resigning one or the other.'

is, in the abstract, perfectly innocent; and it is a better way of spending their time than many others to which they are addicted; but it may become otherwise: and yet, till the abuse has made some progress, the Commanding officer would have no knowledge of it, nor could he interfere. Even at last his interference must be guided by discretion, otherwise he will do more harm than good; and it can in no case be so effectual as that of a respectable clergyman.

I wish, therefore, you would turn your mind a little more to this subject, and arrange some plan by which the number of respectable and efficient clergymen with the army may be increased.[1]

Believe me, &c.,

Wellington

114

TO CHARLES ARBUTHNOT [2]

Elvas, 28 May 1811

My dear Arbuthnot,

. . . I am glad that you are pleased with the result of the campaign in Portugal, and I hope that we shall continue to get on prosperously. But people in England must not be in too great a hurry. They must give us time to do things by degrees, and I hope I shall be able to perform them without great loss; which

---

[1] In November 1811 the Duke of York set the chaplains' branch on a new footing, and assigned them the pay and allowance of a major. In a letter to Wellington, the Adjutant-General wrote: 'It is the Commander in Chief's command, that the Chaplains shall visit the sick and hospitals of their respective divisions or garrisons at least twice in each week, and diligently perform the requisite duties therein; that divine service shall be performed each Sunday: and his Royal Highness particularly enjoins that more men shall not be assembled, for that purpose, at a time, than the voice can reach — a precaution very necessary to insure the attention of the soldier; but that the Chaplain shall perform the service successively to the different corps of his division: and His Royal Highness desires that the service may close with a short practical sermon suited to the habits and understandings of soldiers. To this last part of the service the Commander in Chief attaches much importance, as being in conformity to the custom of the established church; and more than ever required at this time, which is peculiarly marked by the exertions and interference of sectaries of various pescriptions.'

[2] Arbuthnot (1767–1850), educated at Westminster and Christ Church, Oxford, took a job as précis writer in the Foreign Office in 1793, then held diplomatic posts in Stockholm, Lisbon and Constantinople before succeeding Henry Wellesley in 1809 as joint Secretary of the Treasury, an appointment he held until 1823, at which time Wellington observed: 'No individual ever rendered any Government such services as he has to this for a period of now little less than fifteen years'. On January 31st, 1814, Arbuthnot married Harriet Jane, twenty-six years younger than himself, and both became intimate friends of Wellington. Indeed, Arbuthnot spent the last part of his life at Apsley House, and died two years before his host.

after all our boasting we cannot well bear. If there is a war in the north I think we shall make Boney's situation in Spain this year not *a bed of roses*; if there is not a war in the north this year, it is impossible that his fraudulent & disgusting tyranny can be endured much longer; & if Great Britain can only hold out I think we shall yet bring the affairs of the Peninsula to a satisfactory termination. . . .

Believe me, &c.,

Wellington [1]

115

TO LIEUT.-COLONEL JAMES WILLOUGHBY GORDON [2]

Quinta de Granicha,[3] 12th June, 1811

My dear Colonel,

I have received your letter of the 17th May, and I am much obliged to you for the desire you express to render your department useful to us in this country.

The Portuguese Commissariat, and all the departments attached to that army, are in a miserably inefficient state, from two causes : the want of authority to enforce obedience to order and regulation ; the want of money to defray the necessary expenses.

The departments attached to the army are not liable to the military law ; we therefore have no power to punish those guilty of any offence ; and as for expecting punishment from complaint to the Government, or to the civil tribunals, it would be just as reasonable to expect the coming of the Messiah, or the return of King Sebastian.[4]

These unfortunate Governments in the Peninsula had been reduced to such a state of decrepitude, that I believe there was no authority existing within Spain or Portugal before the French invaded these countries. The French invasion did not improve

[1] *The Correspondence of Charles Arbuthnot.*
[2] Lieut.-Colonel, afterwards General Sir James Willoughby, Gordon (1773–1851), had been Military Secretary to the Duke of York, when Commander-in-Chief. In 1811 he was appointed Quartermaster-General in the Peninsula, to Wellington's annoyance.
[3] An estate near Badajoz.
[4] King Sebastian of Portugal (1554–78) was killed in battle against the Moors. Robert Southey relates that many Portuguese confidently expected the reappearance of this king. 'This folly gave occasion to many impositions, which served less to expose the credulity of individuals than to increase the prevalent delusion. One Sebastianist found a letter from King Sebastian in the belly of a fish, appointing him to meet him at night on a certain part of the shore.'

this state of things; and since what is called in Spain the revolution, and in Portugal the restoration, no crime that I know of has been punished in either, excepting that of being a French partizan. Those malversations in office; those neglects of duty; the disobedience of orders; the inattention to regulation, which tend to defeat all plans for military operation, and ruin a state that is involved in war, more certainly than the plots of all the French partizans, are passed unnoticed; and notwithstanding the numerous complaints which Marshal Beresford and I have made, I do not know that one individual has yet been punished, or even dismissed from his office.

The cause of this evil is the mistaken principle on which the Government have proceeded. They have imagined that the best foundation for their power was a low, vulgar popularity, of which the evidence is the shouts of the mob of Lisbon, and the regular attendance at their levées, and the bows and scrapes of people in office, who ought to have other modes of spending their time; and to obtain this bubble, the Government of Portugal, as well as the successive Governments in Spain, have neglected to perform those essential duties of all Governments, viz., to force those they are placed over to do their duty, by which, before this time, these countries would have been out of danger.

The other evil is connected very materially with the first. The Government will not regulate their finances, because it will interfere with some man's job. They will not lay on new taxes, because in all countries those who lay on taxes are not favorites with the mob. They have a general income tax called ten per cent., and in some cases twenty per cent., which they have regulated in such a manner as that no individual, I believe, has paid a hundredth part of what he ought to have paid. Then, from want of money, they can pay nobody, and of course have not even the influence which they ought to have over the subordinate departments.

The hire of mules and carts, the food for the animals and drivers, are never paid; and of course the animals die, and the people desert the service.

The Commissaries have no money to purchase any thing in the country. I will not allow the soldiers to pillage. The Government have no money to pay for the transport of provisions from the magazines on the coast to the army, and are bankrupt in credit, and are unwilling to execute their own law to force means of transport; and the result is that the troops get nothing, and every department and branch of the service is paralyzed.

The remedy which has been proposed from England has been that we should take the Commissariat upon ourselves. I have already done as much as I could in this way; that is, under an arrangement which provides for the expense being subtracted from the subsidy; I have arranged that the Commissary General shall provide for those parts of the army serving with the British divisions. I know that we cannot do more without failure.

In addition to embarrassments of all descriptions surrounding us on all sides, I have to contend with an ancient enmity between these two nations, which is more like that of cat and dog than any thing else, of which no sense of common danger, or common interest, or any thing, can get the better, even in individuals. . . .

Believe me, &c.,

Wellington

❋

[Wellington's headquarters moved on June 14th from the Quinta de Granicha to Albuera, then to Elvas, and by the 20th was installed at the Quinta de S. Joăo, where it stayed for a month. Captain William Tomkinson of the 16th Light Dragoons describes the routine of the Commander of the Forces: 'Lord Wellington rises at six every morning, and employs himself to nine (the breakfast hour) in writing. After breakfast, he sees the heads of departments, viz.: Quarter-Master and Adjutant-General, Commissary-General, Commander of artillery, and any other officers coming to him on business. This occupies until 2 or 3 p.m., and sometimes longer, when he gets on his horse and rides to near six — this, of course, is interfered with when the troops are before the enemy. At nine he retires to write again, or employs himself until twelve, when he retires for the night. His correspondence with England, and the Spanish and Portuguese Government, is very extensive.' [1]]

116

TO —— ——

Quinta de S. Joăo, 27th June, 1811

I have had the honor of receiving your Excellency's letter of the 3rd inst., and it is impossible not to feel for the unhappiness

---

[1] Tomkinson, p. 108.

of the young lady, which you have so well described; but it is not so easy as you imagine to apply the remedy.

It appears to me that I should be guilty of a breach of discretion if I were to send for the fortunate object of this young lady's affections, and to apprise him of the pressing necessity for his early return to England : the application for permission to go ought to come from himself; and, at all events, the offer ought not to be made by me, and particularly not founded on the secret of this interesting young lady.

But this fortunate Major now commands his battalion, and I am very apprehensive that he could not with propriety quit it at present, even though the life of this female should depend upon it; and, therefore, I think that he will not ask for leave.

We read, occasionally, of desperate cases of this description, but I cannot say that I have ever yet known of a young lady dying of love. They contrive, in some manner, to live, and look tolerably well, notwithstanding their despair and the continued absence of their lover; and some even have been known to recover so far as to be inclined to take another lover, if the absence of the first has lasted too long. I don't suppose that your *protégée* can ever recover so far, but I do hope that she will survive the continued necessary absence of the Major, and enjoy with him hereafter many happy days.[1]

I have, &c.,

Wellington [2]

117

TO THE HON. WILLIAM WELLESLEY-POLE

Quinta de S. João, 2nd July, 1811

My dear William,

I received by the last post your letters of the 16th and 18th June, and it appears to me that affairs in England are going on much in the manner that I have expected since the establishment of the Regency.[3] It is impossible, however, that they can last

---

[1] This officer afterwards married the young lady. He returned to the army, and was mortally wounded at the battle of Vitoria.

[2] *Supplementary Despatches*, vii, 171-2.

[3] The death, on November 2nd, 1810, of his favourite daughter Princess Amelia had brought on so severe a recurrence of King George III's madness that on December 19th a Regency Bill was introduced to Parliament and became law on February 5th, despite attacks from the Whig Opposition, whose belief that they would be asked by the Prince Regent to form a new administration was confounded by a last-minute *volte-face* on the Regent's part.

in this manner. The system will do tolerably well as long as there are hopes of the King's recovery; but as soon as there is no prospect of this event, the ministers must possess the real confidence of the Prince, and the countenance and favour of the Regent must be in reality and in appearance with them, or they must resign their situations, or no honest man can support them. . . .

I don't know what people will think of affairs here. I have 50,000 men, including every Portuguese I can get together, and artillery; and about 4000 cavalry, of which 3000 are British. The French have above 60,000 men, including 7000 cavalry, and not including artillery: but they don't like to attack us, and are now breaking up; Soult returning to Andalusia, and the other apparently across the Tagus. I am waiting to see whether I can give one of them a knock: if I can't, I must then wait till Soult will undertake something to the southward, when I shall be able to try my hand on the north of the Tagus. It won't do to keep our troops in the field in Estremadura in the months of August and September, by choice at least.

I am afraid that Blake [1] has stood still since he crossed the Guadiana at Mertola.[2] If he had moved on immediately, he would have struck a fine blow at Seville, which would have given a new course to the war.

The battle of Albuera was a strange concern. They were never determined to fight it; they did not occupy the ground as they ought; they were ready to run away at every moment from the time it commenced till the French retired; and if it had not been for me, who am now suffering from the loss and disorganization occasioned by that battle, they would have written a whining report upon it, which would have driven the people in England mad. However, I prevented that.[3]

Lord Liverpool was quite right not to move thanks for the battle at Fuentes, though it was the most difficult one I was ever concerned in, and against the greatest odds. We had very nearly

---

[1] General Joachim Blake, an Irish soldier of fortune, who became one of the leading Spanish commanders. In January 1812 he capitulated to the French at Valencia and was imprisoned in Vincennes. He died in 1827.

[2] Mértola lies just inside Portugal, some twenty miles from the mouth of the Guadiana and thirty north-west of Huelva.

[3] When, three days after the battle, Wellington reached Elvas and saw Beresford's gloomy account of the seven-hour battle, he exclaimed: 'This won't do; it will drive the people in England mad. Write me down a victory.' (Stanhope, p. 90; Ellesmere, p. 107.) Marshal Soult declared: 'They were completely beaten, the day was mine, and they did not know it and would not run'.

three to one against us engaged; above four to one of cavalry; and moreover our cavalry had not a gallop in them, while some of that of the enemy was fresh and in excellent order. If Boney had been there, we should have been beaten.

Ever yours most affectionately,

Wellington

[On August 29th Wellington entertained to dinner General Graham, who had arrived from Cadiz and his victory at Barrosa to command the 1st Division and to act as second-in-command. Major the Hon. James Hamilton Stanhope, half-brother to Lady Hester, recorded in his unpublished journal : 'Lord Wellington said at dinner that from the account of the great magazines forming on the frontier he believed Bonaparte was coming in person but added "I am damned if he will drive us out"'.

Many years later Wellington said to Samuel Rogers : 'Bonaparte, in my opinion, committed one of his greatest errors when he meddled in Spain ; for the animosity of the people was unconquerable, and it was almost impossible to get us out of that corner. I have often said it would be his ruin ; though I might not live to see it. A conqueror, like a cannon-ball, must go on. If he rebounds, his career is over. At one time I expected him there in Spain in person, and him by himself I should have regarded at least as an accession of 40,000 men.'[1] The Emperor never returned to Spain.

After dinner on that evening of August 29th, 1811, Wellington and his guests went coursing, and in conversation with Stanhope the Peer — a frequent nickname at that period — spoke of 'the enormous number of sick officers, there being 700 absent and only 1400 present. He said their constitutions must all be broken. He got warm and said "By God all my Generals and officers go home. Don't wonder at it. There is no reward in England for service. In France a man gets wealth and dignities but in England a Regiment is just as often given to the man who walks about London as the real soldier. Don't wonder at their going, but they ought to have some consideration for their country and profession. I never want to go home !'

Wellington, having left England in April 1809, did not set foot there again until June 1814.]

[1] Samuel Rogers, *Recollections*, p. 195.

118

TO THE HON. HENRY WELLESLEY [1]

Castello Branco, 2nd August, 1811

My dear Henry,

I have received your letter of the 26th July, & I now enclose the copy of my dispatch to Govt. of yesterday.

The opinion which you say prevails at Cadiz is very little promising; but I don't see in what manner you can combat it, or if you could that it is any concern of yours. Great Britain did not bring Spain into the Contest. On the contrary the war in its commencement & throughout its progress has been carried on by the Spaniards without reference to our opinions, & generally in direct contradiction to our recommendation, & then we are to be blamed & abused because contrary to our own judgements & the plain dictates of military expediency we don't choose to enter upon wild & visionary schemes which we have not the means of accomplishing.

The Spaniards forget that by the folly & treachery of their own Officers they have been brought to the state in which they now find themselves; & we don't remind them sufficiently often of these circumstances; & that the cause for which we are contending is theirs essentially whatever may be the degree of interest which we feel in it.

Who lost the battle of Ocaña [2] contrary to our advice & entreaties, and consequently Andalusia? Who gave up Badajoz treacherously when we were moving to their assistance? Are we to blame if the Spanish armies are not in such a state as that they can be opposed to the Enemy? or if the Cortes have neglected their duty, have usurped the powers of the executive Govt. & have misspent their time in fruitless Debates? Are we in fault because by the mismanagement of the American Colonies the world has been deprived of its usual supply of specie, & G Britain in particular cannot find money to carry on her own operations, or aid the allies?

Let any one Spanish transaction be examined, & the inexperience & folly of the principal people in Spain will be manifest.

[1] Since March 1810 Henry had been at Cadiz as Minister Plenipotentiary to the Spanish Regency.
[2] See note to letter no. 93.

I apprized Castaños [1] of my intention and plan for attacking Ciudad Rodrigo, & him alone; the success of which depends principally upon the length of time during which I can keep it concealed from the enemy. Some Spanish women at Portalegre were apprized of the plan by him; & it must reach the enemy ! ! ! Yet Castaños is one of the best of them. Look at Abadia's [2] conduct in respect to Gallicia. Examine any transaction in which they have been concerned, & it will be found characterized by delay, weakness, folly or treachery! And then we are to be told that our political object is to ruin Spain! . . .

Ever yours most affectionately,

Wellington

119

TO LIEUT.-COLONEL HENRY TORRENS

Freneda,[3] 6th November, 1811

My dear Torrens,

I hear that measures are in contemplation to alter the clothing, caps, &c., of the army.

There is no subject of which I understand so little; and, abstractedly speaking, I think it indifferent how a soldier is clothed, provided it is in a uniform manner; and that he is forced to keep himself clean and smart, as a soldier ought to be. But there is one thing I deprecate, and that is any imitation of the French, in any manner.

It is impossible to form an idea of the inconveniences and injury which result from having anything like them, either on horseback or on foot. Lutyens [4] and his piquet were taken in June, because the 3rd hussars had the same caps as the French *Chasseurs à Cheval* and some of their hussars; and I was near being taken on the 25th September from the same cause.

[1] Don Francisco Xavier de Castaños, Duque de Baylen (1756–1832).

[2] Francisco Xaverio Abadia (1774–1840), a Spanish general of whom Henry Wellesley had written to Wellington on April 27th : 'He appears to me to have more activity, talent and good sense than any man I have seen in Spain'.

[3] A village just inside Portugal. Headquarters were here from October 2nd till January 26th, 1812.

[4] Captain Benjamin Lutyens, 11th Light Dragoons. William Warre described the episode in a letter of June 27th, 1811 : 'Poor Lutyens while retiring from a party which had crossed the Guadiana in his rear, most unfortunately mistook a French body of Cavalry for his own reserve, and did not find out his mistake till too late. He then, however, very gallantly attempted to fight his way through them, but was at last overpowered, losing 5 or 7 killed and 20 wounded, and the remainder of 40 taken with himself and another Officer. One Officer escaped wounded.' (*Letters from the Peninsula*, p. 188.)

At a distance, or in an action, colors are nothing : the profile, and shape of the man's cap, and his general appearance, are what guide us ; and why should we make our people look like the French ? A *cocked-tailed* horse is a good mark for a dragoon, if you can get a side view of him ; but there is no such mark as the English helmet, and, as far as I can judge, it is the best cover a dragoon can have for his head.

I mention this, because in all probability you may have something to say to these alterations ; and I only beg that *we* may be as different as possible from the French in everything.

The narrow top caps of our infantry, as opposed to their broad top caps, are a great advantage to those who are to look at long lines of posts opposed to each other.

Believe me, &c.,

Wellington

120

TO LIEUT.-GENERAL LORD WILLIAM BENTINCK [1]

Freneda, 24th December, 1811

My dear Lord,

I have had the pleasure of receiving your letter of the 14th November ; and I am very much obliged to you for the detail into which you have entered respecting the affairs of which the conduct has been entrusted to you.[2]

I had heard generally of these affairs before, but I have had no opportunities of acquiring information upon them, and have turned my attention but little to them ; and if I could form an opinion upon them I should mistrust it. I have, however, long considered it probable, that even *we* should witness a general resistance throughout Europe to the fraudulent and disgusting tyranny of Buonaparte, created by the example of what has

---

[1] Bentinck (1774–1839) was Governor of Madras from 1804 to 1807 in succession to Lord Clive. He commanded a brigade under Moore at Corunna. In 1827 he returned to India as Governor-General of Bengal, and six years later became the first Governor-General of India.

[2] Bentinck was appointed Commander-in-Chief of the British forces in Sicily, the only piece of Italy not under French control. He forced King Ferdinand IV to accept an English-style constitution. On October 19th, 1837, Wellington talked to the Earl Stanhope about the letters he wrote to Baron Constant and Lord William Bentinck against stirring up revolutionary wars. ' "I should wish nothing better than to have those letters inscribed upon my tomb." He inveighed most strongly against the iniquity of rousing a nation to rebellion merely for the advantage of another nation, and without telling them fairly what they are to expect on their own account.'

passed in Spain and Portugal; and that *we* should be actors and advisers in these scenes; and I have reflected frequently upon the measures which should be pursued to give a chance of success.

Those who embark in projects of this description should be made to understand, or to act as if they understood, that having once drawn the sword they must not return it till they shall have completely accomplished their object. They must be prepared and must be forced to make all sacrifices to the cause. Submission to military discipline and order is a matter of course; but when a nation determines to resist the authority, and to shake off the government of Buonaparte, they must be prepared and forced to sacrifice the luxuries and comforts of life, and to risk all in a contest which, it should be clearly understood before it is undertaken, has for its object to save all or nothing.

The first measure for a country to adopt is to form an army, and to raise a revenue from the people to defray the expense of the army. Above all, to form a Government of such strength as that army and people can be forced by it to perform their duty. This is the rock upon which Spain has split; and all our measures in any other country which should afford hopes of resistance to Buonaparte should be directed to avoid it. The enthusiasm of the people is very fine, and looks well in print; but I have never known it produce anything but confusion. In France, what was called enthusiasm was power and tyranny, acting through the medium of popular societies, which have ended by overturning Europe, and establishing the most powerful and dreadful tyranny that ever existed. In Spain, the enthusiasm of the people spent itself in *vivas* and vain boasting. The notion of its existence prevented even the attempt to discipline the armies; and its existence has been alleged ever since as the excuse for the rank ignorance of the Officers and the indiscipline and constant misbehaviour of the troops.

I therefore earnestly recommend you, wherever you go, to trust nothing to the enthusiasm of the people. Give them a strong and a just, and, if possible, a good, government; but, above all, a strong one, which shall enforce them to do their duty by themselves and their country; and let measures of finance to support an army go hand in hand with measures to raise it.

I am quite certain that the finances of Great Britain are more than a match for Buonaparte, and that we shall have the means of aiding any country that may be disposed to resist his tyranny. But those means are necessarily limited in every country by the difficulty of procuring specie. This necessary article can be obtained in sufficient quantities only by the contributions of the people; and although Great Britain can and ought to assist with money as well in other modes every effort of this description, the principal financial as well as military effort ought to be by the people of the resisting country. . . .

. . . I beg you to present my best compliments to Lady William,[1] and to

Believe me, &c.,

Wellington

[1] In 1803 he married Mary, second daughter of Arthur, 1st Earl of Gosford.

THE YEAR 1812

THE withdrawal of good French troops from Spain for Napoleon's Russian venture, coupled with the wide dispersion of the separate armies across the Peninsula, decided Wellington to undertake a winter siege of Ciudad Rodrigo. Reports that Wellington and his officers were enthusiastically foxhunting bluffed Marmont into the belief that the British were quietly settled in cantonments for the winter. Thus, when troops first appeared before the fortress, the French garrison commander thought it no more than a reconnaissance. Ciudad Rodrigo, high above the swiftly flowing Agueda, was invested on January 7th, and within a week all the outlying suburbs had been captured. Marmont, after the initial deception, was hurrying to the aid of his garrison, whereas Wellington was pushing on the siege with the utmost vigour and without waiting for his siege guns or for a complete opening up of the walls. By the morning of January 19th two breaches had been made, and that night two divisions made the assault, achieving success only after a most desperate struggle. Though Wellington lost nearly a thousand men during the twelve days, the French casualties were double this, and their heavy siege train fell into British hands.

While Wellington was rewarded with a British earldom, a Portuguese marquisate and a dukedom from Spain, the rueful Marmont was at a loss to explain this disaster to the distant Emperor ; and his sole military consolation lay in the fact that Wellington's triumph had not saved Valencia from capitulating.

For the British to hold Ciudad Rodrigo was not enough. They also needed the fortress of Badajoz dominating the Guadiana valley and the southern road to Spain, if they were to go against Marmont's army without exposing Portugal to an invasion by Soult. To avert the chance of this happening, Wellington arranged for General Ballesteros and his Spaniards to move on Seville. On learning that the French under Marmont were preparing to advance, he delayed until March 6th the move of his headquarters from Freneda to Elvas, and even then made pretence of hunting. As he explained to Lord Liverpool : 'I intend to go myself the last, as I know that my removal from one part of the country to the other will be the signal for the enemy that the part to which I am going is to be the scene of active operations'.

Badajoz was invested on March 16th, and by April 6th three breaches had been battered in the formidable ramparts. Then the town was stormed in one of the most costly endeavours of the whole war, and as at Ciudad Rodrigo a fiendish, drunken tumult of disorder tarnished the glory of success. To Lord Liverpool Wellington wrote on April 7th: 'The capture of Badajoz affords as strong an instance of the gallantry of our troops as has ever been displayed, but I anxiously hope that I shall never again be the instrument of putting them to such a test as that to which they were put last night'.

When Soult heard of the event he retired into Andalusia after a forward move, and Marmont retreated towards the Tormes and Salamanca. General Hill, by seizing the bridge of boats at Almaraz — the only Tagus bridge still open to the enemy below Toledo — cut the link between the two French marshals.

No sooner was the siege concluded than Wellington's engineers began to restore Badajoz to a state of defence. He had intended to thrust after Soult into Andalusia with forty thousand troops, but the failure of the Spanish authorities to keep their promises over provisioning Ciudad Rodrigo meant that if he headed for Seville with the fortress unsecured behind him he risked losing every hard-won gain. Instead, he took his army north again, across the Tagus for easier subsistence.

By mid-June, when Napoleon was already marching towards the frontier of Russia with half a million soldiers, Wellington had strengthened Ciudad Rodrigo and had decided to advance upon Salamanca and Valladolid, in the hope of getting as far as Burgos, whence he might, if successful, dominate northern Spain, threaten the French line of communication across the Pyrenees and once and for all get clear of the to and fro by the borders of Portugal and Spain. Believing that he had a better chance of success than ever before, he determined to move forward into Castille and if possible bring Marmont to a general action, while keeping the other French commanders tied down: in the east by an expeditionary force sent from Sicily; in Andalusia by Ballesteros; and in the north of Spain by the Navy who would harass the coastline. Marmont's right flank was to be attacked by a Spanish army in Galicia.

On June 13th Wellington crossed the Agueda with fifty-one thousand men, whereupon Marmont fell back beyond Salamanca, leaving three forts in the city to surrender after a stout resistance. The British, Portuguese and Spanish troops held a strong position on the ridge of San Cristóbal, north of Salamanca, but though sorely tempted to do so, Wellington did not attack his opponents. There followed some days of manœuvring at close quarters, as Marmont tried to cut Wellington off from his base. Both armies were of about equal strength at this time, and when on July 21st the French crossed the Tormes, Wellington, knowing that strong reinforcements were hurrying from Madrid to aid Marmont, decided to withdraw upon Ciudad Rodrigo and even pondered abandoning for the year all thought of an offensive, rather than risk Britain's sole effective army in a disadvantageous battle.

Marmont, however, believing that his enemies were already in retreat, made several errors of which Wellington took swift advantage, inflicting upon the French a resounding defeat by the hillocks of Los Arapiles outside Salamanca, on July 22nd. He caught the French strung out on the move, took seven thousand prisoners and caused more than twice that number of casualties. Had the French not been allowed through default to slip across the river at Alba de Tormes, the victory would have been even more decisive.

Once reassured that King Joseph had turned back towards Madrid again, Wellington advanced to Valladolid, which he entered on the 29th. After a week there he left one division behind and set out for Madrid with thirty-six thousand men. At Segovia he planned to ride in by back streets. Instead, he was waylaid at the entrance by 'a cracked trumpet, an old kettle-drum and two miserable-looking wretches dressed in scarlet robes'. Short of giving deliberate offence, Wellington could do no other than accompany the Spaniards to the market-place where, hatless and impatient, he stood while the populace acclaimed him with '*viva!*'

Still more enthusiastic and boisterous welcomes greeted his entrance to the capital on August 12th. Here he did not linger, but, leaving Hill to prevent any northward move by Soult — in fact the Duke of Dalmatia marched east to Valencia to join King Joseph, who had quitted his capital — he took half his army to Valladolid and thence set off for Burgos, eighty miles away. On September 16th he appeared before the cathedral town and fortress, the strength of which he had seriously underestimated, all the more so since he disposed of three siege guns only. Reluctant to incur the losses of Ciudad Rodrigo and Badajoz, he did not press home the attacks decisively, though in a week when, at the other end of Europe, the Russians were burning Moscow and Napoleon was starting back on the long coach drive to Paris, the British lost two thousand men in minor and vain assaults. Wellington stayed a month. By then two French armies were approaching, while Soult and King Joseph threatened Madrid and Hill's position. Accordingly, Wellington abandoned the siege on October 21st and, closely pursued by French cavalry, retreated south-west — five days to the Douro, which could not be held. On the 30th Hill, unable to keep Soult beyond the Tagus, left Madrid and, on orders from Wellington, crossed the Guadarrama mountains to rejoin the main army. This done, Wellington resumed the retreat. He paused on his favourite defence position at San Cristóbal by Salamanca, but the French did not attack, so he pulled back again, and in three columns the troops, hungry and often disorderly, tramped through mud and driving rain towards Portugal. Six thousand were lost on the road, and this number would have been far greater had it not been for Wellington's firm handling, coolness and presence of mind.

December found the army dispersed in cantonments for the winter, eager for a respite from eleven months' campaigning and a gruelling retreat. The men were in high spirits despite all they had endured, and only regretted that, faced with the prospect of months without fireplaces, they could not winter in Spain, where the villages were cleaner and better provided.

121

TO LADY SARAH NAPIER [1]

Gallegos, January 21, 1812

My dear Madam,—

I am sorry to tell you that your son George was again wounded in the right arm so badly last night, in the storm of Ciudad Rodrigo, that it was necessary to amputate it above the elbow. He, however, bore the operation remarkably well; and I have seen him this morning, quite well, free from pain and fever, and enjoying highly his success before he had received his wound. When he did receive it, he only desired that I might be informed that he had led his men to the top of the breach before he had fallen.

Having *such* sons, I am aware that you expect to hear of those misfortunes which I have more than once had to communicate to you; and notwithstanding your affection for them, you have so just a notion of the value of the distinction they are daily acquiring for themselves, by their gallantry and good conduct, that their misfortunes do not make so great an impression upon you.

Under such circumstances, I perform the task which I have taken upon myself with less reluctance, hoping at the same time that this will be the last occasion on which I shall have to address you upon such a subject, and that your brave sons will be spared to you.

Although the last was the most serious, it was not the only wound which George received during the siege of Ciudad Rodrigo: he was hit by the splinter of a shell in the shoulder on the 16th.

Ever, my dear Madam,
Yours most faithfully

Wellington

[1] Lady Sarah Lennox (1745–1826), fourth daughter of the 2nd Duke of Richmond, married as her second husband in 1781 the Hon. George Napier, and had five sons, of whom the three eldest, Charles James, George Thomas and William Francis Patrick, served in the Army with unusual distinction, all reaching the rank of at least major-general, while the third made an even more lasting reputation as historian of the Peninsular War. Wellington declared in May 1825, 'There is no family more distinguished'. Lady Sarah was blind for the last twenty years of her life.

122

GENERAL ORDER

Gallegos, 22nd Jan., 1812

The Commander of the Forces congratulates the General officers, officers, and troops engaged in the siege of Ciudad Rodrigo, upon the brilliant result of their labours and gallantry, achieved on the night of the 19th instant. He assures them all that he will not fail to report their conduct to H.R.H. the Commander in Chief, and to the Secretary of State, for the information of H.R.H. the Prince Regent, in the terms which it merits.

Wellington

❋

[Dr. James McGrigor,[1] the new Inspector of Hospitals and head of the Medical Department in the Peninsula, arrived at Headquarters at the end of January and in his *Autobiography* described his first interview with Lord Wellington, 'after dining with him on the first day of my joining. . . . His lordship dwelt on the little support he received from some of the heads of departments, whom he freely named, saying he had to do their duties as well as command the army. I replied that it would be my endeavour to prevent his having that trouble with the medical department of the army. We parted on the best terms ; and he desired me to come to him every morning at the same hour, with the other heads of departments, the adjutant-general, quartermaster-general, and commissary-general.

'On my appearing the second morning, I found in the outer apartment the commissary-general, Sir Robert Kennedy, and adjutant-general, Brigadier-General Stewart (with his book under his arm), who, coming up to me, said it was unnecessary for me to come to Lord Wellington, that I might come to his office, and he would transact my business for me with his lordship, whom it was unnecessary for me to trouble. I replied that I preferred doing business directly with Lord Wellington, and that it was by his lordship's desire I came there. At this moment the door of his little inner apartment was opened by Lord Wellington, who, nodding to me, desired me to come in. After this I daily made my appearance to take his orders, and to make my reports on the number of sick and wounded with all the details of their movements. These reports I made to his lordship ever afterwards, whether in the field or in quarters,

---

[1] Afterwards Sir James McGrigor, Bart. (1771–1858). He served as an army surgeon in Flanders, the West Indies and India, and in 1809 was Inspector-General of Hospitals at home before becoming head of Wellington's medical staff. From 1815 to 1851 McGrigor was Director-General of the Army Medical Department. In July 1814 Wellington paid him this tribute in a letter to Torrens : 'I consider him one of the most industrious, able, and successful public servants I have ever met with'.

immediately after his breakfast, which was the time he fixed for seeing the adjutant-general and quartermaster-general, the commissary-general, myself, and occasionally the paymaster-general, and the head of the intelligence department when at head quarters, my brother-in-law, Colonel Colquhoun Grant.

'. . . At first, it was my custom to wait upon Lord Wellington with a paper in my hand, on which I had entered the heads of the business about which I wished to receive his orders, or to lay before him. But I shortly discovered that he disliked my coming with a written paper; he was fidgetty, and evidently displeased when I referred to my notes. I therefore discontinued this, and came to him daily, having the heads of business arranged in my head, and discussed them after I had presented the state of the hospitals.' [1]]

123

TO THE EARL OF LIVERPOOL

Freneda, 11th Feb. 1812

My dear Lord,

. . . I would beg to suggest to your Lordship the expediency of adding to the Engineer establishment a corps of sappers and miners. It is inconceivable with what disadvantage we undertake any thing like a siege for want of assistance of this description. There is no French *corps d'armée* which has not a battalion of sappers and a company of miners. But we are obliged to depend for assistance of this description upon the regiments of the line; and although the men are brave and willing, they want the knowledge and training which are necessary. Many casualties among them consequently occur, and much valuable time is lost at the most critical period of the siege.

I shall be very much obliged to your Lordship if you will desire that the Storekeeper General may take some measures to insure the supply of articles by his department of a better description. Every thing in the way of intrenching and cutting tools supplied by his department is so bad as to be almost useless; and indeed all the stores supplied by this department are nearly of the same description.[2] It would be cheaper for the public to

[1] *Autobiography of Sir James McGrigor*, pp. 261-3.
[2] Years later Major-General Sir George Bell of the 34th Foot wrote in his *Rough Notes of an Old Soldier* : 'The great obstacle in the advance of the siege was caused by the useless and most disgraceful tools furnished by the Storekeeper-General's office in England. The contractor's profits seemed to be more attended to and respected than our chances of success in taking this fortress [Ciudad Rodrigo]; and so it has been the case, again and again, even on to the siege of Sebastopol forty-two years afterwards, to my knowledge.'

HENRY, THIRD EARL BATHURST
From the portrait by Sir Thomas Lawrence

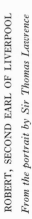

ROBERT, SECOND EARL OF LIVERPOOL
From the portrait by Sir Thomas Lawrence

pay larger prices, if that is necessary, in order to get better goods. The troops would be saved much inconvenience, and a vast expense would be saved, which is now incurred in transporting these stores to the army to replace those worn out in consequence of their being so very bad. It is really shameful that the public should be so badly served. I can't say that the intrenching and cutting tools supplied by the Ordnance are better.

Believe me, &c.,

Wellington

P.S. The cutting tools which we have found in Ciudad Rodrigo belonging to the French army are infinitely better than ours. Is it not shameful that they should have better cutlery than we have?

✻

[In a letter dated February 11th, 1812, Sir James Bland Burges, a former Under Secretary for Foreign Affairs, told his son an authentic anecdote of Lord Wellington. 'It comes from his aide-de-camp, Major Gordon, who brought over the account of the capture of Ciudad Rodrigo. Some little time ago, as a party of officers were dining with him, one of them happened to say that he had just returned from a place where a post of our soldiers was stationed, and that a considerable number of sick were without shelter, and exposed to the severity of the weather. When the party broke up, Lord Wellington ordered his horse and set off with Gordon. They rode to the post in question, about thirty miles off, and arrived there about midnight. They found a great number of sick lying in the open air.

'Lord Wellington immediately knocked up the commanding officer, and asked him why the men were left in such a condition. He said, that there was no accomodation for them in the place.

'"Be so good," said Lord Wellington, "as to show me this house." After he had walked over and inspected it, he told Gordon immediately to remove 150 of the sick into it. He then went to the next officer in rank, and so on, till he had removed the whole of the sick ; and, addressing the officers, he read them a severe lecture on the impropriety of their conduct, and told them that if they or any officer under his command should presume to consult his own convenience or luxury while a single sick man should remain unsheltered, he would make an example of them ; and that, as to themselves, they might procure accomodation as they could somewhere else, for that the sick should remain where he had placed them. He and Gordon then mounted their horses, and returned to head quarters before day, and without any one suspecting they had been absent. On the following evening, however, he told Gordon he suspected, from the

sulky manner in which his orders had been received, that they were likely
enough to be disobeyed; he was therefore determined to pay those
gentlemen another visit.

'Accordingly, they mounted their horses again and arrived past midnight at the post, where they found the sick removed into the open air,
and the officers comfortably reposing in their old quarters. However, he
soon aroused them; for he ordered the sick to be instantly brought in,
put the officers under arrest, marched them to head quarters, where they
were tried for disobedience of orders, and cashiered.' [1]]

On August 10th Wellington transferred his headquarters to Fuente
Guinaldo, a frontier village south of Fuentes de Oñoro and just inside
Spain. Here he spent the next six weeks, and the scene is typical of many
another Wellingtonian headquarters. Everything was quiet and unostenta-
tious, so much so that one would scarcely have suspected the presence
of the Commander of the Forces. There was, so Commissary August
Schaumann tells us, no throng of scented staff officers with plumed hats
and stars, no main guard, no crowd of contractors, actors, valets, cooks,
mistresses, equipages, horses, dogs, forage and baggage wagons, as might
be found at French or Russian headquarters. 'Just a few aides-de-camp,
who went about the streets alone and in their overcoats, a few guides, and
a small staff guard; that was all! About a dozen bullock carts were to be
seen in the large square of Fuente Guinaldo, which were used for bringing
up straw to headquarters; but apart from these no equipages or baggage
trains were visible.' [2]

Another young commissary, English this time rather than Hanoverian,
affords a similar picture in his memoirs. The village of Fuente Guinaldo
that summer of 1811 'presented the veriest piece of still-life, not to be
quite dead, that I ever saw. In the market place were some half-dozen
Spanish women sitting in a row, selling eggs and cabbages, and half-a-
dozen soldiers in their undress were their buyers. Now and then an
officer in a plain blue coat would cross the plaza, on foot or horseback.
And this was all which met the eye.'

Major-General William Wheatley, who had commanded a brigade at
Barrosa with distinction the previous year, wrote home to his wife Jane
on May 4th, 1812, from Fuente Guinaldo : 'Upon my arrival here an
hour since I found Lord Wellington was gone out hunting and is not
expected home till about 4 or 5 o'clock; an aide-de-camp is to let me
know when I may have my audience. . . . My cheeks would almost set
fire to this paper, they are so hot owing perhaps partly to the sun, wind
and rain (for they all come together) and a little portion of nervousness
upon a first visit to my Commander-in-Chief. I got in here at 12 o'clock
and Lord W. does not dine till *seven* p.m. while I breakfasted at the same
hour *a.m.* and so wretchedly poor is this place that I cannot procure

---

[1] *Selections from the Letters and Correspondence of Sir James Bland Burges,
Bart.*, pp. 324–5.
[2] *On the Road with Wellington*, p. 317.

anything better than a small loaf of bread made of Indian corn, yet this is a Spanish village and far superior to anything on the confines of Portugal.']

124

TO MAJOR-GENERAL GEORGE MURRAY

Fuente Guinaldo, 28th May, 1812

My dear Murray,

I received this day your letter of the 2nd, and I cannot express to you how much concerned I am that you have relinquished your situation with this army.[1] I acknowledge that when I first heard of your intention to quit us, my sentiments were not confined to concern and regret; but it is impossible to expect that men will pass their lives in these countries, who have other objects to look to, and I cannot be surprised that, after such continued absence, you should be desirous of spending some time at home.

In answer to your letter I can only express a hope that you relinquish your situation with as much regret as I feel upon losing your assistance; and I assure you that I shall always be happy to receive it again when you feel disposed to give it.

You will have appreciated the difficulty and importance of our late operations. The siege of Badajoz was a most serious undertaking, and the weather did not favor us. The troops were up to their middles in mud in the trenches, and in the midst of our difficulties the Guadiana swelled and carried away our bridge, and rendered useless for a time our flying bridge. However, we never stopped, and a fair day or two set all to rights. The assault was a terrible business, of which I foresaw the loss when I was ordering it. But we had brought matters to that state that we could do no more, and it was necessary to storm or raise the siege. I trust, however, that future armies will be equipped for sieges with the people necessary to carry them on as they ought to be; and that our engineers will learn how to put their batteries on the crest of the glacis, and to blow in the counterscarp, instead of placing them wherever the wall can be seen, leaving the poor officers and troops to get into and cross the ditch as they can.

Hill's late operation is likewise very important, as unless the

---

[1] As Quartermaster-General.

enemy have another bridge, they can no longer pass the Tagus as an army, excepting at Toledo. As you have left us I will not *tantalize* you by entering on our plans for the remainder of the campaign; I think it will be ours at all events, and I hope it may be attended by permanent important consequences.

Believe me, &c.,

Wellington

125

TO THE EARL OF LIVERPOOL

Fuente Guinaldo, 10th June, 1812

My Lord,

The outrages committed by the British soldiers belonging to this army have become so enormous, and they have produced an effect upon the minds of the people so injurious to the cause and likely to be so dangerous to the army itself, that I request your Lordship's early attention to the subject.

I am sensible that the best measures to be adopted on this subject are those of prevention, and I believe there are few officers who have paid more attention to the subject in this view of it than I have done; and I have been so far successful that few outrages are committed by the soldiers who are with their regiments, after the regiments have been a short time in this country. But in the extended system on which we are acting, small detachments of soldiers must be marched long distances through the country either as escorts or returning from being escorts to prisoners, or coming from hospitals, &c; and notwithstanding that none of these detachments are ever allowed to march excepting under the command of an officer or more, in proportion to its size, and that every precaution is taken to provide for the regularity of their subsistence, there is no instance of the march of one of these detachments that outrages of every description are not committed; and I am sorry to say, with impunity.

The foundation of every system of discipline which has for its object the prevention of crimes must be the non-commissioned officers of the army. But I am sorry to say that notwithstanding the encouragement which I have given to this class, they are still as little to be depended upon as the private soldiers themselves;

and they are just as ready to commit irregularities and outrages. I attribute this circumstance very much to the lowness of their pay in comparison with that of the soldiers.

Within my recollection, the pay of the soldiers of the army has been increased from sixpence to one shilling per diem, with other advantages ; while that of the corporals, which was eight-pence, has in the same period been raised only to one shilling and two pence ; and that of the serjeants, which was one shilling, has been raised only to one shilling and sixpence, both with the same advantages as the private soldiers.[1]

Your Lordship will observe that the old proportions have not been preserved ; and the non-commissioned officers of the army not only feel no inclination to preserve a distinction between them and the private soldiers, but they feel no desire to incur the responsibility, and take the trouble, and submit to the privations of their situation for so trifling a difference in their pay, as that of two pence in fourteen pence to corporals, and that of six pence in eighteen pence to serjeants, and they are indifferent whether they continue non-commissioned officers or not.

The remedy for this evil is to increase the pay of the corporals and serjeants, so as at least to restore the old proportions between non-commissioned officers and soldiers before the first increase of pay to the army at the commencement of the last war. This measure becomes particularly necessary in consequence of the opinions generally prevalent in respect to the punishment of soldiers ; which are certainly so far well founded that it must be admitted by all that the best mode of insuring regularity among soldiers is to prevent the commission of crimes.[2] . . .

I have thought it proper to lay these circumstances before your Lordship. I am about to move the army further forward into Spain ; and I assure your Lordship that I have not a friend in that country who has not written to me in dread of the consequences which must result in the army, and to the cause, from a continuance of these disgraceful irregularities, which I declare I have it not in my power to prevent.

I have the honor to be, &c.,

Wellington

[1] These or equivalent ranks in the Foot Guards and Cavalry received a few pence more.

[2] On November 28th, 1813, he wrote : ' I consider all punishments to be for the sake of example, and the punishment of military men in particular is expedient only in cases where the prevalence of any crime, or the evils resulting from it, are likely to be injurious to the public interest '.

126

TO LIEUT.-GENERAL SIR ROWLAND HILL

On the heights near Alba de Tormes,
23rd July, 1812

My dear Hill,

I write to let you know that we beat Marshal Marmont's army yesterday evening near Salamanca, and they are now in full retreat, and we are following them.

Our loss has not been severe, I believe, in men; Marshal Beresford, Generals Leith, Cole, and Victor Alten are wounded; General Le Marchant killed.[1] Sir Stapleton Cotton [2] was likewise wounded last night by a shot from one of our own sentries, who took him for one of the enemy.

We have taken a good many prisoners and cannon, above 3000 of the former, and I should think 20 of the latter, and I understand two eagles. All the troops behaved admirably.

Believe me, &c.,

Wellington

127

TO EARL BATHURST

Flores de Avila, 24th July, 1812

My dear Lord,

I hope that you will be pleased with our battle [Salamanca], of which the dispatch contains as accurate an account as I can give you. There was no mistake; every thing went on as it ought; and there never was an army so beaten in so short a time.[3] If we had had another hour or two of daylight, not a man would have passed the Tormes; and as it was, they would all

---

[1] Major-General James Leith (1763–1816) commanded the 5th Division in the Peninsular War; for Cole see note to letter no. 133; Alten, a Hanoverian, commanded a cavalry brigade; Major-General John Gaspard Le Marchant (1766–1812) died leading a cavalry charge: Oman describes him as 'one of the few scientific soldiers in the cavalry arm whom the British Army owned'.

[2] Major-General Cotton, afterwards Field-Marshal Lord Combermere (1773–1865), commanded a cavalry division.

[3] Wellington's brother-in-law, Major-General Edward Pakenham, commanding the 3rd Division, wrote: 'The Peer was every where in the course of the action, and even surpassed himself in the clearness and energy of his Instructions; — there never lived such a warrior, you may be assured'. Wellington was shot through his cloak and holsters during the action, but not hurt.

have been taken, if Don Carlos de España [1] had left the garrison in Alba de Tormes as I wished and desired; or, having taken it away, as I believe before he was aware of my wishes, he had informed me that it was not there. If he had, I should have marched in the night upon Alba, where I should have caught them all, instead of upon the fords of the Tormes. But this is a little misfortune, which does not diminish the honor acquired by the troops in the action, nor, I hope, the advantage to be derived from it by the country; as I don't believe there are many soldiers who were in that action who are likely to face us again till they shall be very largely reinforced indeed.

I am very anxious that a mark of His Royal Highness' favor should be conferred upon Sir S. Cotton. I believe he would be much gratified at receiving the Red Riband.[2] No cavalry could act better than ours did in the action; and I must say for Sir Stapleton, that I don't know where we should find an officer that would command our cavalry in this country half so well as he does.[3] . . .

Ever My Dear Lord Yours most faithfully,

Wellington

128

TO SIR HENRY WELLESLEY [4]

Madrid, 23rd August, 1812

My dear Henry,

. . . So much depends upon the regular supply of our armies that I hope the Spanish Government will take care to avoid making themselves so far responsible for this important object as to dismiss from the office of Intendant of Castille a man who has hitherto given the greatest satisfaction, and to place in it one entirely inefficient; one who before was a very efficient cause of our withdrawing from the Spanish territory, and whom I was obliged to turn out of my house.

I do not at all like the way in which we are going on, particularly in relation to appointments to offices and great situa-

---

[1] Don Carlos commanded a Spanish division. He became Governor of Madrid.

[2] The insignia of the Order of the Bath were sent to Cotton on August 21st and Wellington invested him at Burgos.

[3] After the great cavalry charge at Salamanca, Wellington rode up and exclaimed with unusual enthusiasm : 'By God, Cotton ! I never saw anything more beautiful in my life. The day is *yours*.'

[4] Henry had been made a Knight of the Bath in March.

tions, in which branch of the Government alone it is, I am afraid, in the power of the existing Regency to do much good. . . .

What can be done for this lost nation ? As for raising men or supplies, or taking any one measure to enable them to carry on the war, that is out of the question. Indeed, there is nobody to excite them to exertion or to take advantage of the enthusiasm of the people or of their enmity against the French. Even the guerillas are getting quietly into the large towns and amusing themselves, or collecting plunder of a better and more valuable description ; and nobody looks forward to the exertions to be made, whether to improve or to secure our advantage.

This is a faithful picture of the state of affairs ; and though I still hope to be able to maintain our position in Castille and even to improve our advantages, I shudder when I reflect upon the enormity of the task which I have undertaken, with inadequate powers myself to do any thing, and without assistance of any kind from the Spaniards or, I may say, from any individual of the Spanish nation.[1] . . .

Ever yours most affectionately,

Wellington

129

TO EARL BATHURST

Madrid, 24th August, 1812

My dear Lord,

I have been going on for more than three years upon the usual allowance of a Commander in Chief, that is ten pounds per diem, liable to various deductions, among others of income tax, reducing it to about eight guineas ; but it will be necessary that Government should now either give me an additional pay under the head of table money, or any other they please, or that they should allow me to charge some of the expenses, such as charities, &c., which I am obliged to incur, in the existing state of this country, or I shall be ruined.

It is not proper, probably, to advert to other services, but I believe there is no service in which a Commander in Chief, with such a charge as I have, is so badly paid as in the British service.

---

[1] On November 1st he was to write to Henry : 'It is extraordinary that the revolution in Spain should not have produced one man with any knowledge of the real situation of the country. It really appears as if they were all drunk, and thinking and talking of any other subject but Spain. How it is to end God knows !'

Indeed, as far as I can learn, there is no instance of an officer holding a permanent command in the British service, whose receipts have been confined to ten pounds per diem, with deductions. They all receive either the allowance of a Government, with that of a Commander in Chief, or an allowance of some other description; but I doubt that the trouble or responsibility or the expenses of any at all equal mine. However, I should not have mentioned the subject, knowing that the public expect in these days to be well served at the lowest possible rate of expense, if I did not find that I was in a situation in which I must incur expenses which I cannot defray without doing myself an injury.
Ever My Dear Lord Yours most faithfully
Wellington

130

TO LIEUT.-COLONEL HENRY TORRENS

Torquemada, 13th Sept. 1812

My dear Torrens,
I received from the Adjutant General by the last post a letter of the 1st of August, in answer to one which I wrote to him on the 15th of April last, in regard to the transmission of invalids from Portugal to England, and the settlement of their accounts.

Since I received His Royal Highness's orders, to which my letter of the 15th of April was an answer, I have had frequent complaints from the Superintendent of Hospitals of the detention in Portugal of soldiers after Medical Boards have invalided them; which detention has invariably been occasioned by the necessity of settling their accounts previous to their being sent to England under His Royal Highness's orders.

Upon receipt of the Adjutant General's letter of the 1st of August, I desired Dr. M'Grigor to put in writing what he had frequently reported to me on this subject, and I now enclose his letter.

In truth, my dear Torrens, the difficulties under which we labor are but little known in England. First: there is no soldier in the army who has at present been paid to a later date than the 24th of April, for want of money. His accounts are settled every month. But, 2ndly; if a soldier has been in hospital since the month of March last, at which time the soldiers had not been paid later than January, and the pay for March not received till

June or July, I should like to know how it is possible for any officer to come to a settlement by a correspondence with one officer, who has to settle the accounts of probably 500 men going to England at the same moment? It is quite impossible; and the consequence is that the poor men are detained here three, four, or five months, to the loss of many, till the correspondence respecting their accounts is finished, during which time many settle all accounts with this world.

It is a great error to suppose that the lower orders are always right in their complaints and the higher orders always in the wrong. My experience has taught me that nine times in ten the soldiers loudest in their complaints and claims have no ground for either the one or the other; and are generally in debt to their Captains. Those who are wounded invariably either throw away or sell their necessaries; and whether the ground is held or not by the army, they claim compensation from the public. Their claim can be settled only by a Board. No officer of a regiment has the power either to admit or to refuse it. Yet, if a soldier makes such a claim at Lisbon, the officer who is to settle the soldiers' claims before they go to England must detain at least as many as one transport will contain, till the claims of one for losses of this description shall be inquired into by post; every letter now requiring three weeks to get an answer. While this is going, many die who might be saved; and after all, a soldier's account can never be settled satisfactorily excepting with his regiment.

I have ordered General Peacocke to carry strictly into execution His Royal Highness's orders; and I shall repeat my directions to him by this post. But I shall be much obliged to you if you will lay before him the enclosed letter; and make known to him what I have above represented.

There is no point in the service to which I have at all times paid so much attention as to the settlement of the soldiers' accounts: I account early settlements to be essential to discipline; but I am quite convinced that it is impossible to attain His Royal Highness's object in this country without detaining here the men three or four months after the necessity for their return to England shall have been pronounced; and the consequences are seen in Dr. M'Grigor's letter.

Believe me, &c.,

Wellington

131

TO THE EARL OF LIVERPOOL

Revilla, 15th Sept., 1812

My dear Lord,

I received by the packet by Coruña your letter of the 28th August, in which you inclosed the copies of the correspondence which you had had with Lord Somerville,[1] respecting the purchase of the manor of Wellington,[2] and the estate of Wellington Park. I am very much obliged to you for your attention to my interests. It rarely happens that a person in your situation has leisure to attend to his own private affairs, much less to those of any other individual; and it is particularly gratifying to me to find that not only your Lordship, but Mr. Perceval had recollected me when a property was offered for sale which I am most anxious to possess.

When the Prince Regent promoted me in the peerage [3] last spring, and made an addition to my pension, I determined, for the sake of my sons, to lay out all the money I had in the purchase of land in Great Britain, and I directed that inquiries might be made for a suitable purchase for me. I likewise intend to lay out in the same manner the sum of money which His Royal Highness has declared his intention to recommend to Parliament to grant me.

The inquiries which have been made, have not hitherto produced any favorable result; and I could not make any purchase with which I should be so well satisfied as that on which you have written to me. I am ready therefore to pay the money as soon as I shall receive your answer to this letter. I am rather inclined however to wish to receive the estate and manor as a gift from the public as part of the 100,000*l.*, if your Lordship should see no objection. But if there should be any, I shall be too happy to make the purchase out of my private funds.

While writing upon this subject, it occurs to me, that as I propose to lay out all the money which the public will grant me in the purchase of land in Great Britain, it would save me some

---

[1] John Southey Somerville, 15th Baron Somerville (1765–1819), sometime President of the Board of Agriculture, invented a plough, was instrumental in introducing merino sheep into Britain and wrote several agricultural works.

[2] Wellington in Somerset, six miles south-west of Taunton.

[3] He was advanced to an earldom after Ciudad Rodrigo, and created Marquess, with a grant of £100,000, after Salamanca.

trouble, and might probably be more advantageous to the public, if the value were granted in land. However, I suggest this to your Lordship, to be attended to only in case there should be no objections.

I beg leave once more to return you my thanks for your kind attention to what would be gratifying to me.

Believe me, &c.,

Wellington

❈

[We have a picture of Lord Wellington at Burgos from the pen of Dr. James McGrigor, his Inspector of Hospitals and senior medical officer. 'In my usual morning visits to his lordship with reports of the sick and wounded of the army, when I met the heads of the departments, and likewise the chief engineer, who had nothing but an unfavourable report to give, Lord Wellington was often in bad humour, for everything went wrong with him. This, therefore, was the period of his life when fortune seemed to turn her back upon him. At length, after daily losses of numbers of men and officers, discontent was not silent even among the officers themselves ; for they saw that, without means, particularly in artillery, they were knocking their heads against stone walls without the least prospect of making any impression upon them.

'One morning I was in his lordship's small apartment, when two officers were there requesting leave to go to England. One of them, an officer in the Engineers, Captain ——, first made his request ; he had received letters informing him that his wife was dangerously ill, and that the whole of his family were sick. His lordship quickly replied, "No, no, sir ! I cannot at all spare you at this moment." Captain ——, with a mournful face and submissive bow, retired. A general officer, of a noble family and who commanded a brigade at Burgos, next advanced, saying, "My lord, I have of late been suffering much from rheumatism—" Without allowing him time to proceed further, Lord Wellington rapidly said, "and you must go to England to get cured of it. By all means. Go there immediately." The general, surprised at his lordship's tone and manner, looked abashed, while he made a profound bow ; but to prevent his saying anything in explanation, his lordship immediately addressed me, inquiring the casualties of the preceding night, and the nature of them.' [1]

There is little doubt that Wellington's handling of the Burgos siege did, at least temporarily, undermine confidence in his hitherto successful leadership, all the more so when this failure came at the end of a brilliant summer campaign. Indeed, all the year had been victorious : Ciudad Rodrigo, then Badajoz, then Salamanca, and the triumphal entry into Madrid.

[1] *The Autobiography and Services of Sir James McGrigor*, pp. 304-5.

'Our want of success at Burgos . . . I think has turned the tide of affairs here,' wrote Ensign John Mills of the Coldstream Guards, 'and Spain, I think, is lost. If ever a man ruined himself, the Marquis has done it. For the last two months he has acted like a madman. The reputation he has acquired will not bear him out. Such is the opinion here.' That was dated November 3rd. Three weeks earlier Captain George Bowles, also of the Coldstream Guards, wrote from Burgos: 'This is one of the longest jobs the noble Marquis has had in hand for some time, and, much as I *revere* him, I must say that in this case he has shown rather more of a quality nearly allied to obstinacy than is to be wished. The fact is that he was repeatedly told by those whom he consulted previous to commencing operations, his means (three eighteen-pounders, four howitzers) were totally insufficient.'

By contrast with these gloomy views we have Brigadier-General F. P. Robinson declaring on October 21st, while in front of Burgos: 'No description of mine can equal this great man. He is everything, and his Army think him so.' Six months later the same senior officer was to write: 'The former want of success [at Burgos] seems to make no impression on our people, they place such confidence in their Hero, that no one questions his conduct. He is their idol, for whom they will offer their lives as freely as they will drink his health, and they will know how readily he can correct any little error in judgement.']

132

TO LORD SOMERS [1]

Villa Toro, 11th October, 1812

My Lord,

As I have before had the honor of writing to you respecting your son, I cannot allow my dispatch to go to England with the melancholy account of the loss which you have sustained, without addressing a few lines to you.

Your son fell, as he had lived, in the zealous and gallant discharge of his duty. He had already distinguished himself in the course of the operations of the attack of the castle of Burgos to such a degree as to induce me to recommend him for promotion; and I assure your Lordship that if Providence had spared him to you, he possessed acquirements, and was endowed with qualities, to become one of the greatest ornaments of his

[1] John, 2nd Baron and (in 1821) 1st Earl Somers (1760–1841). His eldest son, Major Edward Charles Cocks, was killed in the assault on Burgos three days earlier, aged twenty-six. 'He is on every ground the greatest loss we have yet sustained', Wellington assured Beresford.

profession, and to continue an honor to his family, and an advantage to his country.

I have no hope that what I have above stated to your Lordship will at all tend to alleviate your affliction on this melancholy occasion; but I could not deny myself the satisfaction of assuring you that I was highly sensible of the merits of your son, and that I most sincerely lament his loss.

I have the honor to be, &c.,

Wellington

✿

[Major Cocks had for two years commanded a troop of the 16th Light Dragoons with unusual distinction and had thereby earned Lord Wellington's high regard. Then, at the end of May 1812, he had transferred with a majority to the 79th (Cameron Highlanders), being anxious to improve himself in other branches of a profession he adored. At three in the morning of the 8th October this youthful daring figure, kilted, sword in hand, had led the light companies of the Highland Brigade to regain the outer wall which the French had carried in a strong sortie. A ball cut the main artery above the heart.

William Tomkinson, a close friend and brother officer in the 16th Light Dragoons, wrote on the 9th : 'We buried him in the camp ground of the 79th, close to Bellima. Lord Wellington, Sir Stapleton Cotton, Generals Pack and Anson, with the whole of their staff and the officers of the 16th Light Dragoons and 79th Regiment, attended him to his grave. He is regretted by the whole army, and in those regiments in which he has been not a man can lament a brother more than they do him.'

At this funeral Wellington looked so forbidding, so gloomy, that no one ventured to speak to him, and when Colonel Benjamin D'Urban did address a few words, Wellington turned on him and, after a moment's silence, said : 'D'Urban, had Cocks outlived the campaigns, which from the way in which he exposed himself was morally impossible, he would have become one of the first Generals of England'. After this vehement outburst he relapsed into glum silence.[1]

Colonel Frederick Ponsonby later told Samuel Rogers that Wellington 'would often come into my room when he rose and converse for a few minutes. But once — it was during the siege of Burgos — he came and walked about and said nothing. At last he opened the door and said as he went out, "Cocks was killed last night".'

We have, in *Journal of an Officer*, a glimpse of Wellington during the terrible retreat. The scene is near Salamanca on November 15th. 'As we were hastening through the wood of Fragoas about 6 o'clock, Lord Wellington passed by, attended by about fifteen staff-officers and a few

---

[1] 'I think I never saw Lord W. so much affected as he was at Cocks' death', wrote Wellington's friend Thomas Sydenham, who was present.

orderly dragoons : he wore an oil-skin cloak, and looked extremely ill, which was not to be wondered at considering the anxiety of mind and fatigue of body which he was enduring. Shortly after it had become dark we came to the little village of Canero, where Lord Wellington took shelter in a cottage, and many officers of rank were obliged to lie down in their cloaks under hovels near their horses. We pitched our tent in the wood near to the village. The night was dark, cold and wet ; and I had a severe attack of rheumatism, which added much to my distress. We had but little to eat, and nothing to drink ; and it was impossible to light a fire, owing to the violence of the rain.' [1]

George F. Burroughs, Assistant Surgeon to a regiment of dragoons, also gives us a vignette of Lord Wellington near Salamanca : 'The spirit of enthusiasm was raised to the highest pitch, by the electric effect of the words, "Here he comes", which spread from mouth to mouth with the rapidity of lightning. The noble commander passed our columns in review, as usual unaccompanied with any mark of distinction or splendour ; his long horse cloak concealed his under garment ; his cocked hat soaked and disfigured with the rain.' [2]]

133

GENERAL ORDER

Aldehuela de la Boveda, 16th Nov., 1812

1. The Commander of the Forces requests the General officers commanding divisions will take measures to prevent the shameful and unmilitary practice of soldiers shooting pigs in the woods, so close to the camp and to the columns of march as that two dragoons were shot last night ; and the Commander of the Forces was induced to believe this day on the march that the flank patroles were skirmishing with the enemy.

2. He desires that notice may be given to the soldiers that he has this day ordered two men to be hanged who were caught in the fact of shooting pigs ; and he now orders that the Assistant Provosts may attend their divisions on the march, and that they will do their duty, as well in respect to this as other offences.

3. The number of soldiers straggling from their regiments, for no reason excepting to plunder, is a disgrace to the army, and affords a strong proof of the degree to which the discipline of the regiments is relaxed, and of the inattention of the commanding and other officers of regiments to their duty, and to the repeated orders of the army.

[1] Pp. 182-3.
[2] *A Narrative of the Retreat of the British Army from Burgos*, p. 69.

4. The Commander of the Forces considers the commanding officer of any regiment from which there are men absent on a march, to be responsible; and he now desires that the Hon. Lieutenant-General Cole [1] will put in arrest the commanding officer of the — regt. for having allowed soldiers to straggle from the ranks of the — regt. on the marches of yesterday and this day.

Wellington

※

[After the long retreat from Burgos to the frontiers of Portugal, Wellington installed Headquarters in the village of Freneda where he had spent the autumn of 1811 and part of the interval between the sieges of Ciudad Rodrigo and Badajoz. F. Seymour Larpent, his newly arrived Judge Advocate-General, describes Freneda as decayed and dirty, with immense piles of stones in the streets, and holes, and dung all about, and 'houses like a farm kitchen, with this difference that there are the stables underneath'. Freneda had a market-place where Lord Wellington would pace to and fro in conversation with members of his staff,[2] and a church of which the bell went on tolling for hours in a most unattractive manner.

As for the country round, it reminded Larpent of Dartmoor : 'large masses of rock, rounded by the weather, stunted trees, stone-wall enclosures, a succession of ravines, and ruined fortified villages on the hills at a distance. . . . Behind the whole the sierras of Portugal and Spain, now generally covered with snow.' In that last wintry week of November he affords us a clear vignette of Headquarters. 'I found Lord Wellington's secretaries sitting with candles at twelve o'clock in the day, in order to stop their holes and windows with curtains, and burning charcoal fires. Here are no books, no women but ladies of a certain description ; and as to living, you would be surprised what good living is here ; except at Lord Wellington's table, and about two more, and even at those, no port wine, only thin claret, and the country wines and brandy. . . .

'Want of all books and society is the worst. The little conversation here beyond the topics of the day is of a review a year old, or a pamphlet. The dress here is a cap made of velvet, cloth, and fur, with a peak over the eyes (that is a foraging cap) ; the handsomest are all of fur, dark or grey fur, the former the best, with a broad gold band and tassel on the top.

[1] Lieut.-General, afterwards General Sir Galbraith Lowry, Cole (1772–1842) commanded the 4th Division in the Peninsula. He was later Governor of Mauritius and of Cape Colony. He was a younger son of the 1st Earl of Enniskillen. At one time he had been a rival of Wellington for the hand of Kitty Pakenham.

[2] Sergeant Edward Costello of the 95th Rifles relates how a company of his regiment occasionally guarded Wellington's quarters in the house of the alcalde. 'I used to observe him walking through the market-place, leading by the hand a little Spanish girl, some five or six years old, and humming a short tune or dry whistle, and occasionally purchasing little sweets, at the child's request, from the paysannes of the stalls'.

MARSHAL SIR WILLIAM CARR BERESFORD IN 1813

DR. JAMES MCGRIGOR IN 1813

With this is worn a dress great coat, or plain, with military buttons, grey pantaloons ; this is the costume for dinners. Morning dress — overalls, boots, and white or more generally fancy waistcoats ; in winter blue and black velvet, or cloth, with fancy buttons of gold, and narrow stripes of gold as an edging.

'There are four suttlers here, who sell everything, and we are, all things considered, well supplied. We have one little Exeter-change shop, but all very dear ; pepper and mustard dear, a small sauce bottle 7*s*., tea three dollars a pound, cheese 4*s*. a pound, porter 5*s*. a bottle, gin and brandy 7*s*. 6*d*., port wine 6*s*. 6*d*., milk 1*s*. a quart, salt-butter 3*s*. a pound, sugar 1*s*. 8*d*., pork (no other meat) 1*s*. 8*d*. a pound, oil 5*s*. a quart. These are the prices here at *head-quarters*. Remember that distinction ; not the national prices.']

134

TO EDWARD COOKE [1]

Freneda, 25th Nov., 1812

My dear Cooke,

. . . You will certainly be disappointed in your expectations of the result of the campaign here ; and I am afraid others will be so likewise. Yet I acknowledge that what has at last happened ought to have been expected, and was expected and foretold by me when I thought it probable that Soult would raise the siege of Cadiz and would evacuate Andalusia.[2]

I entertained hopes that things might have taken a different turn if I could have succeeded at Burgos, and if Ballesteros [3] had come forward as he ought in the end of September. But I believe those hopes are like many others regarding the war in Spain, and ought more properly to be termed wishes. However, this cause bewitches everybody ; and nobody that I have seen can form and act upon a cool judgment in almost any case.

I ought to have succeeded at Burgos early in October, and then how should I have stood ? I might have driven the Army of Portugal, whose reinforcements were not then organised, beyond the Ebro, and I might have left there or at Burgos an army of 20,000 English and Portuguese (by the way, the worst of

[1] Cooke (1755–1820) became Under Secretary for War in 1807, and was Under Secretary for Foreign Affairs from 1812 to 1817.
[2] Soult did so in September, and marched from Granada with 45,000 to join King Joseph at Valencia. They then both moved west to threaten Madrid.
[3] He failed to keep his promise to advance against the French flank in La Mancha. Francisco Ballesteros commanded a Spanish division.

that description I have yet had, having nearly all the German troops among them), and from 12,000 to 16,000 Spaniards, against what turned out to be 45,000 French. If I could have stayed with them myself, this might have done; but there is nobody else on whom I could have imposed the charge, or who would have liked to undertake it.

I reckon that the King and Soult brought out of Valencia about 45,000 men, of which from 5000 to 7000 cavalry. Hill had on the Tagus about 30,000 of the best we have, and about 10,000 Spaniards of sorts. My plan was to bring Ballesteros upon the left flank and rear of Soult's march out of Valencia, by placing him at Alcaraz in the Sierra, where he would have been safe, at the same time that nobody could move on the great road from Valencia to attack Hill upon the Tagus.

If this game had been well played, it would have answered my purpose. Soult and the King could not have remained in Valencia, and they must have crossed the Ebro, where I should have assembled all the allies, and should have worked upon their right flank.

Had I any reason to expect that it would be well played? Certainly not. I have never known the Spaniards do anything, much less do anything well. Ballesteros has sometimes drawn the attention of a division or two for a moment, but that is all. Everything else you see and read is false and rotten. A few rascals called guerrillas attack one quarter of their numbers and sometimes succeed and sometimes not; but as for any regular operation, I have not known of such a thing, and successful, in the whole course of the war.[1]

Under all these circumstances, probably I ought not to have remained so long at Burgos, and ought to have withdrawn Hill at an earlier period from Madrid, and to have taken earlier measures to retire to the Agueda. The way in which matters stood are as follows: I was deceived respecting the numbers in

[1] Wellington told Lord de Ros years later: 'A Spaniard thinks only of gaining a Victory; but as to considering any result or for what object the effort is to be made he will not trouble himself. Thus his success loses half its value, and if he fails his defeat is a desperate one.'
On November 2nd, 1831, he assured Viscount Mahon: 'The Spaniards make excellent soldiers. What spoils them is that they have no confidence in their officers — this would ruin any soldiers; and how should the Spaniards have confidence in such officers as theirs?' And again on October 22nd, 1837: 'The men are all very fine fellows; but the officers have no knowledge or discipline. *No lo sé* is their answer on every occasion.' Wellington also told Lord de Ros that conceit, want of application and observation and a failure to learn from experience severely handicapped the Spanish officers.

my front in the North. I had no reason to believe that the enemy were so strong till I saw them. Fortunately they did not attack me : if they had, I must have been destroyed.

I raised the siege of Burgos and retired, not because there was any pressure upon me, but because I did not think Hill secure ; and I knew that if he was obliged to retire, I should be lost.

When I saw the enemy in front, it was clear that I was less able to contend with them than Hill was with those in his front, and that the danger threatened him, the apprehension of which as coming from his quarter had induced me to move from Burgos. I therefore ordered him to move ; and I fairly *bullied* the French into remaining quiet upon the Douro for seven days in order to give him time to make his march. Afterwards our situation on the Tormes depended in some degree on the weather. If the rain which fell on the 15th had fallen on the 13th, the French must have attacked me at St. Christoval,[1] or we must have remained in the cantonments on the Tormes ; and after all I don't know that we have sustained any great loss or inconvenience by remaining as long as we could in our positions at Madrid and the Tormes.

In short, I played a game which might succeed (the only one which could succeed) and pushed it to the last ; and the parts having failed, as I admit was to be expected, I have at last made a handsome retreat to the Agueda, with some labor and inconvenience, but without material loss. I believe I have done right.
                    Believe me, &c.,
                                      Wellington

❋

[Dr. McGrigor has described an interview with Wellington as soon as the Commander of the Forces reached Ciudad Rodrigo after the retreat. 'I found him in a miserable small room, leaning over the fire. He was attentively reading some printed paper. He begged me to be seated. I could see that the paper he was reading was Cobbett's Register,[2] just received with the letters from England. After perusing it for a few minutes, he threw it into the fire, and anxiously inquired what reports I had of the sick and wounded. He was in a very bad humour ; he adverted in bitter language to the disorder of the retreat, and indicated especially

---

[1] An ideal defensive position — a treeless ridge of cornfields — a few miles north-west of Salamanca.
[2] William Cobbett, author of *Rural Rides* (1830), started the *Political Register* in 1802, and published it weekly until his death in 1835. As the result of a prosecution in 1810, he spent two years in Newgate Prison.

some divisions of the army, as, also, some officers in particular. Inquiring of me, then, what accounts I could give him of the sick, he reverted anew to the disorder of the retreat, and read to me a severe order, which he said he would issue to the army. This order subsequently made a great deal of noise, not only in the army, but throughout England.' [1] This 'order', in fact a circular letter, now follows.]

135

CIRCULAR LETTER

Freneda, 28th Nov. 1812

Sir,

I have ordered the army into cantonments, in which I hope that circumstances will enable me to keep them for some time; during which the troops will receive their clothing, necessaries, &c., that are already in progress, by different lines of communication to the several divisions and brigades.

But besides these objects, I must draw your attention, in a very particular manner, to the state of discipline of the troops. The discipline of every army, after a long and active campaign, becomes in some degree relaxed, and requires the utmost attention on the part of the Generals and other Officers, to bring it back to the state in which it ought to be for service; but I am concerned to have to observe, that the army under my command has fallen off, in this respect, in the late campaign, to a greater degree than any army with which I have ever served, or of which I have ever read. Yet this army has met with no disaster; it has suffered no privations, which but trifling attention on the part of the Officers could not have prevented, and for which there existed no reason whatever in the nature of the service; nor has it suffered any hardships, excepting those resulting from the necessity of being exposed to the inclemencies of the weather, at a moment when they were most severe.

It must be obvious, however, to every Officer, that from the moment the troops commenced their retreat from the neighbourhood of Burgos on the one hand, and from Madrid on the other, the Officers lost all command over their men. Irregularities and outrages of all descriptions were committed with impunity; and losses have been sustained which ought never to have occurred.

[1] *The Autobiography and Services of Sir James McGrigor*, pp. 315-16.

Yet the necessity for retreat existing, none was ever made in which the troops made such short marches ; none on which they made such long and repeated halts ; and none on which the retreating armies were so little pressed on the rear by the enemy. We must look, therefore, for the existing evils, and for the situation in which we now find the army, to some cause besides that resulting from the operations in which it has been engaged.

I have no hesitation in attributing these evils to the habitual inattention of the Officers of the regiments to their duty, as prescribed by the standing regulations of the service, and by the orders of this army.

I am far from questioning the zeal, still less the gallantry and spirit of the Officers of the army ; and I am quite certain, that when their minds are convinced of the necessity of minute and constant attention to understand, recollect, and carry into execution the orders which have been issued for the performance of their duty, and that the strict performance of this duty is necessary to enable the army to serve the country as it ought to be served, they will give their attention to these points.

Unfortunately, the inexperience of the Officers of the army has induced many to conceive that the period during which an army is on service is one of relaxation from all rule, instead of being, as it is, the period during which, of all others, every rule for the regulation and control of the conduct of the soldier, for the inspection and care of his arms, ammunition, accoutrements, necessaries, and field equipments, and his horse and horse appointments — for the receipt, issue, and care of his provisions, and the regulation of all that belongs to his food and the forage of his horse — must be more strictly attended to by the Officer of his company or troop, if it is intended that an army, a British army in particular, shall be brought into the field of battle in a state of efficiency to meet the enemy in the day of trial.

These are the points, then, to which I most earnestly entreat you to turn your attention, and the attention of the Officers of the regiments under your command, Portuguese as well as English, during the period in which it may be in my power to leave the troops in their cantonments. The Commanding Officers of regiments must enforce the orders of the army, regarding the constant inspection and superintendence of the Officers over the conduct of the men of their companies in their cantonments; and they must endeavour to inspire the non-commissioned officers with a sense of their situation and authority; and the non-commissioned officers must be forced to do their duty, by being constantly under the view and superintendence of the Officers. By these means the frequent and discreditable recourse to the authority of the Provost, and to punishments by the sentence of Courts Martial, will be prevented; and soldiers will not dare to commit the offences and outrages, of which there are too many complaints, when they know that their Officers and their non-commissioned officers have their eyes and attention turned towards them.

The Commanding Officers of regiments must likewise enforce the orders of the army, regarding the constant, real inspection of the soldiers' arms, ammunition, accoutrements, and necessaries; in order to prevent at all times the shameful waste of ammunition, and the sale of it, and of the soldiers' necessaries. With this view both should be inspected daily.

In regard to the food of the soldiers, I have frequently observed and lamented, in the late campaign, the facility and celerity with which the French soldiers cooked, in comparison with those of our army.

The cause of this disadvantage is the same with that of every other description, the want of attention of the Officers to the orders of the army and to the conduct of their men, and their consequent want of authority over their conduct. Certain men of each company should be appointed to cut and bring in wood, others to fetch water, and others to get the meat, &c., to be cooked; and it would soon be found, if this practice were daily enforced, and a particular hour for seeing their dinners, and for the men dining, named as it ought to be, equally as for the parade, that cooking would no longer require the inconvenient length of time which it has lately been found to take; and that the soldiers would not be exposed to the privation of their food, at the moment at which the army may be engaged in operations with the enemy.

You will of course give your attention to the field exercise and discipline of the troops. It is very desirable that the soldiers should not lose the habits of marching; and the division should march ten or twelve miles twice in each week, if the weather should permit, and the roads in the neighbourhood of the cantonments of the division should be dry. But I repeat that the great object of the attention of the General and Field Officers must be, to get the Captains and Subalterns of the regiments to understand and to perform the duties required from them, as the only mode by which the discipline and efficiency of the army can be restored and maintained during the next campaign.

I have the honor to be, &c.,

Wellington

To ——— *or Officer*
commanding the ———

✳

[This well-known letter, which was not intended for circulation beyond commanding officers, aroused deep discontent and resentment among those who had borne the rigours of the retreat. Officers, particularly those in the best regiments, felt that the letter's comments were far too sweeping, however justified they might be in respect of a large section of the army. Writing in 1830, Kincaid of the Rifle Brigade gave his opinion : 'Up to this period Lord Wellington had been adored by the army, in consideration of his brilliant achievements, and for his noble and manly bearing in all things ; but, in consequence of some disgraceful irregularities which took place during the retreat, he immediately after issued an order, conveying a sweeping censure on the whole army. His general conduct was too upright for even the finger of malice itself to point at ; but as his censure, on this occasion, was not strictly confined to the guilty, it afforded a handle to disappointed persons, and excited a feeling against him, on the part of individuals, which has probably never since been obliterated. . . .

'In our brigade, I can safely say, that the order in question excited "more of sorrow than of anger" ; we thought that, had it been *particular*, it would have been just ; but, as it was *general*, that it was inconsiderate. . . .' [1]

Then we find Brigadier-General R. B. Long writing to his brother of Wellington's circular letter : 'The greater part of this is correct, but not the whole. The Troops certainly in many instances did suffer considerable privations, without a possibility of remedy on their part, and when a man has been marching three days without food, fording incessantly rivers, and exposed besides day and night to the inclemencies of very severe weather, sickness and lassitude must ensue, and if means are not provided to assist those who sink under them forward they must be lost. Had I been furnished with a proportion of spare mules for this purpose, I could have saved hundreds of men. But when I see them dead and dying in numbers on the road, I am to presume there must have been a cause for it, and that notwithstanding short marches, halts, etc., the men had to sustain and effect a trial that in many instances human nature was not

[1] *Adventures in the Rifle Brigade*, pp. 194-6.

equal to. I likewise know that there was great derangement in the commissariat for which no Regimental officer could be responsible. But it is likewise evident that subordination was, for various causes, most dreadfully relaxed, and no examples were made to put a stop to it. . . . A great deal of mischief arises also from the absurd mystery and secrecy observed upon occasions which produce considerable embarrassment to Executive officers, without a corresponding advantage to the service. To ask where you are to go ? to halt ? is high treason ; consequently your ignorance upon these subjects prevents your taking such steps as might anticipate embarrassments of various descriptions. If General Officers are not entitled to some degree of confidence, they are, and must be, ciphers in the Army. The difficulties I have experienced from the above cause, in arranging the concerns of my Brigade are not to be told, and have occasioned indeed all my embarrassments.' [1]

An even more hostile opinion is that of Alexander, Lord Saltoun of the 1st Regiment of Foot Guards, who wrote to his mother on February 8th, 1813, about Wellington's letter.

'It should never have gone beyond the orderly books of the army . . . and it is foolish for a General to abuse his army for disorders arising from the want of a proper commissariat, which Frederic the Great says it is his first duty to provide. It is no excuse for him that there is no wood in a country, but it is a very great one for a soldier pulling down a house to cook his provisions with the materials ; and in everything, when one disorder is permitted, another will soon creep in upon the heels of it. I do not mean to say that the army was not in a very bad state, but every man knows, who has ever seen an army, that such must be the case, if that army be ill supplied with bread ; and the saddle should always be put on the right horse. To say nothing of the hardships of the first part of the retreat, which were tolerably severe, the commissary might, and ought to have been at San Muñoz [2] with a supply of bread for the army ; we should then have had ample means of carrying the wounded and those men who were unable to march from fatigue, and their number would have been very much lessened by the seasonable arrival of the bread, which would have enabled many to go through the very severe march we had from that place, for an extra half pound of over-driven beef is a very poor substitute for a pound and a half of bread, especially when that is issued for three days running.' [3]]

[1] *Peninsular Cavalry General*, pp. 237-8.
[2] San Muñoz lies half-way between Salamanca and Ciudad Rodrigo.
[3] *The Frasers of Philorth*, vol. i, p. 241.

136

TO COLONEL HENRY TORRENS

Freneda, 6th Dec., 1812

My dear Torrens,

. . . I have frequently mentioned to you the great inconvenience which I felt from the constant change of officers in charge of every important department, or filling every situation of rank or responsibility with this army.[1] No man can be aware of the extent of this inconvenience who has not got this great machine to keep in order and to direct; and together with the British army, the Spanish and Portuguese concerns, the labor which these constant changes occasion is also of the most distressing description. No sooner is an arrangement made, the order given, and the whole in a train of execution, than a gentleman comes out who has probably but little knowledge of the practical part of his duty in any country, and none whatever in this most difficult of all scenes of military operation. Nobody in the British army ever reads a regulation or an order as if it were to be a guide for his conduct, or in any other manner than as an amusing novel; and the consequence is, that when complicated arrangements are to be carried into execution (and in this country the poverty of its resources renders them all complicated), every gentleman proceeds according to his fancy; and then, when it is found that the arrangement fails (as it must fail if the order is not strictly obeyed), they come upon me to set matters to rights, and thus my labor is increased ten fold.

The officers on the Staff of the British army are effectives in regiments; and considering that it is most important to every army to have good and efficient Staff officers, I do not know that the Colonels of regiments have any right to interfere to prevent the appointment of officers to the Staff from their regiments, or to occasion by their influence the relinquishment of their offices on the Staff when they think proper. If they have this power of interference it is one which may very materially affect the public

---

[1] Wellington had already written on September 13th : 'We have more General Officers to command divisions than we have divisions to be commanded. What we want in them is health, good will, and abilities to perform the duties of their situation. I am sorry to say that the perpetual changes which we are making, owing to the infirmities, or the wounds, or the disinclination of the General Officers to serve in this country, are by no means favorable to the discipline and success of the army ; and do not augment the ease of my situation.'

interests, and it ought not to be exercised lightly or with caprice. At the same time I admit the necessity of keeping regiments well officered, but I should wish to know who is more interested in keeping regiments well officered, than the officer who commands the army ?

Believe me, &c.,

Wellington

THE YEAR 1813

ALL through the spring months of 1813 the Army, steadily reinforced from England, prepared for its greatest, and indeed final, offensive across northern Spain to the Pyrenees. The troops were in excellent condition, stronger and healthier than ever before in the Peninsula ; and Wellington was able to assure Lord Bathurst : 'We have gained in strength 25,000 men since we went into cantonments in the beginning of December, and infinitely more in efficiency'. If only the horses and mules had been as sound, but here the scarcity of green forage caused Wellington delays just when time was of great importance if he was to attack before the enemy divisions trying to subdue Spanish guerrillas in the north rejoined King Joseph, who moved his headquarters from Madrid to Valladolid.

Napoleon, as usual underestimating Wellington's strength, had taken from Spain even more veterans after his return to Paris than he had taken before setting out on the Moscow campaign. Now he was in Germany, facing the Russians, who had entered Berlin, and their ally Prussia, who had re-entered the war. By the end of April Wellington had under his direct command fifty-two thousand British troops, twenty-nine thousand Portuguese and twenty thousand Spaniards. His opponents, reduced to fifty-five thousand, not counting those in the north, were strung out across a two-hundred-mile front between the Tagus and the Douro.

Wellington planned to divide his force and surprise the French by outflanking the Douro, which river formed the enemy's main defence line. While he and General Hill led thirty thousand troops against Salamanca and thereby deceived the enemy into their usual belief that Wellington's presence must denote the main thrust, Sir Thomas Graham would move with the rest of the army secretly northwards through the Tras os Montes — a region considered impassable by the French — and so over the Douro. Then, swinging in a wide hook, Graham would come behind the French defences. Once this had been achieved, Wellington would shorten his communications by using the ports of Bilbao and Santander instead of the ever-receding Lisbon and Oporto.

By the time Hill's corps crossed the Duero [1] on June 3rd, Wellington had his entire force north of that river, and for ten days the army marched north-east across Castile, a cavalry screen hustling the enemy at so respectful a distance that the Allied infantry seldom caught sight of the French falling back through Valladolid and Burgos, where they blew up the castle which had resisted siege eight months before. Wellington, averse to

---

[1] The same river is called the Douro in Portugal and the Duero in Spain.

259

losing men in a frontal attack against prepared positions among the hills south of the Ebro, sent his troops northwards on yet another flanking march, this time toiling for three days over the Cantabrian Mountains and dragging the guns along tracks which the French wrongly deemed impassable until their opponents debouched into the valley by Vitoria. Here King Joseph and Marshal Jourdan, retreating from their now useless defence line on the Ebro, but filled with undue confidence, massed fifty-seven thousand troops and 150 guns behind the river Zadora and then cast away a natural advantage by failing to destroy the bridges.

General Hill feinted in the south, Wellington attacked the enemy's centre, while Graham, with orders to cut off the French retreat along the road leading through Irún to France, went round the northern flank and attacked down the road from Bilbao. The French lost the day, and whereas King Joseph hastily abandoned his ornate travelling coach, Jourdan abandoned his marshal's baton, and both men hurried to the Pyrenees, leaving Vitoria and the battlefield to a litter and confusion seldom paralleled. Pursuit of the vanquished enemy towards Roncesvalles was delayed by slack leadership of the cavalry, by heavy rain, above all by the search for plunder which engaged the zeal of far too many of the troops.

The first assault upon San Sebastián, into which the French had thrown a resolute garrison, was a costly failure, and for want of ammunition Wellington turned the siege into a blockade. On his way back to Headquarters from a visit to his commanders there, the Marquess received urgent news. He had been worried by the fact that, in order to cover operations at San Sebastián and also at Pamplona, another town under siege, the main Allied army had been posted in the passes of the Pyrenees, where the difficulty of communicating between the several divisions was proving a serious disadvantage. He now learnt that, while French troops had advanced in strength against Hill's men holding the vital Maya Pass, Marshal Soult, who had recently been sent from Saxony to the Peninsula as Lieutenant of the Emperor and who was aiming to relieve Pamplona, had ordered thirty-five thousand troops to attack the defile of Roncesvalles, held by only six thousand British. That night the 4th Division withdrew, and so did the 3rd, thereby allowing Soult to reach effortlessly to within six miles of his goal. The Marshal crowed too soon, however. Hill, having once drawn back from the Maya Pass to conform with the retreat from Roncesvalles, was strongly established on the Bidassoa. Confident that Hill would hold his line, Wellington galloped across to the 3rd and 4th Divisions, arriving just in time to cause Soult to jump to the erroneous conclusion that reinforcements had arrived and to postpone for a day the attack he had been about to launch. On July 28th Wellington defeated the French at the battle of the Pyrenees, leaving Soult, who had captured none of the supplies he was counting on for his offensive, to retreat or let his soldiers starve. He chose to retreat.

On August 31st the second major assault upon San Sebastián was successful, although another week passed before the citadel finally surrendered. The passage of the Bidassoa on October 7th meant that British troops were on French soil. Then, on the last day of that month which had seen Napoleon's defeat at Leipzig, starving Pamplona capitulated after a stout and prolonged resistance. November 10th found Wellington's men wading the Nivelle and with irresistible dash forcing the enemy from carefully prepared positions among the crags and forests. The French abandoned St.-Jean-de-Luz and retired into an entrenched camp in front of Bayonne.

The next river to cross was the Nive, flowing from south to north before it turned towards the sea; because there was no bridge it divided the Allied front. For many days torrential rain prevented movement, but on December 9th Hill took four divisions over the river. The French reacted fiercely, attacking first the British left flank between the Nive and the coast, and then, having failed in this effort, seeking to overwhelm Hill's outnumbered force on the heights of St.-Pierre just east of the Nive. Five days of desperate fighting left the French holding Bayonne and blocking the road northwards to Bordeaux, but unable simultaneously to prevent Wellington from advancing east on Toulouse when he was ready to undertake such a campaign.

137

TO LIEUT.-GENERAL THE HON. SIR G. LOWRY COLE

Freneda,[1] 19th March, 1813

Sir,

The mother of the Lady carried off by Lt. Kelly of the 40th Regt.,[2] having complained to me of his conduct & having desired my assistance to remove her daughter from the disgraceful situation in which she is now placed, I consented to grant it, on the condition of a promise on her part that the daughter should not be ill treated & above all should not be confined in a convent.

I enclose the letter from the Lady in which she makes the engagement as above pointed out; and I beg that you will call upon Lt. Kelly to restore the young lady to her family. If he should decline to do so upon your order, I beg you to put him in close arrest, and then to take measures to remove the young lady from his power into that of her family at Sedavim; as I cannot allow any officer of this army to be guilty of such a breach of the laws of Portugal as to carry away a young lady, and retain her in

[1] Wellington arrived here on January 26th after a visit to Lisbon, and remained until May 21st.
[2] The 40th (2nd Somersetshire) Regiment.

the cantonments of the army, contrary to the wishes of her parents and relations.

I beg you to return the enclosed letter.

If you should find it necessary to place Lt. Kelly in close arrest, you will release him as soon as the young lady shall be with her relations at Sedavim; but you will inform Lt. Kelly that he has my positive orders not to cross the Coa.

I have the honor to be &c.,

Wellington

✤

[On Sunday, April 4th, Larpent recorded some Headquarters conversation. 'Lord Wellington looks forward very coolly to another winter here. He said yesterday he should have twenty-five couples of fox-hounds next season. The other day the Commissary-general told him that we had eaten nearly all the oxen in the country, that the cultivation of the lands in Portugal could not go on for want of them, and that he scarcely knew where to turn for a supply of beef, as there was this year no reserve store near Lisbon. Lord Wellington said, "Well, then, we must now set about eating all the sheep, and when they are gone I suppose we must go". And General Murray added, "Historians will say that the British army came and carried on war in Spain and Portugal until they had eaten all the beef and mutton in the country, and were then compelled to withdraw".

'Lord Wellington, yesterday, talking of his soldiers, and English notions, observed that his men were now all so round-shouldered and slouching in their gait, that he was sure, if his regiment here was in its present state to pass in review at Wimbledon Common, the whole would be sent to drill immediately, and declared quite unfit for service. Indeed, he added, that the men had now got into such a way of doing everything in the easiest manner, that he was often quite ashamed of the sentries before his own quarter.']

138

TO EARL BATHURST

Freneda, 14th April, 1813

My dear Lord,

We have had a little rain, and I propose to put the troops in motion on the 1st of May. I am much afraid, however, that our horses will suffer much in the course of the campaign from the extraordinary dryness of the winter and spring, particularly as we have so much new cavalry, all of a description of which the officers are not remarkable for giving much attention to the care of the soldiers' horses. I therefore draw your Lordship's attention thus early to this subject, and to the supply of horses for the artillery.

I acknowledge that I am one of those who are incredulous respecting the difficulties of procuring horses in England for the service of the cavalry and artillery of this army. One thousand horses for the cavalry in this winter and spring would have given the army the service of three, if not four, regiments of cavalry, from which I have been obliged, by orders from the Horse Guards, to draft their horses, very much against their inclination. We are now so deficient in horses for the artillery, that I shall, as usual, take the field with an equipment of artillery far inferior to that of the enemy, and to what I intended to take with me; and we shall have no spare horses whatever.

Surely horses of five and six years old cannot be wanting in England; and, if it is possible to collect in three months in France between 30,000 and 40,000 horses for the remount of the French cavalry and artillery, it cannot be impossible to collect in Great Britain and Ireland one twentieth of the number for the supply of this army. It is very possible that the persons usually employed to supply horses, and the ordinary means, and perhaps even the ordinary price, are not sufficient to procure a large supply at a moment; but England must be much altered if there is any deficiency of horses.

I think the question of price is deserving of some attention. The sum of 25 guineas is paid for a dragoon horse, but he is rising three years old, and is not fit for work, and much less for service, for a year and a half or two years. In estimating his cost to the public at five years old, the age at which we prefer them here, it is not unreasonable to add to the sum about half as much more; if that be true, would there be any thing unreasonably extravagant in giving £40 or 40 guineas for five and six year old horses or mares for the regiments on service, and £45 or 45 guineas for horses for the artillery abroad? If it is not thought expedient to do this, there remains then only to draft the five and six year old horses from the regiments on the home establishment, and to make a great effort to replace them in the regiments by purchases of two and three year old at the usual price. But if this is done, care must be taken that the regiments on the home service do not send us out their old and worn out horses, as they did upon a former occasion, of which there is one instance of the whole remount of one regiment dying in consequence of one day's work.

In suggesting these measures to your Lordship, I am perhaps travelling out of my line; but the success of our operations here depends so much upon the state of our cavalry and artillery, that I cannot avoid to draw your Lordship's attention to these suggestions.

Ever My Dear Lord Yours most faithfully

Wellington

[On May 17th Major Augustus Frazer, commanding the Horse Artillery in the Peninsula, was invited by Wellington to dine at Headquarters. Afterwards he wrote to his wife : 'We sat till half-past eleven, as etiquette forbids any one's moving except the Prince of Orange,[1] who rose about a quarter of an hour before the rest. The party consisted of twenty-eight. The conversation at these tables is necessarily commonplace. Much was said of the Light Division [Wellington had reviewed the Division that day], and more of Ross's Troop, which is certainly in very superior order. A Count de Chaves and his two sons (one a boy) sat opposite Lord Wellington, who sits in the middle of one side of his table. Nothing more amuses me than scenes of this sort; fancy is at work reading the characters of all, and smiling at the eager looks which betray the anxiety to catch a smile from the hero of the day. The Prince of Orange always sits on his right hand. His highness seems affable and good humoured, and is a very general favourite. The boy was soon asleep, and the father followed. I talked with Colonel Arentschild till we were both ready to follow the example, and before we broke up, heat, good cheer, and champagne had made us all drowsy and stupid. All however seemed unnecessarily in fear of the great man ; on his part, he talked with apparent frankness.'[2]

An officer of the Light Division gives us a portrait of Lord Wellington at this period of 1813.

'We know Lord Wellington at a great distance by his little flat cocked-hat (not a fraction of an inch higher than the crown,) being set on his head completely at right angles with his person, and sitting very upright in his hussar saddle, which is simply covered with a plain blue shabrack. His lordship rides, to all appearance, devoid of sash, as, since he has been made a Spanish Field-Marshal, he wears on his white waistcoat, under his blue surtout coat, the red and gold knotted sash of that rank, out of

---

[1] Colonel His Serene Highness Willem Frederick, Hereditary Prince of Orange, born in 1792, was Wellington's aide-de-camp. In 1840 he became King William II of the Netherlands.

[2] *Letters of Colonel Sir Augustus Simon Frazer*, pp. 107-8.

compliment to our allies. From the same motive, he always wears the order of the *Toison d'Or* [1] round his neck, and on his black cockade two others, very small, of the Portuguese and Spanish national colours. His lordship, within the last year, has taken to wearing a white neckerchief instead of our black regulation, and in bad weather a French private Dragoon's cloak of the same colour.

'I give these details respecting our great Captain (who may yet lead us to the gates of Paris), as I always found every minutiae of celebrated characters as much sought after by the inquisitive as the very deeds which have brought them into notice. Often he passes on in a brown study, or only returns the salutes of the officers at their posts ; but at other times he notices those he knows with a hasty "Oh ! how d'ye do", or quizzes good-humouredly some one of us with whom he is well acquainted. His staff come rattling after him, or stop and chat a few minutes with those they know, and the *cortège* is brought up by his lordship's orderly, an old Hussar of the First Germans, who has been with him during the whole of the Peninsular war, and who, when he speaks of him, uses a German expression, literally meaning good old fellow, emphatically implying in that language, attachment and regard.']

139

TO SIR HENRY WELLESLEY

Salvatierra, 22nd June, 1813

My dear Henry,

I have the pleasure to inform you that we beat the French army commanded by the King, in a general action near Vitoria yesterday, having taken from them more than 120 pieces of cannon, all their ammunition, baggage, provisions, money, &c. Our loss has not been severe. They are on their retreat to Pamplona, and we are following them.

I am much concerned to add to this account that of the severe wound and reported death of Cadogan.[2] He had distinguished himself early in the action, as you will see by the detailed report, a copy of which I will send you to-morrow. But he received a wound in the spine as I am informed, and he died last night.

[1] Wellington had received the Spanish Order of the Golden Fleece in 1812.

[2] Lieut.-Colonel the Hon. Henry Cadogan (1780–1813), seventh son of the 1st Earl Cadogan, had been aide-de-camp to Wellington in the Peninsula from 1808 to 1810, and then commanded the 71st (Highland) Regiment of Foot. He had been Henry Wellesley's brother-in-law, his sister Charlotte having married Henry in 1803 and been divorced in 1810. Cadogan's eldest sister Emily Mary had in 1802 married Rev. Gerald Wellesley.

This is Churchill's [1] account, for which I cannot vouch; but it is certain he was wounded, and as I have not heard from himself, I am afraid that the consequence is too true.

His private character and his worth as an individual were not greater than his merits as an officer, and I shall ever regret him. It is a curious instance of his attachment to his profession, and of the interest he felt in what was going on, that after he was wounded and was probably aware that he was dying, he desired to be carried and left in a situation from which he might be able to see all that passed.

The concern which I feel upon his loss has diminished exceedingly the satisfaction I should derive from our success, as it will yours. [2]

Ever yours most affectionately,

Wellington

❋

[We catch sight of Wellington in the hour of his triumph through the eyes of Captain William Stavely, a staff officer attached to the Quartermaster-General, Sir George Murray. After the battle he was ordered into Vitoria to secure quarters for Lord Wellington and the staff. 'While sitting in the evening, much tired waiting for their arrival, Lord Wellington entered the room, and in answer to some remark, as I observed that we had had a glorious day, he replied "Yes, we have got all their artillery"; and on going into an inner room where the dinner was prepared, he said, "Tell Murray I shall march the army off myself in the morning". I asked "At what hour?" "When I get up" was the short reply.' [3]]

140

TO COLONEL SIR JOHN MALCOLM

Near Pampeluna, June 26, 1813

My dear Malcolm,

I am very much obliged to you for your letter of the 22nd May, which I received by the last post, and for the sword which

[1] Captain Horace Churchill, a Guards officer, was General Hill's aide-de-camp during this campaign and at Waterloo. He became a general and was killed at the battle of Gwalior on December 27th, 1843.

[2] In a letter from Dublin dated March 1814, Maria Edgeworth wrote: 'Lady Longford has been here this morning; told us Sir Edward Pakenham was so fatigued by riding an uneasy horse at the battle of Vittoria, he was not able to join for four days. A buckle of Lord Wellington's sword-belt saved him: he wrote four times in one week to Lady Wellington, without ever mentioning his wound.'

[3] *Journal of the Society for Army Historical Research*, autumn 1935: 'One of Wellington's Staff Officers: Lieut.-General William Stavely, C.B.', by Major-General Sir Louis Jackson.

you have given me. . . . I have not much leisure to attend now to Indian concerns, although I always feel an interest about them. I have been frequently astonished at the indifference with which public men in England considered the talents of those who had served in India, possibly because I was partial to those endowed with them, and entertained a higher opinion of those talents than the Ministers. But the fact is so. We must observe, however, that to hold office in England is a favor conferred upon the individual, and is not a right, as it is in India ; and he who has the disposal of the patronage of the Crown must be induced to bestow office by motives of friendship for the individual, by a sense that he can serve his interests, or is more eminently qualified than another to serve the public. Although I had long been in habits of friendship with the public men of the day, and had some professional claims to public notice when I returned to England, I believe I should have been but little known, and should not be what I am, if I had not gone into Parliament. I would, therefore, advise you to go into Parliament if you can afford it, if you look to high public employment. I likewise recommend you not to fix yourself upon Lord Wellesley or any other great man. You are big enough, unless much altered, to walk alone ; and you will accomplish your object soonest in that way. Don't, however, be in a hurry.

You will hear of events here. I have taken more guns from these fellows in the last action than I took at Assye, without much more loss, upon about seventy thousand men engaged. The two armies were nearly equal in numbers, but they cannot stand us now at all.

Ever, my dear Malcolm, yours most sincerely,

Wellington [1]

141

TO EARL BATHURST

Caseda, June 29th 1813 [2]

My dear Lord,

It is desirable that any reinforcements of infantry which you may send to this army may come to Santander, notwithstanding

[1] *The Life and Correspondence of Major-General Sir John Malcolm, G.C.B.*, by John William Kaye, vol. ii, p. 91.

[2] On this day Larpent noted : 'Lord Wellington seemed knocked up yesterday ; he ate little or nothing, looked anxious, and slept nearly all the time of sitting after

that I am very apprehensive of the consequence of marching our vagabond soldiers through the Province of Biscay in that state of discipline in which they and their officers generally come out to us. It may be depended upon, that the people of this Province will shoot them as they would the French, if they should misbehave.

We started with the Army in the highest order; & up to the day of the Battle nothing could get on better. But that event has as usual totally annihilated all order & discipline. The soldiers of the Army have got among them about a million sterling in money, with the exception of about 100,000 dollars which were got for the military chest. The night of the Battle, instead of being passed in getting rest & food, to prepare them for the pursuit of the following day, was spent by the soldiers in looking for plunder. The consequence was that they were incapable of marching in pursuit of the Enemy, & were totally knocked up. The rain came on, & increased their fatigue; and I am quite convinced that we now have out of the ranks double the amount of our loss in the Battle; & that we have lost more men in the pursuit than the Enemy have; & have never in any one day made more than an ordinary march.

This is the consequence of the state of discipline of the British Army. We may gain the greatest Victories; but we shall do no good until we shall so far alter our system as to force the officers of the junior ranks to perform their duty,[1] & shall have some mode of punishing them for Neglect. The new Regts are as usual the worst of all. The 18th Lt Dragoons are a disgrace to the name of a soldier in action as well as elsewhere;[2]

dinner. . . . From this place [Caseda], which is a large village on a hill, we have a full view of a long range of the Pyrenees. . . . I see much snow on them, but no glaciers.'

[1] On July 18th he wrote to Torrens: 'The fact is that if discipline means habits of obedience to orders as well as military instruction, we have but little of it in the Army. Nobody ever thinks of obeying an order; & all the regulations of the Horse Guards as well as of the War Office & all the orders of the Army applicable to this peculiar service are so much waste paper. It is however an unrivalled army for fighting if the soldiers can only be kept in their ranks during the battle.'

[2] Captain William Tomkinson, 16th Light Dragoons, wrote on June 21st: 'The 18th Hussars [their correct designation] got into a great scrape in plundering. They were detected doing so when, I believe, they ought to have been moving forwards. Lord Wellington was so much enraged that he would not recommend any of their subalterns for two troops which were vacant by two captains killed, a thing very unusual. . . . One reason, I heard, was that a carriage belonging to the Etat-Major of the French was ordered to be guarded by a sergeant and some men of the 18th; it contained papers of consequence, which Lord Wellington wished to keep. The sergeant left the carriage, and the papers were lost. This, with their plundering, exasperated him. There might be other reasons.'

268

& I propose to draft their Horses from them & to send the men to England, if I cannot get the better of them in any other manner.

   Ever My Dear Lord Yours most faithfully

              Wellington

142

TO EARL BATHURST

           Huarte, 2nd July, 1813

My dear Lord,

 I enclose the copy of a letter from the Governor of Vitoria, which shows how our men are going on in that neighbourhood. These men are detachments from the different regiments of the army who were sent to Vitoria the day after the battle, each under officers, in order to collect the wounded and their arms and accoutrements. It is quite impossible for me or any other man to command a British army under the existing system. We have in the service the scum of the earth as common soldiers ; [1] and of late years we have been doing every thing in our power, both by law and by publications, to relax the discipline by which alone such men can be kept in order. The officers of the lower ranks will not perform the duty required from them for the purpose of keeping their soldiers in order ; and it is next to impossible to punish any officer for neglects of this description. As to the non-commissioned officers, as I have repeatedly stated, they are as bad as the men, and too near them, in point of pay and situation, by the regulations of late years, for us to expect them to do anything to keep the men in order. It is really a disgrace to have any thing to say to such men as some of our soldiers are.

 I now beg to draw your attention to the mode in which these irregularities affect our numbers. On the 17th June the total British and Portuguese force was 67,036 rank and file ; on the 29th June it is 58,694 rank and file : diminution 8342 rank and file. The British on the 17th June were 41,547 rank and file ; on the 29th June 35,650 rank and file : diminution 5897. The

[1] On November 4th, 1831, Wellington said to Viscount Mahon : 'The French system of conscription brings together a fair sample of all classes ; ours is composed of the scum of the earth — the mere scum of the earth. It is only wonderful that we should be able to make so much out of them afterwards. The English soldiers are fellows who have all enlisted for drink — that is the plain fact — they have all enlisted for drink.'

loss of British rank and file in the battle was 3164, including 200 missing; so that the diminution from irregularities, straggling, &c., since, for plunder, is 2733. The loss of Portuguese rank and file in the battle was 1022, including 73 missing; and their diminution from the same causes is 1423.

While we were pursuing the enemy by the valley of Araquil towards Pamplona, finding so many men straggling from their ranks, I ordered that an hospital might be established to receive them; and, although there are so many men absent from their regiments, there are only 160 in that hospital. The others are plundering the country in different directions.[1]

Ever My Dear Lord Yours most faithfully

Wellington

143

GENERAL ORDER

Irurita, 9th July, 1813 [2]

1. The Commander of the Forces is anxious to draw the attention of the officers of the army to the difference of the situation in which they have been hitherto among the people of Portugal and Spain, and that in which they may hereafter find themselves among those of the frontiers of France.

2. Every military precaution must henceforward be used to obtain intelligence and to prevent surprise. General and superior officers at the head of detached corps will take care to keep up a constant and regular communication with the corps upon their right and left, and with their rear; and the soldiers and their followers must be prevented from wandering to a distance from their camps and cantonments on any account whatever.

3. Notwithstanding that these precautions are absolutely necessary, as the country in the front of the army is the enemy's the Commander of the Forces is particularly desirous that the

---

[1] On July 9th he wrote again to Lord Bathurst: 'I do not know what measures to take about our vagabond soldiers. By the state of yesterday, we had 12,500 men less under arms than we had on the day before the battle. They are not in the hospital, nor are they killed, nor have they fallen into the hands of the enemy as prisoners. . . . I believe they are concealed in the villages in the mountains.'

[2] On this day Larpent wrote: 'Yesterday the chimney of the house of Lord Wellington's patron was on fire from the dressing of Lord Wellington's dinner. . . . It was with difficulty at last put out, when the fire-bell had collected all the town buckets full of water, and a wet blanket had been pushed down the chimney, which, being half wood, made the event very uncertain. . . . Lord Wellington was out in the rain with his hat off, and a silk handkerchief over his head, giving directions.'

inhabitants should be well treated, and private property must be respected, as it has been hitherto.

4. The officers and soldiers of the army must recollect that their nations are at war with France solely because the ruler of the French nation will not allow them to be at peace, and is desirous of forcing them to submit to his yoke; and they must not forget that the worst of the evils suffered by the enemy in his profligate invasion of Spain and Portugal have been occasioned by the irregularities of the soldiers, and their cruelties authorised and encouraged by their chiefs towards the unfortunate and peaceful inhabitants of the country.

5. To revenge this conduct on the peaceable inhabitants of France would be unmanly and unworthy of the nations to whom the Commander of the Forces now addresses himself, and at all events would be the occasion of similar and worse evils to the army at large than those which the enemy's army have suffered in the Peninsula, and would eventually prove highly injurious to the public interests.

6. The rules, therefore, which have been observed hitherto in requiring, and taking, and giving receipts for supplies from the country, are to be continued in the villages on the French frontier, and the Commissaries attached to each of the armies of the several nations will receive the orders from the Commander in Chief of the army of their nations respecting the mode and period of paying for such supplies.

Wellington

[On July 14th Wellington set up headquarters at Lesaca, eight miles south-east of Irún, and stayed until the first week of October. On August 8th Larpent wrote this description of the village: 'This small, dirty place is a curious scene of bustle just now; crowded with Spanish fugitives — the head-quarters no small body, with all our stragglers and those of Longa's,[1] who are more numerous (he having a quarter here now, and looking like an English butcher in a handsome hussar dress), with abundance of Spanish and Portuguese officers (for both troops are near), as well as with English, with wounded and prisoners passing, with mules and muleteers innumerable, besides all the country people who come here to turn all they have got into money. Noises of all sorts; thrashing all going on in the rooms up stairs; the corn then made into bread and sold in one corner; "*aqua ardente*" being cried all about; lemonade

---

[1] Colonel Don Francisco Longa commanded a Spanish division at Vitoria and afterwards.

(that is, dirty water and dark-brown sugar) the same ; here a large pig being killed in the street, with its usual music on such occasions ; another near it with a straw fire singeing it, and then a number of women cutting up and selling pieces of other pigs killed a few hours before. Suttlers and natives with their Don Quixote wineskins all about, large pigskins, and small ditto, and middling ditto, all pouring out wine to our half-boozy, weary soldiers ; bad apples and pears, gourds for soup, sour plums, &c., all offered for sale at the same moment. Perpetual quarrels take place about payment for these things between the soldiers of the three allied nations and the avaricious and unreasonable civilian natives ; mostly, however, between Spaniards and Spaniards. The animals eating green Indian corn almost against every house here and in the churchyard, which contains four tents from the want of stables and of quarters. Not the least curious or noisy in this confusion are about fifteen men and women with fresh butter 4s. the pound, who are come from near St. Andero and beyond it — a stout race dressed in a curious, peculiar manner, who contrive to bring butter on their heads in baskets for above a fortnight together, and sell it at last in a state that I am very glad to eat it for breakfast for ten days after it arrives. It forms a sort of very mild cream cheese, in fact.'

In his *Military Sketch Book* William Maginn wrote of Lesaca : 'Here I have seen the indefatigable Commander of the Forces working with an energy which often threatened his life. He rode so much one week, that he was confined for several succeeding days to his bed ; and I have seen his fifteen valuable chargers led out by the groom to exercise, with scarcely any flesh on their bones — so active and vigilant was their noble rider, and so much were his horses used. Every day during the siege of San Sebastian I saw him, unattended by his staff, riding by my window, in a narrow street of Renteria,[1] on his way to the besieged fortress, accompanied by an old artillery or engineer officer, — I believe Sir. R. Fletcher,[2] — and dressed in a plain grey frock, white cravat, and cocked hat — evidently intent on the matters of the siege ; this was upwards of thirty miles a day for a *ride*, between breakfast and dinner ; but he has often rode double that distance, over the worst roads and in the worst of weather.' [3]]

[1] On the road between Irún and San Sebastián.
[2] Lieut.-Colonel Sir Richard Fletcher (1768–1813) was Wellington's chief engineer. He was in charge of constructing the Lines of Torres Vedras, and played a leading part in the sieges of Ciudad Rodrigo, Badajoz and San Sebastián, at which last he was killed.
[3] Vol. ii, pp. 157-8.

144

TO EARL BATHURST

Lesaca, 8th August, 1813

My dear Lord,

. . . It is a very common error, among those unacquainted with military affairs, to believe that there are no limits to military success. After having driven the French from the frontiers of Portugal and Madrid to the frontiers of France, it is generally expected that we shall immediately invade France ; and some even here expect that we shall be at Paris in a month. None appear to have taken a correct view of our situation on the frontier, of which the enemy still possess all the strongholds within Spain itself ; of which strongholds, or at least some of them, we must get possession before the season closes, or we shall have no communication whatever with the interior of Spain. Then in France, on the same great communications, there are other strongholds, of which we must likewise get possession.

An army which has made such marches, and has fought such battles, as that under my command has, is necessarily much deteriorated. Independently of the actual loss of numbers by death, wounds, and sickness, many men and officers are out of the ranks for various causes. The equipment of the army, their ammunition, the soldiers' shoes, &c., require renewal ; the magazines for the new operations require to be collected and formed, and many arrangements to be made, without which the army could not exist a day, but which are not generally understood by those who have not had the direction of such concerns in their hands. Then observe, that this new operation is only the invasion of France, in which country every body is a soldier, where the whole population is armed and organized, under persons, not, as in other countries, inexperienced in arms, but men who, in the course of the last twenty five years, in which France has been engaged in war with all Europe, must, the majority of them, at least, have served somewhere.

I entertain no doubt that I could to-morrow enter France, and establish the army on the Adour, but I could go no farther certainly. If peace should be made by the Powers of the North, I must necessarily withdraw into Spain, and the retreat, however short, would be difficult, on account of the hostility and the warlike disposition of the inhabitants, particularly of this part of the country, and the military direction they would receive from the gentry their leaders. To this add, that the difficulty of all that must be done to set the army to rights, after its late severe battles and victories, will be much increased by its removal into France at an early period; and that it must stop short in the autumn if it now moves at too early a period.

So far for the immediate invasion of France, which, from what I have seen of the state of the negotiations in the north of Europe,[1] I have determined to consider only in reference to the convenience of my own operations. . . .

Ever My Dear Lord Yours most faithfully

Wellington

145

TO LIEUT.-GENERAL LORD WILLIAM BENTINCK

Lesaca, 5th Sept., 1813

My dear Lord,

. . . . There is no man better aware than I am of the state of every officer's reputation who has to command [Spanish] troops with such miserable means of support as these have, particularly in these days in which such extravagant expectations are excited by that excessively wise and useful class of people, the editors of newspapers. If I had been at any time capable of doing what these gentlemen expected, I should now, I believe, have been in the moon.

They have long ago expected me at Bordeaux; nay, I understand that there are many of their wise readers (amateurs of the military art) who are waiting to join the army till head quarters shall arrive in that city; and when they shall hear of the late Spanish battle, I conclude that they will defer their voyage till I shall arrive at Paris. But you may depend upon this, first, that I shall neither myself form, nor encourage in others, extravagant expectations; secondly, that you shall have my full support in any measure that you think proper to adopt under your instructions; and thirdly, that if you do your own duty (as I am sure

[1] On June 4th an armistice was concluded at Pläswitz between France and Russia, through Austria's mediation. On August 12th, Austria declared war again on France.

you will) according to the best of your judgment, and satisfy
yourself, you will satisfy your employers, and eventually the
British public. . . .

Believe me, &c.,

Wellington

146

TO —— ——

Lesaca, 10th Sept., 1813

My dear Sir,

I received last night your letters of the 22nd July and 9th
September, and I acknowledge that I wish you had followed the
advice of —— ——, and had omitted to send me either; and I
will detain both till I shall have received your answer upon what
I am now about to state to you.

I have never interfered directly to procure for any officer
serving under my command those marks of His Majesty's favor
by which many have been honored; nor do I believe that any
have ever applied for them, or have hinted through any other
quarter, their desire to obtain them. They have been conferred,
as far as I have any knowledge, spontaneously, in the only mode,
in my opinion, in which favors can be acceptable, or honors and
distinction can be received with satisfaction. The only share
which I have had in these transactions has been by bringing the
merits and services of the several officers of the army distinctly
under the view of the Sovereign and the public, in my reports
to the Secretary of State; and I am happy to state, that no
General in this army has more frequently than yourself deserved
and obtained this favorable report of your services and conduct.

It is impossible for me even to guess what are the shades of
distinction by which those are guided who advise the Prince
Regent in the bestowing those honorable marks of distinction,
and you will not expect that I should enter upon such a discussion. What I would recommend to you is, to express neither
disappointment nor wishes upon the subject, even to an intimate
friend, much less to the Government.

Continue, as you have done hitherto, to deserve the honorable distinction to which you aspire, and you may be certain
that if the Government is wise, you will obtain it. If you should

not obtain it, you may depend upon it that there is no person of whose good opinion you would be solicitous, who will think the worse of you on that account.

The comparison between myself, who have been the most favored of His Majesty's subjects, and you, will not be deemed quite correct; and I advert to my own situation only to tell you, that I recommend to you conduct which I have always followed.

Notwithstanding the numerous favors that I have received from the Crown, I have never solicited one; and I have never hinted, nor would any one of my friends or relations venture to hint for me, a desire to receive even one; and much as I have been favored, the consciousness that it has been spontaneously by the King and Regent, gives me more satisfaction than anything else.

I recommend to you the same conduct, and patience; and, above all, resignation, if, after all, you should not succeed in acquiring what you wish; and I beg you to recall your letters, which you may be certain will be of no use to you.

Believe me, &c.,

Wellington

147

TO SIR CHARLES STUART

Vera, 11th October, 1813

My dear Sir,

I have just received your letter of the 2nd; and as Marshal Sir William Beresford had before apprised me of the dissatisfaction of the Portuguese Government with the British Government, I am glad to see on what ground this dissatisfaction rests.

Our newspapers do us plenty of harm by that which they insert; but I never suspected that they could do us the injury of alienating from us a Government and nation, with which, on every account, we ought to be on the best of terms, by that which they omit. I, who have been in public life in England, know well that there is nothing more different from a debate in Parliament than the representation of that debate in the newspapers. The fault which I find with our newspapers is, that they so seldom state an event or transaction as it really occurred (unless when they absolutely copy what is written for them), and their observations wander so far from the text, even when they have a dispatch or other writing before them, that they appear to be absolutely incapable of understanding, much less of stating the truth on any subject.

The Portuguese Government and nation, therefore, should be very cautious how they allow themselves to judge of the estimation in which they are held by the Prince Regent and his Ministers, and by the British nation, by the newspaper statements. They may depend upon it that here the Portuguese army and nation are rising in estimation every day, and I recommend to them to despise every insinuation to the contrary.

Dom Miguel Forjaz [1] is the ablest statesman and man of business that I have seen in the Peninsula; but I hope that he will not be induced, by such folly as the contents and omissions of our newspapers, to venture upon the alteration of a system which, up to the present day, has answered admirably, has contributed in a principal degree to our great and astonishing success, and has enabled the Portuguese Government and nation to render such services to the cause, and has raised their reputation to the point at which it now stands. . . .

. . . All that I can say is that if we are to begin to disagree about such nonsense as the contents or the omissions of the newspapers, I quit the Peninsula for ever.

Believe me, &c.,

Wellington

[The third week of November found Wellington's headquarters on the coast at St.-Jean-de-Luz. More than a month elapsed before Larpent penned a description. 'This place has been a very flourishing town, and of considerable trade, but is much in decay; this partly before the late wars, from the bar having decreased, so that only small vessels can get in now, and the evil still increases. At low water the river only ripples over the bar of sand, scarcely a foot deep, and at times the river is choked up by the sand, so that it cannot make its way out, and floods the town.

'Sacoa is a very safe harbour; for small vessels drawing under ten feet, quite safe. They lie there high and dry, according to the tide. The houses of the former merchants are rather magnificent, though some are in ruins, and their number, for the size of the town, considerable. It has

[1] Dom Miguel Pereira Forjaz, Conte de Feira (1769–1827), was, after the Convention of Cintra, appointed Secretary to the Regency of Portugal, with responsibility for war and foreign affairs.

Wellington declared: 'Monsieur de Forjaz, I have always said, was the ablest man I had to do with in the Peninsula. . . . To say the truth, I never knew either in Portugal or Spain any general or any statesman who showed great practical talent except Forjaz.'

been called a sort of little Paris for the Basques. Near the sea the water has been, and is, gaining on the town and bay. There are many ruins ; one is part of an old convent, now beyond the sea-wall, and almost in the sea, and some say a whole street has been washed away. The great sea-wall made by Bonaparte, six hundred yards long, was constructed to save the town, and makes a good dry walk.

'Sibour is also a very large village, or small town, of inferior houses, where at present two brigades of Guards are, and two other regiments of Lord Aylmer's brigade, besides some staff cavalry, &c. Most of the better houses have French papers from Paris, and it looks very well. The whole forms one landscape, like tapestry — sea-ports from Vernet or Claude,[1] &c. ; some in colours, some in bistre or an imitation of Indian ink, some Chinese, but in better perspective. The brown and black are very pretty. Most of the walls are papered. The lower parts of the houses are all a sort of warehouse (where they are not shops) ; this serves us for stabling, but they are flagged, which having no straw is noisy, and they smell much also. Almost all the men of a better sort went away from St. Jean de Luz ; several women, for the most part old, stayed, and many have since returned ; but no society, or anything of that sort, is as yet on foot here. The deputy mayor, who stayed, sold all the wine he could appropriate, his own, and all unclaimed, as well as other things, and is, I believe, making money of us very fast. The town is now all a market or fair, and full of Spaniards and Portuguese, as well as French and Bascos, all pillaging poor John Bull, by selling turkeys for 25s. and 30s., and fowls for 12s. and 14s.'

Larpent had spent a day in St.-Jean-de-Luz at the beginning of September when he had been captured by the French and held as a prisoner for a month until Wellington could effect an exchange. At that time the town had been the headquarters of Marshal Soult. Now the Judge Advocate-General was struck by the change in appearance — a change which reflected the difference between the two nations at war.

'When I was last there, all was gay and glittering, full of chattering officers in their best uniforms, with gold lace and ornaments, and prancing country steeds with housings and trappings of all kinds. The shops were crowded with sky-blue and scarlet caps embroidered with silver and gold, and pantaloons the same, smart cloaks, trinkets, &c. The road was covered with long cars, bringing in supplies drawn by mules gaily ornamented, and with bells, and waggoners with blue frocks, and long smacking whips, whilst the quay was nearly deserted, only a few boats to be seen which had just returned from an unsuccessful attempt to send in shot and shells to St. Sebastian ; the sailors idle, and scarcely the appearance of a port visible. Bread and vegetables were abundant ; other eatables, not so.

'Now we have, on the contrary, a different scene ; not a piece of finery is to be seen, no gay caps, no pantaloons, no ornaments. The

[1] Carle Vernet (1758–1836) and Claude Gellée (1600–82), French painters.

officers all in their morning great coats ; Lord Wellington in his plain
blue coat, and round hat, or perhaps in his sky-blue Salisbury hunting
dress. The streets, full of Spanish mules, with supplies, and muleteers,
&c., all running against you, and splashing you as you walk ; every shop
crowded with eatables — wines, sauces, pickles, hams, tongues, butter,
and sardines. The quay is now always a busy scene, covered with some
rum casks, and flour casks, and suttler stores ; the sailors all in our pay,
at work constantly and making fortunes ; the pilots in full hourly employment, bringing in vessels here or at Sacoa. The latter is full of masts and
sails from Passages, Bilbao, Lisbon, or the west of England. The prices
are still enormous, and of course the activity is the result. The French
peasants are always on the road between this place and Bayonne, bringing
in poultry, and smuggling out sugar in sacks on their heads.']

148

TO EARL BATHURST

St. Jean de Luz, 21st Nov., 1813

My dear Lord,
    . . . I have had a good deal of conversation with people here,
and at St. Pé, regarding the sentiments of the people of France
in general respecting Buonaparte and his Government; and I
have found it to be exactly what might be supposed from all that
we have heard and know of his system. They all agree in one
opinion, viz., that the sentiment throughout France is the same
as I have found it here, an earnest desire to get rid of him, from a
conviction that as long as he governs they will have no peace.[1]

    The language common to all is, that although the grievous
hardships and oppression under which they suffer are intolerable, they dare not have the satisfaction even of complaining;
that, on the contrary, they are obliged to pretend to rejoice, and
that they are allowed only to lament in secret and in silence their
hard fate. . . .

    I have not myself heard any opinion in favor of the House of
Bourbon. The opinion stated to me upon that point is, that 20
years have elapsed since the Princes of that House have quitted
France; that they are equally, if not more, unknown to France

[1] To General Graham, who had gone to England, he reported on the 18th :
'We have been remarkably well received by the French, indeed full as well as in
any part of Spain ; and I am happy to add that our troops and the Portuguese
have behaved very well. . . . None but the persons in office, and the higher class
of the officers of the army, are attached to him [Buonaparte].'

than the Princes of any other Royal House in Europe; but that
the allies ought to agree to propose a Sovereign to France instead
of Napoleon, who must be got rid of, if it is hoped or intended
that Europe should ever enjoy peace; and that it was not material
whether it was of the House of Bourbon or of any other Royal
Family.

I have taken measures to open correspondence with the
interior, by which I hope to know what passes, and the sentiments of the people, and I will take care to keep your Lordship
acquainted with all that I may learn. In the mean time, I am
convinced more than ever that Napoleon's power stands upon
corruption, that he has no adherents in France but the principal
officers of his army, and the *employés civils* of the Government,
and possibly some of the new proprietors; but even these last I
consider doubtful.

Notwithstanding this state of things, I recommend to your
Lordship to make peace with him if you can acquire all the
objects which you have a right to expect. All the powers of
Europe require peace possibly more than France, and it would
not do to found a new system of war upon the speculations of
any individual on what he sees and learns in one corner of
France. If Buonaparte becomes moderate, he is probably as
good a Sovereign as we can desire in France; if he does not we
shall have another war in a few years; but if my speculations are
well founded, we shall have all France against him; time will
have been given for the supposed disaffection to his Government
to produce its effect; his diminished resources will have decreased his means of corruption, and it may be hoped that he
will be engaged singlehanded against insurgent France and all
Europe.

There is another view of this subject, however, and that is,
the continuance of the existing war, and the line to be adopted
in that case. At the present moment it is quite impossible for
me to move at all: although the army was never in such health,
heart, and condition as at present, and it is probably the most
complete machine for its numbers now existing in Europe, the
rain has so completely destroyed the roads that I cannot move;
and, at all events, it is desirable, before I go farther forward, that
I should know what the allies propose to do in the winter, which
I conclude I shall learn from your Lordship as soon as the King's
Government shall be made acquainted with their intentions by

WELLINGTON AND HIS STAFF CROSS THE BIDASSOA INTO FRANCE, OCTOBER 9TH, 1813

From an aquatint by M. Dubourg after the painting by J. F. Rigaud

the King's diplomatic servants abroad. As I shall move forward, whether in the winter or the spring, I can inquire and ascertain more fully the sentiments of the people, and the Government can either empower me to decide to raise the Bourbon standard, or can decide the question hereafter themselves, after they shall have all the information before them which I can send them of the sentiments and wishes of the people.

I can only tell you that, if I were a Prince of the House of Bourbon, nothing should prevent me from now coming forward, not in a good house in London, but in the field in France; and if Great Britain would stand by him, I am certain he would succeed. This success would be much more certain in a month or more hence, when Napoleon commences to carry into execution the oppressive measures which he must adopt in order to try to retrieve his fortunes.

I must tell your Lordship, however, that our success, and every thing, depends upon our moderation and justice, and upon the good conduct and discipline of our troops: Hitherto these have behaved well, and there appears a new spirit among the officers, which I hope will continue, to keep the troops in order. But I despair of the Spaniards. They are in so miserable a state, that it is really hardly fair to expect that they will refrain from plundering [1] a beautiful country, into which they enter as conquerors; particularly, adverting to the miseries which their own country has suffered from its invaders. I cannot, therefore, venture to bring them back into France, unless I can feed and pay them; and the official letter which will go to your Lordship by this post will show you the state of our finances, and our prospects. If I could now bring forward 20,000 good Spaniards, paid and fed, I should have Bayonne. If I could bring forward 40,000, I do not know where I should stop. Now I have both the 20,000 and the 40,000 at my command, upon this frontier, but I cannot venture to bring forward any for want of means of paying and supporting them. Without pay and food, they must plunder; and if they plunder, they will ruin us all.

I think I can make an arrangement of the subsidy to cover the expense of 20,000 Spaniards; but all these arrangements are

---

[1] This is confirmed by Sir Thomas Picton, who wrote on January 3rd to a friend: 'The Spaniards, instead of being of any service to us in our operations, are a perfect dead weight, and do nothing but run away and plunder. We should do much better without these vapouring poltroon rascals, whose irregular conduct indisposes every one towards us.'

easily settled, if we could get the money. Where we are to get the money, excepting from England, it is impossible for me to devise; as the patriotic gentlemen at Lisbon, now that they can buy no Commissariat debts, will give us no money, or very little, for the draughts on the Treasury, and the yellow fever has put a stop to the communication with Cadiz and Gibraltar; and if we had millions at all three, we could not get a shilling for want of ships to bring it.

Ever My Dear Lord Yours most faithfully

Wellington

PART SIX

VICTORY IN FRANCE AND FLANDERS: 1814–1815

THE YEAR 1814

In January, whereas the armies of Austria, Prussia and Russia invaded northern France, there was little activity on Wellington's front. Soult, strongly reinforced since Christmas, held a line along three swollen rivers : Adour, Bidouse and Nive, with his right flank protected by the entrenched camp and fortress of Bayonne, and his left flank extending to Pied de Port. Not until February 12th did Wellington resume his offensive. Then, leaving Sir John Hope to blockade Bayonne with thirty thousand men, he moved eastwards with forty-five thousand, and within a week had compelled the French to fall back forty miles to the Gave d'Oloron. On the 27th, one day after Hope had got half his force across the Adour between Bayonne and the sea and had thus completed the blockade of that city, Wellington beat Soult at Orthez on the Gave de Pau. Here the French, having been outflanked earlier on the Gave d'Oloron, fought for six hours to oppose a crossing, but had then to retreat north-east, stopping again at Aire on the Adour to fight a while before withdrawing further still.

Wellington's troops advanced over the Languedoc plain towards Toulouse, where, after brief engagements at Vic-Bigorre and at Tarbes, Soult dug himself in behind the flooded Garonne. This crossing presented Wellington with a formidable problem. The first two attempts, just after Paris had surrendered to the armies of Blücher and Schwarzenberg, were in vain, but then Beresford, who on March 12th had entered Bordeaux with a column and secured the Gironde estuary as well as dealing with a mayor and populace who declared in support of King Louis XVIII and sported the white cockade of the Bourbons, got over the Garonne. No sooner was this done than the bridge broke under the pressure of flood water and his eighteen thousand men were cut off. Eventually Wellington reunited his army on the north bank and on April 10th was fought the battle for Toulouse. The British triumphed, though not without heavy loss, and while Soult withdrew south-east towards Carcassonne, Wellington entered the city.

On the evening of that day, April 12th, he learnt that the Emperor Napoleon had abdicated. The war was over, except at Bayonne, which did not surrender for another fortnight.

Colonel Frederick Ponsonby, who brought the news of Napoleon's abdication from Bordeaux to Toulouse, later told John Cam Hobhouse that when he arrived he found Wellington 'pulling on his boots in his shirt. He had entered Toulouse an hour. "I have extraordinary news for you." "Ay, I thought so. I knew we should have peace ; I've long expected it."

285

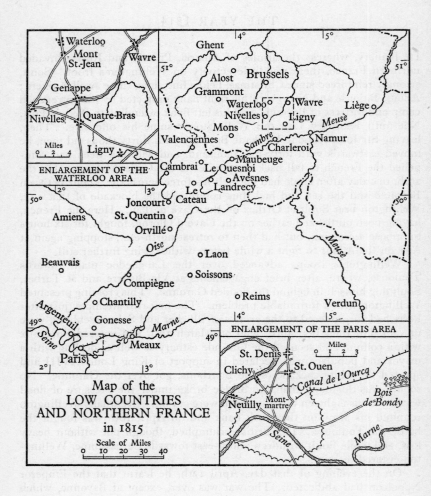

ENLARGEMENT OF THE
WATERLOO AREA

Waterloo
Mont
St.-Jean
Wavre
Genappe
Nivelles
Quatre-Bras
Miles
0   2   4
Ligny

Ghent
Alost
Brussels
Grammont
Waterloo
Wavre
Liège
Nivelles
Ligny
Mons
Meuse
Valenciennes
Sambre
Charleroi
Namur
Cambrai
Maubeuge
Le Quesnoi
Avesnes
Joncourt
Le
Landrecy
Cateau
St. Quentin
Amiens
Orvillé
Oise
Laon
Meuse
Beauvais
Soissons
Compiègne
Reims
Chantilly
Verdun
Argenteuil
Gonesse
Marne
Seine
Meaux
Paris

Map of the
LOW COUNTRIES
AND NORTHERN FRANCE
in 1815
Scale of Miles
0   10   20   30   40

ENLARGEMENT OF THE PARIS AREA

Miles
0   1   2   3
St. Denis
Clichy
St. Ouen
Canal de l'Ourcq
Neuilly
Mont-
martre
Bois
de Bondy
Seine
Marne

'"No ; Napoleon has abdicated."

'"How abdicated ? Ay, 'tis time indeed. You don't say so, upon my honour ! Hurrah !" said Wellington, turning round on his heel and snapping his fingers.' [1]

On April 19th Wellington concluded conventions for the suspension of hostilities ; the Spaniards and Portuguese made ready to return to their homes ; and many of the British divisions embarked at Bordeaux to fight at New Orleans, or else were scattered in Ireland, England, India, Holland and Antigua. Wellington travelled to Paris as Ambassador and for a week shared in the deliberations of the Allied Powers there. Then he was sent to Madrid to represent to the restored King Ferdinand VII and his ministers the need for averting civil war by adopting a less despotic and more liberal policy. He left Madrid again on June 5th and on the 14th took leave of his army at Bordeaux.

Back in London on June 23rd, a Field-Marshal and a Duke, and endowed by the Government with half a million pounds, he received congratulations from the House of Commons and took his seat in the House of Lords as baron, viscount, earl, marquess and duke — an unprecedented occasion. After a brief tour of the defences of the Netherlands, Wellington returned to Paris as Ambassador to the Court of the Tuileries, and spent the rest of 1814 in the restive French capital.

149

TO EARL BATHURST

St. Jean de Luz, 10th January, 1814

My dear Lord,

. . . In regard to the operations on the Rhine,[2] I confess that I feel no confidence in any thing that is doing. The allies are not strong enough, nor sufficiently prepared, to invade France at all, or to do more than cross the Rhine in one great corps, and there blockade some one, two, or three fortresses, by taking their cantonments for the winter. By the hesitation and delays of their Generals, I think they are sensible of the truth of this observation ; but they have not strength to resist the cry of all the foolish people who, without knowing what they are talking about, are perpetually writing and talking of invading France. . . .

. . . The allies do not appear to me to have reflected that every

---

[1] Lord Broughton, *Recollections of a Long Life*, vol. i, pp. 189-90.
[2] Napoleon had crossed the Rhine into France at the end of October. The Allies, with 265,000 men, did so on the last day of 1813. Blücher declared : 'We must march to Paris. Napoleon had paid his visit to every capital in Europe, and we can do no less than return the compliment.'

thing was lost in Europe by the loss of one or two great battles, and that every thing has been restored to its present state by their military success.

It has always occurred to me, however, upon the battle of Leipsic,[1] that if Buonaparte had not placed himself in a position that every other officer would have avoided, and had not remained in it longer than was consistent with any notions of prudence, he would have retired in such a state, that the allies could not have ventured to approach the Rhine. They must not expect battles of Leipsic every day; and that which experience shows them is, that they ought, above all things, to avoid any great military disaster. Their object is peace, upon a certain basis, upon which they have agreed. Although I am quite certain that Buonaparte has no intention to make peace, notwithstanding his speeches and declarations, I am equally certain that the people of France will force him to peace, if the allies suffer no disaster. This is clear, not only from his public language, but from every thing that he does, from the reports circulated, &c. &c. (one of which, by the by, was, that Lord Castlereagh had landed at Morlaix); and it is obvious that if the allies can only continue some operation during the winter, till the garrisons behind them shall fall, and their reinforcements shall reach them, and that they are so connected as that they cannot be beat, they must attain their object.

I agree very much with your Lordship about Louis XVIII, in the existing situation of affairs. But if you cannot make peace with Buonaparte in the winter, we must *run* at him in the spring; and it would be advisable to put one of the Bourbons forward in that case.

Ever My Dear Lord Yours most faithfully

Wellington

[1] Here, on October 16-19th, 1813, some 300,000 Russian, Austrian, Prussian and Swedish troops had routed Napoleon's army of 190,000 Frenchmen, Saxons and Italians.

150

TO THE MARQUESS WELLESLEY

St. Sever, 1st March, 1814

My dear Wellesley,

I write you two lines just to let you know that we beat Marshal Soult, near Orthez, on the 27th.[1] The action was for some time very warm, but I never saw troops get such a beating as they did; and they were saved at all only by the night. I expect to have my posts on the Garonne immediately.

Ever yours most affectionately,

Wellington [2]

151

TO COLONEL HENRY TORRENS

St. Sever, March 8th, 1814

Sir,

I have the honour of enclosing papers which have been transmitted to me by Lieutenant-General Sir Rowland Hill, being a letter from Major-General Byng,[3] two from Sir William Stewart, and a division order by the latter on the conduct of the troops; and complaining particularly of Colonel McDonald of the 57th and of Colonel Sir Nathan[1] Peacocke of the 71st.[4]

I concur in all the complaints of the irregularity of the troops. Till lately I could not say too much in favor of their conduct;

[1] Major Harry Ross-Lewin, 32nd Foot, saw Lord Wellington that morning: 'He had been reconnoitring the enemy, and, seating himself on the grass in his well-known short white cloak, he took out some paper, and began to write; but some drizzling rain that was then falling incommoded him. Another officer and I, perceiving the inconvenience he suffered, immediately procured an umbrella, which my companion fixed near him so as to shelter the paper, his lordship having thanked him for his attention.'
John Colborne related that on the day before the battle of Orthez 'I remember seeing Lord Wellington in a little white cloak, sitting on a stone, writing. Charles Beckwith, who was standing near me, said, "Do you see that old White Friar sitting there? I wonder how many men he is marking off to be sent into the next world."'
[2] *Supplementary Despatches*, viii, 607.
[3] Major-General John Byng, afterwards Field-Marshal the Earl of Strafford (1772–1860), commanded a brigade at Vitoria and one of the Guards brigades which held Hougoumont at Waterloo.
[4] Sir Nathaniel Levett Peacocke was cashiered in April for his cowardice at the battle of St.-Pierre, when he went to the rear on the pretence of getting ammunition. Colonel Duncan McDonald was also dismissed the service, because his regiment arrived a day late for the battle of Orthez, having been sent to St.-Jean-de-Luz to receive new clothing.

but I am sorry to say that since their late operations they have been as bad, if not worse than ever; and I have no doubt the inhabitants of this country, however at first well inclined towards us, will be as much our enemies as the Spaniards and Portuguese ever were to the French army.

I attribute the conduct of the troops entirely to the regimental officers. They neither read nor understand nor endeavor to carry into execution any of the orders of the army which have for their object the prevention of the committal of crimes. In ordinary circumstances, that is to say, when the army is quietly encamped in a position or in cantonments, all goes on well enough, and the ordinary regimental discipline is sufficient to keep the soldiers in tolerable order; but when an exertion of any kind is to be made, the whole machine falls to pieces.

The officers and non-commissioned officers have no authority over their men; indeed the latter are as bad as the soldiers: and when we come after a victory to pursue our enemy, we find that our loss from irregularity is greater in the pursuit than his in the flight.

Then there is no crime recorded in the Newgate Calendar [1] that is not committed by these soldiers, who quit their ranks in search of plunder; and if the Staff Corps were three times as numerous and active as they are, they would not be sufficient either to prevent the mischief or detect those guilty of it.

I have no hesitation in attributing the evil to the utter incapacity of some officers at the head of regiments to perform the duties of their situation, and the apathy and unwillingness of others; to the promotion of officers in regiments by regular rotation, thus holding forth no reward to merit or exertion, and leaving all in a state of equal indifference and apathy whether their superiors have, or not, reason to be displeased with them; and to the difficulty, if not impossibility, of punishing any officer for *neglect of duty*, when he is to be tried by others, each and all of whom have been guilty of the same, if not of greater neglects. In general such neglects are punished by sentencing the Commander-in-Chief to reprimand the officer, which is just so much waste paper; or if the more extended punishment of suspension from rank and pay for three or six months is sentenced, it is considered another mode of being idle and generally absent;

---

[1] *The Newgate Calendar, or Malefactors' Bloody Register*, begun in 1773, was a record of the more notorious criminals housed in Newgate Gaol.

and at the end of the period the officer returns to his regiment in as good a situation as ever.

This evil might perhaps in some degree be remedied by placing those at the bottom of the list who should have been suspended from rank and pay by sentence of a General Court Martial; but it must likewise be observed that any additional severe consequences attached to this punishment would only render still more frequent the more favorite one with courts martial, that of reprimand by the Commander-in-Chief.

There is not much difficulty in posting a British army for a general action, or in getting the officers and men to do their duty in the action. The difficulty consists in bringing them to the point where the action can be fought, and in the exertion to be made afterwards to derive all the advantages which any other troops in the world would derive from victory. These exertions require order and discipline among the men; and habits of obedience to order, attention, exertion, and intelligence and authority among the officers. But both fail; and I have always found that we lose more men in a pursuit than we do in any general action. . . .

Wellington [1]

152

TO SIR HENRY WELLESLEY

Aire, 16th March, 1814

My dear Henry,

The baggage of King Joseph, after the battle of Vitoria, fell into my hands, after having been plundered by the soldiers; and I found among it an imperial, containing prints, drawings, and pictures.

From the cursory view which I took of them, the latter did not appear to me to be any thing remarkable. There are certainly not among them any of the fine pictures which I saw in Madrid, by Rafael and others; and I thought more of the prints and drawings, all of the Italian school, which induced me to believe that the whole collection was robbed in Italy rather than in Spain. I sent them to England; and, having desired that they should be put to rights, and those cleaned which required it, I have found that there are among them much finer pictures than

---

[1] *Supplementary Despatches*, viii, 607.

I conceived there were; and as, if the King's palaces have been robbed of pictures, it is not improbable that some of his may be among them, and I am desirous of restoring them to His Majesty, I shall be much obliged to you if you will mention the subject to Don J. Luyando,[1] and tell him that I request that a person may be fixed upon to go to London to see them, and to fix upon those belonging to His Majesty.

This may be done either now or hereafter when I shall return to England, as may be most expedient.

In the mean time, the best of them are in the hands of persons who are putting them to rights, which is an expense necessary for their preservation, whether they belong to His Majesty or not.[2]

Ever yours most affectionately,

Wellington

I will get the catalogue of the pictures which I have got copied, and will send it to you. It will probably enable the Spanish Government to form an opinion, without inspection, which of the pictures belong to the King.

153

TO SIR HENRY WELLESLEY

Toulouse, 30th April, 1814

My dear Henry,

In consequence of the desire expressed by Lord Castlereagh that I should go to Paris to confer with him, I am about to set out for that place; and I propose to be back here by the time I can receive an answer to this letter; that is, in about ten or twelve days.

I have likewise to inform you that Lord Castlereagh has expressed a desire that I should accept the embassy to Paris,

---

[1] Luyando was Minister of State and head of the Spanish Foreign Department. In May 1814 he fell under the King's displeasure and was dismissed.

[2] After the battle of Vitoria King Joseph's abandoned carriage was found to contain more than 165 pictures stolen from the Spanish Royal Collections and cut or removed from their frames. The Duke notified the King of Spain that he intended to return them, but instead he was asked to keep 'that which has come into your possession by means as just as they are honourable'. The paintings, now in Apsley House, London, include works by Breughel, Vermeer, Pieter de Hooch Velasquez, Murillo, Van Dyck and Rubens.

which I have not declined. I must serve the public in some manner or other; and, as under existing circumstances I could not well do so at home, I must do so abroad. Lord Castlereagh has, however, left it to me to go home, &c., as I might please; only to have it understood that I was to have charge of the concerns at Paris.

I therefore propose to return here immediately after I shall have seen Lord Castlereagh, in order to superintend the breaking up, and embarkation, and return of the armies of the different nations to their respective countries; and I shall then go to Madrid.

I shall be very anxious to hear of the King's decision and conduct in regard to the constitution.

Do not mention to any body the intention that I should be the ambassador at Paris.[1]

Ever yours most affectionately,

Wellington

154

TO H.R.H. THE DUKE OF YORK

Bordeaux, 14th June, 1814

Sir,

As the allied troops have marched for their own country, and the British cavalry and the horses of the artillery have marched to embark in the British channel, and a part of the infantry have embarked here, besides those sent upon foreign expeditions, and the remainder are collected here and at Bayonne for embarkation as soon as vessels arrive to take them away, I propose to leave Lieut. General the Earl of Dalhousie [2] to direct and superintend the embarkation, and to return to England immediately. I am the more induced to take this step, as I have understood that it is the gracious intention of the Prince Regent to employ me in his

[1] Castlereagh wrote to Liverpool from Paris on May 5th: 'Lord Wellington arrived yesterday without notice, in time, in his blue coat, to see the Russian and Prussian Guards defile by Louis XVIII. The Emperor of Russia visited him in the evening, and he afterwards appeared at a ball given by Charles [his brother, Sir Charles Stewart], where he was the great object of admiration. He looks perfectly well, and does not show the effects of his campaigns as much as I expected in his countenance.'

[2] George Ramsay, 9th Earl of Dalhousie (1770–1838), commanded the 7th Division in the Peninsula and South of France. He later became Governor of Canada and then Commander-in-Chief, India.

service in another manner, and that it is desirable that I should return to England at an early period.

I have the honor to be, &c.,

Wellington

155

GENERAL ORDER

Bordeaux, 14th June, 1814

1. The Commander of the Forces being upon the point of returning to England, again takes this opportunity of congratulating the army upon the recent events which have restored peace to their country and to the world.

2. The share which the British army have had in producing those events, and the high character with which the army will quit this country, must be equally satisfactory to every individual belonging to it, as they are to the Commander of the Forces, and he trusts that the troops will continue the same good conduct to the last.

3. The Commander of the Forces once more requests the army to accept his thanks.

4. Although circumstances may alter the relations in which he has stood towards them for some years so much to his satisfaction, he assures them he will never cease to feel the warmest interest in their welfare and honor, and that he will be at all times happy to be of any service to those to whose conduct, discipline, and gallantry their country is so much indebted.

156

TO W. WALLER [1]

London, July 11th, 1814

Sir,

I have received your letter of the 8th instant in which you have desired that I should appoint your son to a situation in the Embassy to Paris.

There is no situation in the Embassy to Paris, excepting that of Secretary, that is paid, that I am aware of; and under this circumstance you will probably think it proper to turn your attention to some other line for your son.

[1] He lived at 34 Devonshire Place, London.

I would likewise beg to observe to you that at the same time that I entertain the highest respect for you and don't doubt that your son has been educated for a situation such as you desire he should fill, it requires something more than the recommendation of a father, however respectable, to induce me to employ any Gentleman confidentially in the public service.

I have the honor to be,
Your most humble Servant
Wellington

157

TO WILLIAM HAMILTON [1]

Paris, 29th August, 1814

My dear Sir,

Upon my arrival here I found that Sir Charles Stuart had brought the Princesse de Borghese's agents as low as they could come, and I have come into her house,[2] having determined on the purchase from what passed on the subject in London.

The price agreed upon is 800,000 *francs* for the house and furniture complete, and 63,000 for the stable, which is a separate concern, and requires some repairs. The whole will come to about 870,000 *francs*; and considering the size and situation of the house, the number of persons it will accommodate, and the manner in which it is furnished, the purchase is a remarkably cheap one.

I have not settled in what number of instalments the payments are to be made; but I understand there will be no objection to as many as we please, and I will make the number as great as possible.

I have a list of the furniture, which I propose to have verified by one of the gentlemen attached to the embassy, and then send

[1] Hamilton (1777–1859) was Under-Secretary of State for Foreign Affairs from 1809 to 1822. He superintended the transportation to England of Lord Elgin's Grecian marbles.

[2] No. 39, Rue du Faubourg St.-Honoré, was built in 1720. After 1800 it belonged to Pauline Bonaparte, youngest of Napoleon's sisters, who was created Princesse de Borghese. She sold it to Wellington for the British Embassy, which it is to this day.

In his autobiography *Old Men Forget*, Duff Cooper, the late Lord Norwich, himself Ambassador there, wrote of the house: 'It is a perfect example of what a rich gentleman's house should be. Neither palatial nor imposing, but commodious and convenient, central and quiet. . . . The house is very much as she [Pauline] left it and her plate still adorns the dinner-table on great occasions.'

it home to the office. I presume that Government would be desirous of not having any addition made to the furniture, nor any alteration to the house, without the positive authority of the Secretary of State, nor any repair without previous estimate to be submitted to the Secretary of State as soon as possible.

I should certainly have willingly paid £2000 or 48,000 *francs* a year for this house if I could have hired it, and shall have no objection to have that sum stopped from my salary for it.

Believe me, &c.,

Wellington

158

TO WILLIAM WILBERFORCE [1]

Paris, 15th Sept., 1814

My dear Sir,

. . . You do me justice in believing that I will pursue, with all the zeal of which I am capable, the object of the abolition of the slave trade by France. I really believe that the King and his principal Minister are sincere in their professions to us, and in their intentions to perform their engagement to abolish the trade entirely in five years, and in the mean time to prevent the trade on the northern coast of Africa, and to restrict it generally by the subjects of France as much as possible. I have not yet, however, received an answer in writing to the note I gave in about three weeks ago upon these subjects, which I am assured is to be attributed to the severe illness and death of the Minister of Marine,[2] to whose department what I proposed had been necessarily referred.

I regret this delay the more, as M. de Talleyrand,[3] with whom Lord Castlereagh and I had talked over all the propositions in my note, and who had discussed them with the King, is going to the Congress of Vienna.

There are but few persons now in France who have turned their attention to the slave trade, and those few are proprietors

---

[1] Wilberforce (1759–1833) had succeeded after twenty years of struggle in getting his bill for the abolition of slavery passed by Parliament and given royal assent in 1807. In 1814 he was M.P. for Bramber.

[2] Monsieur Malouet.

[3] Charles Maurice de Talleyrand-Périgord, Prince of Benevento (1754–1838), having been Minister for Foreign Affairs under the Directory, the Consulate and the Empire, had now been appointed to the same post under Louis XVIII, and was to play a leading part at the Congress of Vienna.

in the colonies or speculators in the trade, and interested in carrying it on. I am sorry to say that there is a very large interest of the former in the House of Peers ; and it is not easy to believe what an influence the proprietors of St. Domingo have on all the measures of the Government. The proposition to abolish the slave trade is foolishly enough connected with other recollections of the revolutionary days of 1789 and 1790, and is generally unpopular. It is not believed that we are in earnest about it, or have abolished the trade on the score of its inhumanity. It is thought to have been a commercial speculation, and by some to have been occasioned by the continental system ; and that, having abolished the trade ourselves with a view to prevent the undue increase of colonial produce in our stores, of which we could not dispose, we now want to prevent other nations from cultivating their colonies to the utmost of their power.

These impressions can be overcome only by time and perseverance ; but till they are overcome, I acknowledge that I do not think the King has the power to do more than prevent the trade of his subjects on that part of the coast from which we have expelled it. . . .

Believe me, &c.,

Wellington

159

TO WILLIAM WILBERFORCE

Paris, 4th Nov., 1814

My dear Sir,

I received your letter of the 18th October, to which I did not reply immediately, as General Macaulay [1] was going to England and I knew would let you know the state of things here.

Lord Liverpool will have informed you that orders have at last been issued to prevent the trade in slaves by French subjects on the coast of Africa north of Cape Formoso.[2] Much remains still to be done to secure the execution of those orders, to provide

---

[1] A brother of Zachary Macaulay, the philanthropist and anti-slave trade reformer, and an uncle to Lord Macaulay, Colin Macaulay had known Wellington in India. He was one of the officers imprisoned in chains by Hyder Ali at Seringapatam in 1781. He acted as secretary to the political and diplomatic commission which accompanied General Harris's army against Seringapatam in 1799. Later Macaulay served as Resident in the state of Travancore.

[2] Cape Formoso lies on the coast of Nigeria, some 250 miles east of Lagos.

for the condemnation of those and their vessels found disobeying them, and for the care of the slaves captured in the vessels which may be taken in breach of the orders; to all which points I am attending.

But we must keep the subject out of discussion and publication in England if we propose to do any real good. His Majesty's servants cannot be more zealous than they are; they deserve confidence and ought to be trusted; and I am quite convinced that the publications and discussions do more harm than good.

We have now brought the abolition practically to the state in which it was before peace was made with France, with this additional advantage, that France has engaged to abolish entirely in five years. We must not relax in our endeavors to do more; but it is really necessary to leave this interest, like others, in the hands of those whose duty it is to take care of it.

I have had no reason to complain of the newspapers lately on the subject of the slave trade, and I hope they will continue not to notice it for some little time longer.

Believe me, &c.,

Wellington

160

TO THE COMTE DE JAUCOURT [1]

Paris, 11th Dec., 1814

The Duke of Wellington presents his compliments to His Excellency the Comte de Jaucourt and encloses a letter from an English gentleman, employed here in collecting materials for an edition of Demosthenes, who has such bad health as to be unable to attend the public libraries; and who, therefore, requests permission to have them from the King's libraries to his own house.

This gentleman states himself to be a Fellow of Trinity College, Cambridge, and he is probably therefore a respectable character; but the Duke is not acquainted with him, and therefore forwards this request to his Excellency as it has come to his hands, renewing to M. le Comte de Jaucourt the assurances of his high consideration and respect.

[1] The Comte de Jaucourt was Minister of Foreign Affairs.

161

TO THE DUKE OF RICHMOND

Paris Decr 18th 1814

My dear Duke

I avail myself of the opportunity afforded by March's [1] return to Brussels to write you a few lines, which I should have done at an earlier period if I had not frequently heard that you intended to come here.

March will tell you how much William [2] is grown. He now understands French sufficiently well to be able to learn other things; and he will begin immediately. I am perfectly satisfied with him in every respect.

I have never been able to find out Mrs & Miss Finucane; let me know where they live if you should know.

There is no publick news here of any description. Matters appear to go on tolerably well; and as far as I can judge the Royal Family are popular with the people, particularly in the Southern Provinces of France. But the discontent of the Nobility and of every body above the very lowest classes who has been in France in the last 15 years is terrible; and I entertain but little doubt that if there was any difference between the King & the Legislature or any serious disturbance of any kind, the Govt. would be overturned or there would be a Civil War. If the Govt. were overturned the people would submit as quietly to the New Govt. as it did to that now existing.

I don't think there is any real objection to the Bourbons; and their conduct has been remarkably wise & prudent. That to which the discontented really object is the harmful system on which the Bourbons appear to wish to found their authority, and their Claim to the Confidence of other Nations. It is impossible to believe without seeing the extent to which individuals are ruined in France. There is scarcely any Man who can exist without the assistance of the Salary of Publick employment; and France reduced, or rather France not engaged in War cannot afford to pay all those who must live on the publick Revenue or

---

[1] Charles Gordon Lennox, Earl of March, (1791-1860) was Assistant Military Secretary to Wellington. He succeeded his father as 5th Duke of Richmond in 1819.
[2] William Pitt Lennox, fourth son of the Duke of Richmond, was born in September 1799.

work for their subsistence. Then those who have plundered the World, and still think they could do the same cannot endure the Notion of living upon a reduced half pay in their villages, which gives them only a bare subsistence.

That which I have above stated will shew you the cause of the discontents in this Country, of the Rumours of War &c &c. Some years will elapse before this Country will be tranquil, if it should ever be so ; and I hope we & the neighbouring nations will not forget to be on our Guard against the Evils by which it is yet in the power of this restless people to overwhelm us.

Believe me My dear Duke Ever Yours most sincerely

Wellington

Remember me most kindly to the Duchess &c.[1]

[1] The National Library of Ireland, the Richmond Papers.

THE YEAR 1815

On January 24th Wellington left Paris to replace Lord Castlereagh as Britain's representative at the Congress of Vienna. The Foreign Secretary claimed that his own presence in London for the opening of Parliament in February was essential, but this was partly a pretext to remove Wellington from the dangers of the French capital. As the Duke himself wrote many years later : 'Lord Liverpool and the Ministers in England had for some time been alarmed respecting the threat of the French newspapers respecting myself, and had been anxious to remove me from Paris. I felt no such alarm ; but I confess that I believe that if I had been at Paris a few months afterwards, when Buonaparte landed in France from Elba, and King Louis XVIII quitted Paris to go to the Netherlands, I should have been seized, and at all events prevented from joining the army in Flanders.'

While in Vienna Wellington drafted memoranda, wrote numerous letters, attended receptions and gave interviews or conversed with a galaxy of crowned heads, princes and plenipotentiaries. But he remained little more than a month.

All seemed peaceful, and then, early in March, came the astounding news that Napoleon had escaped from Elba and landed in France. The Powers conferring in Vienna declared him an outlaw. Armies were mobilized. Wellington, who at first underestimated the danger, went off to Brussels and took command of what was to be the Allied right wing. Soon he was complaining of the troops and staff placed at his disposal ; the foreign regiments were not of the first quality, while most of his Peninsular veterans were in America or on their way back.

By June Wellington's army of ninety-three thousand, more than half of them foreigners of little experience, were guarding two possible lines of approach into the Low Countries from the south-west, and watched the frontier running towards the Channel coast, whereas Blücher's 117,000 Prussians were extended between Liège in the east and Charleroi south of Brussels. The Allies had decided not to march on Paris until the Austrian and Russian armies drew near to France's eastern frontier, when a simultaneous offensive would be launched. For his part, the Emperor Napoleon, guessing correctly that Paris was bound to be the Allies' principal objective, and being too impatient to wage a defensive campaign, had resolved to forestall his opponents and carry the war into Belgium.

Napoleon joined his troops on the 14th and next day the French crossed the frontier, drove the Prussians from the Sambre and broke their defence line by Charleroi. One vital message to the anxious Wellington was detained, and not until seven that evening did word reach him that

Blücher's army was falling back towards the north-east after sharp fighting. Accordingly the Duke ordered his divisions to concentrate in an arc between Grammont and Nivelles, and later news caused him to have the troops in Brussels got under arms, ready to move out when and whither events should dictate.

All through the afternoon of June 16th was fought the battle of Quatre-Bras, where Marshal Ney was prevented from attacking Blücher's right flank, but where Wellington was prevented from going to the aid of his Prussian allies who were assaulted and worsted at Ligny. Early on the 17th, to match the Prussian withdrawal, he ordered his own troops in Quatre-Bras to retire upon Waterloo and the ridge of St.-Jean, a dozen miles nearer to Brussels. The move was carried out in pouring rain and was only sporadically hampered by belated French cavalry thrusts.

The Battle of Waterloo began towards noon on the 18th. All afternoon the fight went on about La-Haye-Sainte, until the farm was lost. All afternoon the Guards hung on valiantly to Hougoumont. Blücher kept a promise he had made to Wellington on the previous morning and pressed in from the east to ensure and clinch the victory. By nightfall the battle was over, its course summed up by Wellington in the words : 'They pommelled us and we pommelled them. We pommelled the hardest, and so we won.'

Napoleon fled from the scene, reached Charleroi on the 19th and Laon next day. Here he held a council of war, at which his desire to assemble the remains of his army and renew the struggle was vetoed by his generals. Instead he went on to Paris and abdicated in favour of his son, who was promptly rejected by the Chamber of Representatives. On July 3rd Napoleon was at Rochefort, seeking a passage to America but thwarted in his design by the vigilance of British warships, to one of which, H.M.S. *Bellerophon*, he surrendered on the 15th. In August he was sent into exile on the island of St. Helena, where he arrived on October 17th and remained until his death in 1821.

Meantime, on June 21st, the Allied army crossed into France, block-aded key towns in the north and captured Cambrai, the only place where real resistance was offered, on the 24th. On July 3rd was signed the Convention of Paris, which stipulated, besides a suspension of arms, that the Allies were to occupy the capital and that all French troops should withdraw south of the Loire. Difficulties were raised, notably by Fouché, against the return of Louis XVIII to the throne, but after negotiations and the appointment of Fouché as Minister of Police, the Allies occupied Paris and on July 8th King Louis entered the city. Wellington had his work cut out to moderate Blücher and the Prussians from revengeful acts and also to urge upon the Allies a moderate and lenient policy towards vanquished France.

On November 20th a convention was signed, providing for the with-drawal of all foreign troops apart from an army of occupation of 150,000 men, to be maintained at French expense, and, among other clauses, for the payment of a large indemnity. The occupation lasted three years, with Wellington in charge. Finally the British contingent left France in November 1818.

✻

[Lord William Pitt Lennox and Colonel Fremantle accompanied Wellington from Paris to Vienna, and the former has left us an account of the journey. 'The Duke travelled in an English carriage, with his valet, Tesson, on a seat on the roof, and a courier in advance. Anxious to lose no time on the road, we breakfasted and dined in the carriage, our meals consisting of game, pies, cold fowls and tongue, *pâtés de foie gras*, with the choicest pure claret from the Duke's own cellars.

'With the exception of four hours during the night, we never stopped upon the road between Paris and Vienna, and here the Duke's powers of falling at once to sleep came into effect; for no sooner had we reached the inn, than, the courier having made preparations, his Grace went in immediately to bed, and at the hour named for starting, he appeared perfectly refreshed, having slept, dressed, and breakfasted during that brief period; while we, the two *attachés*, looked what is called, with more truth than elegance, "extremely seedy", having passed our time in eating supper, and then lying down in our clothes before the hot German stove, until it was time to make our toilet previous to departure.' [1]

They travelled by way of Strasbourg, Augsburg, Munich and Braunau, and on arrival in Vienna the Duke lodged in a 'splendid mansion' in the Mineritzin Platz.

There is an account of Wellington's arrival in Vienna in a letter written to George Jackson, a minor diplomat, by a certain Count Otto Löwenstern.

'The people of Vienna, whose curiosity at first was so troublesome, had at last brought themselves to look on emperors and kings, to say nothing of the smaller fry of royalty, as scarcely more worthy of attention than ordinary mortals; but the arrival of the Duke of Wellington has roused them from this state of apathy, and all Vienna is on the *qui vive* to get a glimpse of him.

'The *Redoute* was thronged the night of his arrival and some of our royalty were present, but, oh the disappointment ! — not the Duke. The next day February 4th he paid his visits of ceremony *en grand uniforme de Feldmarschall*, and in the evening assisted at the Redoute. About seven thousand persons were there, and as many more could not get in. The Duke, wearing a plain dress, was not recognized at first, but as soon as his presence was made known he became the object of attention too general and *trop empressé*, and people crowded about him with very little ceremony and politeness. Lord Stewart was with him and a lady in mask and domino, supposed to be either Lady Castlereagh or Lady Cathcart.' [2]]

[1] *Three Years with the Duke*, pp. 90-1.
[2] *The Bath Archives*, vol. 2, p. 469.
Lady Castlereagh had been Amelia Anne, a daughter of the 2nd Earl of Buckinghamshire. Lady Cathcart had been Elizabeth Elliot, daughter of a Governor of New York.

162
TO COLONEL JOHN CAMERON [1]

Vienna Feby 5th 1815

Sir,

I received your letter of the 18th January this morning, and I have transmitted it to the Secretary of State with my recommendation of you.

The Government fixed the occasions on which Medals should be granted to the Army, and framed the Rules according to which I was bound to make the lists of those to whom they were to be granted; and not having received their orders to recommend for Medals for the service at Arroyo Molinos, Alba de Tormes or at Bejar or at Ayre or at Arrivete it was impossible for me to recommend you for a Medal for your services on those occasions; neither was it possible for me to recommend you for a Medal at Fuentes d'Honore, or in the Pyrenees according to the rules by which I was ordered and bound to make out the lists of those I recommended.

I have not an accurate recollection of the lists for Bayonne, the Nivelle, Orthes & Thoulouse; but of this I am very certain, that I have never failed to do justice to your services, as it was my earnest desire to render it to every officer and soldier I had the honor of commanding.[2]

I have had nothing to say to the selection of the officers recently appointed Knights Commanders of the Order of the Bath.[3] I did not know their names till I saw the list of them in the Gazette.

If you had known these facts I hope that the same spirit of Justice by which I have always been animated would have induced you to spare me the pain of reading the reproaches & charges of Injustice contained in your letter, and that you would have defended me with the 92nd Regt; and would have shown

---

[1] Cameron commanded the 92nd Regt.

[2] On August 15th, 1815, Wellington wrote to Frances, Lady Shelley about his bestowal of the Order of Maria Theresa which had caused offence, 'I have given it to those officers who, in my opinion, are best entitled to it, for general conduct throughout the campaign, and not for any particular battle. I think I have selected the best officers in the army. I never give anything to favor; nor do I listen to solicitation. My sole object is to be just, and I don't in the least care what is said.'

[3] On January 2nd the Order of the Bath had been remodelled into three classes: Grand Cross, Knight Commander and Companion.

them that the Regulation & not I deprived you of those marks of honor which they wished to see you obtain.

As these facts are in the knowledge of every body, it is scarcely possible to believe that you were not aware of them, and I attribute the harshness of your letter solely to the irritation which you naturally feel in considering your own case.

However, the expression of this irritation, however unjust towards me and unpleasant to my feelings, has not made me forget the services which you and your brave Corps rendered upon every occasion on which you were called upon; and although I am afraid it is too late I have recommended you in the strongest terms to the Secretary of State.

> I have the honor to be, Sir,
> Your most obedt. humble Servant,
> > Wellington

163

TO VISCOUNT CASTLEREAGH

Vienna, 26th March, 1815

My Lord,

. . . I entirely concur in opinion with His Majesty's Government; and it is the decided opinion of the Sovereigns and Ministers here, that no measure of war ought to be adopted in regard to France, whatever may be our strength, excepting on the invitation of the King.

Your Lordship, however, may depend upon it that, whatever may be the determination and strength of the Allies, and however their declarations may be construed, Buonaparte and the French nation will not allow them to remain at peace, and they must be prepared either to give up all their conquests to the Rhine, or for active hostilities.

It is the desire for war, particularly in the army, which has brought Buonaparte back, and has formed for him any party, and has given him any success; and all my observations when at Paris convinced me that it was the King alone who kept Europe at peace, and that the danger which most immediately threatened His Majesty was to be attributed to his desire to maintain the peace, contrary to the wishes, not only of the army, but of the majority of his subjects, of some of his Ministers, and even of some of his family.

Your Lordship will then judge what chance there is of maintaining the peace if Buonaparte should be entirely successful, considering his disposition for war, adverting to the opinions he has delivered and entertains upon the peace, and to the necessity under which he labours to cultivate his popularity with the army, and to endeavor, at least, to flatter the vanity of the nation by military success. Depend upon it, my Lord, that if he succeeds in establishing himself we have no chance of peace, excepting by resigning all our conquests to the Rhine at least; and our chance then depends upon his moderation.

However, His Majesty's Government may rely upon it that I shall continue to act precisely according to their wishes, as far as I shall be acquainted with them. . . .

I have the honor to be, &c.,

Wellington

164

TO EARL BATHURST

Bruxelles, 4th May, 1815

My dear Lord,

. . . To tell you the truth, I am not very well pleased either with the manner in which the Horse Guards have conducted themselves towards me. It will be admitted that the army is not a very good one; and, being composed as it is, I might have expected that the Generals and Staff formed by me in the last war would have been allowed to come to me again : but instead of that, I am overloaded with people I have never seen before; and it appears to be purposely intended to keep those out of my way whom I wished to have. However, I'll do the best I can with the instruments which have been sent to assist me.[1]

Ever, my dear Lord, yours most sincerely,

Wellington

✽

[About a fortnight before Waterloo Thomas Creevey was walking in the Park at Brussels when he met Lord Wellington. ' " Let me ask you, Duke, what you think you will make of it ? " He stopt, and said in the most natural manner :—" By God ! I think Blücher and myself can do

---

[1] To one correspondent he wrote on May 22nd : 'I command a very small British army, with a very large British Staff, to which my superiors are making additions every day'. To another he declared : 'I have more Generals and officers of all nations than I know how to employ'.

the thing." — "Do you calculate," I asked, "upon any desertion in Buonaparte's army ?" — "Not upon a man," he said, "from the colonel to the private in a regiment — both inclusive. We may pick up a marshal or two, perhaps ; but not worth a damn." — "Do you reckon," I asked, "upon any support from the French King's troops at Alost ?" — "Oh !" said he, "don't mention such fellows ! No : I think Blücher and I can do the business." — Then, seeing a private soldier of one of our infantry regiments enter the park, gaping about at the statues and images :— "There," he said, pointing at the soldier, "it all depends upon that article whether we do the business or not. Give me enough of it, and I am sure." '[1]]

165

TO LIEUT.-GENERAL LORD LYNEDOCH [2]

Bruxelles, 13th June, 1815

My dear Lord,

I have received your letter of the 7th instant, and I shall be very happy to belong to the military club [3] proposed to be established, in which will, of course, be included the Peninsula Club, respecting which we before corresponded.

There is nothing new here. We have reports of Buonaparte's joining the army and attacking us ; but I have accounts from Paris of the 10th, on which day he was still there ; and I judge from his speech to the Legislature that his departure was not likely to be immediate. I think we are now too strong for him here.

Believe me, &c.,

Wellington

✳

[The next letter, written early on Waterloo day, is to Lady Frances Webster, who in 1810 had married a Hussar officer named James Wedderburn Webster (1789–1840) and was then travelling in Belgium with her parents, her father being Arthur, 1st Earl of Mountnorris. Webster had been with Byron in Athens in 1810. Three years later Byron, while staying with the Websters at Rotherham, became involved with Lady Frances, whom he described to Lady Melbourne as 'pretty, but not surpassing — too thin, and not very animated ; but good-tempered — and a something interesting enough in her manner and figure'.

[1] *The Creevey Papers*, p. 228.
[2] Lieut.-General Sir Thomas Graham had been created Baron Lynedoch in April 1814.
[3] This became the United Service Club in London.

He stated in letters that Lady Frances did not and would not live with her husband, whom she did not love and who loved other women. Webster, declared Byron, 'is a little *indiscreet* blusterer who neither knows what he would have, nor what he deserves. . . . He is passionately fond of having his wife admired, and at the same time jealous to jaundice of everything and everybody.'

Princess Dorothea Lieven, wife of the Russian Ambassador in London, thought Webster had reason to be jealous. Writing on April 18th, 1821, she described Lady Frances as 'a young and rather pretty woman, although she is a little too washed-out for my taste. But my taste has nothing to do with it, and other people admire her; for instance, the Duke of Wellington, who had certain passages with her at Brussels five or six years ago, and nearly forgot in her company that he had the battle of Waterloo to win. There was talk of a law-suit; but he avoided the scandal by paying down some thousands of guineas.'

Lady Shelley, by contrast, watched the Duke at a ball in Paris and recorded on August 16th, 1815 : 'His manner is the most paternal of any one I ever saw; and so far removed from any nonsense, that I am convinced his attachment to Lady Frances is platonic. Of this I am certain : if there is any love in the case, it is only on the lady's side. His manner to her in public is simple and kind.'

It appears that in February 1816 Webster obtained £2000 in damages for a libel accusing Lady Frances and the Duke of adultery.]

166

TO LADY FRANCES WEDDERBURN WEBSTER

Waterloo, Sunday morning, 3 o'clock,
18th June, 1815

My dear Lady Frances,

As I am sending a messenger to Bruxelles, I write to you one line to tell you that I think you ought to make your preparations, as should Lord Mountnorris,[1] to remove from Bruxelles to Antwerp in case such a measure should be necessary.

We fought a desperate battle on Friday,[2] in which I was successful, though I had but very few troops. The Prussians were very roughly handled, and retired in the night, which obliged me to do the same to this place yesterday. The course of the operations may oblige me to uncover Bruxelles for a

---

[1] Arthur, 1st Earl of Mountnorris (1744–1816) and formerly Viscount Valentia, married as his second wife Sarah, a daughter of Sir Henry Cavendish. They had a son and two daughters.
[2] This refers to Quatre-Bras.

moment, and may expose that town to the enemy; for which reason I recommend that you and your family should be prepared to move to Antwerp at a moment's notice.

I will give you the earliest intimation of any danger that may come to my knowledge; at present I know of none.

Believe me, &c.,

Wellington

Present my best compliments to Lord and Lady Mountnorris.

167

TO THE DUKE OF BEAUFORT [1]

Bruxelles, 19th June, 1815

My dear Lord,

I am very sorry to have to acquaint you that your brother Fitzroy is very severely wounded, and has lost his right arm. I have just seen him, and he is perfectly free from fever, and as well as anybody could be under such circumstances. You are aware how useful he has always been to me; and how *much* I shall feel the want of his assistance, and what a regard and affection I feel for him; and you will readily believe how much concerned I am for his misfortune. Indeed, the losses I have sustained have quite broken me down; [2] and I have no feeling for the advantages we have acquired. I hope, however, that your brother will soon be able to join me again; and that he will long live to be, as he is likely to become, an honor to his country, as he is a satisfaction to his family and friends.

Believe me, &c.,

Wellington

[1] Henry Charles, 6th Duke of Beaufort. Lord Fitzroy Somerset (1788–1855), the youngest of eight brothers, was Wellington's Military Secretary. In 1852 he was created 1st Baron Raglan and commanded British forces in the earlier stages of the Crimean War.

[2] Lady Mornington told Mrs. Charles Bagot that when she first saw the Duke at Brussels after the battle and congratulated him, he put his face between his hands to hide his tears and said, 'Oh ! Do not *congratulate* me. I have lost all my dearest friends.' He also told her : 'The finger of God was on me all day — nothing else could have saved me'.

168

TO THE HON. WILLIAM WELLESLEY-POLE

Bruxelles, June 19th, 1815

My Dear William,

You'll see the account of our Desperate Battle and victory over Boney ! !

It was the most desperate business I ever was in ; I never took so much trouble about any Battle ; [1] & never was so near being beat.

Our loss is immense particularly in that best of all Instruments British Infantry. I never saw the Infantry behave so well.

I am going immediately.

Can we be reinforced in Cavalry or Infantry or both ?

We must have Lord Combermere [2] as Lord Uxbridge [3] has lost his leg. He was wounded when talking to me during the last attack, almost by the last shot.

Ever Yours most affectionately

W.[4]

❋

[Thomas Creevey met Wellington soon after the Duke reached Brussels on June 19th, and went up to the room where he was writing his despatch. 'The first thing I did, of course, was to put out my hand and congratulate him upon his victory. He made a variety of observations in his short natural, blunt way, but with the greatest gravity all the time, and without the least approach to anything like triumph or joy. "It has been a damned serious business," he said. "Blucher and I have lost 30,000 men. It has been a damned nice thing — the nearest run thing you ever saw in your life. . . ." He repeated so often its being *so nice a thing — so nearly*

[1] Mrs. Charles Bagot records that in Paris during July Wellington declared : 'I have taken a good deal of pains with many of my battles, but I never took half the pains I did at Waterloo'. Sir Augustus Frazer says that the Duke told Lord Fitzroy Somerset on the evening of June 18th : 'I have never fought such a battle, and I trust I shall never fight such another'.

In his *Recollections* Samuel Rogers states that within half an hour of the return of Lady Mornington and her daughter to Brussels, the Duke came in and, walking up and down the apartment in a state of great agitation, burst into tears and uttered these words : 'The next greatest misfortune to losing a battle is to gain such a victory as this'.

[2] Sir Stapleton Cotton had been raised to the peerage in April 1814.

[3] The former Lord Henry Paget, now Earl of Uxbridge, and soon to be Marquess of Anglesea (1768–1854), had commanded the cavalry under Sir John Moore, but not under Wellington in the Peninsular, because he had gone off with Henry Wellesley's wife.

'By God ! I've lost my leg,' cried Uxbridge. 'Have you, by God ?' was the Duke's laconic reply.

[4] *Camden Miscellany*, vol. xviii.

run a thing, that I asked him if the French had fought better than he had ever seen them do before. — "No," he said, "they have always fought the same since I first saw them at Vimeira." Then he said :—"By God ! I don't think it would have done if I had not been there." ¹]

169

TO THE EARL OF ABERDEEN ²

Bruxelles June 19th 1815

My Dear Lord

You will readily give credit to the existence of the extreme grief with which I announce to you the death of your gallant brother, in consequence of a wound received in our great battle of yesterday.

He had served me most zealously & usefully for many years, & on many trying occasions ; but he had never rendered himself more useful, & had never distinguished himself more than in our late actions. He received the Wound which occasioned his Death, when rallying one of the Brunswick Battns which was shaking a little ; and he lived long enough to be informed by myself of the glorious result of our actions to which he had so much contributed by his active & zealous assistance.

I cannot express to you the regret & sorrow with which I look round me & contemplate the loss which I have sustained, particularly in your brother. The glory resulting from such actions, so dearly bought is no consolation to me ; and I cannot suggest it as any to you, and his friends ; but I hope that it may be expected that this last one has been so decisive as that no doubt remains that our exertions and our individual losses will be rewarded by the early attainment of our just object. It is then that the glory of the actions in which our friends & relations have fallen will be some consolation for their loss.

Believe me My Dear Lord Your's
most sincerely Wellington

Your brother had a black horse given to him I believe by Lord Ashburnham,³ which I will keep till I hear from you what you wish should be done with it.

---

¹ *The Creevey Papers*, pp. 236-7.
² George, 4th Earl of Aberdeen (1784–1860). His brother, Sir Alexander Gordon, was aide-de-camp to Wellington.
³ Bertram, 3rd Earl of Ashburnham.

[Writing in his journal on September 3rd that year, Wellington's old friend of India days, Sir John Malcolm, related how at dinner in Paris the Duke spoke with great affection of Colonel Gordon, his late aide-de-camp. 'He said he had been long with him, and his manly qualities had attached him very much. He said that Gordon had during the action, two or three times (when he was using his glass), led his horse out of the severe fire to which he was exposed, and showed throughout the day a great solicitude to preserve his (the Duke's) life. "When I was at supper at the village of Waterloo", said the Duke, "he was brought in, and I thought, as he had only lost his leg, we should save him. I went to see him, and said I was sorry he was so severely wounded, at the same time taking hold of his hand. "Thank God you are safe", was his reply. I then said, "I have no doubt, Gordon, you will do well." He raised himself, and then fell back in the manner that indicated his being completely exhausted. "Poor fellow," the Duke added, "he probably felt there was no chance. He died next morning at eight."' [1]]

170

GENERAL ORDER

Nivelles, 20th June, 1815

1. As the army is about to enter the French territory, the troops of the nations which are at present under the command of Field Marshal the Duke of Wellington, are desired to recollect that their respective Sovereigns are the Allies of His Majesty the King of France, and that France ought, therefore, to be treated as a friendly country. It is therefore required that nothing should be taken either by officers or soldiers, for which payment be not made. The Commissaries of the army will provide for the wants of the troops in the usual manner, and it is not permitted either to soldiers or officers to extort contributions. The Commissaries will be authorised, either by the Field Marshal or by the Generals who command the troops of the respective nations, in cases where their provisions are not supplied by an English Commissary, to make the proper requisitions, for which regular receipts will be given ; and it must be strictly understood that they will themselves be held responsible for whatever they obtain in way of requisition from the inhabitants of France, in the same manner in which they would be esteemed accountable for purchases made for their own Government in the several dominions to which they belong.

[1] *The Life and Correspondence of Major-General Sir John Malcolm*, vol. ii, p. 121.

WATERLOO : AT THE APPROACH OF THE IMPERIAL GUARDS, WELLINGTON TURNS TO HIS OWN
GUARDS AND SHOUTS 'NOW, MAITLAND! NOW'S YOUR TIME!'

From the painting by T. Jones Barker

2. The Field Marshal takes this opportunity of returning to the army his thanks for their conduct in the glorious action fought on the 18th inst., and he will not fail to report his sense of their conduct in the terms which it deserves to their several Sovereigns.

Wellington

171

TO H.R.H. THE DUKE OF YORK

Orvillé, 28th June, 1815

Sir,

I have had the honor of receiving your Royal Highness's letter of the 23rd instant, and I am highly flattered by your Royal Highness's approbation, and gratified by your attention to this army.

Your Royal Highness will see, from what happens every day, that our victory is decisive, and I hope we shall bring the concerns of this country to a satisfactory close without striking another blow.

I will immediately recommend to your Royal Highness certain officers for the third class of the Order of the Bath. At the same time, I wish to suggest what follows for your Royal Highness's consideration.

We have now 240 Orders, that is, of the first and second class, of the Order of the Bath for Admirals and General Officers; and, putting the navy out of the question, excepting to consider them as entitled to half of the numbers, the remainder will be for General Officers, or 120 orders for officers of that rank. Now I would ask your Royal Highness whether there are now, or, considering the size of the British army, or the other calls there are upon that army for officers for other armies, it is possible that there can ever be in the British army 120 General Officers so distinguished as to merit the first and second class of the Order of the Bath. We cannot expect again to have so long or so extensive a system of warfare as we have had for the last twenty-two years; yet even now, if Colonels and Lieut. Colonels with five medals, had not got the second class of the Order, your Royal Highness would have found it difficult to fill your go vacancies of that class.

That which I would propose is, that the second class, instead of being 180, should be reduced to 80 ; and the mode in which I would make the reduction should be by appointing only to the vacancies occasioned by the death or promotion of the original number of Admirals and General Officers.

I would then give only the third class, not as third class, but as Knights Companions. I would form another third class hereafter, to be composed of Colonels in the army, Post Captains in the navy, and Lieut. Colonels in the army, of more than three years' standing ; the two last having already been Knights Companions, and the Knights Companions should be the fourth class.

The new third class might be limited or not, as your Royal Highness might think proper. But I think the formation of it might be delayed till some future period.

I confess that I do not concur in the limitation of the Order to Field Officers. Many Captains in the army conduct themselves in a very meritorious manner, and deserve it ; and I never could see the reason for excluding them either from the Order or the medal.

I would likewise beg leave to suggest to your Royal Highness the expediency of giving to the non-commissioned officers and soldiers engaged in the battle of Waterloo, a medal.[1] I am convinced it would have the best effect in the army ; and, if that battle should settle our concerns, they will well deserve it.

I have the honor to be, &c.,

Wellington

172

TO MARSHAL LORD BERESFORD

Gonesse,[2] 2nd July, 1815

My dear Beresford,

I have received your letter of the 9th of June. You should recommend for the Spanish medal for Albuera according to the rules laid down by the King of Spain for the grant of it. I

---

[1] The silver Waterloo medal, designed by Thomas Wyon, was issued in 1816–17 to all who took part in the battle, and also to those engaged at Ligny and Quatre-Bras.

[2] Gonesse is about ten miles north of Paris, on the Senlis road. On the same day he wrote to the Earl of Uxbridge : 'We are going on very well. We have shut the French into Paris and their lines ; Blücher has crossed the Seine. Buonaparte is off, I believe, to Havre. They offer an armistice ; but I won't grant it unless I shall be certain it will lead to a permanent settlement.'

should think it should be given only to those who were there and actually engaged.

I am, as soon as I shall have a little time, going to recommend officers for the Order of San Fernando,[1] and will apply to you for a Portuguese list.

You will have heard of our battle of the 18th. Never did I see such a pounding match. Both were what the boxers call gluttons. Napoleon did not manoeuvre at all. He just moved forward in the old style, in columns, and was driven off in the old style. The only difference was, that he mixed cavalry with his infantry, and supported both with an enormous quantity of artillery.

I had the infantry for some time in squares, and we had the French cavalry walking about us as if they had been our own. I never saw the British infantry behave so well.

Boney is now off, I believe, to Rochefort, to go to America. The army, about 40,000 or 50,000, are in Paris. Blücher on the left of the Seine, and I with my right in front of St. Denis, and the left upon the Bois de Bondy.[2] They have fortified St. Denis and Montmartre very strongly. The canal de l'Ourcq is filled with water, and they have a parapet and batteries on the bank; so that I do not believe we can attack this line. However, I will see.

Believe me, &c.,

Wellington

173

TO MARSHAL PRINCE BLÜCHER

Gonesse, 4th July, 1815

Mein lieber Fürst,

I enclose your Highness the unanimous resolutions of the Houses of Lords and Commons of the United Kingdom of Great Britain and Ireland, whereby they offer to your Highness, and the brave army under your command, their grateful thanks for your and their conduct in the battle of the 18th June; and the extract of a letter which I have received upon the same subject from the Speaker of the House of Commons.

I beg leave to congratulate your Highness upon this occasion;

---

[1] A Spanish military order, instituted in 1811.
[2] Bondy, a village some seven miles east of Paris on the road to Meaux.

and to assure your Highness that, as an Englishman and as the General of an Allied Army, engaged in the same battle, I concur entirely in these votes of thanks to your Highness and your army ; and that I shall never cease to feel grateful for the cordiality with which we have concerted and conducted our operations, and particularly for the effectual co-operation and assistance of your Highness and your army in the battle of the 18th June, for which I now transmit you the thanks of the Houses of Lords and Commons.

Believe me, &c.,

Wellington [1]

174

GENERAL ORDER

Gonesse, 4th July, 1815

1. The Field Marshal has great satisfaction in announcing to the troops under his command, that he has, in concert with Field Marshal Prince Blücher, concluded a military convention with the Commander in Chief of the French army in Paris, by which the enemy are to evacuate St. Denis, St. Ouen, Clichy, and Neuilly, this day at noon ; the heights of Montmartre to-morrow, at noon ; and Paris the next day.

2. The Field Marshal congratulates the army upon this result of their glorious victory. He desires that the troops may employ the leisure of this day to clean their arms, clothes, and appointments, as it is his intention that they should pass him in review.

Wellington

✳

[On July 7th the Duke of Wellington entered Paris. Lord Teignmouth described the scene. 'It was his intention to have reviewed the troops and marched through the city the day before, but he was evidently deterred by prudential motives, and was apprehensive of unpleasant occurrences. You will be anxious to hear in what manner he was received. I accompanied him with a numerous train of officers, whilst not a single British soldier was admitted. He did not go far beyond the gate, but immediately went to his headquarters,[2] which adjoin the Place de la Concorde. A few

---

[1] William Gavin, Quartermaster of the 71st Highland Regiment, saw the Duke at Argenteuil. 'The Engineers were laying a Pontoon bridge across the Seine. Lord Wellington was sitting on a beam of timber answering a dispatch from Marshal Blücher.'

[2] The Palais de l'Élysée.

316

cries of "Vivent les Anglais" were heard, and fewer still of "Vive le Roi"·
Some of the Royalists made a fruitless attempt to excite some friendly
acclamations, and were hailed with cries of "A bas le garde du corps".
The tri-coloured standard and cockade are displayed in all directions.
The opinion of many is that Louis XVIII will never be crowned. However, the silence of the people may be attributed to fear of expressing their
sentiments before the government is decided. The Prussians marched
through Paris yesterday [7th] ; they are excessively fine troops.' [1]]

175

GENERAL ORDER

Paris, 18th July, 1815

The Field Marshal has been informed that the officers of the
army force the doorkeepers of the theatres to open the doors of
the private boxes, which is contrary to rule, and to the good
order so creditable to the British army, of which it is the example.

The boxes of the theatres are in general private property,
and nobody can enter those thus situated, or those which are
hired, excepting the proprietors, or those who have hired them.

The Field Marshal is convinced that it is only necessary to
give this information to the officers of the army to induce them
to refrain from conduct which cannot be justified.

Wellington

176

TO SIR HENRY WELLESLEY

Paris, 19th July, 1815

My dear Henry,

You will have heard of our great battle in Flanders, and of
its final result in the surrender of Buonaparte to the *Bellerophon*,
off the Isle d'Aix ; [2] and if the Allies will only be a little moderate,
that is, if they will prevent plunder by their troops, and take only
what is necessary for their own security, we may hope for permanent peace.

[1] *Reminiscences of Many Years*, vol. i, pp. 91-2.
[2] Napoleon went on board H.M.S. *Bellerophon* on July 15th. The Ile d'Aix
lies off the mouth of the Charente, near La Rochelle.

But I confess that I am a little afraid of them. They are all behaving exceedingly ill.

Ever yours most affectionately,

Wellington

✻

[On July 24th Sir John Malcolm — his brothers James and Pulteney had also been created Knights Commander of the Bath — arrived in Paris after visiting Brussels and the field of Waterloo. He was invited to dine with Wellington that same evening, and recorded in his journal an account of their meeting and conversation.

'We found the Duke with a large party seated at dinner. He called out, in his usual manner, the moment I entered, "Ah ! Malcolm, I am delighted to see you." I went and shook hands, introduced Lord John Campbell, and then sat down. I mention this trifle because it showed me at once that his astonishing elevation had not produced the slightest change. The tone — the manner — everything was the same.

'After dinner, he left a party he was with when I entered, and, shaking me by the hand, retired to one end of the room, where he shortly stated what had occurred within the eventful month. "People ask for an account of the action", he said. "I tell them it was hard pounding on both sides, and we pounded the hardest. There was no manoeuvring", he said ; "Buonaparte kept his attacks, and I was glad to let it be decided by the troops. There are no men in Europe that can fight like my Spanish infantry [he meant the British regiments which had fought in Spain] ; none have been so tried. Besides", he added with enthusiasm, "my army and I know one another exactly. We have a mutual confidence, and are never disappointed." — "You had, however", I observed, "more than one-half of your troops of other nations." — "That did not signify", he said, "for I had discovered the secret of mixing them up together. Had I employed them in separate corps I should have lost the battle. The Hanoverians", he added, "are good troops, but the new Dutch levies are bad. They, however, served to fill gaps, and I knew where to place them."

'. . . I remarked that he had taken advantage of an event which staggered credulity — that of an English army occupying the capital of France — to act in a manner that was calculated to soften the asperity and lessen the hatred of the two rival nations. "That very observation", he replied, "was made to me some days ago by Talleyrand." — "I trust, however", I added, "that France will be deprived of *the means of attacking other nations*, particularly the newly-created Kingdom of the Netherlands, for they may be termed, as a nation, the most elastic in the world." He said that was true, and care should be taken ; but I thought that he seemed to think dismantling the frontier places was better than giving them up.' [1]]

[1] *The Life and Correspondence of Major-General Sir John Malcolm*, vol. ii, pp. 100-2.

177

TO JOHN WILSON CROKER

Paris, 8th August, 1815

My dear Sir,

I have received your letter of the 2nd, regarding the battle of Waterloo. The object which you propose to yourself is very difficult of attainment, and, if really attained, is not a little invidious. The history of the battle is not unlike the history of a ball. Some individuals may recollect all the little events of which the great result is the battle won or lost; but no individual can recollect the order in which, or the exact moment at which, they occurred, which makes all the difference as to their value or importance.

Then the faults or the misbehavior of some gave occasion for the distinction of others, and perhaps were the cause of material losses; and you cannot write a true history of a battle without including the faults and misbehavior of part at least of those engaged.

Believe me that every man you see in a military uniform is not a hero; and that, although in the account given of a general action, such as that of Waterloo, many instances of individual heroism must be passed over unrelated, it is better for the general interests to leave those parts of the story untold, than to tell the whole truth.[1]

If, however, you should still think it right to turn your attention to this subject, I am most ready to give you every assistance and information in my power.

Believe me, &c.,

Wellington

178

TO JOHN WILSON CROKER

Paris, 17th August, 1815

My dear Sir,

I have received your letter of the 11th, and I regret much that I have not been able to prevail upon you to relinquish your plan.

[1] On November 14th he wrote to one senior officer: 'In general I am very averse to bringing forward instances of misconduct, after such a battle as that of Waterloo. Many a brave man, and I believe even some very great men, have been found a little terrified by such a battle as that, and have behaved afterwards remarkably well.'

You may depend upon it you will never make it a satisfactory work.

I'll get you the list of the French army, Generals, &c.

Just to show you how little reliance can be placed even on what are supposed the best accounts of a battle, I mention that there are some circumstances mentioned in General Alava's [1] account which did not occur as he relates them.

He was not on the field during the whole Battle, particularly not during the latter part of it.

The battle began I believe at eleven.

It is impossible to say when each important occurrence took place, nor in what order. We were attacked first with infantry only; then with cavalry only; lastly & principally with cavalry and infantry mixed.

No houses were possessed by the Enemy in Mont St. Jean, excepting the farm in front of the left of our centre on the road to Genappe can be called one. This they got I think at about 2 o'clock, & got it from a circumstance which is to be attributed to the neglect of the officer commanding on the spot.

The French cavalry were on the plateau in the centre between the two high roads for nearly ¾ of an hour, riding about among our squares of infantry, all firing having ceased on both sides. I moved our squares forward to the guns; and our cavalry which had been detached by Lord Uxbridge to the flanks was brought back to the centre. The French cavalry were then driven off. After that circumstance, repeated attacks were made along the whole front of the centre of the position by cavalry and infantry till seven at night. How many I cannot tell.

When the enemy attacked Sir Thos Picton [2] I was there, and they got as far as the hedge on the cross road, behind which the Netherland Troops had been formed. The latter had run away, and our troops were on our side of the hedge. The French were driven off with immense loss. This was the first principal attack. At about two in the afternoon, as I have above said, they got

[1] Don Miguel Ricardo de Alava (1771–1843) was probably the only man present at both Trafalgar and Waterloo. His uncle, Vice-Admiral Don Ignatio Maria d'Alava, was wounded aboard his flagship, the *Santa Ana*. Having fought the British at sea, he served with them on land, from 1809 onwards, as Spanish Commissioner at Wellington's headquarters in the Peninsula, and at Waterloo. He became Spain's representative at the Court of the Bourbons, and was later an exile in England.

[2] Lieut.-General Sir Thomas Picton (1758–1815) had commanded the 3rd Division in the Peninsula and South of France, and led the 5th Division in the Waterloo campaign. Wounded at Quatre-Bras, he was killed on June 18th.

possession of the farm house on the high road, which defended this part of the position; and they then took possession of a small mound on the left of the high road going from Brussels immediately opposite the gate of the farm; and they were never removed from thence till I commenced the attack in the evening. But they never advanced farther on that side.

These are answers to all your queries. But remember, I recommend to you to leave the battle of Waterloo as it is.

Believe me, &c.,

Wellington

[Amid the acclamation and the triumphs, Wellington had his critics, not least of whom was Captain Cavalié Mercer of the Royal Horse Artillery. In his experience 'the Duke never attended to any justification if anything went wrong', and he appeared to have no partiality for the Horse Artillery. 'It is difficult to say why, but his Grace certainly treated us harshly and on many occasions unjustly. Of his harshness *voici un exemple*. Captain Whinyates having joined the army with the rocket troop, the Duke, who looked upon rockets as nonsense, ordered that they should be put into store, and the troop supplied with guns instead. Colonel Sir. G. Wood, instigated by Whinyates, called on the Duke to ask permission to leave him his rockets as well as guns. A refusal. Sir George, however, seeing the Duke was in a particular good humour, ventured to say, "It will break poor Whinyates' heart to lose his rockets." "D—n his heart, sir; let my order be obeyed", was the answer thundered in his ear by the Duke, as he turned on the worthy Sir George.'

On August 26th, 1815, Mercer had this to write in his journal: 'An officer holding a command in his army (particularly of cavalry or artillery) was in constant jeopardy — constantly struggling to reconcile two contradictions: 1st, to conciliate the natives, and thus prevent complaints; and 2nd, to keep his men comfortable and horses *fat* (that is the word), which could only be done at the expense of the natives. These, encouraged by the Duke's orders, proclamations, etc., were never backward in complaining — indeed, they soon became insufferably insolent: and whilst affecting to admire and praise the *grand Vellangton*, and draw comparisons between him and Blucher and his Prussian *thieves* (for they so invariably termed them) — "*voleurs Prussiens*" — they in reality laughed at us; whilst even the private soldiers of the Prussian army were (to their face, at least) treated with the most reverential deference. A sad contrast there was between our relative situations. As for gratitude, the wretches have not one grain of it. Many actually imagine that motives of fear have induced the Duke to adopt this (to them) strange line of conduct.' [1]]

---

[1] *Journal of the Waterloo Campaign*, pp. 353-4.

179

TO THE EARL OF MULGRAVE

Paris, 21st December, 1815

My dear Lord,

I received yesterday your Lordship's letter of the 10th, regarding the claim of the Field officers of the artillery, present in the battle of Waterloo, to the same measure of favour granted to those in the battle of Vitoria.

In my opinion, you have done quite right to refuse to grant this favour, and that you have founded your refusal on the best grounds. I cannot recommend that you should depart from the ground you have taken. To tell you the truth, I was not very well pleased with the artillery in the battle of Waterloo.

The army was formed in squares immediately on the slope of the rising ground, on the summit of which the artillery was placed, with orders not to engage with artillery, but to fire only when bodies of troops came under their fire. It was very difficult to get them to obey this order. The French cavalry charged, and were formed on the same ground with our artillery, in general within a few yards of our guns. In some instances they were actually in possession of our guns. We could not expect the artillery-men to remain at their guns in such a case. But I had a right to expect that the officers and men of the artillery would do as I did, and as all the Staff did, that is to take shelter in the squares of the infantry till the French cavalry should be driven off the ground, either by our cavalry or infantry. But they did no such thing; they ran off the field entirely, taking with them limbers, ammunition, and everything; and when, in a few minutes, we had driven off the French cavalry, and had regained our ground and our guns, and could have made good use of our artillery, we had no artillerymen to fire them; and, in point of fact, I should have had no artillery during the whole of the latter part of the action, if I had not kept a reserve in the commencement.

Mind, my dear Lord, I do not mean to complain; but what I have above mentioned is a fact known to many; and it would not do to reward a corps under such circumstances. The artillery, like others, behaved most gallantly; but when a misfortune of this kind has occurred, a corps must not be rewarded. It is on account of these little stories, which must come out, that I object to all the propositions to write what is called a history of the battle of Waterloo.

If it is to be a history, it must be the truth, and the whole truth, or it will do more harm than good, and will give as many false notions of what a battle is, as other romances of the same description have. But if a true history is written, what will become of the reputation of half of those who have acquired reputation, and who deserve it for their gallantry, but who, if their mistakes and casual misconduct were made public, would not be so well thought of ? I am certain that if I were to enter into a critical discussion of everything that occurred from the 14th to the 19th June, I could show ample reason for not entering deeply into these subjects.

The fact is, that the army that gained the battle of Waterloo was an entirely new one, with the exception of some of the old Spanish troops.[1] Their inexperience occasioned the mistakes they committed, the rumours they circulated that all was destroyed, because they themselves ran away, and the mischiefs which ensued ; but they behaved gallantly, and I am convinced if the thing was to be done again, they would show what it is to have had the experience of even one battle.

Believe me, &c.,

Wellington

P.S. — I am very well pleased with the Field officers for not liking to have their application referred to me. They know the reason I have not to recommend them for a favour.[2]

180

TO THE EARL OF CLANCARTY [3]

Mont St. Martin,[4] 3rd Dec., 1817

My dear Clancarty,

. . . You may depend upon it that I will do everything in my power to get a medal for Monsieur de Sales. The truth regarding the battle of Waterloo is this : there exists in England an

[1] Wellington means his British regiments which had fought in Spain.
[2] *Supplementary Despatches*, xiv, 618-20.
[3] Richard Le Poer Trench, 2nd Earl of Clancarty (1767–1837), was British Ambassador to the Netherlands.
[4] Mont-St.-Martin was Wellington's H.Q. near Cambrai.

insatiable curiosity upon every subject which has occasioned a *mania* for travelling and for writing. The battle of Waterloo having been fought within reach, every creature who could afford it, travelled to view the field; and almost every one who came who could write, wrote an account. It is inconceivable the number of lies that were published and circulated in this manner by English travellers; and other nations, seeing how successfully this could be done, thought it as well to adopt the same means of circulating their own stories. This has been done with such industry, that it is now quite certain that I was not present and did not command in the battle of Quatre Bras, and it is very doubtful whether I was present in the battle of Waterloo. It is not so easy to dispose of the British army as it is of an individual: but although it is admitted they were present, the brave Belgians, or the brave Prussians, won the battle; and neither in histories, pamphlets, plays, nor pictures, are the British troops ever noticed. But I must say that our travellers began this warfare of *lying*; and we must make up our minds to the consequences. . . .

Believe me, my dear Clancarty,
Ever yours most sincerely,
Wellington [1]

[1] *Supplementary Despatches*, xii, 155-6.

BIBLIOGRAPHY

(A) MANUSCRIPT SOURCES

The Richmond Papers in the National Library of Ireland, Dublin.

Additional Manuscripts (37308, 37415) in the British Museum, London.

Colonel the Hon. James Hamilton Stanhope: 'Private Memoranda and Journal from the beginning of 1810 to the 26th of July 1812 when I returned to England'. In the possession of the Earl Stanhope, K.G., D.S.O., M.C.

Lieutenant William Lambton: Unpublished Journal (Additional Manuscripts 13664, British Museum, London).

(B) PUBLISHED SOURCES

Arbuthnot: *The Correspondence of Charles Arbuthnot.* Edited by A. Aspinall (Royal Historical Society, Camden Third Series, 1941).

Bagot, Mrs. Charles: *Links with the Past* (Edward Arnold, 1901).

Barrington, Sir Jonah: *Personal Sketches of His Own Times* (2 vols., George Routledge, 3rd ed., 1869; 1st ed., 1827).

Beatson, Lieut.-Colonel Alexander: *Views of the Origin and Conduct of the War with Tippoo Sultaun; comprising a Narrative of the Operations of the Army under the Command of Lieutenant-General George Harris, and of the Siege of Seringapatam* (1800). Beatson, formerly A.D.C. to the Marquess Wellesley, was Surveyor-General to the Army.

Biddulph, Colonel John: *The Nineteenth and their Times* (John Murray, 1899).

Blakiston, Major John: *Twelve Years' Military Adventure in Three Quarters of the Globe, 1802–1814* (2 vols., Henry Colburn, 1829).

Broughton, Lord (John Cam Hobhouse): *Recollections of a Long Life.* Edited by his Daughter-in-Law, Lady Dorchester (2 vols., John Murray, 1911).

Buckham, P. W.: *Personal Narrative of Adventures in the Peninsula* (1827).

Burghersh: *Correspondence of Lord Burghersh, afterwards Eleventh Earl of Westmorland, 1808–1840.* Edited by Rachel Weigall (John Murray, 1912).

Burghersh: *Correspondence of Lady Burghersh with the Duke of Wellington.* Edited by Lady R. Weigall (John Murray, 1903).

Burroughs, George F.: *A Narrative of the Retreat of the British Army from Burgos; in a Series of Letters* (Bristol, 1814).

Byron: *Lord Byron's Correspondence, chiefly with Lady Melbourne, Mr. Hobhouse, the Hon. Douglas Kinnaird, and P. B. Shelley.* Edited by John Murray (2 vols., John Murray, 1903).

Camden Miscellany: 'Some Letters of the Duke of Wellington to his Brother William Wellesley-Pole'. Edited by Professor Sir Charles Webster (vol. xviii, Royal Historical Society, 1948).

Chad : *The Conversations of the First Duke of Wellington with George William Chad.* Edited by the 7th Duke of Wellington (The Saint Nicholas Press, Cambridge, 1956).

Colebrooke, Sir T. E. : *The Life of the Honourable Mountstuart Elphinstone* (2 vols., John Murray, 1884).

Costello, Edward : *Adventures of a Soldier written by Himself* (Colburn & Co., 2nd ed., 1852).

Cowell, Lieut.-Colonel Sir John Stepney : *Leaves from the Diary of an Officer of the Guards* (Chapman & Hall, 1854).

Creevey: *The Creevey Papers. A Selection from the Correspondence & Diaries of the late Thomas Creevey, M.P. Born 1768 — Died 1838.* Edited by the Right Hon. Sir Herbert Maxwell, Bart. (2 vols., John Murray, 1903).

Croker : *The Croker Papers: Correspondence and Diaries of John Wilson Croker.* Edited by Louis J. Jennings (3 vols., John Murray, 1884).

Dictionary of National Biography: Index and Epitome. Edited by Sidney Lee (Smith, Elder & Co., 1903).

East India Military Calendar, the; containing the Services of General and Field Officers of the Indian Army, by the Editor of the Royal Military Calendar (3 vols., Kingsbury, Parbury, & Allen, 1823–25).

East-India Register and Directory for 1805, the ; corrected to the 8th November, 1804, containing Complete Lists of the Company's Servants, Civil, Military, and Marine, at the Different Presidencies of the East-Indies. Compiled by John Mathison & Alexander Way Mason, of the Secretary's Office, East-India House.

Edgeworth : *The Life and Letters of Maria Edgeworth.* Edited by Augustus J. C. Hare (2 vols., Edward Arnold, 1894).

Elers : *The Memoirs of George Elers.* Edited by Lord Monson and George Leveson Gower (Heinemann, 1903).

Fortescue, Sir John W. : *Following the Drum* (William Blackwood, 1931). This contains extracts from the diary of Ensign Mills.

Frazer : *Letters of Colonel Sir Augustus Simon Frazer, K.C.B., commanding the Royal Horse Artillery in the Army under the Duke of Wellington, written during the Peninsular and Waterloo Campaigns.* Edited by Major-General Edward Sabine (Longmans, 1859).

Guedalla, Philip : *The Duke* (Hodder & Stoughton, 1931).

Hickey: *Memoirs of William Hickey.* Edited by Alfred Spencer (4 vols., Hurst & Blackett, 1925).

Hutton, James : *Selections from the Letters and Correspondence of Sir James Bland Burges, Bart.* (John Murray, 1885).

Jackson, Sir George : *The Bath Archives. A Further Selection from the Diaries and Letters of Sir George Jackson from 1809 to 1816* (2 vols., Richard Bentley, 1873).

Jackson, Major-General Sir Louis : 'One of Wellington's Staff Officers : Lieut.-General William Staveley, C.B.' (*Journal of the Society for Army Historical Research*, Autumn 1935).

Journal of an Officer during the Recent Campaign in Portugal and Spain under Lord Viscount Wellington (T. Johnson, 1810).

Kaye, John William : *The Life and Correspondence of Major-General Sir John Malcolm, G.C.B.* (2 vols., Smith, Elder & Co., 1856).

Bibliography

Kincaid, Captain J.: *Adventures in the Rifle Brigade, in the Peninsula, France, and the Netherlands, from 1809 to 1815* (T. & W. Boone, 1830).

Larpent: *The Private Journal of F. Seymour Larpent, Judge-Advocate General, attached to the Head-Quarters of Lord Wellington during the Peninsular War, from 1812 to its close.* Edited by Sir George Larpent, Bart. (2 vols., Richard Bentley, 1852).

Lennox, Lord William Pitt: *Memoir of Charles Gordon Lennox, Fifth Duke of Richmond* (Chapman & Hall, 1862).

Lennox, Lord William Pitt: *Three Years with the Duke, or Wellington in Private Life*, by an ex-aide-de-camp (Sanders & Otley, 1853).

Leslie: *Military Journal of Colonel Leslie, K.H., of Balquhain whilst serving with the 29th Regt. in the Peninsula, and the 60th Rifles in Canada, &c., 1807–1832* (Aberdeen University Press, 1887).

List of all the Officers of the Army and Royal Marines on Full and Half-Pay: with an Index; and a Succession of Colonels (1812).

London Kalendar, The: or, Court and City Register, for England, Scotland, Ireland, and the Colonies, for the Year 1816 (William Stockdale, 1816).

McGrigor: *The Autobiography and Services of Sir James McGrigor, Bart.*, late Director-General of the Army Medical Department (Longmans, 1861).

Maginn, William: *The Military Sketch Book: Reminiscences of Seventeen Years in the Service Abroad and at Home.* By an Officer of the Line (2 vols., Henry Colburn & Richard Bentley, 2nd ed., 1831).

Maxwell, Sir Herbert: *The Life of Wellington. The Restoration of the Martial Power of Great Britain* (2 vols., Sampson Low, Marston & Co. Ltd., 1899).

Maxwell, W. H.: *Life of Field-Marshal His Grace the Duke of Wellington* (3 vols., H. H. Bailey & Co., 1839–41).

Mercer, General Cavalié: *Journal of the Waterloo Campaign kept through the Campaign of 1815* (Peter Davies, 1927 ; 1st ed., 1870).

Mills, Ensign John: See *Following the Drum*, by Sir John W. Fortescue.

Napier: *Passages in the Early Military Life of General Sir George T. Napier, K.C.B., written by Himself.* Edited by his Son, General W. C. Napier (John Murray, 1894).

Napier, Sir W. F. P.: *History of the War in the Peninsula and in the South of France from the Year 1807 to the Year 1814* (6 vols., Thomas & William Boone, new ed. revised, 1851).

Notes relative to the Late Transactions in the Metahetta Empire. Fort William, December 15, 1803. With an Appendix of Official Documents (J. Debrett, 1804).

Oman, C. W. C.: *Wellington's Army, 1809–1814* (Edward Arnold, 1913).

Oman, Sir Charles: *A History of the Peninsular War* (7 vols., Oxford at the Clarendon Press, 1902–30).

Ray, Gordon N.: *The Buried Life: A Study of the Relation between Thackeray's Fiction and his Personal History* (published for the Royal Society of Literature by Geoffrey Cumberledge, Oxford University Press, 1952).

Robinson: 'A Peninsular Brigadier'. Letters of Major-General Sir F. P. Robinson, K.C.B., dealing with the Campaign of 1813. Edited, with an Introduction, by C. T. Atkinson (*Journal of the Society for Army Historical Research* December 1956).

Rogers : *Recollections of Samuel Rogers.* Edited by W. Sharpe (Longman, Brown, Green, 1859).

Salisbury : *A Great Man's Friendship. Letters of the Duke of Wellington to Mary, Marchioness of Salisbury, 1850–1852.* Edited by Lady Burghclere (John Murray, 1927).

Saltoun, Alexander Fraser, 17th Lord : *The Frasers of Philorth* (3 vols., Edinburgh, 1879).

Schaumann, August Ludolf Friedrich : *On the Road with Wellington. The Diary of a War Commissary in the Peninsular Campaigns.* Edited and Translated by Anthony M. Ludovici (Heinemann, 1924).

Scott, John : *Paris Revisited in 1815, by Way of Brussels* (Longman, Hurst, Rees, Orme & Brown, 2nd ed., 1816).

Shelley : *The Diary of Frances Lady Shelley, 1787–1817.* Edited by her Grandson, Richard Edgcumbe (2 vols., John Murray, 1912–13).

Stanhope, Philip Henry, 5th Earl : *Notes on Conversations with the Duke of Wellington, 1831–1851* (Oxford University Press, 1938 ; first public ed., 1888). During Wellington's lifetime Stanhope was Viscount Mahon.

Teignmouth, Lord : *Reminiscences of Many Years* (2 vols., David Douglas, Edinburgh, 1878).

Thorn, Major William : *Memoir of the War in India, conducted by General Lord Lake, Commander-in-Chief, and Major-General Sir Arthur Wellesley, Duke of Wellington, from its Commencement in 1803 to its Termination in 1806, on the Banks of the Hyphasis* (T. Egerton, 1818).

Tomkinson, Lieut.-Colonel William : *The Diary of a Cavalry Officer in the Peninsular and Waterloo Campaigns, 1809–1815.* Edited by his Son, James Tomkinson (Swan Sonnenschein & Co., 1894).

Vivian, the Hon. Claud : *Richard Hussey Vivian, First Baron Vivian. A Memoir* (Isbister & Company Limited, 1897).

Ward, S. G. P. : *Wellington's Headquarters: A Study of the Administrative Problems in the Peninsula, 1809–1814* (Oxford University Press, 1957).

Wellington : *The Dispatches of Field Marshal the Duke of Wellington during his Various Campaigns.* Compiled by Lieut.-Colonel Gurwood (12 vols., John Murray, 1834–38).

Wellington : *The General Orders of Field Marshal the Duke of Wellington, in Portugal, Spain and France, from 1809 to 1814; in the Low Countries and France in 1815, and in France, Army of Occupation, from 1816 to 1818.* Compiled by Lieut.-Colonel Gurwood (W. Clowes & Sons, 1837).

Wellington : *The Mysore Letters and Dispatches of the Duke of Wellington, 1799–1805.* Printed verbatim from the Original Manuscripts (Bangalore : Mysore Government Press, 1862).

Wellington : *Supplementary Despatches and Memoranda of Field Marshal Arthur Duke of Wellington, K.G.* Edited by his Son, the Duke of Wellington (15 vols., John Murray, 1858, etc.).

Welsh, Colonel James : *Military Reminiscences, extracted from a Journal of nearly Forty Years' Active Service in the East Indies* (2 vols., Smith, Elder & Co., 1830).

PERSONAL INDEX

This index should be used in conjunction with the List of Contents and the List of Recipients of Letters, since the addressee of a letter does not appear in the index as such.

GENERAL INDEX

The following contractions are here used : W.=Wellington ;
n.=footnote.

PRINTED BY R. & R. CLARK, LTD., EDINBURGH

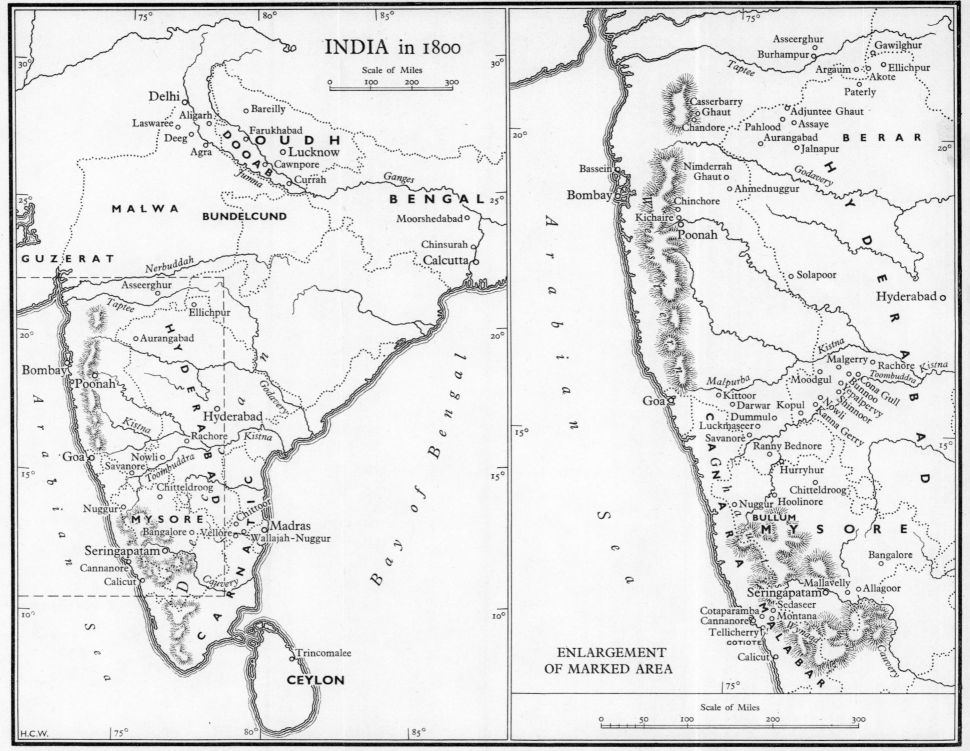

INDIA in 1800

Scale of Miles
0   100   200   300

Left map labels:

Delhi
Laswaree
Aligarh
Deeg
Agra
Bareilly
Farukhabad
OUDH
Lucknow
Cawnpore
Currah
Jumna
DOOAB
Ganges
BENGAL
Moorshedabad
Chinsurah
Calcutta
MALWA
BUNDELCUND
GUZERAT
Nerbuddah
Asseerghur
Taptee
Ellichpur
HYDERABAD
Aurangabad
Bombay
Poonah
Hyderabad
Kistna
Rachore
Kistna
Godavery
Goa
Nowli
Savanore
Toombuddra
Chitteldroog
Nuggur
MYSORE
Bangalore
Vellore
Chittoor
Madras
Wallajah-Nuggur
Seringapatam
Cannanore
Calicut
Cauvery
CARNATIC
Deccan
Trincomalee
CEYLON

Arabian Sea
Bay of Bengal

H.C.W.

Right map — ENLARGEMENT OF MARKED AREA:

Asseerghur
Burhampur
Gawilghur
Argaum
Ellichpur
Akote
Paterly
Taptee
Casserbarry Ghaut
Chandore
Adjuntee Ghaut
Pahlood
Assaye
Aurangabad
Jalnapur
BERAR
Bassein
Nimderrah Ghaut
Ahmednuggur
Godavery
Bombay
Kichaire
Chinchore
Poonah
Solapoor
Hyderabad
HYDERABAD
Kistna
Malgerry
Rachore
Kistna
Toombuddra
Malpurba
Moodgul
Cona Gull
Goa
Kittoor
Darwar
Kopul
Bunnoo
Yepalpervy
Shinnoor
Dummulo
Nowli
Kanna Gerry
Luckmaseer
Savanore
Ranny Bednore
Hurryhur
Chitteldroog
Nuggur
Hoolinore
BULLUM
MYSORE
Bangalore
Mallavelly
Allagoor
Seringapatam
Sedaseer
Cotaparamba
Montana
Cannanore
Wynaad
Tellicherry
COTIOTE
MALABAR
Calicut
Cauvery
CANARA

Arabian Sea

ENLARGEMENT
OF MARKED AREA

Scale of Miles
0   50   100   200   300

Antony Brett-James: *Wellington at War 1794-1815* (Macmillan)

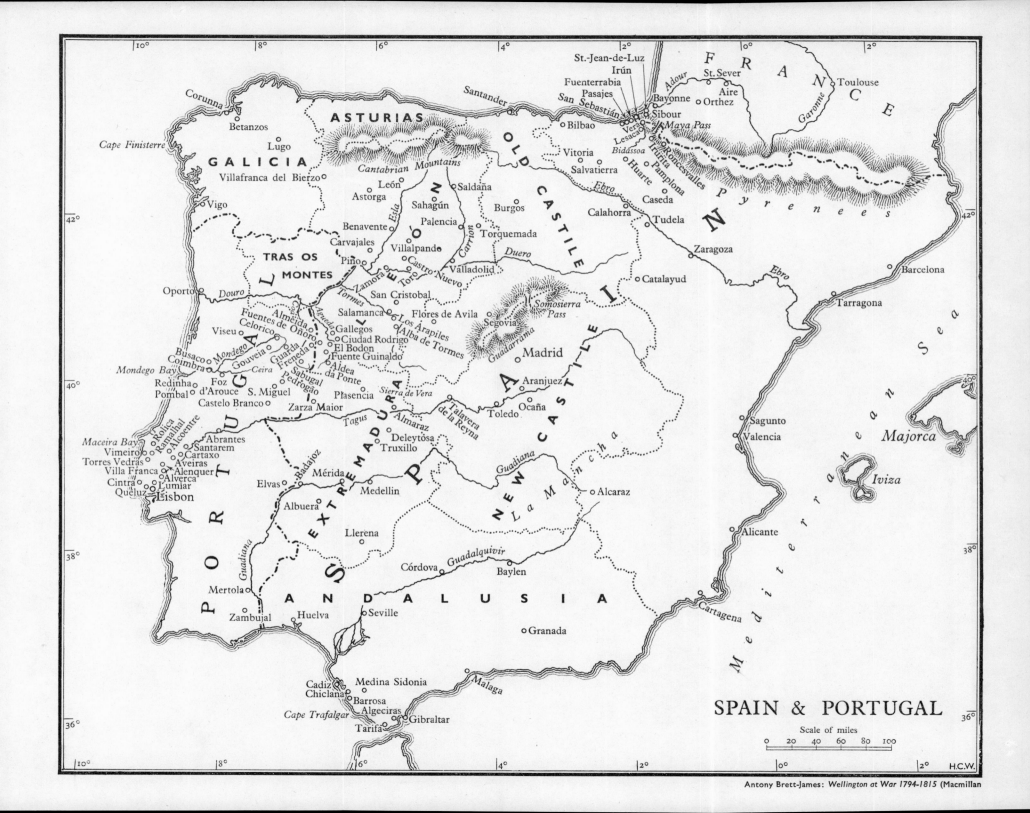

SPAIN & PORTUGAL

Scale of miles

0   20   40   60   80   100

Antony Brett-James: *Wellington at War 1794-1815* (Macmillan

H.C.W.